Teaching Film

Modern Language Association of America
Options for Teaching

For a complete listing of titles,
see the last pages of this book.

Teaching Film

Edited by
Lucy Fischer
and Patrice Petro

The Modern Language Association of America
New York 2012

Library of Congress Cataloging-in-Publication Data:

Teaching film / edited by Lucy Fischer and Patrice Petro.
p. cm.—(Options for teaching ; 35)
Includes bibliographical references and index.
ISBN 978-1-60329-114-9 (hardcover : alk. paper)—
ISBN 978-1-60329-115-6 (pbk. : alk. paper)
1. Motion picture—Study and teaching (Higher). I. Fischer, Lucy.
II. Petro, Patrice, 1957–
PN1993.7.T37 2012
791.43071'1—dc23 2011050858

Options for Teaching 35
ISSN 1079-2562

Cover illustration of the paperback edition: *The Kiss*, by P. J. Cook. 2003. Acrylic on wood. © P. J. Cook

Printed on recycled paper

Published by The Modern Language Association of America
26 Broadway, New York, NY 10004-1789
www.mla.org

We dedicate this volume to the Society for Cinema and Media Studies and to its members, who have done so much, as teachers and scholars, to broaden our understanding of the field, past and present.

Contents

Part V: Style and Craft

Part VI: Film and Media in the Digital Age

Acknowledgments

We would like to thank David G. Nicholls, the former director of book publications for the MLA, for his help in moving this volume through its various stages of editing and production. We are indebted to Sara Pastel, also of the MLA, for her excellent work as copyeditor. We would also like to thank all our contributors, who remained extraordinarily patient during a very long gestation period for this book. Jason Bittel and Katherine Coyle, graduate student assistants at the University of Pittsburgh, helped prepare the manuscript and kept us on track with our contributors; Eric Herhuth, project assistant at the University of Wisconsin, Milwaukee, did the same. Finally, we would like to acknowledge the long-standing support of our colleague E. Ann Kaplan, who first suggested to the MLA that we serve as editors for this project. Needless to say, it has been a personal and professional pleasure to work together on this volume.

Lucy Fischer and Patrice Petro

Introduction: "Memories of Underdevelopment"

This is the second volume on the subject of film pedagogy that the Modern Language Association (MLA) has published in its series Options for Teaching. The first was Barry Keith Grant's *Film Study in the Undergraduate Curriculum*, which, interestingly and tellingly, was released in 1983 under the banner Options for the Teaching of English. Hence for many years, at least according to the MLA, film studies was a subset of English and subsumed under the category of language and literature. Clearly, the field has advanced considerably since then, both in its scholarly and academic standing. The Society for Cinema and Media Studies (SCMS), the field's preeminent scholarly association, was established in 1959 and has held annual conferences since 1960. Today it boasts nearly three thousand members from institutions of higher education around the world, all of whom would agree that cinema and media studies constitutes a distinct although highly complex and porous discipline.

While as of this writing the MLA lists some thirty titles in its series Options for Teaching, several, including Grant's volume, are out of print. The majority focus on literature or language, concentrating on such highly specific areas as children's literature, representations of the Holocaust or Spanish Civil War, the African novel, the graphic novel, and Stuart and

Tudor women writers. *Teaching Film*, by contrast, has the formidable task of confronting the entirety of the film pedagogical landscape, an impossible and unattainable undertaking. We can only gesture toward broad areas, issues, and questions that we trust will receive more detailed consideration in the future.

Despite the absence of a single comprehensive volume on teaching film, the film studies field, internationally, has produced a substantial body of work on the subject. The British Film Institute, for example, which has a strong commitment to outreach and education, has a publication series that does for cinema and television what the MLA series does for literature, with volumes on such focused topics as teaching short films (Quy), teaching black cinema (Jones), and teaching film and television documentary (Benyahia). Furthermore, a few US film journals (such as *Cinema Journal*, sponsored by SCMS) have historically devoted occasional sections of an issue to teaching, in which media instructors offer their syllabi and thoughts on curriculum design. As for books, in the United States there have been almost none dedicated exclusively to film pedagogy. Instead there have been a plethora of works that can be used in the classroom (e.g., anthologies, basic histories, formal analyses, and film history texts), but these are addressed more to the student than to the teacher (although a few come with teachers' guides). Thus the writing on approaches to teaching film has been piecemeal and dispersed and, therefore, difficult for teachers to know of or track down. Unlike the United Kingdom, the United States has no national institution dedicated to the teaching and preservation of cinema to which college professors can turn for source materials and advice. Moreover, film studies has not had the established and long-standing position of other humanities fields in the US academy—a fact that has made its teaching more challenging than other subjects.

We have called our introduction (with no small sense of irony) "Memories of Underdevelopment"—an allusion to *Memorias del subdesarrollo*, the famous Cuban film of 1968 by Tomás Gutiérrez Alea that tracks the tension between the private life of a male intellectual and the revolution that surrounds him. On the one hand, our summoning of this title (which, like the reenergized emergence of academic film studies, dates to the late 1960s), seeks to underscore the ways that our field still suffers from a certain lack of recognition and its attendant deprivations. On the other hand, the revolution is here, and film studies has been in the advanced guard—at times leading the way in the humanities. It is this dual sense of past and present, disadvantage and advantage, development and perceptions of underdevelopment that we seek to invoke in this volume and explore in this introduction.

Primary among the field's "memories of underdevelopment" is the question of its recognition in academia. As Krin Gabbard explains in a 2006 article for the *Chronicle of Higher Education*, when the National Research Council (NRC) released its 1995 report on the disciplines, film studies was unranked but not entirely ignored. At that time, it was declared to be "an emerging discipline," along with race, ethnicity, and postcolonial studies and feminist, gender, and sexuality studies. Ten years later, in 2005, the NRC began seeking new information to move film studies into its next set of rankings. Gabbard reports that Charlotte V. Kuh, the director of the NRC's task force that constructs its taxonomies and ranks disciplines, again declares film studies to be an emerging discipline, now one also of "ambiguous provenance." As Gabbard wryly remarks:

> Although the term might suggest something more exotic, it merely acknowledges that the advanced study of cinema takes place in departments of comparative literature, French, theater, and communications as well as in programs prominently labeled cinema and media studies.

Indeed, our field is known by many names—not only those noted by Gabbard but also film studies, screen studies, and visual culture, to name a few. Likewise, the field is dispersed across a range of academic departments, programs, institutional divisions, and scholarly organizations (SCMS, but also the MLA, the University Film and Video Association, the Latin American Studies Association, the German Studies Association, the Popular Culture Association, the International Communications Association, and the College Art Association, among others). While this academic polymorphism and mobility serves film studies well in an age that questions the boundaries of disciplinarity, such indeterminacy often leads to institutional invisibility and, as a result, film studies has often fallen between the cracks—with all the perils that metaphor involves.

The Division on Film (which includes history, criticism, and theory) is among the largest of the MLA Division Executive Committees. Much of this membership comes not only from film studies departments but also from English, comparative literature, and foreign language and literature departments. While there is something appealing in the designation of an "emerging discipline," since it evokes an ideal of a discipline that is in a constant state of flux and becoming, there are obvious drawbacks and pitfalls to such a liminal and undefined status as well. Indeed, the fundamental interdisciplinarity of our field, coupled with its institutional diffusion, has made it nearly an absent signifier to some of our peers and nearly unclassifiable within the NRC's system of taxonomies and disciplinary rankings; thus, at least for the NRC, cinema and media studies remains, more than half a century after the establishment of a scholarly association in its name, officially in a merely provisional (or embryonic) state.

In this regard, it is important to note that courses in film studies have been offered at US universities since at least 1915. In his *Scenes of Instruction: The Beginnings of the U.S. Study of Film*, Dana Polan explores the history of film studies as an academic field, situating his research within scholarship in other disciplines in the humanities, sciences, and social sciences that have also questioned and investigated disciplinarity since the 1990s. He points out that while film theory has been scrutinized by scholars in our field, the tracing of our institutional history has remained largely ahistorical and impersonal. His study therefore focuses precisely on the human practice of film studies, paying particular attention to pedagogy and the development of approaches to university instruction. In the process, he provides a more complicated understanding than the traditional narrative of how film studies came into being in US higher education, which commonly has the field forming in the 1950s, culminating in 1959 with the founding of the Society of Cinematologists (formerly SCS, the forerunner of the SCMS), and then proliferating in the spirit of 1960s counterculture. Polan turns his attention to the period ignored by this conventional narrative, concentrating on the years between 1915 and 1935. He begins in 1915, when the earliest film classes coincided with the release of the first feature films and with a proliferation of writing about film. He ends with 1935, the year Iris Barry founded New York's Museum of Modern Art's (MoMA) circulating film library, which overnight constituted a veritable canon for students of film and was available to be viewed in classes.

Polan's book is only one of several recent works that explore the institutional and intellectual foundations of US film studies, spanning not just the academy but also government, the museum, and the publishing industry. These works include Peter Decherney's *Hollywood and the Culture Elite: How the Movies Became American*; Haidee Wasson's *Museum Movies: The Museum of Modern Art and the Birth of Art Cinema*; and a collection of essays, edited by Lee Grieveson and Wasson, entitled *Inventing Film Studies*. Wasson's study of MoMA also elaborates on the ties between the United States and Europe (especially the United Kingdom), and Michael

Zryd's contribution to *Inventing Film Studies* looks at experimental film and the development of film studies in the United States and Canada.

This volume, by necessity, eschews a coverage model of the pedagogical field, but it does attempt to point toward the most important issues in film teaching, exploring questions of digital media; social history; genre; style; authorship; mode (documentary, avant-garde, animation); national, transnational, postcolonial, regional, and world practices; relations between film production and critical studies; and representations of race, gender, sexual preference, and body type. In so doing, the essays also provide valuable bibliographies, filmographies, and lists of resources, both print and digital.

Moreover, the contributors survey and examine specific challenges involved in film pedagogy—ranging from the sometimes unreasonable expectations of students (that courses will be easy, that films shown will be recent, that all media examined will be American-made and in English) to the problems involved with film resources. Decherney, for instance, discusses the hornet's nest that has been film copyright, which, until recently, has haunted film instructors' uses of film clips and even frame grabs in the classroom and on the lecture circuit. Almost every other author speaks about the endless and frustrating difficulties of attaining adequate, viewable prints for classroom use of the films or television programs they wish to show, even with the proliferation of new technologies, Internet databases, and access to media online. Libraries generally do not engage in interlibrary loan of such materials, and neither do archives. Furthermore, rare films cannot be photocopied for classroom use.

Though not addressed in this volume, it is also worth mentioning (apropos the theme of underdevelopment) that we in film studies have nowhere near the collection of scholarly databases at our disposal that faculty members in more traditional fields do—another element that can affect our teaching (and our students' research, especially at the graduate level). The instructor of art history, for example, has for many years been able to go to *ARTstor* (assuming one's library subscribes); select images of works by innumerable painters, sculptors, and sometimes photographers; and create instant slide shows to use in class, with all supporting documentation readily available. No such resource exists for the film studies teachers looking for film clips or frame enlargements (although recently *Cinema Image Gallery* has begun to provide online pictures of posters, lobby cards, and the like). For most film instructors, a do-it-yourself ethic has had to prevail. Thus the film teacher may resort to searching *YouTube*, where, if lucky, he or she can find a desired clip, but of indeterminate origin and often poor quality. Similarly, while we all feel fortunate to have the International Federation of Film Archives (FIAF) bibliography of international film periodicals or the *Literature Film Index*, such sources only catalog articles starting with the early 1970s, when film made its serious debut in the academy. As for the previous six and a half decades, one is again on one's own. While we are pleased to have the *AFI [American Film Institute] Catalog* online (although incomplete by several decades), we have no such library-based, digital catalog for other national cinemas. While the scholar of literature can do a keyword search for all the occasions that William Shakespeare or Johann Goethe has used a particular word, no such databases exist for the long shot in Orson Welles or the tracking shot in Max Ophüls. Neither does the film teacher have access to anything comparable to such literary databases as *19th Century British Pamphlets*; *Black Women Writers*; Gale's *Literary Index*, *Literary Criticism Online*, and *Literature Resource Center*; *MagillOnLiterature*; or *North American Women's Drama*. Online, vetted encyclopedias of cinema have only recently become available for ascertaining basic facts about films, directors, movements, or national cinemas. Hence, the teacher of film has been left to the vagaries of relatively unsubstantiated sources like *Wikipedia* or the *Internet Movie Database* or, of course, to books. Despite scholarly advances in the field and the improved access to materials initiated by the birth of video, DVD, and the Internet, film teachers and researchers are still pioneers—in the best and worst senses of that term.

And yet, for all the underdevelopment of our resources and the ongoing frustrations about perceptions of our field, film studies has nonetheless continued to expand and thrive at a time when more traditional disciplines have lost momentum, membership, and fresh ideas. Our scholarly associations continue to grow by leaps and bounds, as young scholars are avidly drawn to our field, infusing it with new ideas, directions, and research. As this volume demonstrates, film studies has an impressive cadre of distinguished scholars (among the first and second generations of doctorates to be trained in the area) who have dedicated their careers to developing, refining, and augmenting their field. The stellar quality of the essays included here is evidence enough that film studies has arrived (or, dare we claim, emerged)—that is, it has become an object of serious intellectual inquiry. It is also a field that, while perhaps not yet as disciplined as some would like, offers a wealth of ideas about what teaching film and media involves, both its challenges and satisfactions, in a knowledge-building act of collective self-definition.

Organization of This Volume

This volume gathers together thirty-four essays divided into six distinct and yet overlapping parts: "Theory and Representation," "Geographies of Cinema," "Interdisciplinarities," "Genre and Mode," "Style and Craft," and "Film and Media in the Digital Age." The contributions range from practical reconsiderations of introductory or advanced courses to more conceptual inquiries into the state of the discipline. *Teaching Film* opens by addressing and rethinking some of the basic categories through which cinema and media studies are commonly understood and taught. Part 1, "Theory and Representation," begins with questions of film criticism and theory—ranging from auteur studies to broader philosophical questions of the ontology, epistemology, and discursive structure of the medium—reflecting the growing sophistication of the field. The section then goes on to explore a variety of ways to teach issues of representation, moving across and within categories of gender, race, sexuality, and normativity.

The essays in part 2, "Geographies of Cinema," consider a variety of approaches to teaching within an expanded international frame, surveying geographies across categories of nationalism, regionalism, postcolonialism, transnationalism, and globalization. Here, the impulse derives from the wealth of new work on cinema as a transnational phenomenon and examines cinematic traditions within both geographically larger (South Asia, Latin America, and the Caribbean) and smaller (Japan, Germany, and Eastern Europe) scales of nation and region. The essays aim to ascertain how best to teach geographies of cinema while remaining attentive to the aesthetic shapes and alternative public spheres that have proliferated in our global era.

The study of world cinema has been further complicated and enhanced by the range of interdisciplinary approaches that have enriched cinema and media studies since 1960 and before. In the third part of *Teaching Film*, "Interdisciplinarities," these formations are explored in depth, whether they concern teaching film and literature, teaching film across languages, or teaching film in relation to politics, historiography, or law and public policy. Each of the essays aims to expand film pedagogy beyond the critical, theoretical, or geographic approaches already established by engaging with intellectual paradigms as well as students and scholars across traditional disciplinary divides.

The fourth and fifth parts of the volume turn to long-standing issues in film and media studies. The essays gathered together in "Genre and Mode" explore the theoretical, historical, and institutional constructions of various film genres (e.g., the musical and film noir)—how they are created and, in turn, how they are remaking our media landscape. Also included here are essays on the broader modes of the medium, such as animation, documentary, and avant-garde film, all of which have historical roots in the turn of the twentieth century and continue to enrich and broaden our understanding of cinema today. In "Style and Craft," we have included a range of essays on teaching film in relation to such formal elements as sound, music, and mise-en-scène, as well as in relation to the crafts of performance, filmmaking, and screenwriting. These essays open up vital and revealing dimensions of teaching film today by considering cinema as both an aural as well as visual medium and by exploring how stardom complicates earlier notions of authorship and genre. Finally, the essays included here on teaching film to students in various majors and degree programs remind us that we face myriad institutional settings in our colleges and universities. Whether speaking about teaching film in a production school or teaching screenwriting in an English department, these essays provide a wealth of new ideas for engaging students in the very best traditions of the humanities and liberal arts.

In the final section of the volume, "Film and Media in the Digital Age," we highlight the challenges and opportunities for teaching film with access to today's technology. Once merely a buzzword, "media convergence" has now become a literal description of the ubiquity and codependency of film, telephone, radio, television, and the Internet. And yet, even as home video and the Internet appear to rival the influence of film and television, these media also open up new opportunities for critical analysis and viewing experience. The essays in this section endeavor to engage a new generation of educators and students by exploring both the promises and challenges of new media. They also reflect the long-standing concerns of film studies as an interdisciplinary field committed to teaching the moving image in an era of rapid technological, educational, and geopolitical change.

While this introduction and most of the essays that follow focus on issues of theory and content as related to film studies pedagogy, in truth, these are not the only kinds of knowledge that the film teacher needs.

Whether first-time instructors or those suddenly teaching at a new site, film pedagogues find themselves confronted by a host of questions and problems—even before opening their classroom door. Although film and media teachers assign many readings, their primary object of study is audio-visual, and, therefore, they cannot simply walk into class holding a book in their hand and say, "Please turn to page thirty-one." The following section seeks to address some of the material circumstances of film and media instruction in the hope that it will save the new (and even semi-experienced) film instructor time, energy, tears, and frustration.

Practical Pedagogy: Everything You Wanted to Know about Teaching Media but Were Afraid to Ask

This volume is decidedly not meant to be a one-shot how-to manual for becoming an instant instructor of film studies. Before one presumes to teach a film or other media class, one needs the kind of background (institutional or otherwise) that one expects of any other college-level teacher. Yet even those well versed in film or media history, theory, and criticism can be woefully unprepared for entering the actual classroom.

The list below is meant to serve as a field guide for the uninitiated. We hope that by consulting this material before considering offering a course, an instructor can avoid the pitfalls and mishaps that often plague the new teacher of media. This advice applies only to face-to-face teaching, not to online teaching, which requires an entirely different approach. It also presumes that your institution does not have a film archive at your disposal, since it is very rare for an institution to have one.

Check the availability of titles you wish to use in your syllabus. There are huge gaps in the availability (in any format) of many (particularly silent) films. We recommend that either you or a media specialist at your institution investigate this issue well before you commit to teaching a particular course. Unfortunately, there is no single database that provides this information, but the *Internet Movie Database*, *Amazon*, foreign cultural offices, and *Google* are helpful (as are word of mouth). Some films and excerpts are available on *YouTube* or other video sites—though the legality of using them is unclear. In the case of avant-garde or political media, certain niche distributors handle these materials (e.g., Women Make Movies, Filmmakers Cooperative, Canyon Cinema).

Consider the budget you will need to teach a course and how you will get the funds you require.

Beware of different film versions or formats. Some distributors will offer better prints of films than others, and some can be unusable in class. For foreign films, check out whether a film is subtitled or dubbed. Also check out which region standard it utilizes; some DVDs or videotapes of foreign films will not play on US equipment. For silent films, some have been colored or tinted (like the originals); some have accompanying music tracks, either original or new. Watch out for titles that apply to numerous films (remakes or otherwise); it's easy to select the wrong one.

Check out the various formats on which films were released (e.g., DVD, Blue-Ray, videotape, 16mm, foreign, or American modes). Which formats do the equipment at your institution support? Clearly, 16mm projectors are now few and far between, and 16mm prints are old and often damaged. Similarly, videotape and laser disc are outdated formats, though in some cases they are the only forms available. It is worth checking if your institution has a multistandard player.

Decide whether you will rent or purchase the media for your class. Some 16mm films are still available for rental and unavailable in other formats (especially some independent films). For the most part, it is impractical these days to purchase 16mm films, unless your university already has a large and valuable collection with the necessary storage facility. Given that DVDs are relatively inexpensive (for mass-produced films, not independents), most universities choose to build up a collection of these materials.

Consider how the media will be handled. If purchased, where will it be stored, how will it be stored, and who will catalog and maintain it? Who will have access to it, and how will access be controlled?

Investigate the rooms available for your class. A room for teaching film and media should (1) be equipped with an adequate locked media closet (otherwise, you will have to bring in equipment for each class); (2) have blackout shades or curtains, especially important if you are teaching in the daytime; (3) have video projection or a large-screen monitor of a size that is workable for the number of students you will teach; (4) have dimmable lights; (5) be soundproof enough not to bother other classes; and (6) have a raked floor.

Investigate the equipment in the room in which you will teach. These days one should have a DVD player (US format and international format), a videotape player (US and possibly international format), 16mm equipment (if you will use it), a video projector or large-screen monitor, computer hookup, and possibly a laser disc player (if you need to use materials available only in this format). Ideally, there would also be a built-in computer, but one can always bring a laptop and cables if necessary. All equipment should be securely locked up to prevent theft.

Think about class scheduling. Will you show films in the regular class session or require a separate screening? If the latter, you need to list hours that encompass both class and screening—unless you are going to require students to acquire and screen films on their own. If you are screening films in a single class you need at least three hours and fifty minutes to allow for adequate discussion and a break, given that features can be over two hours.

Investigate current resources. Does your university library or your department already have a film collection that you can use for your courses? Does your library have an adequate collection of books in film studies to sustain student research, at either the undergraduate or graduate level? Does your library subscribe to a sufficient number of media journals or have them available online (e.g., through *JSTOR* or *Project Muse*)? Does your library subscribe to necessary databases (e.g., *FIAF*, *AFI Catalog*, *Film Literature Index*)? Does your library have needed historical journals on microfilm, on microfiche, or in databases?

Train yourself on equipment before you teach. Much time can be wasted in class if you are not proficient in using the technology. Furthermore, not being prepared does not impress students.

Train yourself on tools like *PowerPoint* and computerized film-editing programs for creating, embedding, and projecting film stills (useful for illustrating shot composition) and film excerpts.

Be prepared for technological breakdowns. Have a DVD cleaning cloth to wipe DVDs. Have a cell phone and the number of an audiovisual specialist handy at all times.

Works Cited

Benyahia, Sarah Casey. *Teaching Film and TV Documentary*. London: British Film Inst., 2008. Print. Teaching Film and Media Studies.

Decherney, Peter. *Hollywood and the Culture Elite: How the Movies Became American*. New York: Columbia UP, 2005. Print.

Gabbard, Krin. "Cinema and Media Studies: Snapshot of an 'Emerging' Discipline." *Chronicle of Higher Education.* Chronicle of Higher Educ., 17 Feb. 2006. Web. 30 Dec. 2009.

Grant, Barry Keith, ed. *Film Study in the Undergraduate Curriculum.* New York: MLA, 1983. Print. Options for Teaching 5.

Grieveson, Lee, and Haidee Wasson, eds. *Inventing Film Studies.* Durham: Duke UP, 2008. Print.

Jones, Peter. *Teaching Black Cinema.* London: British Film Inst., 2008. Print. Teaching Film and Media Studies.

Polan, Dana. *Scenes of Instruction: The Beginnings of the U.S. Study of Film.* Berkeley: U of California P, 2007. Print.

Quy, Simon. *Teaching Short Films.* London: British Film Inst., 2008. Print. Teaching Film and Media Studies.

Wasson, Haidee. *Museum Movies: The Museum of Modern Art and the Birth of Art Cinema.* Berkeley: U of California P, 2005. Print.

Part I

Theory and Representation

Introduction to Part 1

One of the major textbooks used in upper-level American film studies courses is Leo Braudy and Marshall Cohen's *Film Theory and Criticism*, first published in 1974 and now in its seventh edition. That this volume has become a staple of media education makes clear the import of theoretical issues in contemporary film studies. The title of the work makes an important distinction between criticism and theory—criticism (originally associated with film reviews and intellectual magazine pieces) focuses on the explication of particular filmic texts, and theory (traditionally associated with academic study) focuses on comprehending the broad ontology and discursive structure of the medium. In a sense, one might chart the entire history of Euro-American film theory through the various versions of this text and which articles have been dropped or added. Interestingly, some early-twentieth-century writing on the cinema has remained essential: Siegfried Kracauer's meditation on cinematic realism, Erwin Panofsky's description of the filmic space-time continuum, and André Bazin's sense that the photographic medium is tied to death. Certainly, one long-lasting theoretical influence on American film studies, which has led to various "directors courses," is the French auteur theory, developed by

Cahiers du cinéma critics in the late 1940s. It not only ascribed authorship to the filmmaker but also sought to elevate cinema to an art form comparable to others. This theory, really more of an approach, was soon discredited, since cinema is a highly collaborative form with contributions by countless practitioners. Nonetheless, the auteur theory still operates as a useful and powerful organizing principle for many teachers and students dealing with the totality of film history and style.

As film studies evolved in the late twentieth century, more sophisticated questions took precedence; scholars examined the breadth of the medium, its conditions of address, and the manner in which its formal elements were organized into discursive structures. Part of this investigation involved a return to early film theory (e.g., the work of Béla Balázs, Rudolph Arnheim, and Sergei Eisenstein) to mine their texts for important insights regarding film art, the close-up, montage, and visual cognition. Starting in the 1970s, however, new approaches were generated in an attempt to find more scientific means of characterizing the cinematic medium. Drawing on semiotics and the work of Ferdinand de Saussure, among others, critics like Christian Metz questioned whether film discourse approached the level of a language, developing inquiries that ultimately drew parallels but no one-to-one relationship. Theorists like Peter Wollen turned to structuralism (pioneered by Claude Lévi-Strauss) to explain the construction of certain genres, like the western. Others (like Jean-Louis Baudry and Raymond Bellour) turned to psychoanalysis (be it Freudian or Lacanian) to comprehend the manner in which cinema acts on the spectator through, for instance, its apparatus or oedipal dynamics. More recently, writers like Carl Plantinga and Gregory Smith have turned to cognitive studies for a different explanation of how the viewer perceives and responds to a film—both intellectually and affectively. Though essential, teaching theory is a difficult task, especially since students often expect that discussing films in class will rise only to the level of newspaper reviewing. Its challenges are addressed by many of the essays in this section.

At times, theoretical questions about the cinema have dovetailed with notions of representation—the manner in which certain entities (persons, races, nations, even locales) are portrayed on-screen. This concern is central to a mass art form that reaches millions of people and affects their vision of the world. With the rise of the second-wave women's movement in the United States and Europe in the 1970s, attention turned to the image of women on-screen. Works by Molly Haskell and Marjorie Rosen were key to this debate. Soon, however, such analyses of plots and characterizations, concentrating only on the story line of a film, came to be viewed as superficial and limited, and more attention came to be paid to theoretical issues concerning cinema's depiction of the female—especially questions of the gaze that was seen as male-oriented and often voyeuristic or sadistic. Here Laura Mulvey's essay "Visual Pleasure and Narrative Cinema" was crucial, linking questions of feminist politics to psychoanalysis (representation to theory).

The influence of feminist theory on the field was profound. Thus as feminist critics had once accused film studies of being male-focused, so in later years scholars critiqued it for concentrating on the white or European worldview, a charge that accompanied the growth of multicultural study in the university. Accordingly, questions of race surfaced in all areas of film studies, with special attention in the United States given to Asian, Latino, African American, and Native American subcultures as seen in relation to more hegemonic white society. Like gender and race, sexual orientation soon became a pressing issue in the United States and had an intense influence on film theory, with courses on queer or LGBT cinema proliferating, often centered on sexuality and the body. Now attention has turned to disability studies (also focused on corporeality) in the university, with film and other media seen as strong influences on the manner in which society views people living with disabilities. Hence, scholars like Martin Norden and Sally Chivers have published works on the topic, and courses examining the issue have appeared.

In the essays that follow, questions of both film theory and representation are raised and discussed within the context of specific courses, highlighting their structures, pedagogical assumptions, and challenges.

Works Cited

Arnheim, Rudolph. *Film as Art.* Berkeley: U of California P, 1957. Print.

Balázs, Béla. *Theory of the Film: Character and Growth of a New Art.* Trans. Edith Bone. New York: Dover, 1970. Print.

Baudry, Jean-Louis. "The Apparatus: Metapsychological Approaches to the Impression of Reality in Cinema." Braudy and Cohen 171–88.

Bazin, André. *What Is Cinema?* Trans. Hugh Gray. Berkeley: U of California P, 1968. Print.

Bellour, Raymond. *The Analysis of Film.* Ed. Constance Penley. Bloomington: Indiana UP, 2000. Print.

Braudy, Leo, and Marshall Cohen. *Film Theory and Criticism.* 7th ed. New York: Oxford UP, 2009. Print.

Chivers, Sally, ed. *The Problem Body: Projecting Disability on Film.* Columbus: Ohio State UP, 2010. Print.

Eisenstein, Sergei. *Film Form and the Film Sense.* Ed. and trans. Jay Leyda. New York: Meridian, 1957. Print.
Haskell, Molly. *From Reverence to Rape: The Treatment of Women in the Movies.* New York: Holt, 1974. Print.
Kracauer, Siegfried. *Theory of Film: The Redemption of Physical Reality.* New York: Oxford UP, 1960. Print.
Metz, Christian. *Film Language: A Semiotics of the Cinema.* Chicago: U of Chicago P, 1990. Print.
Mulvey, Laura. "Visual Pleasure and Narrative Cinema." *Screen* 16.3 (1975): 6–18. Print.
Norden, Martin. *The Cinema of Isolation: A History of Physical Disability in the Movies.* New Brunswick: Rutgers UP, 1994. Print.
Panofsky, Erwin. "Style and Medium in the Motion Pictures." [1934/1936]. *Film Theory and Criticism.* 3rd ed. Ed. Gerald Mast and Marshall Cohen. New York: Oxford UP, 1985. 215–33. Print.
Plantinga, Carl, and Greg M. Smith, eds. *Passionate Views: Film, Cognition, and Emotion.* Baltimore: Johns Hopkins UP, 1999. Print.
Rosen, Marjorie. *Popcorn Venus.* New York: Avon, 1974. Print.
Wollen, Peter. *Signs and Meaning in the Cinema.* Bloomington: Indiana UP, 1974. Print.

Timothy Corrigan

Teaching Film Auteurs

In the 1960s, the movies arguably made their most significant headway into the classrooms of US colleges and universities first and foremost as the products of directors refigured as authors. Directors of the European new-wave cinema, like Jean-Luc Godard, Ingmar Bergman, and Michelangelo Antonioni, offered films whose aesthetic and textual challenges aligned them with modernist literature and art. They and their films became comparable to the canonical writers and texts taught in English and foreign language departments, from Bertolt Brecht's plays to the novels of William Faulkner and Marguerite Duras. The focus on auteurs at once facilitated and reduced how film has been taught, while also identifying critical and theoretical flashpoints that open film studies to other rich issues.

Auteur cinema, *auteurism*, and *author cinema* were first coined by and associated with writers for the French journal *Cahiers du cinéma* in the 1950s and the French new-wave films of Godard, François Truffaut, and Agnès Varda of that same period. In the pervasive cultural shifts that followed World War II, including the prominence of existential philosophies and wide criticism of institutional systems of many kinds, these writers and filmmakers attacked the so-called boulevard cinema that seemed merely to repeat industrial formulas of the past and instead hailed films that represented the creative or individual vision of auteurs.[1] In this sense, auteurism appeared originally as a fundamentally differential and evaluative term that distinguished the art of film from film as mass entertainment.

The early champions of auteurism attribute to the director the primary role in determining the look and meaning of film. Especially in the postwar period, film critics and filmmakers begin to imagine the director able to use the camera, as Alexandre Astruc famously put it in his 1948 essay, as a "*caméra-stylo*," or camera pen, analogous to the expressive tool of the writer:

> [T]he cinema is quite simply becoming a means of expression, just as all the other arts have been before it. . . . After having been successively a fairground attraction, an amusement analogous to boulevard theatre, or the means of preserving the images of an era, it is gradually becoming a language. By language, I mean a form in which and by which an artist can express his thoughts, however abstract they may be, or translate his obsessions exactly as he does in the contemporary essay or novel. This is why I would like to call this new age of cinema the age of the *caméra-stylo* (camera pen). This metaphor has a very precise sense. By it I mean that the cinema will gradually break free from the tyranny of what is visual, from the image for its own sake, from the immediate and concrete demands of the narrative, to become a means of writing just as flexible and subtle as written language. (159)

These claims would be technologically underpinned by the arrival of portable, lightweight camera technology, introduced as the Arriflex system in Germany in 1936 and as the Éclair 35mm Cameflex in France in 1947. More than coincidentally, these different *caméra-stylos* would feature reflex-viewing systems linking the pragmatics of filmmaking with the potential for the conceptual reflexivity of a personal auteur cinema and its "idea of the cinema expressing ideas" (159).

From this historical beginning and foundation, an auteurist model for film introduces two important and fundamental questions to the classroom: To what extent can film be considered the product of a single expressive and creative individual or agency? To what extent can film be considered a language or like a language? The two questions overlap since an expressive agency is commonly associated with the articulation of a personal style or ideas whose vehicle is a discourse or a film language.[2] Thus, from the start, the common practice with an auteurist critical perspective would be to investigate, for instance, the films of Fritz Lang as a consistent personal vision that expresses itself according to identifiable cinematic figures or forms, seen across his films—in this case, perhaps shared themes about the dark impulses of society and a consistent stylistics of blocking groups of characters within the mise-en-scène of these films.

The *Cahiers* writers and French new-wave filmmakers implicitly recognized that the historical precedents for auteurism originated in the very first decades of the twentieth century, when Hollywood developed a Fordist division-of-labor model in which the director, more so than the film's cinematographer or editor, handled the main responsibilities for the actual filmmaking.[3] Directors like D. W. Griffith or Charlie Chaplin, for example, made their creative role a key ingredient in the financing, production, and promotion of their early films. Accordingly, as film critics, Godard and others would return to the power of older filmmakers (and others like John Ford and Nicholas Ray) and partly reinvent Hollywood and film history by describing them as distinctively individual auteurs whose creativity and style distinguished them from directors who simply followed industrial formulas. Later, Alfred Hitchcock would, in a tongue-in-cheek fashion, signal his presiding presence through cameo appearances in his films, suggesting that the director as auteur represents the central vision of his films. More recently, filmmakers as diverse as Woody Allen and Clint Eastwood have been identified as American auteurs because they write, direct, and appear in their own films. Significant variation on the notion of a film auteur is evident in these directors and the historical periods they worked in, but approaching their films through the auteurist perspective established in the 1950s allows viewers to analyze the films' consistent style and thematics.

Critical perspectives defining auteurism have varied considerably over the last fifty years. Building on the French foundation of a director's identifiable stylistic and thematic concerns in different films, four approaches have become the primary critical categories over the last fifty years, each with pragmatic advantages and disadvantages. First, in the United States, Andrew Sarris became the most prominent proponent of auteurism as an evaluative measure of a film, basing his model in a humanist perspective that worked to elevate the cultural status of the movies. In his collection *The American Cinema: Directors and Directions, 1929–1968*, Sarris isolates as criteria of value the director's technical abilities, a distinguishable personality visible in the films, and the presence of an interior meaning that makes auteur films art. Second, in the wake of structuralist and poststructuralist theories in the 1970s and 1980s, when, ironically, theories of the death of the author appeared in the work of writers like Roland Barthes and Michel Foucault, auteurism remained an important critical practice but became associated less with the person or style of the filmmaker than with different semiotic and structural clusters in films whereby the director-auteur appears as the vehicle for the arrangement of certain interpretive cues. In his influential book *Signs and Meaning in the Cinema*, Peter Wollen advocates a structural approach to authorship as an act of decipherment that places the film author's name in quotation marks to designate a critical construct rather than a biographical individual. For example, John Ford's films return again and again to the antinomy, or opposition, between garden and wilderness, and a viewer can see this common "Ford" structure developed differently in films from *My Darling Clementine* (1946) to *The Man Who Shot Liberty Valance* (1962).

Third, more recent approaches to auteurism have paid increasing attention to how the figure of the auteur in a film or group of films requires historical and cultural differentiations. Not only have the changing industrial and technological mechanisms that support filmmaking altered the power and the way filmmakers can express an identity, but the social and cultural contexts (including gender, race, and sexuality) for enacting a singular cinematic vision have changed and continue to change significantly. These differences can and, for many, should be taken into account in discussing how a film mobilizes an auteurist force: the recent films of the Iranian director Abbas Kiarostami require a historical and cultural contextualization that would distinguish his brand of auteurism from, say, the auteurist vision in the 1960s films of the Brazilian director Glauber Rocha; women directors such as Penny Marshall or Chantal Akerman may require a different critical measure of how female identity becomes articulated in film. Finally, an important determinant from the beginning, the commercial and industrial significance of auteurism has become especially visible since 1990 as the auteurist label has become a particularly important and successful tool for marketing and promoting a film. Today, the promotion of a film often clearly claims the presiding vision of a director, sometimes as part of its official title, as in *Quentin Tarantino's Kill Bill: Volume One* (2003), and sometimes as an explicit confrontation with other authorial visions, as in the marketing of Kenneth Branagh's *Hamlet* (1996) as an engagement with both Shakespeare and Laurence Olivier. A film directed by Quentin Tarantino often considers Tarantino's name its most salient feature and, perhaps more so than ever before in film history, distribution strategies have expanded that power by using and highlighting a director's name as part of the discovery, production, and distribution of new films.

This commercial use and manipulation of auteurism does not simply debunk or undermine the traditional association of auteurism with singular creativity. Rather, it adds another critical dimension for teaching and understanding film as both an artistic and economic activity in which the name of the auteur can be positioned to generate certain expectations for a film's reception.

Each of these auteurist methods and their frequent overlapping provide rich entryways into film analysis and, used with subtlety, can provide the framework for sophisticated courses such as The Cinema of Jane Campion, in which one teaches not only her films but also how different kinds of critical thinking produce different readings. In this case, one approach may allow a viewer to evaluate and distinguish the development of Campion's body of work from her short films and breakthrough features *Sweetie* (1989) and *An Angel at My Table* (1990) through international successes like *The Piano* (1993) and *The Portrait of a Lady* (1996) in terms of their evolving thematic and stylistic common ground and difference, such as the distinctive use of sound and a continuing investigation of female interiority. As a productive interpretation of these films, another approach may look for structural arrangements that link her films together, possibly exploring contrasting figures of confinement and nature. A third use could develop an auteurist perspective to analyze how Campion's films articulate specific cultural and historical forces, including her place as a female director and her status as a New Zealand filmmaker working first in the context of the new Australian cinema and later international coproductions.

Finally, a fourth auteurist angle on these films would attend not only to the works themselves but also to the ways marketing campaigns have used Campion's reputation—as a woman filmmaker and as a director of art films—to establish certain expectations for the reception of the films. There are alternative ways to use an auteurist model as a critical perspective on Campion's films (or those of any auteur), and tailoring an approach or using a variety of approaches to discuss a filmmaker's work is perhaps the most sophisticated and subtle way to take pedagogical advantage of this critical method.

An equally valuable pedagogical use of an auteurist lens in a film course is to surface its pitfalls and contradictions, since demonstrating which critical dimensions of film practice are not adequately served by an auteur model makes students sensitive to the complexities of film studies. Auteur theory provokes two primary challenges for film studies: To what extent is film a collaborative industrial practice that belies auteurist assumptions?

And how does a critical viewer reconcile the tension between auteurism and genre, two often opposed critical methods?

The fundamental problem in reading films as the product of an auteur is the tendency to valorize biography and essentialism in discussing the relationship between a filmmaker and a film. While this critical temptation appears almost justified in discussions of Spike Lee's *Malcom X* as a felicitous meeting of racial views, it becomes transparently problematic in the films of the Coen brothers, who collaborate on their films. More generally, the commonplace recognition that film is almost always a collaborative practice—with producers, screenwriters, editors, and stars often playing equal or larger roles in the look and meaning of a completed film—means any subtle reading of an auteurist film benefits enormously from taking these other contributions into account. Indeed, considering the other major figures in a film's production has sometimes allowed instructors and students alike to move away from the dominant assumption that only directors warrant the label auteurs and provided legitimate evidence for reading a movie or group of movies as the product of others as the presiding auteur, such as the star (Marlene Dietrich, for instance), the producer (like Irving Thalberg), or even the choreographers (in Busby Berkeley films and other musicals). In her well-known essay on *Citizen Kane*, Pauline Kael analyzes perhaps history's most celebrated auteur and auteurist film, Orson Welles and *Citizen Kane* (1941), by arguing that the writer Herman Mankiewicz rather than Orson Welles should be credited for the elaborate narrative construction of the film and that the cinematographer Gregg Toland is most responsible for the film's dramatic visual style.

A second common critique of auteurism is frequently formulated in the opposition of auteur criticism and genre criticism. While auteur criticism privileges the individual creative power in a film, genre studies emphasizes the repetition of industrial and artistic formulas put in place by a long film history and an industry always attuned to audience expectations. With a critical model based in film genres, the achievement of a work such as *His Girl Friday* (1940) or *The Big Sleep* (1946) may be less about the creative vision of the director Howard Hawks than about the timely combination of generic conventions and icons associated with the screwball comedy or film noir and a production unit aiming at a certain target audience. Even the films of more current auteurs, such as Martin Scorsese or Mira Nair, need to be considered not simply from the point of view of a romantic aesthetic of expressive vision but also in terms of how they mobilize and refashion standard generic formulas. Teaching a film that seems to place its generic and auteurist status in contention, such as Scorsese's *The Departed* (2006) or Nair's *Monsoon Wedding* (2001), can be one of the most productive ways to teach both methods, as well as the general importance of methodic choices in reading and understanding a film from any perspective.

In today's convergent cultures of new media, the Internet, and the movies, the long and diverse history of auteur criticism has perhaps become more, not less, important in the classroom. As in the past, changing social, industrial, and technological conditions are now transforming how a tradition of auteur criticism can and will be used. Most prominent, the rapid globalization of media (including film) and the shift of movie distribution and reception to new media venues (from the Internet to iPods) have potentially altered in fundamental ways what it means to be a single artist expressing a particular perspective. In today's climate, anyone and everyone may choose to be an auteur, but what that ultimately means requires precise historical, technological, and cultural analysis.

Notes

1. The best known statement of this position is Truffaut's "A Certain Tendency in French Cinema."

2. While debates about the description of film as language are as old as the cinema itself, the 1960s and 1970s witnessed a rigorous and widespread debate about this question, most famously in the work of Christian Metz, Pier Paolo Pasolini, and Umberto Eco.

3. This early industrial shift is described in detail in David Bordwell, Janet Staiger, and Kristin Thompson's *The Classical Hollywood Cinema* (113–28).

Works Cited

Astruc, Alexandre. "The Birth of a New Avant-Garde: La Caméra-Stylo." *Film and Literature: An Introduction and Reader.* Ed. Timothy Corrigan. Upper Saddle River: Prentice, 1999. 158–62. Print.

Bordwell, David, Janet Staiger, and Kristin Thompson. *The Classical Hollywood Cinema: Film Style and Modes of Production to 1960.* New York: Columbia UP, 1985. Print.

Kael, Pauline. "Raising Kane." *The* Citizen Kane *Book.* New York: Bantam, 1971. 1–87. Print.

Sarris, Andrew. *The American Cinema: Directors and Directions, 1929–1968.* New York: Da Capo, 1996. Print.

Truffaut, François. "A Certain Tendency in French Cinema." *Cahiers du Cinéma in English* 1 (1966): 30–40. Print.

Wollen, Peter. *Signs and Meaning in the Cinema.* Bloomington: Indiana UP, 1972. Print.

Edward Branigan

Teaching Film Theory

Texts have by no means disappeared, but they are not the sole object of scrutiny. Theory now dramatizes and explores such topics as the discourses through which individual texts are constituted, the types of subjectivity they manifest, the work of representation they accomplish, the history in which they are situated, and the tactics of reading they mandate.

—William Cain, "Contemporary Theory, the Academy, and Pedagogy"

[T]heory is ever present in our daily lives. Whenever we make judgments of knowledge or value, we invoke, consciously or not, a system of assumptions, definitions, concepts, and beliefs: in short, a theory.

—D. N. Rodowick, "Gray Is Theory"

[I]t is often easier to discover a truth [a fact] than to assign it to its correct place.

—Ferdinand de Saussure, *Course in General Linguistics*

Film Theory Is from Mercury, Film Criticism from Pluto

Film historians do not question the general validity of historiography, the philosophy of history. By contrast, the academic discipline of film theory—the philosophy of film—is beset with detractors, suspicions, and muddled commentaries. Part of the problem is that film theory is not properly distinguished from film criticism in the same way that general methods and theories for conceptualizing history are kept distinct from historical studies of a specific period in a specific setting. Film criticism concentrates on one or a few specific films through careful description, analysis, interpretation, and evaluation. Film criticism depends on theories of interpretation—hermeneutics—that have a long history in the humanities (Hernadi, *Cultural Transactions* and "Literary Interpretation"). Unfortunately, what passes for film criticism often ignores this history or offers confused versions of it and instead favors a patchwork of allusions to bits of various film theories.

In any event, criticism of individual films is not film theory (Branigan, "On the Analysis"; Bordwell, *Making* 4–7, 211–12, 250–53; Thompson), nor does a filmmaker need to know film theory to make films, just as a speaker of English need not know linguistics to use language. A further analogy: theories in physics are not designed to build rockets or bicycles even if, when building them, some physics may be helpful. Moreover, what could it mean to assert that a newly discovered film has conclusively proven, or disproven, a film theory (Mullarkey)?

Film theory concerns the conditions and possibilities of film by addressing all films, or at least a very large number of produced films, including films not yet created. Thus if a film theorist were to make a mistake in describing a scene, it would not be fatal to a theoretical argument, since the example could be converted into a hypothetical film scene. It would, however, be a serious matter if a critic were to mistakenly describe a scene from a film under analysis. What is at stake in film theory is the scale or scope of our thinking (or, in the analogy posed by the title of this section, a kind of distance from the sun, or film). Film theory does not provide a recipe or justification for the interpretation(s) of a particular film but rather examines large-scale institutions, conditions of or for intelligibility, and networks of changing values from which texts can and may emerge. Is film theory, then, a system of some sort or even a science (Buckland, Introduction; Turvey; Elsaesser and Buckland)?

How should one characterize the tenuous relationship between theory and criticism? Are individual films neatly encompassed within a theoretical system as a bull's eye is within a target? Not necessarily. When film is considered as a discursive practice or text, it becomes a trajectory that is linked to social, historical, and language issues exposed by a theory. A text is designed to interact with a person's memory and to elicit meanings and responses. Thus film as a text is more complicated than what is on the screen. It also moves closer to topics studied in literary theory, when literature is treated as a text. Shared topics include issues of cultural production, ideology, narrative structure, point of view, dialogue, and character. A verbal narrative begins with temporal structures (e.g., verb tenses) and works toward creating space, while a filmic narrative begins with a series of spaces—the camera must be somewhere—and works toward creating a sense of time. Space, time, causality, agency, and value are mental constructs capable of being addressed by both film and literary theories.

There are several ways to avoid creating simple nested and hierarchical relationships whereby texts (or authors) are at the top or bottom, opposite to theory (Rodowick, "Elegy"; Branigan, *Projecting*; Wartenberg and Curran; Aitken; Lehman, "Introduction"; Branigan, "To Zero"). In addition, hierarchies are susceptible to "surface-depth" interpretations, where either a film is real and concrete while theory is abstract and illusory, or film is only an imperfect, constructed appearance—like dream work or Freud's secondary elaboration—while theory states real, though concealed, laws that resemble blueprints or building blocks of thinking. A hierarchical model is reflected in the concept of a substance, which is assumed by some theorists to be an elusive, underlying material or quality providing specificity to film. I believe that teaching film theory requires a set of concepts about the concepts in a given film theory; these metaconcepts must be capable of addressing large-scale issues and clarifying the semantic structures of a theory. Film theory is not about the fact of film but about the meanings and implications of how we have chosen to talk about the fact of film. Perhaps one should spend less time excavating deep realities (e.g., searching for a presumed substance) as a defense against *trompe-l'œil* and *trompe-l'esprit* and more time mapping a specific linguistic and social topography that generates (or revises or discards) concepts.

Metaconcepts

I prefer to employ basic philosophical categories as a way of framing the similarities and differences among types of film theories (see app.): ontology (metaphysics, realism), epistemology (logic, philosophy of mind and language), aesthetics, and ideology (political philosophy). This framework demonstrates to students how specific claims by a film theorist connect to broad philosophical issues and topical debates. I spend about ten hours of lecture on the general issues raised by each philosophical category before talking about film or film theorists. My course on classical film theory (c. 1916–76)—six hours of lecture and one discussion section per week for ten weeks with three teaching assistants—is designed to lay the foundation for a subsequent course on contemporary film theory and perhaps also for courses on media, cultural theory, and cultural criticism.

Some media theorists seem to think that the advent of new media has produced entirely new objects that radically change the structure of thought and the design of desire, when instead their focus should be less on the materiality of an object and more on investigating the effects of changes in contemporary social behavior and changes in styles of media criticism. What is new in new media is not a matter of philosophy or the latest technology but of sociology.

Philosophical categories allow the instructor to powerfully connect claims by a film theorist to problems and decisions in ordinary life, quite apart from fictional stories in films and what is said about them by theorists; or rather, it provides an opportunity to show that films and theories relate to daily practice, such as goals, expectations, and judgments, whether important or prosaic, made every day (Rodowick, "Gray" 255; Gledhill and Williams). In a strict sense, films consume only a tiny sliver of one's time during a year. Nevertheless, films remain important because of profound ties to our perception of the world—to how we transform mere occasions and disconnected actions into familiar and standardized events and scenarios that demand our participation. Philosophers are vitally concerned with this question of how we choose to live, articulate, and construct a world of significance. Language and consciousness do not exist in a vacuum, but are embodied (Noë; Clark).

A variety of schemes have been proposed for analyzing film theories. An orthodox view divides film theories according to historical periods into formalist versus realist approaches beginning in 1915, followed by modernist approaches (structuralism and beyond) beginning in 1970, overlaid on silent versus sound aesthetics. Subcategories, gradations, nationalities, and controversies then locate particular theorists (Plantinga; Bordwell, "Film") within a vast historical-conceptual collage (Stam; Stam, Burgoyne, and Flitterman-Lewis; Andrew, *Concepts*). A popular polarization contrasts the Anglo-American tradition with Continental philosophy

(Trifonova; Allen and Smith) or seeks a synthesis (Buckland, *Cognitive Semiotics*).

Some schemes present a logical grid with which to classify and analyze film theories. Dudley Andrew has modified Aristotle's four types of causation to yield four metacategories: raw materials or medium of film, creative methods and techniques, significant forms and shapes, and purpose and value (*Major Film Theories*). Tim Bywater and Thomas Sobchack employ a variation on these four categories. Warren Buckland has conducted an intriguing series of "rational reconstructions" of film theories using a four-part scheme borrowed from the linguist Rudolf Botha ("Film as 'Specific Signifying Practice'"; "Theorizing"; "What"; "Rational Reconstruction"; "Death"). Noël Carroll employs "the argumentative style of analytic philosophy" to seek "clarifications" of certain abstractions "found in philosophical aesthetics" that bear on claims made by film theorists (5, 263, 263). Gregory Currie's work is in a similar vein. Christopher Falzon explores the history of philosophy for insights into film. Melinda Szaloky explores a modern, Continental brand of philosophical aesthetics. Francesco Casetti finds a perfect grid of three kinds of film theory, each with five distinctive internal features and five distinctive external features. Thomas Elsaesser and Malte Hagener divide film theories into a seven-part grid derived from qualities or modes of mind and body.

Language, Tropes, Topoi

Brian Henderson probes film theories from a different angle. He suggests turning away from compiling the abstract elements of a language of film—followed by an inevitable spiral of ever-greater generalizations—and instead moving toward a "structural method" that carefully analyzes the language of film theories (xiii, 5). In effect, he is asking how film theories are made out of the resources provided by our current language, where *language* is a summation of the ways we are expressing what is important to us and what we choose to notice.

> [F]ilm theory consists of fragments of systems (or of fragments posing as systems), themselves riddled with gaps and contradictions, which seem at times to define different objects as well as to assert different standpoints. However, none of these propositions is inconsistent with the assumption that there are discursive regularities in film theory, that problematic, concepts, propositions, even theoretical structures recur in a virtually constant way and are in fact the basis of those controver-

sies that constitute the field and even, perhaps, of the inconsistencies that characterize it. (xii)

The idea here is that conflict and indeterminacy are being regulated and manipulated in a theoretical discourse, not abolished. Dana Polan argues that theory must be theorized as being immersed within cultural institutions, power structures, and discursive formations. For Mary Ann Doane, the *excess*, *leakage*, and *contingency* of theory is due to the *resistance* of the object film and to the free-floating—transient but intense—attention mandated by cinephilia. Christian Metz goes one step further by investigating the investigator's imaginary, that which desires to write film theory. He claims, "Interwoven into every analytical undertaking is the thread of a self-analysis" (79). Metz discovers therein a state of "voyeuristic sadism sublimated into epistemophilia" (16). He knows well that this thread (or threat?) of a self-analysis extends to efforts both to understand film theories and to teach them.

In a complementary way, I believe that the assorted discourses in a film theory routinely work to fashion shifts in vocabulary through exploiting so-called radial structures of overlapping ambiguities that are intrinsic to language (Branigan, *Projecting*, "To Zero"). These radial structures are not logical and deterministic but partially motivated, convenient, and, to a degree, intractable and open to future situations. A point is reached where the problem of extending a given theoretical language game to new circumstances becomes irresolvable within the language. Thus one cannot project with certainty future applications of a word or theory (Wittgenstein, "Yellow Book"). Prominent examples of these necessarily hazy and unacknowledged but productively radial concepts would include the following: shot, frame, image, camera, motion, motion picture, medium, editing, style, realism, performance, auteur, voice, motivation, intention, point of view, and narration.

Henderson captures this spirit when he says that "determining when and how the term 'shot' became standardized is a prime task for research—a matter of historical and theoretical importance" (xxi). Such a research program develops from the conviction that a given notion of shot—what counts as a shot and what one does with the notion—will begin to determine what it is possible to say within a theoretical paradigm within a historical moment. In what context is a shot defined by a splice? Does a shot depict only the past when a camera was turned on and off? Are fictions and abstractions in a film due to the editing of these kinds of shots (Branigan,

Projecting 76–80, 297n109)? In particular, would a splice be sufficient (or even necessary) to define a point-of-view shot? (The answer is no.) Moreover, do we watch a film by imagining that we are seeing objects through the lens of a real or hypothetical camera—providing us a tunnel-like point of view (93–94, 167, 176–78)? Isn't our view of filmic space and time significantly more mobile and general than allowed by the notion of shots defined by splices? One might wonder whether there are analogous problems in thinking about the units of the sound track (Branigan, "Soundtrack").

The way in which a word like *shot* finds its place in a film theory illustrates that one discourse through which an individual film is constituted is the discourse provided by film theory, itself an amalgam of discourses that emerges from the ways a community sees itself (Saussure 68; Cain 8). A focus on language and its anthropology—that is, pragmatics—leads to the view that film theory is a means of doing things with words that is one among several verbal tasks that might be undertaken with the object film. Critical and analytic languages also create models that are limited by the measured instability of words and concepts (Bordwell, *Making*). Thus a closer examination of the variety of language uses might reveal a new, more natural connection between criticism and theory (Vescio). Theory is different from other verbal tasks with film, not because it is absolute or a priori or foundational (that is, theory does not dictate criticism of a film), but because theory has a distinctive value within academic activities. Part of its value is that it analyzes, clarifies, and promotes opportunities for the formation of social value, including its own.

Classroom Practice

In the classroom, I aim to foster a keen sensitivity for the rhetorical strategies of film theories by closely examining the construction of several sentences or paragraphs, word by word, for each theorist. This is done on a blackboard, not with *PowerPoint*, because I need a workspace where students can watch as I erase, reorganize, and trace through a process of successive readings and revisions. This way, students can feel the delicate weight of a metaphor and the precision of every word chosen by a theorist together with the manner in which each word contributes to the interlocking patterns of an argument. Students are surprised by much of this procedure, including lengthy discussions of prepositions (Branigan, "Of Prepositions") and the words *the*, *a*, and especially *and*. Consider, for example, the conjunction that appears in the title of Rudolf Arnheim's chapter "Film and Reality," the first chapter of his *Film as Art*, and the prepositions that appear in a claim like the following: "our perception *of* film *as* Art is *about* what we perceive *in* reality" (9; emphasis added).

Especially important is to teach students about metaphor and the effects of "conceptual blending" (Fauconnier and Turner). There are many wonderful metaphors in film theory that carry a reader in a half-dozen or so different, productive directions, such as Jean-Louis Baudry's description of the film screen as "bordered with black like a letter of condolence" (293–94) and Noël Burch's treatment of editing as an art of "plastic" (32). Equally important, however, are the plentiful and subtle, quiet comparisons that appear in most paragraphs. For a theorist, above all, thinking in a disciplined manner requires a disciplined use of words, root metaphors, links, and mental pictures.

A fine way to learn about theory is to write about theory by adopting a defined set of verbal strategies. I ask students in their final course paper to practice theory by responding, for example, as Metz might to an André Bazin quotation or to dissect a quotation from an unfamiliar theorist by adopting the rhetoric of a familiar theorist. I insist that students use specific page references when mentioning even obliquely a theorist's argument. I believe that thinking in terms of pages and passages helps students think concretely about the abstractions of theory.

My midterm and final exams are variants of a take-home exam. I hand out in advance a large number of questions from which I will select a few for the in-class exam. My handout for the final exam is 6,700 words and focuses strongly on analyzing short theoretical passages from several points of view to carefully weigh the advantages and disadvantages of an argument, including how it has been designed to fit within the theory as a whole. I stress that a theory is about not just ideas and conclusions but also the language and metaphors within which it exists.

Acquiring a keen sensitivity to language is also essential for watching films and learning how to argue with an image. I believe that the visual patterns we come to see on a film screen have been projected through our linguistic behavior—our language games or situational awareness, as Ludwig Wittgenstein might say (*Philosophical Investigations*)—as well as projected through a multitude of embodied, schematic descriptions and competing figures of mind. In short, how we choose to talk about cinema is a clue to what we will see and, later, think we remember seeing.

I prefer to assign original writings by film theorists to my students while almost completely avoiding secondary sources that interpret or gloss or rework the theorists. There are several fine anthologies of commentary on film theories, but I resist them, since I believe students need to confront the theories directly. I stress that one must read for continuities among apparently very disparate works along with a search for new beginnings. (For classical theory, I require about 1,300 pages of reading in ten weeks.) I am convinced that an instructor must emphasize that there are many positive values to be found in every essay. I believe that an introductory theory course must be stoutly affirmative in its tone, otherwise, when undercutting a theorist's argument through perpetual attacks and complaints (which are not to be confused with an infrequent, spare, and judicious critique), students too easily become dispirited or cynical and lose interest.

The major obstacle for students in a theory class is their acquiring the skills necessary to read and arrange ideas. My primary framework is outlined in the appendix below, although I introduce several other techniques for modeling rhetorical systems. For most students, the details and major conclusions of a film theory will evaporate in the months and years following a course; nonetheless, if students can acquire the skills for reading theory, then pertinent ideas and arguments can be reclaimed whenever needed. I urge students not to focus overmuch on a theorist's conclusions but to think about how the theorist is thinking. If one understands a theorist's method of thinking, one will be able to apply the ideas to new problems and to new films. I have found that the screening of films mainly deflects from the verbal nature of theory and leads to misunderstandings about the relationship between theory and film. I do eventually show a few clips and slides in class—to surprised but appreciative students.

Teaching theory is one of the great rewards of the profession. Though initially perplexed and challenged by philosophical ways of thinking, most students value the strength that comes from finding their way among precise and intricate lines of reasoning. This skill has many applications in life. Even in the limited case of moving images, an understanding of how film theories are constructed will illuminate not just the marvel of film, but the predispositions, plans, and values implicit in our actions and words.

Note

My thanks for support and careful reflections on this essay from Dudley Andrew, David Bordwell, Warren Buckland, Francesco Casetti, Chris Dzialo, Lucy Fischer, John Kurten, John Mullarkey, Patrice Petro, David Rodowick, Jeffrey Scheible, Philipp Schmerheim, Melinda Szaloky, and Charles Wolfe.

Works Cited

Aitken, Ian. *European Film Theory and Cinema: A Critical Introduction*. Bloomington: Indiana UP, 2001. Print.

Allen, Richard, and Murray Smith, eds. *Film Theory and Philosophy*. New York: Oxford UP, 1997. Print.

Andrew, Dudley. *Concepts in Film Theory*. New York: Oxford UP, 1984. Print.

———. *The Major Film Theories: An Introduction*. New York: Oxford UP, 1976. Print.

Arnheim, Rudolf. *Film as Art*. Berkeley: U of California P, 1957. Print.

Baudry, Jean-Louis. "Ideological Effects of the Basic Cinematographic Apparatus." *Narrative, Apparatus, Ideology: A Film Theory Reader*. Ed. Philip Rosen. New York: Columbia UP, 1986. 286–98. Print.

Bordwell, David. "Film: Film Theory." *Encyclopedia of Aesthetics*. Ed. Michael Kelly. Vol. 2. New York: Oxford UP, 1998. 197–201. Print.

———. *Making Meaning: Inference and Rhetoric in the Interpretation of Cinema*. Cambridge: Harvard UP, 1989. Print.

Branigan, Edward. "Of Prepositions: Lost and Found." *Velvet Light Trap* 64 (2009): 95–98. Print.

———. "On the Analysis of Interpretive Language." *Film Criticism* 17.2-3 (1993): 4–21. Print.

———. *Projecting a Camera: Language-Games in Film Theory*. New York: Routledge, 2006. Print.

———. "Soundtrack in Mind." *Projections* 4.1 (2010): 41–67. Print.

———. "To Zero and Beyond: Noël Burch's *Theory of Film Practice*." Lehman, *Defining* 149–68.

Buckland, Warren. *The Cognitive Semiotics of Film*. Cambridge: Cambridge UP, 2000. Print.

———. "The Death of the Camera: A Review and Rational Reconstruction of Edward Branigan's *Projecting a Camera*." *New Review of Film and Television Studies* 4.3 (2006): 311–30. Print.

———. "Film as 'Specific Signifying Practice': A Rational Reconstruction of Stephen Heath's 'On Screen, in Frame: Film and Ideology.'" *Semiotica*, forthcoming.

———. "Film Semiotics." *A Companion to Film Theory*. Ed. Toby Miller and Robert Stam. Oxford: Blackwell, 1999. 84–104. Print.

———. Introduction. *Film Theory and Contemporary Hollywood Movies*. Ed. Buckland. New York: Routledge, 2009. 1–16. Print.

———. "A Rational Reconstruction of the 'Cinema of Attractions.'" *The Cinema of Attractions Reloaded*. Ed. Wanda Strauven. Amsterdam: Amsterdam UP, 2006. 41–55. Print.

———. "Theorizing Melodrama: A Rational Reconstruction of 'Tales of Sound and Fury.'" *Mind the Screen: Media Concepts According to Thomas Elsaesser*. Ed. Jaap Kooijman, Patricia Pisters, and Wanda Strauven. Amsterdam: Amsterdam UP, 2008. 32–42. Print.

———. "What Does the Statistical Style Analysis of Film Involve?" *Literary and Linguistic Computing* 23.2 (2008): 219–30. Print.

Burch, Noël. *Theory of Film Practice*. Trans. Helen R. Lane. New York: Praeger, 1973. Print.

Bywater, Tim, and Thomas Sobchack. "The Ideological/Theoretical Approach: Using Basic Principles to Uncover Deeper Meanings." *An Introduction to Film Criticism: Major Critical Approaches to Narrative Film.* New York: Longman, 1989. 163–93. Print.

Cain, William E. "Contemporary Theory, the Academy, and Pedagogy." Sadoff and Cain 3–14.

Carroll, Noël. *Philosophical Problems of Classical Film Theory.* Princeton: Princeton UP, 1988. Print.

Casetti, Francesco. *Theories of Cinema, 1945–1995.* Trans. Francesca Chiostri and Elizabeth Gard Bartolini-Salimbeni. Rev. ed. Austin: U of Texas P, 1999. Print.

Clark, Andy. *Being There: Putting Brain, Body, and World Together Again.* Cambridge: MIT P, 1997. Print.

Currie, Gregory. *Image and Mind: Film, Philosophy, and Cognitive Science.* New York: Cambridge UP, 1995. Print.

Doane, Mary Ann. "The Object of Theory." *Rites of Realism: Essays on Corporeal Cinema.* Ed. Ivone Margulies. Durham: Duke UP, 2002. 80–89. Print.

Elsaesser, Thomas, and Malte Hagener. *Film Theory: An Introduction through the Senses.* New York: Routledge, 2010. Print.

Elsaesser, Thomas, and Warren Buckland. "Film Theory, Methods, Analysis." *Studying Contemporary American Film: A Guide to Movie Analysis.* London: Arnold, 2002. 1–25. Print.

Falzon, Christopher. *Philosophy Goes to the Movies: An Introduction to Philosophy.* New York: Routledge, 2002. Print.

Fauconnier, Gilles, and Mark Turner. *The Way We Think: Conceptual Blending and the Mind's Hidden Complexities.* New York: Basic, 2002. Print.

Gledhill, Christine, and Linda Williams. "Part 1: Really Useful Theory." *Reinventing Film Studies.* Ed. Gledhill and Williams. London: Arnold, 2000. 5–95. Print.

Henderson, Brian. *A Critique of Film Theory.* New York: Dutton, 1980. Print.

Hernadi, Paul. *Cultural Transactions: Nature, Self, Society.* Ithaca: Cornell UP, 1995. Print.

———. "Literary Interpretation and the Rhetoric of the Human Sciences." *The Rhetoric of the Human Sciences: Language and Argument in Scholarship and Public Affairs.* Ed. John S. Nelson, Allan Megill, and Donald N. McCloskey. Madison: U of Wisconsin P, 1987. 263–75. Print.

Lehman, Peter, ed. *Defining Cinema.* New Brunswick: Rutgers UP, 1997. Print.

———. "Introduction: What Is Film Theory?" Lehman, *Defining* 1–13.

Metz, Christian. *The Imaginary Signifier: Psychoanalysis and the Cinema.* Trans. Celia Britton, Annwyl Williams, Ben Brewster, and Alfred Guzzetti. Bloomington: Indiana UP, 1982. Print.

Mullarkey, John. *Refractions of Reality: Philosophy and the Moving Image.* New York: Palgrave, 2008. Print.

Noë, Alva. *Out of Our Heads: Why You Are Not Your Brain, and Other Lessons from the Biology of Consciousness.* New York: Hill, 2009. Print.

Plantinga, Carl. "Cognitive Film Theory: An Insider's Appraisal." *CiNéMAS* 12 (2002): 15–37. Print.

Polan, Dana. "Film Theory Re-assessed." *Continuum: The Australian Journal of Media and Culture* 1.2 (1987): n. pag. Web. 21 Dec. 2010.

Rodowick, D. N. "An Elegy for Theory." *October* 122 (2007): 91–109. Print.
———. "Gray Is Theory (Except in Black and White or Color); or, The Paradoxes and Pleasures of Film Theory." Sadoff and Cain 245–57.
Sadoff, Dianne F., and William E. Cain, eds. *Teaching Contemporary Theory to Undergraduates.* New York: MLA, 1994. Print.
Saussure, Ferdinand de. *Course in General Linguistics.* Trans. Roy Harris. Chicago: Open Court, 1986. Print.
Stam, Robert. *Film Theory: An Introduction.* Oxford: Blackwell, 2000. Print.
Stam, Robert, Robert Burgoyne, and Sandy Flitterman-Lewis. *New Vocabularies in Film Semiotics: Structuralism, Post-structuralism, and Beyond.* New York: Routledge, 1992. Print.
Szaloky, Melinda. "Making New Sense of Film Theory through Kant: A Novel Teaching Approach." *New Review of Film and Television Studies* 3.1 (2005): 33–58. Print.
Thompson, Kristin. *Breaking the Glass Armor: Neoformalist Film Analysis.* Princeton: Princeton UP, 1988. Print.
Trifonova, Temenuga, ed. *European Film Theory.* New York: Routledge, 2008. Print.
Turvey, Malcolm. "Can Scientific Models of Theorizing Help Film Theory?" Wartenberg and Curran 21–32.
Vescio, Bryan. "Reading in the Dark: Cognitivism, Film Theory, and Radical Interpretation." *Style* 35.4 (2001): 572–91. Print.
Wartenberg, Thomas E., and Angela Curran, eds. *The Philosophy of Film: Introductory Text and Readings.* Oxford: Blackwell, 2005. Print.
Wittgenstein, Ludwig. *Philosophical Investigations.* Trans. G. E. M. Anscombe, P. M. S. Hacker, and Joachim Schulte. Rev. 4th ed. Oxford: Wiley-Blackwell, 2009. Print.
———. "The Yellow Book." *Wittgenstein's Lectures: Cambridge, 1932–1935.* Ed. Alice Ambrose. Amherst: Prometheus, 2001. Sec. 18. Print.

Appendix:
Some Components of a Film Theory

Ontology studies the nature of an artifact—its determining features and traits. What is film? That is, what is a film made out of that makes it a film rather than something else? For example, of which of the following might it be made: celluloid, light beams, photographs, images, experiences of images, editing, time, movement, ideas, feelings? How broadly or narrowly should *film* be defined and where does the definition lead? An example of a (misleading) ontological claim is the following: "I believe that film is essentially a visual medium." Some additional issues in ontology:

> Which are the essential materials or necessary forms and functions in a film as opposed to the merely contingent or accidental features of a film? Running time, for example, does not define what it is to be a film, since a film does not need to have a particular running time to be a film.

What is the role of an artist's intention? This problem concerns authorship, the source of an artifact; that is, perhaps what the artifact is depends on who made it come into being with a certain, definite purpose. The purpose, then, supposedly explains and defines what it is to be that film. Thus the question arises, is art something private or public?

What is the relationship of film to other arts and materials and sources? Perhaps what film is depends on its differences from and similarities to some close relatives. And what exactly brings about such a close grouping of certain things, and of which close relatives? only the arts?

Epistemology studies the conditions of knowing and interpreting. How is a spectator able to comprehend a film? through which logic? What allows us to say, "I understand the scene," or "This is what the scene really means"? How do we become conscious of something in watching a film? What makes meanings occur to us? Are they given to us, or do we make them? In general, epistemology addresses the following question: how are we able to think and know something about something else in, through, from, with, despite, or outside a film? After all, many of the things that we see and think about while watching a film are not in the movie theater.

Of what is knowledge made? The doctrine of empiricism holds that knowledge is obtained and built up directly through sense data, sensation, and experience (data-driven, bottom-up). As a method, it relies on close scientific observation and experiment to discover the facts of the world and of film. By contrast, the doctrine of rationalism holds that knowledge is obtained indirectly through reason, inference, and logic (goal-driven, top-down). As a method, rationalism relies on speculative inquiry to uncover the hidden, nonobvious laws of the world and film.

What is the role of memory in watching a film?

In what way does something come to possess a meaning: does it happen by convention? causality? resemblance? intention? expression? communication? What are the large-scale ways of enforcing a meaning? through rhetoric, genre, and narrative form?

What is interpretation? In what way does a film solicit from us certain abstract generalizations, such as the claim that a scene is about the mutability of joy or shows the unexpectedness of the dance of time or illustrates how remorse attaches to fate?

What is truth? How is reference made to a state of affairs in the world? What will count as mere appearance?

What causes sensation, pleasure, and emotion? Is the cause external or internal?

Aesthetics involves evaluative judgments made about an artifact, such as "I thought the scene was not effective."

What is the proper use of techniques and devices?

What makes a scene forceful or mediocre? Are there special aesthetic emotions (e.g., the sublime)?

What criteria justify or drive our values and norms: that is, to what sort of ethics do we subscribe? What accounts for the ranking of the fifteen to twenty major evaluative principles in criticism, like celebrating narratives that are reflexive, visceral, novel, ironic, or transgressive over narratives that are transparent or linear?

Ideology examines the psychology of belief—how attitudes are formed and come to possess legitimacy and authority (e.g., "I think the film is sexist").

What is the relation of film to society and politics? to its economic institutions, including issues of censorship, propaganda, and documentaries?

What is the relation of film to its creation: technology; tools and instruments; capital; labor; film finance, production, distribution, and exhibition; and, notably, the various institutions and specialized tools of film criticism?

What are the socially constructed roles of gender, sexual orientation, race, ethnicity, class, and nationality?

What is the relation of film to history: how has film been used and regarded?

Realism: what makes a film realistic? convincing and plausible? Is part of a film's link to the world already built in and natural—a matter of ontology; for instance, because film is photography not painting? Are a spectator's prior beliefs and expectations important to a feeling of realism or epistemology? Is realism a matter of narrative or documentary conventions so that it is not at all natural but must be learned? Is it a genre? Does realism involve persuasion or craft (aesthetics)? Does it involve the accurate transmission of an author's vision? the transmission of a dominant ideology, what most people feel is ordinary and real? Perhaps on this basis a science fiction or fantasy film may well seem realistic.

If several of the above factors are important in creating realism, then how important is each factor? The basic question here concerns how realism as a method or style or strategy of representing something in an art medium is connected to that which is being referred to in the real world. Of course, what a person decides is real in the world, and capable of being represented realistically by a film, is a problem, since the real may be invisible, emotional, immaterial, spiritual, poetic, unknowable, and so forth. In tackling these issues, it may be useful to make distinctions among such words as *real*, *reality*, *realization*, *realism*, and *reel*.

Maureen Turim

Teaching Feminist Film Theory; or, Women and Film

The enormously broad and varied work on issues of women's representation in film and the historical emergence of women making films has made teaching women in film and feminist film theory an exhilarating but daunting task. Are we talking about one course or a series of courses? What needs to be done now? Do we need to provide a history of critical approaches, a survey of key films, or rather a focus on a particular question, such as the woman's body or women in the workplace? Should the course be organized by historical periods or as a comparison of theoretical approaches? Any of these solutions may be viable. In this essay I emphasize the importance of grounding any such course in a close study of filmic expression. The question I ask students to keep in mind is, How are women woven into the form of this film, its images and sounds? Then as we move through the semester, I ask them to look for repetitions and deviations from our expectations, built by historical patterns.

If feminist film studies began by insisting that gender matters and is now taking into account what it might mean to undo gender, we are all scrambling to decide what to retain from our theoretical heritage. Urgently, we update our approaches to race, international perspectives, and queer theory. On a theoretical level, I suggest both demonstrating the structural functions of sexual difference in narrative and denaturalizing the dichotomy of genders as an absolute difference in society. I close by directly addressing feminist theory, which, while it has triumphed and come into its own as central to theories of film and culture, still needs to be salvaged from oversimplification and from the stereotypes used to denigrate it.

In this light, let's for now recall some basics. Films, like much cultural production, build a conception of women, but in a complex weave of narrative, image, and sound, a rich and seductive plentitude. It is hard for some students to see that films represent creative choices and constructions that entail discourses or arguments. Film analysis at its best incisively demonstrates this process and deconstructs assumptions that view the status of women as natural or simply true. Other students find depictions of women appalling, looking critically at childlike waifs, oversexualized bimbos, and evil femme fatales, sometimes failing to see the nuances of intelligence and desire that may emerge in or alongside these stereotypes.

Film analysis should be different from casual reception. The hardest part about teaching such an ideologically loaded subject is moving students through their intuitive reactions to characters in film toward a more complex view of character construction by films, in the context of history and theory. Pedagogically, we may wish to build on what students already know, yet we also need to suggest that freedom, rights, and self-determination for women entail more than many have come to understand. Many students do not realize how recently women earned the right to vote or the even more recent date when sexual harassment in the university and the workplace became illegal.

My first argument, then, is that successful courses on women and film must take into account, then move beyond, the enunciations so prevalent in class discussions: "I liked or admired" versus "I hated or found repulsive" a given character, image, or action. These comments will recur; each time they should be taken as an opportunity to delve more deeply into the film and its context.

It is to instill the sense of women in both history and film history that some women in film courses are organized with a strong historical component, especially for the part that focuses on American film. I have often used a text devoted to women's history outside film. When I team-taught the course Women and Film at the University of Wisconsin with Fina Bathrick and Diane Waldman, my favorite historical overviews were William Henry Chafe's *The American Woman: Her Changing Social, Economic, and Political Roles, 1920–1970* and Mary P. Ryan's *Womanhood in*

America: From Colonial Times to the Present. Ryan, in her overview of over two hundred years of women's history, makes especially useful, if brief, comments on the connection between filmic representation and social history, as when she examines young women shop clerks in Hollywood narratives in juxtaposition to her treatment of the development of department stores, consumerism, and salesladies. Today, these histories of US women are out of print, as is Nancy Woloch's *Women and the American Experience*, and we are more likely to concentrate on individual historical articles that coincide with the films or use essays on the films that demonstrate the historical and sociological context. For those who are still seeking a history text, I suggest the following: Chafe, *The Paradox of Change: American Women in the Twentieth Century*; Ryan, *Mysteries of Sex: Tracing Women and Men through American History*; or Glenda Riley, *Inventing the American Woman: An Inclusive History*. We must ask students to put together social historical context and filmic representation and to think through the connections as an ongoing investigation.

Such emphasis on history, including the rich heritage of silent film and the sound films of the 1930s through the 1950s, is unlike the approach Sarah Gilligan uses in her book *Teaching Women and Film*. Here, she offers an annotated course outline that looks at the contemporary role of women in the film industry, at audiences, at genre, as well as at representation, stars, and gender. Her case studies are all drawn from recent film, and her approach focuses on the film industry and reception studies. She supplies useful methodological investigations in this vein and suggests assigning students worksheets instead of essays to write. She suggests her approach is particularly valid because it is easiest for students to grasp the issues in films with which they are already familiar.

The decision to focus on the recent past rather than to include the sweep of film history may be governed by an instructor's background, but I do not agree with Gilligan's argument that one should concentrate on the recent past because those films are already familiar to students. I would like to encourage more teaching of early American and international film, whenever possible. I think learning to analyze films from different periods greatly helps students analyze films from the recent past and present. I find using D. W. Griffith's shorts, such as *The Lonedale Operator* (1911) or *The Painted Lady* (1912), works well. Later introducing works by early women filmmakers, such as Lois Weber's *The Blot* or *Too Wise Wives*, both from 1921, or Alice Guy-Blaché's *Matrimony's Speed Limit* (1913), begins to establish the complexity of the silent period. Dorothy Arzner's *The Wild*

Party (1929) illustrates how a woman director emerges in the early sound period, staging Clara Bow as a hard-partying flapper converted to serious young woman through a romance with her professor. This film allows instructors to speak of the ideological work that romance performs in films about women. The pre–Hays Code fallen-women films such as William A. Seiter's *Big Business Girl* or Alfred E. Green's *Baby Face*, both from 1931, show the transition to sound and the discourse surrounding workplace sexuality and gender issues in the early 1930s.

Currently, the task of teaching a historical course on women in film is made more difficult by a paucity of adequate textbooks dedicated to such a course. Long-standing texts for women and film courses include *Women's Pictures: Feminism and Cinema*, by Annette Kuhn, now out of print, and *Women and Film: Both Sides of the Camera*, by E. Ann Kaplan. Central to both texts are the issues of melodrama and classical film representation in contrast to women filmmakers' attempts to answer to this tradition, including the "counter-cinema" of feminist and Brechtian inspiration and international progressive cinema. Each book introduces students to feminist theory, women's genres, and women directors. Kaplan's book may be frustrating to use, however, since it is structured through the analysis of a small set of selected films, which may not be the ones you use or the ones students have seen. In my experience students only want to read analyses of films they have seen. Many professors assign only Kaplan's introductory essay or only an essay pertaining to a film they decide to use, preferring other essays for other film choices.

The numerous anthologies on women and film present the same selection problem, leading many professors to turn to reserve readings, course Web postings, or duplicated course readers. Most useful would be a general text that is based less on extended analyses of a few examples and more on comparative treatments of genres, periods, or issues, taking as its central issue the historical changes of women's representation.

A historically oriented women-in-film class must also address the racism of film history. In teaching exclusion, marginalizing, and stereotyping of women of color and ethnicity, one risks reproducing such issues, since there are so few films that offer a progressive focus on other than white or Christian women. Such films as Oscar Micheaux's *Within Our Gates* (1920) and Herbert Biberman's *Salt of the Earth* (1954) might be used to trouble the impression left by Victor Fleming's *Gone with the Wind* (1939), Michael Curtiz's *Mildred Pierce* (1945), or even both John Stahl's and Douglas Sirk's versions of *Imitation of Life* (1934, 1959) that other women's stories fit only into the interstices of the white woman's narrative.

Another question is, How do we teach the history and theory of female spectatorship? The examination of spectatorship gained great traction in feminist theory as a means of approaching, indeed of validating, the study of melodrama and soap operas—genres that, it could be argued, were significant to masses of women. Female spectators, a group to which early cinema sought to appeal, became important in early debates about cinema history. Lesbian spectatorship, which appropriates films and stars in a way that works against the grain of straight readings, constitutes another significant element of spectator studies. Although arguments concerning female spectatorship often operate mainly through textual readings of films, the marketing of female stars—of all stars—to women has taken place largely through film magazines and has been an aspect of studying spectatorship and fandom as institutions. So I emphasize getting my students to ask what research needs to be undertaken to address spectatorship historically. Too often such research is neglected, so that writers primarily extrapolate from their subjective reaction. Alternatively, spectator studies point to the writing of critics, but I caution students that they need a context broader than a critic's review, since reviews are not self-evident markers of reception.

I like to take a case history of a film that challenges certain spectatorship assumptions, especially regarding a critic's reception, posing a question such as, Why did Pauline Kael wax euphoric about Bernardo Bertolucci's *Last Tango in Paris* (1972)? Kael's watershed review poses a set of complicated questions for feminist film theory and history, appearing as it does alongside the flourishing of second-wave feminism. Kael ignored aspects of the film's misogyny, yet she recognized something of what we can now see as the role this film played in ushering in what has been called the cinema of sensation, or films' preoccupation with bodily pleasure and the breaking of taboos. There is a direct line from *Last Tango* to recent films such as *Romance* (1999), by Catherine Breillat (who had a walk-on role in *Last Tango* alongside her sister), a line that traces the more desperate aspects of female heterosexual desire. Yet the film evokes familiar self-sacrificial demands of its female character, only to twist these at the end to render her a dishonest betrayer of the self she explored throughout the film. *Last Tango*, mixed object that it is, speaks to a different order, of changes yet to come, and perhaps even to the historical tendency of feminist viewers to respond selectively, dropping many of their feminist concerns.

In addressing spectatorship, I introduce what I call the "solipsistic fallacy," the assumption that most other spectators had or should have the same reaction one has. Differences of opinion that appear in class discussions can demonstrate the diversity of spectatorship. The questions of spectatorship now become, How do spectators at a historical moment and from any given class, ethnic, or gender position interpret the constellation of signifiers that a film uses to construct its notions of female being? How do we get inside raw box office numbers to understand groups of spectators? How do we treat the unconscious and the multidimensionality of spectatorship?

The means to answer those questions involve extrafilmic historical and sociological sources, entailing theoretical speculation and a supported argument. One intriguing example is Kuhn's *Dreaming of Fred and Ginger: Cinema and Cultural Memory.* Teaching women in film, as is the case with teaching women in literature, sometimes feels like introducing students to the entire history of culture: from breast fetishism to taboos on lesbian desire, from suffrage and separate spheres to the racist aspects of domestic employment. The difference here is that while students may expect a course on Jane Austen or the history of women writers to entail questions of history, they may not bring the same expectations to a course on Jane Campion or women in film.

How does one then teach Campion's *The Piano* (1993)? The film is an obvious choice for a women in film course, because of its major female auteur (director-screenwriter) and compelling female characters, the mute mother and daughter-witness thrust into a male frontier that usurps native lands, in a melodrama focusing on female self-expression and female sexuality. A massive bibliography has already emerged on just this film, much of which addresses the Victorian and colonial context on one hand and desire on the other. Many of these essays play close, if intermittent, attention to filmic expression, recognizing that the film's camerawork, editing, sound, and music are key to the thematic issues much of the writing addresses. Gilligan's *Teaching Women and Film* mentions *The Piano* but only discusses it briefly. Harriet Elaine Margolis has edited *Jane Campion's* The Piano, and Felicity Coombs and Suzanne Gemmell have edited *Piano Lessons: Approaches to* The Piano. Maria Margaroni's essay on the film in *Camera Obscura* uses Kristevian theories of melancholia, though some might find that Julia Kristeva is somewhat problematically presented in this piece, particularly because of a rather literal interpretation of her reference to matricide.

An easy way to incorporate *The Piano* into a women and film class would be to use it to showcase the problems of feminism in postcolonial contexts. Instructors could also start the course with this film, to show how important methodology is to the project of the class. Introducing students to the various readings of the film, contradictory and partial, might be useful. Perhaps starting with just two readings, an instructor could select one that focuses on how well Campion orchestrates the melodrama to display the vivid release and then violent repression of female desire and contrast it to another that critiques the melodramatic form for putting female choices in impossible binary terms. Such an approach could open up the semester to thoughtful explorations. Film form of any complexity suggests multiple discourses, and if we can urge our students to see that there is not one template of feminist reading, then we have made progress.

Including world cinemas is increasingly important in a women and film course. Certainly one possibility is including a unit on the history of one or more national cinemas. Patrice Petro has made cogent arguments about the centrality of gender in *Joyless Streets: Women and Melodramatic Representation in Weimar Germany*; she amplifies the topic in her comparison with American cinema in *Aftershocks of the New: Feminism and Film History*. Margarethe von Trotta, Jutta Bruckner, Ulrike Ottinger, Monika Treut, Doris Dörrie, Helma Sanders-Brahms, and Helke Sander are among the German filmmakers whose works might also be considered. For French cinema, one might center on Agnès Varda's films, especially *Cleo from 5 to 7* (1962) and *Vagabond* (1985), or include the women directors Marguerite Duras, Claire Denis, Brigitte Rouan, Diane Kurys, and Breillat. Alternatively, one could organize this unit to address the entire European Union or the Hispanic transnational cinema. Perhaps even more vital to helping students rethink feminism beyond the US-European frame would be dedicating a section of the course to global cinema; one could group works that address feminism in the context of Islam, drawing on the great Iranian women filmmakers and a growing cadre of Arab women making films that propose a complex look at women caught among the forces of tradition, modernity, and reactionary movements. One of my favorite ways of addressing international women's issues is to structure a unit comparing representations in East and South Asia, comparing the films of China, Japan, Korea, and India. Postcolonialism could also serve as the organizing theoretical issue, linking women's representation from many continents.

In addition, I would argue for inclusion of avant-garde films by women. Two resources are *Women and Experimental Filmmaking*, edited by Jean Petrolle and Virginia Wright Wexman, and *Women's Experimental Cinema: Critical Frameworks*, edited by Robin Blaetz. The essays in these volumes suggest approaches to such filmmakers as Maya Deren, Germaine Dulac, Marie Menken, Joyce Wieland, Gunvor Nelson, Carolee Schneemann, Barbara Rubin, Amy Greenfield, Barbara Hammer, Chick Strand, Peggy Ahwesh, Leslie Thornton, Su Friedrich, Abigail Child, Chantal Akerman, Nina Menkes, Lourdes Portillo, Rea Tajiri, Cheryl Dunye, Sally Potter, Yvonne Rainer, Safi Faye, Trinh T. Minh-ha, Faith Hubley, Caroline Leaf, Marjorie Keller, Charlotte Robertson, and Rose Lowder. There are also many sources on Maya Deren, including a book edited by Bill Nichols. For those instructors unfamiliar with this large body of film art made by women, including even one film, such as Deren's *Meshes of the Afternoon* (1943), would introduce students to the potential force of women's expression in cinema. Similarly, Věra Chytilová's anarchistic comedy *Daisies* (1968) could serve to introduce issues of feminist political rebellion within creative filmmaking. Lucy Fischer's *Shot/Countershot: Film Tradition and Women's Cinema* suggests that pairing experimental films with traditional films addressing some of the same issues may be fruitful. Women filmmakers showing in your area might be invited to class; including a screening with the filmmaker present gives an added dimension to this aspect of the course.

The role of feminist documentary in the last fifty years has been enormous, and Diane Waldman and Janet Walker's anthology, *Feminism and Documentary*, is a useful introduction to the genre. The section on innovative autobiographies overlaps with the area of avant-garde film and might be used as a transition from one unit of the course to another. Many of the films discussed address race and ethnicity as well as labor and class and so offer another way to bring these crucial matters into the course.

Let me conclude with a longer discussion of the role of theory. A cluster of concepts concerning the gaze, voyeurism, exhibitionism, fetishism, masquerade, and performance remain key to teaching both feminist theory and women and film. All these concepts engage issues of females as objects of desire and issues of female desire itself (that is, the subjectivity of desiring females). Now is the time to reengage with these crucial concepts, going beyond reductionist versions of them and avoiding the glosses on the original essays that sometimes discredit the importance of the concepts per se. What could be more central to teaching women in film than understanding how one looks at women and how women look out at the world and what the image of a woman might mean from the standpoint of sexuality's relation to power? I do suggest, however, that we link these psychoanalytic concepts with philosophical investigation of the same issues. Rather than retain all aspects of the historical psychoanalytic formulations, we should update psychoanalysis in the light of feminism, queer theory, and other theoretical advances. Elizabeth Cowie's *Representing the Woman: Cinema and Psychoanalysis* makes some useful steps in the direction of redefining and applying the concepts.

If all fetishism does not constitute a sadistic view of women, it is still important to speak of those moments in which sadism might underlie a fetishistic representation of women. If a woman is sometimes portrayed as the dominatrix, does that necessarily mean that viewers are more likely to respond to her as masochists? The challenge for us is to look at the myriad enunciations of power and gender in film history, indeed, in many individual films, and to ask hard questions about the relation between the psyche and the image of the body, as well as questions about the social construction of power.

The opening scene of Kimberly Peirce's *Boys Don't Cry* (1999), in which the character Brandon Teena, born Teena Brandon and played by Hilary Swank, slips a sock into his pants then adjusts it for more plausibility, provides an invitation into discussing the reinvention of the gendered body and what this means for women. That this scene is set before a mirror and rhymes with a later mirror scene in the film provides the opportunity to introduce issues I address in my essay "Looking Back at the Mirror" and to connect this scene to framing in the rearview mirror at other moments in the film. *Boys Don't Cry* is a useful film for teaching patriarchal oppression as it applies to both women and men and for teaching Judith Butler's performative theories of gender. My classes have puzzled over both the stripping scene and the later rape scene, shocked or unnerved by their violence. So I turn the discussion to the structure of the film, hoping that by now the class can see how scenes in a film interact theoretically. The film depicts the trial by the group for lying degenerating into a punishing trial by fire of Brandon for being between genders, for having the body of one gender and the desire to be another. When a student asks, Doesn't everyone exist in the gaps between assumed gender characteristics and personal, invented, and performed desires, and doesn't this film establish identification with an image of that struggle? then I know the course was worth the effort.

Works Cited

Blaetz, Robin, ed. *Women's Experimental Cinema: Critical Frameworks.* Durham: Duke UP, 2007. Print.

Chafe, William Henry. *The American Woman: Her Changing Social, Economic, and Political Roles, 1920–1970.* New York: Oxford UP, 1972. Print.

———. *The Paradox of Change: American Women in the Twentieth Century.* New York: Oxford UP, 1991. Print.

Coombs, Felicity, and Suzanne Gemmell, eds. *Piano Lessons: Approaches to* The Piano. Sydney: Libbey, 1999. Print.

Cowie, Elizabeth. *Representing the Woman: Cinema and Psychoanalysis.* Minneapolis: U of Minnesota P, 1997. Print.

Fischer, Lucy. *Shot/Countershot: Film Tradition and Women's Cinema.* Princeton: Princeton UP, 1989. Print.

Gilligan, Sarah. *Teaching Women and Film.* London: BFI Educ., 2003. Print.

Kael, Pauline. Rev. of *Last Tango in Paris*, dir. Bernardo Bertolucci. *New Yorker* 28 Oct. 1972: 130. Print.

Kaplan, E. Ann. *Women and Film: Both Sides of the Camera.* New York: Methuen, 1983. Print.

Kuhn, Annette. *Dreaming of Fred and Ginger: Cinema and Cultural Memory.* New York: New York UP, 2002. Print.

———. *Women's Pictures: Feminism and Cinema.* London: Verso, 1994. Print.

Last Tango in Paris. Dir. Bernardo Bertolucci. United Artists, 1972. MGM Home Entertainment, 2007. DVD.

Margaroni, Maria. "Jane Campion's Selling of the Mother/land: Restaging the Crisis of the Postcolonial Subject." *Camera Obscura* 53 (2003): 93–125. Print.

Margolis, Harriet Elaine, ed. *Jane Campion's* The Piano. Cambridge: Cambridge UP, 2000. Print.

Nichols, Bill, ed. *Maya Deren and the American Avant-Garde.* Berkeley: U of California P, 2001. Print.

Petro, Patrice. *Aftershocks of the New: Feminism and Film History.* New Brunswick: Rutgers UP, 2002. Print.

———. *Joyless Streets: Women and Melodramatic Representation in Weimar Germany.* Princeton: Princeton UP, 1989. Print.

Petrolle, Jean, and Virginia Wright Wexman, eds. *Women and Experimental Filmmaking.* Urbana: U of Illinois P, 2005. Print.

The Piano. Dir. Jane Campion. Miramax, 1993. Artisan Home Entertainment, 1999. DVD.

Riley, Glenda. *Inventing the American Woman: An Inclusive History.* Wheeling: Davidson, 1995. Print.

Ryan, Mary P. *Mysteries of Sex: Tracing Women and Men through American History.* Chapel Hill: U of North Carolina P, 2006. Print.

———. *Womanhood in America: From Colonial Times to the Present.* New York: New Viewpoints, 1975. Print.

Turim, Maureen. "Looking Back at the Mirror." *Psychoanalyses/Feminisms.* Ed. Peter L. Rudnytsky and Andrew Gordon. Albany: State U of New York P, 2000. Print.

Waldman, Diane, and Janet Walker, eds. *Feminism and Documentary.* Minneapolis: U of Minnesota P, 1999. Print. Visible Evidence 5.

Woloch, Nancy. *Women and the American Experience.* New York: Knopf, 1984. Print.

Paula J. Massood

Teaching African American Film: Race, Politics, and Aesthetics

> Nothing has done so much to awaken race consciousness of the colored man in the United States as the motion picture.
> (Foster, qtd. in Sampson 174)[1]

William Foster's observation above suggests that people of color recognized the power of the cinema far earlier than implied by the establishment of film programs in the 1960s or more recent courses on race and representation. In fact, Foster's exhortation for black entrepreneurs and audiences to grab hold of the new technology and use it for the betterment (social, spiritual, economic) of the race suggests an early overall cognizance of the affective power of the medium, one that Hugo Münsterberg would acknowledge a few years later in his *The Photoplay: A Psychological Study* (1916). To be sure, Foster was a showman and entrepreneur, not a theorist, but his identification of the medium with intellectual and political awakening has been a constant in African American considerations of film and filmmaking, pervading larger discussions of race and representation. In what ways did film awaken race consciousness, and how does it continue to do so?

Like African American writings on film, African American filmmaking is often considered a relatively recent phenomenon (a belief based in part on the ubiquity of films by Spike Lee and other modern filmmakers). Yet just about every moment in American film history has been inflected by an African American presence either in front of or behind the camera. As early as 1894, for example, Thomas Edison was capitalizing on the popularity of minstrelsy in his first films, which either featured popular stage actors such as James Grundy or which drew on familiar character types and comic scenarios—the pickaninny, the cakewalk—from the vaudeville circuit. In these early examples, American cinema borrowed racial caricatures from American theater and literature and extended them into a medium whose photographic base solidified such representations of black inhumanity. This "making real" of black inferiority developed over time, from comic figures to more threatening brutes, in concert with the American studio system, often leaving little space for alternative versions of African American life.

It would be a mistake, however, to write the tale of African American film as one of complete victimhood or exclusion. Furthermore, it is historically limiting to suggest, as many scholars do, that black American filmmaking began with responses to D. W. Griffith's racist *The Birth of a Nation* (1915) when, in fact, there has been an active black presence in American film—albeit one that existed on the periphery of the industry—from almost the beginnings. African American entrepreneurs like Foster, for example, saw the potential of the new medium of film as early as 1910—years before Griffith's screed against the Civil War—when he founded Foster Photoplay Company in Chicago. The filmmaking concern was geared toward providing African American audiences with "nondegrading Black-cast comedies" featuring African American entertainers from the vaudeville circuit and theater troupes like Chicago's Pekin Players (Sampson 174).

The sheer breadth of the topic of African American film leaves one wondering how to approach it in a classroom, particularly in an interdisciplinary setting made up of students who possess little or no knowledge of film form and history. Often the temptation has been to cover the topic either through issues of representation or through a form of narrative analysis that attaches value judgments on good or bad characters, story lines, or directorial talent (without an acknowledgement of the text's conditions of production). While such approaches have produced seminal studies of African American film—and here Donald Bogle's *Toms, Coons, Mulattoes,*

Mammies, and Bucks and Thomas Cripps's *Slow Fade to Black* are prime examples—they tend to overlook two facets of black American filmmaking that define how we understand and analyze black film. The first is African American film's relation to Hollywood. While this methodology suggests a purely industrial or empirical approach to an art form, it can address the issues of access, reception, and aesthetics that are bound up in the fabric of an industry that from its very beginnings has been dependent on economics for its survival. The second aspect concerns the ways in which African American film has been and continues to be an aesthetic and political tool of self-expression and self-constitution. Therefore, I find that the best approach to teaching African American film in a classroom—whether it be a semester-long survey class, a focused genre or director's course, or a course on another subject altogether—is introducing students to the historical roots of black filmmaking. In what follows I present a brief example of such material as an introduction to the overarching questions we ask of African American film.

The Foster Photoplay Company provides a compelling introduction to the industrial, aesthetic, and political issues laid out above. It was the first production company owned and operated by African Americans, and its first film, *The Railroad Porter* (1912), is considered the first black-directed film. In addition, its existence suggests the early—and self-conscious—engagement of black entrepreneurs with the medium.[2] Before establishing his production company, Foster held a variety of jobs in show business, including serving as the publicity agent in New York for the Bert Williams and George Walker productions of *In Dahomey* and *Abyssinia* and booking acts for the Pekin Theatre in Chicago. Foster, using the pseudonym Juli Jones, also wrote columns on the entertainment circuit for black newspapers such as the *Indianapolis Freeman* and the *Chicago Defender* (Sampson 172). His move into film production was a natural progression from his theater activities, combining his knowledge of the black vaudeville circuit with his well-documented interest in the state of the black entertainment industry. Foster saw film as a means to "offset so many insults to the race" (qtd. in Everett 54). But he was interested also in the medium's potential for entertainment and profit, and he predicted in 1913, shortly after the release of *The Railroad Porter*, that "for [the] promoter, manufacturer, producer and actor the field that will bring the biggest returns to Negroes for several investments is the motion picture industry" (qtd. in Sampson 175).

Soon other companies—financed by blacks or whites—were following Foster's example and producing films for black audiences, and the race film industry, the first independent black filmmaking, was born.[3] Many firms, like Foster's, were established by entrepreneurs who saw an opportunity to make money in a burgeoning new entertainment sector, and the content of the early films, mostly short comedies featuring black vaudevillians, suggests a relatively conventional approach to the medium. And yet race films were also created out of necessity, since the early American film industry—both in its initial iterations on the East Coast and its more organized structure on the West Coast—was closed to African American personnel in front of or behind the camera.[4] Spectatorship could be just as restricted because many theaters in both the North and the South were segregated, offering either separate screenings or separate seating areas for black and white patrons.

The growth of the race film industry also suggests that African American audiences were aware of the effects of film imagery very early in the medium's history and that they had a stake in watching themselves onscreen.[5] As early as 1913, for example, Foster mentions that "picture houses [have] been obliged to 'take off' pictures because . . . their colored patrons protested [that] the traditional caricature of their kind projected on the screen was not true to life" (qtd. in Sampson 174). The black press, picking up from its already extensive coverage of the theatrical circuits, soon began covering film, and reviewers stated their high expectations for films geared toward black audiences. What was a profit-making endeavor quickly became a battleground in defining African American identity. For race film companies, this battle was fought on the level of narrative as tension developed between entertainment and uplift: should audiences be content watching the same characters that were drawn from minstrelsy, or should they be exposed to more uplifting stories of black achievement? And how might the decision over content affect a company's ability to remain vital while competing against more technically accomplished Hollywood fare?

The release of *The Birth of a Nation* in 1915 resulted in state and national protests and censorship battles over Griffith's depictions of black depravity and inhumanity. The film's release also added to the desire among African American filmmakers to create alternative representations of black people, a desire closely aligned with the black elite's project to define a "New Negro" in the twentieth century.[6] During this crucial stage in the development of film form, the country was experiencing an industrial expansion. Northern industrial cities opened their factories to an influx of southern, formerly agrarian, workers. The Great Migration resulted in an

African American population that was increasingly urban and for whom Civil War–era melodramas, such as Griffith's, were outmoded. Film, in this environment, was seen as an important educational tool for the newly arrived migrants to the city, especially by the black middle class who took a progressive and pedagogical approach to the new technology.

Two of the most influential African American–owned outfits at this time were the Lincoln Motion Picture Company, established by George and Noble Johnson in 1915, and the Micheaux Book and Film Company, founded by Oscar Micheaux in 1918. Noble Johnson was a Hollywood character actor who, with his brother George, created the Lincoln Motion Picture Company with the intention of making "positive family films, each structured around a black hero's struggle to accomplish some admirable ambition" (Berry 50). Firmly ensconced in the uplift ideology embraced by W. E. B. Du Bois's "Talented Tenth," the company was celebrated in the black press for its "dedication to technical merits and thematic integrity in depicting black life and culture" and for presenting characters who were intelligent, accomplished, and dignified (Everett 117). The company, funded by the money Noble Johnson earned through his studio work, produced three films—*The Realization of a Negro's Ambition* (1916), *A Trooper of Troop K* (1917), and *The Law of Nature* (1917)—in quick succession before he left to fulfill his contractual obligations with Universal. Lincoln continued operations for a few years more before ceasing operations in 1923 because of financial difficulties. While uplift narratives were critical successes, such content still had to compete with Hollywood films, most of which were generously capitalized and featured popular stars.

Lincoln's most serious competitor was the Micheaux Book and Film Company. A former railroad porter, homesteader, and novelist, Micheaux was also an entrepreneur, a provocateur, and a race man who, like Foster, tried to combine the two facets of African American silent filmmaking, entertainment and uplift. Micheaux moved into filmmaking after George and Noble Johnson refused his request to direct the Lincoln adaptation of his novel, *The Homesteader* (1917). Micheaux had no prior experience in filmmaking, but he directed the adaptation himself and released *The Homesteader* in February 1919. The film, a semi-autobiographical story about a homesteader in South Dakota, was a critical success; *Half-Century Magazine*, for example, suggested that it ranked "in power and workmanship with the greatest of white western productions" (qtd. in McGilligan 131). The film's premiere run was short-lived, however. After receiving complaints from members of the black church that the film vilified black preachers, the Chicago censorship board banned future screenings of *The Homesteader* in the city because of its "tendency to disturb the public peace" (qtd. in McGilligan 130). The ban was overturned a few days later, but it was just one of many incidents in Micheaux's career—which extended from the silent to the sound era and included over forty films—where the filmmaker was criticized for his presentation of the less savory aspects of African American life at a time when the black bourgeoisie was trying to prove its equality.[7]

It may have been his skill at garnering publicity through controversy or his ability to make films for very little money that made Micheaux's film company the only one to survive the transition to sound in 1927. Most companies were undercapitalized and forced to compete against a Hollywood product that was technically superior and the beneficiary of monopolistic distribution and exhibition practices. When Al Jolson, in blackface, adapted stage minstrelsy for sound film in *The Jazz Singer* (1927), the fate of the race film companies, especially those making the more earnest uplift melodramas, was sealed. Moreover, Hollywood's borrowings from the vaudeville stage, combined with a belief in the general harmony of African American voices, resulted in a demand for black singers and entertainers in Hollywood, reducing the pool of talent available to independent producers, who could not compete with studio wages.[8]

It was not long, however, before the race film industry reappeared, though with marked changes in its organization and content, suggesting the decisions and compromises producers faced to compete with Hollywood. In this context, Micheaux's sound career serves as an interesting example. Although Micheaux was the sole African American producer to survive the transition to sound, he did not emerge unscathed. Notorious for his cost-cutting and low-budget productions, even Micheaux felt the effects of the changes in the industry. By 1928 the Micheaux Book and Film Company was forced into bankruptcy. It was only by accepting the backing of white investors—the theater owner Frank Schiffman and the manager Leo Brecher—that Micheaux was able to start afresh with a new company, the Micheaux Film Company.[9] This new financial backing enabled him to make his first sound film, *The Exile*, in 1931.

Micheaux's partnership with Schiffman was part of a larger trend in race film production, in which white-financed companies were established and began producing films that could directly compete with Hollywood for the attentions of black audiences. A main battleground in this offense was film content. Whereas earlier companies like the Lincoln produced uplift melodramas, sound-era race films were, for the most part, African American adaptations of popular Hollywood genre films, notably the gangster film and the western. Many also included song-and-dance numbers featuring cabaret performers, in a direct engagement with Hollywood's use of black entertainers.

While Micheaux's films bore financial constraints, other race film companies, like the aptly named Million Dollar Productions, began producing some of the "most stylish black films" of the late 1930s (Sampson 222). Million Dollar Productions was established in 1937 by Leo and Harry Popkin, West Coast entrepreneurs, who teamed up with Ralph Cooper, former emcee of the Apollo Theater and a talented singer and dancer who had been frustrated by his limited options with the studios. Cooper joined with the Popkins once he and his producing partner, George Randol, ran into financial trouble on their first film, a gangster film called *Dark Manhattan* (1937). The Popkins helped finance and distribute the film and then made three more films with Cooper, including the gangster films *Bargain with Bullets* (1937) and *Gang War* (1939) and the musical *The Duke Is Tops* (1938), starring Lena Horne. While such genre films have often been dismissed as nothing more than black versions of Hollywood films, many were popular with critics and audiences of the time; for example, *Bargain with Bullets* was described as "a step forward for the Negro in the film world" at the time of its release (qtd. in Sampson 353).

This shift in content from edifying uplift tales to Hollywood's demoralizing and demeaning popular attractions has led at least one scholar to describe this period in black film as an "identity crisis" (Taylor 24). The questions raised by these genre films indicate the tensions inherent in African American filmmaking, centered on the films' relation to the American film industry and on whether breaking with Hollywood guarantees a departure from the industry's legacy of stereotype. Larger questions loom: Does independence equal political and representational authenticity (if such a thing exists)? Is Hollywood always already hobbled by technical and narrative conventions that can only support a white, male, heteronormative point of view?

Such questions may seem limited to the race film industry, but they remain relevant even decades after the last race film was released in 1948 (Micheaux's *The Betrayal*). During the late 1960s, for example, black independent filmmaking reappeared in two forms, both of which asked many of the same questions as did Foster, Micheaux, and Cooper. On the one hand was provocateur Melvin Van Peebles, whose *Sweet Sweetback's*

Baadasssss Song (1971) borrowed its guerrilla-like approach to production, marketing, and exhibition straight from Micheaux. *Sweetback*'s eponymous sex worker turned revolutionary reflected the changes of the time: he was highly sexualized, as befit post–production code American filmmaking, and more militarized than past African American heroes, reflecting changes in the civil rights movement following a series of violent urban rebellions and the assassination of Martin Luther King, Jr., and of Malcolm X. The film struck a chord with audiences, earning millions, despite its use of experimental aesthetics that included jump cuts, narrative repetitions, an asynchronous sound track, and an overall low-budget look.[10]

The critical and aesthetic response to the film indicates that Van Peebles faced a similar set of expectations as Micheaux. Some critics, like Huey Newton, viewed the film as revolutionary, especially supporting its message of black resistance (particularly Sweetback's assault of LAPD officers who had taken him into custody). Others, particularly those writing for more mainstream outlets like *Ebony*, were troubled by the film's violence, its graphic sexuality, and the fact that it made a hero of a criminal (see Massood, "*Sweet Sweetback*"; Hartmann). Like decades before, the argument among critics focused on the power of film as an orchestrator of demeaning stereotypes versus a model of film that enables positive African American self-definition.

The second branch of black independent filmmaking in the late 1960s and 1970s was the Los Angeles school of filmmakers, a group of young African and African American film students associated with the University of California, Los Angeles, who were committed to creating a new aesthetic for black filmmaking that rejected Hollywood narrative and technical conventions (which they viewed as interpolating black audiences into a particular master narrative of white supremacy). Inspired by the films emerging from nations in Latin America and on the African continent, filmmakers like Charles Burnett, Haile Gerima, Billie Woodberry, and (a bit later) Julie Dash and Zeinabu irene Davis adapted experimental aesthetics from such film movements to their specific context, one in which, they felt, African Americans occupied a similar position in the United States that colonized peoples occupied elsewhere. They were also inspired by Van Peebles's filmmaking, particularly *Sweetback*, but they chose less militant subject matter, instead focusing on stories of families and women trying to survive in Los Angeles's South Central and Watts neighborhoods (see Massood, "Aesthetic"). Charles Burnett's *Killer of Sheep* (1977) uses a combination of avant-garde techniques and documentary realism to tell a lyrical story of a man's attempts to remain connected to his family and friends while holding down a job in an abattoir that does not pay him enough to support his family.

Of the two filmmaking styles, it was Van Peebles's that made the greatest mark on Hollywood; drawing on *Sweetback*'s financial success, Hollywood quickly produced several low-budget black action films (or blaxploitation films), like *Shaft* (1971) and *Super Fly* (1972), that replicated Van Peebles's trickster characters and underworld narratives without his political punch. Despite the visibility that blaxploitation gave to African American talent, it was not long before religious and political groups were advocating against the films because of their representation of black criminality, venality, and buffoonery. The LA school films, despite their proximity to Hollywood, received little distribution and remained (and continue to remain) virtually unknown outside a small circle of audiences consisting of film scholars and festival attendees. The films, like those produced by earlier race filmmakers, could not compete against Hollywood's glossy production values and recognizable narrative conventions.

The discussion of independent filmmaking in the 1960s and 1970s offers an example of the ways in which aesthetic, industrial, and political issues introduced in the early twentieth century are relevant to later African American film and how a focus on such themes equips students with a complex understanding of race and representation in the late twentieth and early twenty-first centuries. In my classes, I encourage students to think historically and to understand African American filmmaking as part of a continuum in which some things—like technology and access to the industry—may change, but many of the central questions remain the same.

Spike Lee's *Bamboozled* (2000) and Lee Daniels's *Precious: Based on the Novel* Push *by Sapphire* (2009) serve as two constructive examples of contemporary African American films that raise, either directly or indirectly, questions about race and representation similar to those being asked decades ago. *Bamboozled* directly addresses the history of stereotype and caricature in its story of an African American television producer who writes a modern-day blackface minstrel show in an attempt to be fired from an unfulfilling job. Instead of offending audiences as intended, the show is a success and the producer is confronted by the knowledge that he has updated images of African American buffoonery, making them acceptable to audiences in a new millennium. I encourage students to identify and analyze *Bamboozled*'s many references to film and popular culture and to link these historical examples to the present-day media environment. The film's underlying question—has African American representation changed since the beginnings of American filmmaking?—is a useful topic for in-class discussion and also provides the foundation for a longer, more formal writing assignment.

Precious, on the other hand, is an example of a film that approaches questions of stereotype and caricature less directly. While the film was extremely successful at the box office and among most critics (earning numerous award nominations and two Oscars), there remains an uncanny element in some of the responses to *Precious* that return us to the cinema's assumed potential for veracity that often lies at the heart of discussions of African American representation. Several cultural critics have focused on the practice of color casting, claiming, as Jada F. Smith has on *The Root*, that the film replicates Hollywood's long practice of "colorism," in which good characters are light-skinned, while bad characters are dark-skinned (a criticism also directed at Micheaux during his career). Elsewhere critics have engaged in a heated argument about the film's representation of black men, with some, like Ishmael Reed, suggesting that *Precious* lacks positive male characters and comparing it unfavorably to *The Birth of a Nation*. Whether one agrees with either assessment, such arguments suggest that African American film representation remains a fraught subject, one that continues to rest on the identification of stereotypes. Students who have a knowledge of the history of African American representation may be better equipped to place a film like *Precious* into a broad context that asks more complex questions than whether the film presents good or bad images of African American life. Moreover, they may be able to identify and analyze the underlying assumptions of critical responses to African American film. When Foster predicted in 1913 that "the motion picture is here to stay. The Negro is sure to do his part of the work and certain to reap his portion of the reward" (qtd. in Sampson 175), he was addressing the cinema's potential as a business enterprise, a medium for uplift, and a tool to aid in the redefinition of African American representation. Students should be encouraged to consider similar questions in the classroom, whether the film is made in 1913 or 2012.

Notes

1. This quotation originally appeared in the *Indianapolis Freeman* 20 Dec. 1913.

2. Unfortunately, no extant copies of *The Railroad Porter* remain. While no footage exists of the film, the filmmaker and scholar Zeinabu irene Davis used the

plot summaries in reviews written during the time to re-create a scene from *The Railroad Porter* in *Compensation*, her 2000 independent feature that splits its temporal focus between early- and late-twentieth-century Chicago.

3. In 1913, for example, the Afro-American Film Company was founded in New York by white investors with the African American businessman Hunter C. Haynes as head of production. The Afro-American Film Company, like Foster's Photoplay Company, produced short comedies featuring popular black vaudevillians. Haynes left Afro-American to form his own Harlem-based company, the Haynes Photoplay Company, in 1914. The company produced the short comedy *Uncle Remus' First Visit to New York* and a newsreel featuring the popular boxers Sam Langford and Joe Walcott before going out of business.

4. Jacqueline Stewart suggests that whites in blackface began replacing African American actors in American films after about a decade (55).

5. The most comprehensive coverage of the critical response to early film is contained in Everett.

6. The term *New Negro* was first coined in 1895 in the *Cleveland Gazette* and was used to describe a group of New Yorkers who successfully passed civil rights legislation. By the turn of the century, the term was regularly used to refer to the black bourgeoisie.

7. Micheaux's story is richer and more complex than what can be covered in this brief essay. Several excellent studies of his films represent some of the most interesting work being done in African American film scholarship. See esp. Bowser and Spence; Bowser, Gaines, and Musser; Green, *Straight Lick* and *With a Crooked Stick*; Gaines.

8. Besides using African American performers in standard films, some Hollywood studios began producing musicals with all-black casts. Two of the earliest titles were *Hearts in Dixie* (1929) and *Hallelujah!* (1929). For more on the genre, see Knight; Weisenfeld; Massood, *Black City Cinema*.

9. Micheaux's relationship with Schiffman was fraught, and the partnership dissolved after Schiffman sued Micheaux in 1933 for money owed.

10. Such aesthetics were drawn from international film movements, including Soviet film from the twenties and the French new wave.

Works Cited

Berry, S. T. *The Fifty Most Influential Black Films: A Celebration of African-American Talent, Determination, and Creativity.* New York: Citadel, 2001. Print.

Bogle, Donald. *Toms, Coons, Mulattoes, Mammies, and Bucks: An Interpretive History of Blacks in American Films.* 1973. 3rd ed. New York: Continuum, 1994. Print.

Bowser, Pearl, Jane Gaines, and Charles Musser, eds. *Oscar Micheaux and His Circle: African-American Filmmaking and Race Cinema of the Silent Era.* Bloomington: Indiana UP, 2001. Print.

Bowser, Pearl, and Louise Spence. *Writing Himself into History: Oscar Micheaux, His Silent Films, and His Audiences.* New Brunswick: Rutgers UP, 2000. Print.

Cripps, Thomas. *Slow Fade to Black: The Negro in American Film, 1900–1942.* 1977. New York: Oxford UP, 1993. Print.

Everett, Anna. *Returning the Gaze: A Genealogy of Black Film Criticism, 1909–1949.* Durham: Duke UP, 2001. Print.

Gaines, Jane. *Fire and Desire: Mixed-Race Movies in the Silent Era.* Chicago: U of Chicago P, 2001. Print.

Green, J. Ronald. *Straight Lick: The Cinema of Oscar Micheaux.* Bloomington: Indiana UP, 2000. Print.

———. *With a Crooked Stick: The Films of Oscar Micheaux.* Bloomington: Indiana UP, 2004. Print.

Hartmann, Jon. "The Trope of Blaxploitation in Critical Responses to *Sweetback.*" *Film History* 6.3 (1994): 382–404. Print.

Knight, Arthur. *Disintegrating the Musical: Black Performance and American Musical Film.* Durham: Duke UP, 2002. Print.

Massood, Paula J. "An Aesthetic Appropriate to Conditions: *Killer of Sheep*, (Neo)-Realism, and the Documentary Impulse." *Wide Angle* 21.4 (1999): 20–41. Print.

———. *Black City Cinema: African American Urban Experiences in Film.* Philadelphia: Temple UP, 2003. Print.

———. "*Sweet Sweetback's Baadasssss Song.*" *Fifty Key American Films.* Ed. John White and Sabine Haenni. London: Routledge, 2009. 152–58. Print.

McGilligan, Patrick. *Oscar Micheaux: The Great and Only.* New York: Harper Perennial, 2007. Print.

Reed, Ishmael. "Hollywood's Enduring Myth of the Black Male Sexual Predator: The Selling of *Precious.*" *CounterPunch.* CounterPunch, 4–6 Dec. 2009. Web. 1 Jan. 2010.

Sampson, Henry. *Blacks in Black and White: A Source Book on Black Films.* 2nd ed. Lanham: Scarecrow, 1995. Print.

Smith, Jada F. "Does Hollywood Still Have a Brown Paper Bag Test?" *The Root.* Washington Post, 12 Nov. 2009. Web. 1 Jan. 2010.

Stewart, Jacqueline. *Migrating to the Movies: Cinema and Black Urban Modernity.* Berkeley: U of California P, 2005. Print.

Taylor, Clyde. "Crossed Over and Can't Get Black: The Crisis of 1937–39." *Black Film Review* 7.4 (1993): 22–27. Print.

Weisenfeld, Judith. *Hollywood Be Thy Name: African American Religion in American Film, 1929–1949.* Berkeley: U of California P, 2007. Print.

Patricia White

Teaching Queer Cinema with Independent Media

One of the most exciting dimensions of teaching film (and popular culture) is learning what students already know and then generating an informed and critical epistemology from the familiar. Teaching LGBT (lesbian, gay, bisexual, and transgender) representation in film and media presents rich opportunities to build on student familiarity—with such mainstream breakthroughs as Ang Lee's *Brokeback Mountain* (2006) and *Queer Eye for the Straight Guy* (2003–07)—and to formalize the knowledge and challenge the assumptions that students have about LGBT history, lives, and struggles for representation. With the commercial success of gay-themed work and the acceptance of such out celebrities as Ellen Degeneres, the recent past is a teachable moment of both social transformation and market logic, and students of diverse backgrounds have illuminating perspectives on and important stakes in making sense of it. By focusing on film and media by and about LGBT producers, teachers can connect questions of political and aesthetic representation and expose students to independent media sources.

In the post-network-television era of convergence between media platforms like cable and the Internet, the young citizens who are our students have many media alternatives, but their exposure to alternative media—noncommercial, politically engaged, formally inventive film and video work by feminists, people of color, or LGBT, transnational, and other media producers—is not guaranteed by this apparent democratization. Such exposure is more likely to come in the classroom, facilitated by critical pedagogy. Similarly, a seeming liberalization of representations of gender and sexuality—*The L Word* gesture—obscures more challenging practices and histories unless teaching these is made a priority.

This contribution discusses how a vital curricular area—the mutually constitutive fields of gender and sexuality studies and film and media studies—has been defined and enriched by an emphasis on independent media and questions of self-representation, as well as how higher education can respond to changes in the mediascape, including in the distribution of independent film and video. I draw on my teaching experience and the assumption that a focus on questions of gender and sexuality is a productive entry point to film and media in a broader curriculum.

Teaching film today necessarily entails teaching media. Even if the object of study is a discrete cinematic text, access to it and information about it engage and are embedded in other media—principally students' computers, linked by a campus server to course management software, the library, and the Web. Changes in media delivery systems like Web streaming and video on demand, the proliferation of "niche" cable networks, and Web 2.0's culture of user-generated content correlate with changes in media content, but not always in predictable ways. The advent of *YouTube* has had a profound impact on teaching film, as anyone involved in higher education is likely to confirm, and, like any anarchic and libidinally driven realm of cultural practice, the site is rife with queer content. Given the voyeuristic structures that have always attended lesbian representation in particular, *YouTube* is not an unproblematic place to do research on the topic. In teaching the course Learning from *YouTube*, Alex Juhasz finds that getting a whole lot of something does not necessarily mean getting what you need in a form you can use.[1] Quickly, her class gained "a more keen awareness of how censorship and corporations function well on the site while community and art do not."

Queer media is defined by a range of film forms; changing relations of production, address, and reception; historical, subcultural, national, and transnational contexts; and cultural and political rifts and alliances between gay men and lesbians, feminist and queer theorists, politicos and aesthetes. To learn about these things, students often have to unlearn what they think they know about queer media from networks like Bravo and television shows like *Will and Grace* (1998–2006). Student openness to queer content in mainstream movies has undoubtedly increased since early in my career, when I encountered skepticism when teaching homoeroticism in Alfred Hitchcock's *Rebecca* (1940) or Howard Hawks's *Red River* (1948). The number of *Brokeback* mash-ups on the Internet is adequate testimony to this fact.[2] Learning from *YouTube* could occur if instructors used the site in the context of the rich homoerotic tradition of the western—from *Red River* to Andy Warhol's *Lonesome Cowboys* (1968), which, though an obscure avant-garde film, is also a cult film and a parody, genres that thrive on the site and elsewhere on the Web. But like art and community, history is not a priority of the site. For me, there is a kind of pathos in how much ingenuity goes into queering popular culture sources—while I often find fan videos deeply compelling (and suspect that having been bewitched by the television show *That Girl* [1966–71] in my childhood would have led to similar efforts if I had had the tools), I feel that students' exposure to alternative traditions would channel some of this creativity toward less-well-worn grooves.

Media proliferation contributes to the rhetoric of democratization, while real inequities in access remain or deepen in the era of deregulation and globalization: just count the number of films by women released in the summer months, nonwhite actresses in leading roles, subtitled films on *Logo*, independent documentaries on public television. For anyone teaching the history and stakes of women's and LGBT media, mainstream (corporate-owned and -driven) outlets are woefully inadequate. Despite a congressional mandate for the funding and broadcast of risk-taking independent media addressing underserved audiences, the percentage of work by independent producers remains miniscule even as the television grid expands. Deregulation and privatization will not redress these inequities. One important classroom strategy is teaching media policy and political economy.

Another is to seek out independent work; in what follows I discuss the robust counterpublic sphere of feminist and LGBT filmmaking (see Warner), its relationship with the academy, and some specific challenges facing education in this area now. I do not wish to imply that work by LGBT producers is the only way to approach these topics, much less that independent media favors a mimetic relation between maker and content. Self-representation, however, is a useful rubric for organizing a syllabus that also redresses the marginalization of many of these artists. In the film and media studies classroom students can encounter independent media with an awareness of its formal as well as institutional and economic specificities, such as funding, format, and distribution. For me, film (and media) pedagogy includes a wider range of work than theatrical features and so foregrounds the social contexts of film and media production and reception.

Although syllabi across the humanities curriculum include Laura Mulvey's "Visual Pleasure and Narrative Cinema," the most widely anthologized essay in the field, few emphasize that Mulvey proposes an answer to the bind she astutely describes: the paradigm of "woman as image, man as bearer of the look" defining commercial, narrative cinema will be overturned by independent (experimental) women's filmmaking (11). While it is challenging to teach viewers who have grown up within a culture of maximum visual stimulation to appreciate Mulvey's films or the anti–visual pleasure modernist aesthetic she advocates, it is rewarding to introduce them to works that foreground form. In a related tactic, instructors can unfold historically for students all the sites in which women and queers have taken up formal experimentation to challenge dominant modes: Berlin and Paris avant-gardes between the world wars, the post–World War II American underground, and video activism during the AIDS epidemic, to name a few. Students certainly identify with Mulvey's polemical prose, and her call for new relations of production strikes a chord with the prevalent do-it-yourself ethic. Foregrounding these questions also offers an opportunity to address economic and institutional questions about film production: Who funds movies? Who has the skills to make them? What audiences are addressed? How do audiences access the work and acquire the skills to respond to it?

As my invocation of Mulvey's framework indicates, for me teaching LGBT media is intimately tied with feminist film theory and women's access to the means of production. With the upsurge of queer visibility since the 1990s, both the issues of gaze and image that Mulvey raises (and attendant issues of heteronormativity in her framing of the topic) and questions of gender equity are paramount. I often begin classes on gender and sexuality in film by discussing with students the Guerrilla Girls' campaign with Movies by Women, "Unchain the Women Directors," a public art project that raised awareness of how male-dominated film production remains. Although the statistics used to paint the dire picture of women's underrepresentation as directors (7% in 2005) are compiled from the year's two hundred top-grossing films—a different stratosphere from independent, nontheatrical production—they are sobering ones. Working from what students are likely to know something about, I frame a unit on new queer cinema—B. Ruby Rich's moniker for the flourishing of independent LGBT features with bold aesthetic and political visions in the early 1990s—through the work of the producer Christine Vachon. It was through close collaboration with Vachon and her partners at Killer Films that Todd Haynes has emerged as a first-rank auteur (see Morrison). Killer has also put its stamp on new queer cinema through Tom Kalin's *Swoon* (1992) and *Savage Grace* (2008); Nigel Finch's historical drama *Stonewall* (1995); the documentarian Mary Herron's feature debut, *I Shot Andy Warhol* (1995); John Cameron Mitchell's adaptation of his play *Hedwig and the Angry Inch* (2001), among other independent features. Most notably, Vachon's commitment to the novice women filmmakers Rose Troche and Guinevere Turner (*Go Fish* [1994]) and Kimberly Peirce (*Boys Don't Cry* [1999]) constitutes a key intervention in the gender inequities of queer public culture. These two benchmark features have been the subject of fine analyses by LGBT scholars that are productively taught in conjunction with Vachon's no-nonsense books on independent film production.[3] Here issues of representation—both political and aesthetic—intersect, and students' investments, no matter what their identities, make for lively classroom exchanges.

Theatrical features that influenced students' youthful identification through accessibility on DVD are a useful way in to teaching students about queer self-representation. The DVD as equalizing commodity form can do some significant cultural work, given the radical discrepancies in budget and scale among feature-length films. Cheryl Dunye's 16mm independent production *The Watermelon Woman* (1996), for example, resembles her early free-form, low-fi videos that mix talking heads and fictionalized scenarios. But as the first feature by an African American lesbian to be theatrically released (however modestly), it broke historical barriers and the DVD distribution threshold—fittingly for a "meta" movie about self-representation and alternative histories (see Reid-Pharr; Zimmer).

Access to work on DVD inevitably drives the selection of texts for teaching as well, but we need not be confined to American studio releases. Queer theory, like feminism, has become increasingly committed to transnational inquiry, and audiovisual works are central to these developments. Instructors may choose to highlight the prominent queer voices among art cinema auteurs—from Rainer Werner Fassbinder, Pier Paolo Pasolini, Luciano Visconti, and Chantal Akerman to Lino Brocka, François Ozon, Tsai Ming-liang, and Apichatpong Weerasethakul. Or they may wish to engage questions of globalization by focusing on queer representation in East Asian cinema through Tony Rayns's writing or on Deepa Mehta's *Fire* (1996) in relation to films made by South Asian queers through Gayatri Gopinath's work. Teaching this work is facilitated by the global marketing of Asian cinema on DVD and LGBT-owned DVD labels like Wolfe Video.

Richard Dyer, the most significant scholar in defining LGBT film studies, opens "Believing in Fairies: The Author and the Homosexual," his contribution to Diana Fuss's groundbreaking anthology *Inside/Out*, by recounting a student's "gotcha" comment: "Richard doesn't believe in authors—unless they are women!" and adds blacks and queers to the list. Dyer's typically succinct and elegant diagnosis of the contradictory investments of the queer pedagogue remains accurate. Although his research and much of the field is profitably invested in the study of queer representations in and reception of mainstream culture, the history and concept of self-representation is the guiding principle of Dyer's *Now You See It: Studies in Lesbian and Gay Film*. His chapters foreground nonmainstream contexts from silent avant-garde cinema to Weimar to the 1960s underground and 1970s lesbian feminist and gay liberation movements and provide a useful breakdown for a syllabus on the subject. As a curricular organization in teaching LGBT film, authorship certainly departs from the media watchdog group GLAAD's (the Gay and Lesbian Alliance against Defamation's) interest in mainstream representations and visibility—and, again, the field should not exclude scrutiny of dominant culture or focus on film to the exclusion of work on television and the Internet (see Gross; Becker; the online journal *Flow*). But whether or not it is a quaint fixation, a holdover from the days of identity politics, the commitment to authorial criteria—films by queers and women—is a fruitful approach to alternative media and its social contexts, if it avoids prescriptive aesthetics.

Independent filmmaking in the United States comprises documentary, experimental, short, and feature film and video made by producers working outside corporate structures to fund, produce, and often distribute their work, as well as the many organizations that support them. Beyond the teaching of specific works, pedagogy can engage with these groups' online resources, such as *IndieWire*, *Filmmaker*, and *The Independent*.[4] Other institutions such as the Independent Television Service, media arts centers, community-based video organizations, and film and video festivals are important barometers of aesthetic, political, and cultural currents that teachers and students can explore. Yet even in the age of convergence, not-for-profit educational distributors are the strongest bridge between alternative media and higher education.

Students learn to take a wider view of independent film than the theatrical feature through exposure to documentary, experimental film and video, and short work from the collections of distributors like Women Make Movies and Frameline. Documentaries like *Screaming Queens: The Riot at Compton's Cafeteria* (2006), by Victor Silverman and Susan Stryker, and *Boy I Am* (2006), on female-to-male transgender identity, by Sam Feder and Julie Hollar, are in productive dialogue with the scholarship students read for feminist and LGBT studies classes. The recognition of formal traditions beyond talking heads and narrative commonplaces is as eye-opening as the subject matter and perspective. Teaching Barbara Hammer's 1970s lesbian videos provides a direct dose of lesbian feminist culture, enriched when historicized and taught with the work of the younger experimental filmmaker Su Friedrich and the even younger video artist Sadie Benning. The compelling voices of black gay men echo in two key works from the late 1980s: Marlon Riggs's *Tongues Untied* (1989) is an hour-long video on "black men loving black men"—a phrase that is repeatedly invoked in the film—identity, and HIV, structured around performance and poetry. Isaac Julien's *Looking for Langston* (1988) highlights some of the same black gay poets to illuminate the intersections of race and desire in queer subcultures and histories and the protection of legacies.

Riggs is only one of many artists of this period of efflorescence in queer cultural production to have been lost to AIDS. Video had a key role in AIDS activism. In *An Archive of Feelings*, the queer theorist Ann Cvetkovich argues that cultural production is one important response to queer trauma and looks at lesbian video artists' work. Many aspects of the AIDS video movement tested out assumptions about collectivity and community, democratization of media, and government indifference long before the advent of the Internet; the online ACT UP Oral History Project, by the filmmaker Jim Hubbard and the writer and activist Sarah Schulman, includes numerous interviews with filmmakers and video artists that can be taught in conjunction with their work.

Julien remains a key figure in LGBT independent film, and it is fitting that his experimental biopic *Derek* (2008) celebrates another avant-garde British queer auteur, Derek Jarman, who died of HIV in 1994 and who connected queer aesthetics and politics in a radical and public way. The preservation of his contribution is crucial. *Derek* is narrated by Jarman's friend and featured actor Tilda Swinton and was produced by the film theorist Colin MacCabe. The presentation of *Derek* in lesbian and gay film festivals recalled Jarman's participation in these events as the new queer cinema was emerging. It is a reminder of the political and experimental promise they still hold.

The space of the classroom where these works are taught is distinct from the sector of LGBT independent production and the organizations that sustain it, but the vital worldwide network of hundreds of film and video festivals can be studied through the informative roundtable discussions published on festivals in the journal *GLQ*.[5] Participants speak of the festivals' function as a queer counterpublic sphere, raising questions about the local and transnational, consumerism and oppositionality, globalization and corporatization, community and virtuality. The accessibility of online festival programs can also enrich class discussions and facilitate curatorial assignments.[6]

Yet nontheatrical work by independent artists featured in festivals is usually not accessible to individual viewers on DVD. Any work in distribution is most often available from educational distributors with institutional pricing structures, and faculty members need to advocate for these works' acquisition by university libraries. Learning why artists' work and independent documentaries cannot be purchased or downloaded for home video prices is an education in economies of scale, the politics of visibility, and media justice—for teachers and professors as well as students. Independent media is not funded by corporations or government grants or foundations, sold to television or major cultural organizations, or advertised to anything like the extent that would be necessary to subsidize mass-market distribution. Colleges and universities, through institutional purchases from independent distributors, are the key sites through which students have access to alternative work and artists are compensated for their work. Work is usually sold with public performance rights, so that free campus screenings are permitted (unlike other library holdings). The institutional price returns a much larger percentage to the filmmaker than a low-cost sale. Educators can connect with the media arts community not only to bring new works into the curriculum and scholarly debate but also to engage in media advocacy efforts.

My affiliation as a board member with Women Make Movies, the leading feminist distributor of films by and about women, exposes me to a continuous flow—or gush—of new work by and about women from around the world that drives my teaching in feminist and LGBT media, from the reissued work of Mulvey and Peter Wollen to documentaries about women and the Middle East to a range of works by lesbians of color. New releases, especially documentaries, motivate my curricular revisions, but their sheer number can be difficult to absorb into existing course structures. Hence I encourage other kinds of campus programming and design assignments that engage students in documenting our library's holdings to teach others about these resources—whether they are professors designing courses using media across the curriculum or students looking for alternatives to the mainstream media. Teaching specific works is always facilitated by scholarship on a particular title, such as Trinh T. Minh-ha's experimental documentaries or Kim Longinotto's observational ones. The University of Minnesota Press's Visible Evidence series has been an important catalyst for scholarship on independent documentary, and blogs and online reviews help redress the inattention of major outlets.

Educational distribution in the United States is endangered, as is independent media, by lack of public funds. Organizations such as Women Make Movies, California Newsreel, Third World Newsreel, Icarus Films, and New Day Films have their roots in the politicized alternative media culture of the 1960s and 1970s or, in the case of the San Francisco–based Frameline's LGBT distribution service, in the phenomenal success of LGBT film festivals. While these not-for-profit organizations generate revenue to sustain themselves and remunerate their artists, changes in the market—first the wide availability of consumer-priced video and now Internet distribution—pose challenges to their marketing models. Committed to the widest possible exposure for the filmmakers they represent, such oraganizations may be undermined by new initiatives that do not generate enough revenue to sustain independent production. It is a precarious balance for which university faculty members and libraries are primary institutional supports. By making the case for independent media within our institutional settings and encouraging wide use of holdings and acquisitions, professors have a concrete role in supporting this sector.

Film studies emerged as a discipline in the era of a political countercinema and feminist theory in the 1970s, was challenged and catalyzed by multiculturalism in the 1980s, and offered rich terrain for queer theory in the 1990s. Commitment on the part of those teaching film and media could greatly influence pedagogical contexts in the early-twenty-first-century culture of convergence, but only if we are self-conscious about our institutional setting as one among many frameworks that govern access to alternative media and to self-representation. The counterpublic sphere of independent media that has been shaped over this same period, consisting of documentarians, community video activists, media artists, and networks of media art centers, is both threatened and enhanced by developments in new media. Independent producers need to maintain the rights to and earn revenues from their work as new models for streaming and on-demand distribution are tried out and video-sharing sites proliferate. The independent media community and university information technology and library personnel are entering into dialogue on these issues and practices. Teachers and scholars should understand something of these debates and developments and the effects on their work. In this latest round of left pessimism versus techno optimism, we need a little of both.

Queer media is everywhere. To prevent the second half of the saying, "now you see it . . . now you don't" from coming true, we as educators have to work to preserve histories and sustain alternative practices by addressing them in the classroom. A commitment to studying gender and sexuality means making marginalized perspectives central, and film and media studies offers a way to look at some of our culture's most powerfully invested representations and visions. Its pedagogy should be attuned to the stakes of media production, distribution, and reception, as well as form and content.

Notes

1. Visit the course at www.youtube.com/MediaPraxisme.

2. *Star Wars: The Empire Brokeback* had 759,724 views as of 22 August 2008.

3. See Aaron, esp. Pick, "New Queer Cinema and Lesbian Films" 103–18; "The *Boys Don't Cry* Debate" in Stacey and Street (257–95); Vachon with Edelstein; and Vachon with Bunn.

4. A sign of just how tough the times have been is the cessation in publication of *The Independent* (which started in 1978), when the Association of Independent Film and Videomakers went under in 2006.

5. See "Queer Film and Video Festival Forum, Take One"; "Queer Film and Video Festival Forum, Take Two"; White, Rich, Clarke, and Fung.

6. A few of the longest-running North American events are Frameline in San Francisco, Out Fest in Los Angeles, MIX and The New Festival in New York, Inside/Out in Toronto, and Image + Nation in Montreal.

Works Cited

Aaron, Michele, ed. *New Queer Cinema: A Critical Reader.* Edinburgh: Edinburgh UP, 2004. Print.

Becker, Ron. *Gay TV and Straight America.* New Brunswick: Rutgers UP, 2006. Print.

Cvetkovich, Ann. *An Archive of Feelings: Trauma, Sexuality, and Lesbian Public Cultures.* Durham: Duke UP, 2003. Print.

Dyer, Richard. "Believing in Fairies: The Author and the Homosexual." *Inside/Out.* Ed. Diana Fuss. New York: Routledge, 1991. 185–201. Print.

———. *Now You See It: Studies in Lesbian and Gay Film.* London: Routledge, 1990. Print.

Gross, Larry. *Up from Invisibility: Lesbians, Gay Men, and the Media in America.* New York: Columbia UP, 2001. Print.

Guerrilla Girls. "Unchain the Women Directors." *Guerrilla Girls.* Guerrilla Girls, 2006. Web. 14 Feb. 2011.

Juhasz, Alex. "Learning from *Youtube.*" *MIT·Press.* MIT P, Feb. 2011. Web. 25 Sept. 2011.

Morrison, James, ed. *The Cinema of Todd Haynes: All That Heaven Allows.* London: Wallflower, 2007. Print.

Mulvey, Laura. "Visual Pleasure and Narrative Cinema." *Screen* 16.3 (1975): 6–18. Web. 14 Feb. 2011.

"Queer Film and Video Festival Forum, Take One." *GLQ* 11.4 (2005): 579–603. Print.

"Queer Film and Video Festival Forum, Take Two." *GLQ* 12.4 (2006): 599–625. Print.

Reid-Pharr, Robert F. "Makes Me Feel Mighty Real: *The Watermelon Woman* and the Critique of Black Visuality." *F Is for Phony: Fake Documentary and Truth's Undoing.* Ed. Alexandra Juhasz and Jesse Lerner. Minneapolis: Minnesota UP, 2006. 130–42. Print.

Stacey, Jackie, and Sarah Street, eds. *Queer Screen.* London: Routledge, 2007. Print.

Vachon, Christine, with Austin Bunn. *A Killer Life: How an Independent Producer Survives Deals and Disasters in Hollywood and Beyond.* New York: Simon, 2006. Print.

Vachon, Christine, with David Edelstein. *Shooting to Kill: How an Independent Producer Blasts through the Barriers to Make Movies That Matter.* New York: Avon, 1998. Print.

Warner, Michael. *Publics and Counterpublics.* New York: Zone, 2002. Print.

White, Patricia, B. Ruby Rich, Eric O. Clarke, and Richard Fung. "Queer Publicity: A Dossier on Lesbian and Gay Film Festivals." *GLQ* 5.1 (1999): 73–93. Print.

Zimmer, Catherine. "Histories of *The Watermelon Woman*: Reflexivity between Race and Gender." *Camera Obscura* 68 (2008): 41–66. Print.

Raphael Raphael

Teaching Film and Disability Studies

Cinema has always been obsessed with disability. This fascination has been deeply ambivalent; the disabled body has evoked both attraction and disgust. Whether as an object of laughter, a source of fear, a site to negotiate concerns about war and technology, or a locus to explore new possibilities of human corporeality, disability has figured prominently in the ways that cinema has imagined the body. From Edison Manufacturing Company's *Fake Beggar* (1898) and many of D. W. Griffith's first Biograph shorts to *Coming Home* (1978), *Forrest Gump* (1994), and *There's Something about Mary* (1998), imagining the disabled body has been an important part of structuring the language of film. Despite this centrality, disability is only now emerging as an important axis of embodiment (along with race, gender, and sexuality) considered in film criticism and in our film studies classrooms. This essay calls then for bringing greater attention to something that has been there all along. Introducing what the film and disability theorist Christopher R. Smit refers to as a "disability lens" to our analysis of film offers a valuable way to recast and enrich our explorations of film history and theory ("Desiring"). Given disability studies' rich historical insights into the visual rhetoric of disability, the discipline offers valuable potential intersections with film studies. After a brief introduction to some of the central concerns of disability studies, this essay surveys some examples of the ways in which film theory and criticism have engaged with disability, then closes with a few suggestions for integrating a disability lens into the film studies curriculum.

Disability Studies

The discipline of disability studies shares much with feminist theory, including activist origins. It emerged out of the successes of the disability rights movement of the 1970s and is now part of the humanities curriculum in the university, only recently taking root in the academy after the passage of the 1990 Americans with Disabilities Act (ADA). While feminism sought to "politiciz[e] the materiality of bodies and rewrit[e] the category of woman," disability studies seeks to do the same with the disabled body (Thomson, *Extraordinary Bodies* 21). A central question it asks is, Exactly what does it mean to be disabled? Is disability a self-evident truth of the body, or is it a social construction that is historically and culturally fluid and, as such, can be reimagined? Disability studies articulates these very different ways of viewing the body in culture as the "medical model" and the "social model," respectively (see chart below).

Medical Model versus Social Model of Disability

Medical Model	Social Model
Fixed truth of the body	Fluid, historically or culturally specific
Individual concern	Collective concern or responsibility
A condition to escape or cure	Unique or multivalent experience

The discipline of disability studies is largely concerned with interrogating the dominance of the medical model in literature and culture, dislodging its naturalness and making explicit the distributions of power it conceals (Thomson, *Extraordinary Bodies* 9). While the medical model views disability as a self-evident, individual "tragedy," disability studies sees it instead as a complex social construction that, along with other markers of identity, such as race and gender, can distribute power and also deny it. Merely having an impairment does not make one disabled; that is, needing eyeglasses to function is unlikely to result in discrimination, while wearing a visible hearing aid may. Moreover, someone who uses a wheelchair may be disabled in an environment that does not accommodate it and no longer "disabled" in an environment that does. Both views also result in radically different imperatives for action. While the medical model seeks to "fix" the individual body, the social model seeks to "fix" society. Closely related to the discipline's activist origins and its ties with feminism, disability studies is also deeply invested in visuality.

Disability studies shares with film studies an essential concern for spectatorship and the ways that visuality structures disability. In her essay "The Politics of Staring," the disability studies theorist Rosemarie Garland Thomson identifies the extreme contradictions of the visibly disabled body, which has a history of conspicuous display "while being politically and socially erased" (56). This contradictory past includes the freakshow, the popular late-nineteenth- and early-twentieth-century form of entertainment in which bodies marked as disabled and racially other were displayed for profit.[1] As a mode of spectatorship privileging body spectacle, the freakshow was influential on the emerging form of film, particularly the cinema of attractions; however, the influence of this debased cultural practice was largely disavowed by an industry (and history) eager to distance itself from prurient forms of early spectatorship. In addition to this largely erased history, widely circulated images of disabled bodies used for charity fund-raising (particularly those of disabled children) have also helped shape the conspicuous presence of disability in American culture. At the same time, people with disabilities have often been excluded from public view, stigmatized, and denied access to resources and political power. As late as 1974, there were so-called ugly laws in many states that made it illegal for visibly disabled people to appear in public (Thomson, *Extraordinary Bodies* 7).[2] This tension has choreographed a unique form of spectatorship, a stare rather than a gaze; the disabled body is marked simultaneously with "to-be-looked-at-ness, and not-to-be-looked-at-ness" (Thomson, "Politics" 56).

These contradictions have made representations of the disabled body charged, ambivalent sites. On the one hand, disability is "constructed as the embodiment of corporeal insufficiency and deviance . . . becom[ing] a repository for social anxieties about such troubling concerns as vulnerability, control and identity," a "lightning rod" of physical discomfort and fear of death (Thomson, *Extraordinary Bodies* 6, 15). On the other hand, Thomson suggests these representations may offer possibilities of great empowerment, imbuing the disabled body with "radical potential . . .

as a sign for difference" (38). So while disability may serve to "enforce normality" and is tied to fundamental notions of citizenship, such as self-sufficiency and independence, it may also disrupt these scripts, celebrating different possibilities of embodiment (Davis, *Enforcing*). Regardless, the medium of film has served as a privileged space to stare at the disabled body.

Film Criticism of Disability within Disability Studies

While film criticism within disability studies has been enriched by attention to the visual politics of disability, it has not always acknowledged this ambivalence. Much of the film criticism generated within disability studies scholarship is similar to other early identity-based analysis, such as those produced by feminist, race, and gay and lesbian theorists. These early analyses of disability provide a valuable cataloging of stereotypes but are largely limited to considering incidences of positive and negative images. As such, much of the investigation of representations of disability in film could be enriched by additional critical dialogue with film theory, following the shift that has moved other identity-based analyses beyond "image of" studies to greater consideration of textual analysis, spectatorship, and audience.

Paul Longmore exemplifies this type of analysis in his essay "Screening Stereotypes," the work credited with inaugurating analysis of cinematic representations of disability. It is as important to disability studies scholarship as Laura Mulvey's "Visual Pleasure and Narrative Cinema" is to film studies scholarship. Longmore's influential article identifies some of the most recurring archetypes of disability in film and provides the first comprehensive model to study its representations in film. These types generally associate the disabled body with criminality or monstrosity (e.g., a host of Bond villains or Peter Sellers's comically evil Dr. Strangelove). Alternatively, the disabled character may be part of a compensation drama or a "super-crip" narrative of remarkable overcoming, as in Jim Sheridan's *My Left Foot* (1989).

In all these varied types, Longmore sees a common aim: to reassure society by isolating disabled characters and then blaming them for their own isolation. Within the logic of the stereotypes, people with disabilities are isolated not because of social dynamics (e.g., the stigma associated with disability or systematic prejudice) but instead because of their own moral or emotional defects. Even when disabled characters are treated as sympathetic, they are still incapable of successful integration in society, and the logic of the narrative often calls for their death, frequently by suicide. In the last moments of *The Elephant Man* (1980), David Lynch's celebrated biopic about John Merrick, the famous "freak" performer of Victorian-era England, Merrick chooses to quietly end his life. The problematic sexuality of people with disabilities is also presented as part of their isolation. They are either perversely hypersexual or, as is more often the case, asexual, wholly incapable emotionally or physically of a sexual relationship, as in *Whose Life Is It Anyway?* (1981), in which the newly disabled quadriplegic Ken Harrison (Richard Dreyfuss) wishes to end his life, in large part because of his loss of sexual functioning.

Although Longmore's important work illuminates ableist[3] assumptions in dominant cinema and provides a valuable topography of representations of people with disabilities, his study is limited by assumptions of spectator passivity and a strict allegiance to a realist aesthetic framework. While Mulvey famously returned to her initial assumptions, modifying them to accommodate the pleasure of actual spectators (see "Afterthoughts" and the often neglected "Changes"), Longmore has not. His initial framework—and its concerns for positive and negative images—continues to resonate throughout film criticism within disability studies.

An important example of Longmore's legacy is Martin Norden's *Cinema of Isolation.* Norden's influential study places Longmore's assumptions into a comprehensive film history. He locates the auteurs Griffith, Alfred Hitchcock, Frank Capra, and Tod Browning within the "pantheon of movie directors who have drawn repeatedly from the world of physical disability" (xi). Norden sees an uneven narrative of progress in dominant representations of disability, with a move through three historical phases: early "freakish" body spectacles, like the silent disability-themed Lon Chaney vehicle *The Unknown* (1927) or Browning's *Freaks* (1932); postwar narratives of adjustment, such as *Best Years of Our Lives* (1946); and increasingly "positive" and complex portraits of disability beginning in "New Hollywood," such as *Coming Home.* The stereotypes Norden identifies include "obsessive avengers" (52), wronged characters who seek revenge on the able-bodied, as in *Freaks*, and "sweet innocents" (33), pure and docile characters often rewarded with a miracle cure, as in *Heidi* (1937). While Richard Dyer has pointed out how racial hierarchies are embedded in film stock and lighting, Norden suggests that the formal properties of film—for example, high or low angle framing and set design, the presence of staircases—help choreograph the coding of disability. He illustrates how the cinematographer Haskell Wexler interrupted this coding in *Coming Home* by using a specially designed wheelchair-height dolly that "normalized" disabled characters, eliminating the high angle shots that would normally structure their relationships with other characters, making the nondisabled people appear more dominant in framing, as in the 1954 film *Rear Window* (268).

Although adding a critical historical overview, Norden leaves Longmore's fundamental assumptions of spectator passivity and Manichaean binary oppositions in place. He does not account for the unstable viewing positions (and pleasures) that actual disabled and nondisabled spectators may find even in such "negative" representations as *Freaks*; nor does he account for the ways spectators may find earnest "positive" representations of disability equally repugnant. For such accounts, it is essential to turn to the audience. Jacqueline Bobo's work on the reading practices of black women suggests that spectators who are accustomed to being denied access to positive representations develop their own unique strategies to negotiate meaning in films; similarly, with *Freaks*, disabled viewers might take pleasure from the rare opportunity to identify with a spectrum of disabled protagonists in a studio film, disregarding elements of the film that they might find offensive. A "new wave" of disability film scholarship has begun to address these unexpected pleasures while entering into closer dialogue with critical film theory.

New Directions in Disability Film Scholarship

Christopher R. Smit and Anthony Enns's *Screening Disability: Essays on Cinema and Disability* announces itself as part of this new wave of disability film scholarship that challenges notions of the passive spectator and problematizes the initial insights of Longmore and Norden's work, calling for greater emphasis on reception and greater recognition of the complexity of texts (Smit, Preface ix–xi). Within their volume (which grew out of the first conference on cinema and disability at the University of Iowa in 1999), *Freaks* emerges as a particularly resonant and ambivalent text, one that has been embraced and reviled by both disabled and nondisabled spectators since its opening in 1932 (see Haller and Larsen). Smit and Enns's volume highlights other areas in need of further attention, including international cinema.[4] The volume also seeks to complicate earlier studies of disabled sexuality. Drawing on theories of the cyborg, James Cherney's "Sexy Cyborgs: Disability and Erotic Politics in Cronenberg's *Crash*" examines the ways *Crash* (1996) may "undermine the political power of the ableist repression of sexual desire for the other" and imagine new sexual identities for the disabled body (179).

In addition to more substantive dialogue with film theory, trends in recent analysis of representations of disability include critical intersections with other theoretical frameworks. In "*As Good As It Gets*: Queer Theory and Critical Disability," Robert McRuer uses queer theory and a critical disability framework to consider the ways in which compulsory heterosexuality intersects with compulsory able-bodiedness in the 1997 comedy *As Good As It Gets*.[5] There has also been limited consideration of intersections between race and ability. John Nickel's "Disabling African American Men: Liberalism and Race Message Films" suggests that the charged site of the disabled black male body was a powerful postwar symbol for liberal paternalism's benevolence, making profound changes in the country's racial landscape more palatable to white audiences. Both McRuer and Nickel, however, still overlook the multiple subject positions that viewers may inhabit and remain committed to positive/negative image paradigms. This legacy of the work of Longmore and Norden continues even as analysis of disability makes further connections with film theory and its consideration of texts, spectators, and audiences, as well as representations of sexuality and race.

Some of the most provocative work in intersections between film and disability studies has come from the scholarship of David Mitchell and Sharon Snyder. Building on their earlier work on narrative theory and disability (see *Narrative Prosthesis*), in "Body Genres and Disability Sensations" they reevaluate Linda Williams's schema of "body genres" (melodrama, horror, and pornography). While Williams's theory might be said to overlook disability in her examination of these genres of excess, Mitchell and Snyder place it at their center. Substituting comedy for pornography, they argue "disability is as crucial as gender in the primal structuring fantasies of [melodrama, horror, and comedy]" (162). Disabled bodies have served as a "form of visual shorthand" that are "constructed cinematically and socially to function as delivery vehicles in the transfer of extreme sensations to audiences" (164, 162).

Although adopting Williams's structure, Mitchell and Snyder do not follow through on her central insights. While Williams suggests that these genres of excess are ambivalent and, far from being solely misogynist, may offer privileged sites to challenge gender roles, Mitchell and Snyder, echoing Longmore and Norden, see no such potentially utopian uses of the genres with respect to disability. Their attention to comedy could also profit from dialogue with feminist film scholarship suggesting that comedy, with its inversions and antiauthoritarian bent, may also serve to challenge cultural scripts (see Rowe). Given the frequent coupling of disability with the genre, examining ways in which comedy might unsettle cultural roles of disability warrants further attention. Mitchell and Snyder instead privilege "new disability documentary cinema" as offering a true "site of resistance and political revision" (174, 169). In the autobiographical documentary *When Billy Broke His Head* (1995), Billy Golfus exposes the institutional and social hurdles faced by people with disabilities, including Golfus's struggle to have his father accept his disability. Another example is Mitchell and Snyder's celebrated *Vital Signs: Crip Culture Talks Back* (1995). While not addressing the sliding points of identification the genres may offer, their contribution questions whether the attributes generally associated with disabled characters are instead functions of internal generic codes.

Many areas warrant further attention. There has been little work on audience and reception and very little consideration of how disabled spectators respond to films (see Ross). Star studies of performers with star texts about their disabilities, such as Marlee Matlin or Marty Feldman, would be valuable contributions, including those who made their careers by feigning disability, such as Lon Chaney, or by hiding it, as did the RKO star Herbert Marshall (who lost a leg in World War I) and Harold Lloyd (who used a prosthesis to disguise loss of fingers from a set explosion). Because disability is a global concern, another important area in need of further exploration is international representation of disability. Although, as Michael Davidson reminds us, the study of disability cannot be considered divorced from nation, since "disability is as much about national and cultural power differential as it is a matter of medicine and bodies" ("Universal Design" 119; see also Kim and Jarman).

Toward a "Disability Lens" in the Film Studies Classroom

While much remains to be understood about the fluid and ambivalent role disability has played in cinema—and that cinema has played in the pleasures of disabled spectators—by adopting a critical disability lens informed by the rich intersections between film theory and criticism and disability studies, we can begin to more fully appreciate cinema's complicated obsession with disability, both as heuristic and teaching tool. In the appendix below, I offer a few thematic clusters of films as starting points toward integrating a disability lens into any film studies classroom, suggesting sample films exploring disability across historical periods, genres, and nations. I include some usual suspects frequently found in film studies curriculum, such as *Rear Window* and *Psycho*, as well as independent disability documentaries. Although this list might be helpful in a stand-alone survey course of disability representation (a rarity at present), it is intended for use piecemeal in existing film studies curriculum.

The purpose of a disability lens is not to function as an addition but to bring attention to what already exists across the curriculum, inviting students to be aware of the ambivalent, often contradictory ways that cinema's concern for issues of ability have been used in our imagining of the body. As testament to the success and visibility of other identity-based analysis, particularly feminist and critical race theory, our students are likely to be aware that they have some investment in those categories. Disability, however, for many students, remains a simple, "natural" truth that goes without saying; you're disabled or you ain't. As such, interrogating the ways in which cinema participates in—and challenges—these cultural scripts may have other benefits as well, perhaps contributing to more inclusive classrooms. In addition to enriching our explorations with film theory and history, investigations that include the axis of ability may suggest for the first time to many disabled and nondisabled students that disability, instead of an isolated phenomenon, is something in which we are all deeply invested.

Notes

1. For a history of the phenomenon, see Bogdan.

2. "Ugly laws" is the name of convenience given by historians to a series of ordinances instituted in the United States, particularly in the late nineteenth century, that barred from public view anyone "diseased, maimed, mutilated or deformed in any way, so as to be an unsightly or disgusting object" (qtd. in Schweik 59).

3. A core concern of disability studies, "ableist" refers to ideologies that assume a nondisabled experience and perspective, thereby marginalizing the disabled (see Davis, *Enforcing* 161).

4. See Enns for a discussion of the role of disabled masculinity in the specific context of post–Tiananmen Square national anxieties in Hong Kong; see also Davidson, "Universal Design."

5. For other intersections between queer identity and disability, see Davidson, "Phantom Limbs."

Works Cited

Bobo, Jacqueline. "Black Women's Responses to *The Color Purple*." *Jump Cut* 33 (1988): 43–51. Print.
Bogdan, Robert. *Freakshow: Presenting Human Oddities for Amusement and Profit.* Chicago: U of Chicago P, 1988. Print.
Cherney, James. "Sexy Cyborgs: Disability and Erotic Politics in Cronenberg's *Crash*." Smit and Enns 165–80.
Davidson, Michael. "Phantom Limbs: Film Noir and the Disabled Body." *GLQ: A Journal of Lesbian and Gay Studies* 9.1-2 (2003): 57–77. Print.
———. "Universal Design: The Work of Disability in an Age of Globalization." Davis, *Disability Studies Reader* 117–28.
Davis, Lennard, ed. *The Disability Studies Reader.* 2nd ed. New York: Routledge, 2006. Print.
———. *Enforcing Normalcy: Disability, Deafness, and the Body.* London: Verso, 1995. Print.
Dyer, Richard. *White: Essays on Race and Culture.* London: Routledge, 1997. Print.
Enns, Anthony. "The Spectacle of Disabled Masculinity in John Woo's 'Heroic Bloodshed' Films." Smit and Enns 151–63.
Erb, Cynthia. "'Have You Ever Seen the Inside of One of Those Places?': *Psycho*, Foucault, and the Postwar Context of Madness." *Cinema Journal* 45.4 (2006): 45–63. Print.
Haller, Beth A., and Robin Larsen. "Public Reception of Real Disability: The Case Of *Freaks*." *Journal of Popular Film and Television* 29.4 (2002): 164–72. Print.
Kim, Eunjung, and Michelle Jarman. "Modernity's Rescue Mission: Postcolonial Transactions of Disability and Sexuality." *Canadian Journal of Film Studies* 17.1 (2008): 52–68. Print.
LeBesco, K. "There's Something about Disabled People: Contradictions of Freakery in the Films of the Farrelly Brothers." *Disability Studies Quarterly* 24.4 (2004): n. pag. Web. 2 Sept. 2011.
Longmore, Paul. "Screening Stereotypes: Images of Disabled People in Television and Motion Pictures." "*Why I Burned My Book" and Other Essays on Disability.* Philadelphia: Temple UP, 2003. 131–46. Print.
McRuer, Robert. "*As Good As It Gets*: Queer Theory and Critical Disability." *GLQ* 9.1-2 (2003): 79–105. Print.
Mitchell, David, and Sharon Snyder. "Body Genres and Disability Sensations." *Cultural Locations of Disability.* Chicago: U of Chicago P, 2006. 156–81. Print.
———. *Narrative Prosthesis.* Ann Arbor: U of Michigan P, 2001. Print.
Mulvey, Laura. "Afterthoughts on 'Visual Pleasure and Narrative Cinema' Inspired by *Duel in the Sun*." *Framework* 15-17 (1981): 12–15. Print.
———. "Changes." *Discourse* 7 (1985): 11–30. Print.
———. "Visual Pleasure and Narrative Cinema." *Screen* 16.3 (1975): 6–18. Print.

Nickel, John. "Disabling African American Men: Liberalism and Race Message Films." *Cinema Journal* 44.1 (2004): 25–48. Print.
Norden, Martin. *Cinema of Isolation*. New Brunswick: Rutgers UP, 1994. Print.
Ross, Karen. "But Where's Me in It? Disability, Broadcasting and the Audience." *Media, Culture and Society* 19.4 (1997): 669–77. Print.
Rowe, Kathleen. *The Unruly Woman: Gender and the Genres of Laughter*. Austin: U of Texas P, 1995. Print.
Sandahl, Carrie. "Disability and Comic Violence in *There's Something about Mary*." *Disability Studies Quarterly* 19.3 (1999): 192–95. Print.
Schweik, Susan. "Begging the Question: Disability, Mendicancy, Speech and the Law." *Narrative* 15.1 (2007): 58–70. Print.
Smit, Christopher R. "Desiring Difference in Tod Browning's *The Unknown*." Society for Cinema and Media Studies Annual Conference. Loews Philadelphia Hotel. Mar. 2008. Address.
———. Preface. Smit and Enns ix–xviii.
Smit, Christopher R., and Anthony Enns, eds. *Screening Disability: Essays on Cinema and Disability*. Oxford: UP of Amer., 2001. Print.
Thomson, Rosemarie Garland. *Extraordinary Bodies: Figuring Physical Disability in American Culture and Literature*. New York: Columbia UP, 1997. Print.
———. "The Politics of Staring: Visual Rhetorics of Disability in Popular Photography." *Disability Studies: Enabling the Humanities*. Ed. Sharon L. Snyder, Brenda Jo Brueggemann, and Thomson. New York: MLA, 2002. 56–75. Print.
Williams, Linda. "Film Bodies: Gender, Genre, and Excess." *Film Genre Reader 2*. Ed. Barry Keith Grant. Austin: U of Texas P, 1995. 140–58. Print.

Appendix: Thematic Film Clusters

History

Cinema of Attractions, Silent Films

Fake Beggar (1898)
Don't Pull My Leg (1908)
The Unknown (1927)

Classical Hollywood

Freaks (1932)
Best Years of Our Lives (1946)
The Men (1950)

New Hollywood

Midnight Cowboy (1969)
Johnny Got His Gun (1971)
Coming Home (1978)

Contemporary

Born on the Fourth of July (1989)
Crash (1996)
The Station Agent (2003)

Genre

Melodrama

Orphans of the Storm (1921)
Magnificent Obsession (1954)
The Elephant Man (1980)

Comedy

See No Evil, Hear No Evil (1989)
There's Something about Mary (1998)
Stuck on You (2003)

For debate about the comedies of the Farrelly brothers, see Sandahl, LeBesco.

Science Fiction or Horror

Psycho (1960) (see Erb)
Gattaca (1997)
X-Men (2000)

Film Noir

Rear Window (1954)
Touch of Evil (1958)

See Davidson, "Phantom Limbs," for consideration of disability and film noir.

Documentary

When Billy Broke His Head (1995)
Vital Signs: Crip Culture Talks Back (1995)
The Real Helen Keller (2000)

International Cinema

India

Boot Polish (1954)
I Have Found It [*Kandukondain Kandukondain*] (2000)

Germany

Even Dwarfs Started Small (1970)
Chinese Roulette (1976)

France

Automobile Accident (1904)
The One-Legged Man (1908)
The Diving Bell and the Butterfly (2007)

Senegal

The Little Girl Who Sold the Sun [*La petite vendeuse de soleil*] (1999)

Iran and Iraq

Turtles Can Fly (2004)

Part II

Geographies of Cinema

Introduction to Part 2

In recent years, the concept of the nation as an expression of specific cultural values has undergone extensive scholarly critique, and many of us in cinema and media studies have been deeply engaged in this critique, especially as it impacts our teaching. In a recent collection of essays entitled *World Cinemas, Transnational Perspectives*, the editors Nataša Ďurovičová and Kathleen Newman propose to reconsider film history beyond the nation-state by focusing instead on a variety of transnational formations, stretching from the local to the global, across various categories—including statehood, language, cultural and ethnic affiliation or citizenship—as well as across various economies of scale, involving uneven exchanges and alliances among small and large film industries and practices. As Ďurovičová and Newman explain, the notion of the transnational is crucial to dislodging the dominant approach to teaching world cinema, which typically takes the form of teaching discrete national units in which various national cinemas are analyzed at peak moments in their history (German expressionism, Soviet montage, French impressionism and surrealism, Italian neorealism, and so on). The "geopolitical imaginary of the discipline of film studies," they argue, must now be upgraded to a transnational perspective, which they theorize as above the level of the national but below the level of the global (ix).

While understanding that nationalisms of various kinds continue to form part of national imaginations across the world, the essays included in this section take up the challenges described by Ďurovičová and Newman and show that the cinema has always and everywhere been both a deeply local and a highly global transnational industry, long before the term *globalization* came into vogue. To be sure, the authors of the essays also emphasize the abiding internationalism of the cinema, the particular mix of national, transnational, and postcolonial commitments and opportunities to which various national movements give rise, and underscore the widespread adoption of world cinema survey courses in university and college curricula. They argue, however, that most university film courses nonetheless remain organized according to the assumption that Hollywood cinema is "the cinema" (and not even a national cinema at that) against which all other non-Western, postcolonial, or "regional" cinemas must vie for attention and inclusion. While Hollywood films dominate the curricula of introductory courses, whether under the guise of genre, auteur, or film history surveys, more ambitious world cinema courses confront problems of tokenism in an effort to avoid the "one-week/one-continent" mode of including non-Western cinema in film history surveys. Among the many challenges to teaching the complex interrelation of national, transnational, and world cinemas today is thus the very real problem of coverage, or rather of getting beyond a coverage model, since it produces a limited and impoverished understanding of the cinema in relation to its audiences and its multiple locations.

The essays included in this section propose a variety of ways to move beyond these difficulties and to rethink the geopolitical imaginary of cinema by focusing on specific case studies of courses that explore questions of colonialism, postcolonialism, and regionalism (in relation to teaching South Asian cinema, Latin American and Caribbean cinemas, and European cinemas in the wake of the fall of the Berlin Wall and the emergence of the European Union); transnationalism (through the work of exilic, émigré, diasporic, refugee, and ethnic filmmakers); as well as nationalism, now located within frameworks of regionalism, transnationalism, and world cinema. Indeed, even the most seemingly "national" of national cinemas (such as the Japanese cinema) circulates well beyond the nation-state, demonstrating how local distinctiveness abounds in the global circulation of moving images and technology.

Given the rapid and pervasive changes in this global circulation—with new media platforms that enable instant access and full saturation of moving images across borders of all kinds—the essays in this section necessarily highlight the dynamics of the production and reception of independent, international, and commercial films in national, regional, postcolonial, and transnational contexts. In the process, they also address questions of culture, identity, and historical change, with particular attention to postcolonial and postcommunist identities and the ways in which digital media and production have expanded the theories and practices of cinema beyond debates over representation to embrace the diverse uses of cutting-edge tools, networks of activism, and regional and global indigenous networks of distribution and exhibition. Just as the restoration of damaged prints opens up the history of lost or censored films to new students and scholars and is the result of international archival cooperation, so, too, does the increase in transnational and global cultural exchanges, financing, and distribution challenge and transform the teaching of cinema history, which must now be understood within a broader geographic frame.

Work Cited

Ďurovičová, Nataša, and Kathleen Newman, eds. *World Cinemas, Transnational Perspectives.* New York: Routledge, 2009. Print.

Neepa Majumdar

Teaching Indian Cinema

Long before Bollywood appeared on the academic and popular horizon of the United States, commercial films from Bombay and Madras already had a hegemonic presence in many parts of the world, such as the Middle East, Southeast Asia, Africa, and Eastern Europe. Both in India and in places like Nigeria, Turkey, and Eastern Europe, Hindi- and Tamil-language films from India have functioned in relation to the local cinema cultures in much the same way as Hollywood has functioned in relation to other cinemas worldwide. A cinema that arguably has had a larger international presence than Hollywood, at least in terms of audience numbers, Indian cinema has been the other dominant mainstream cinema against which various counter-cinemas have struggled, including India's own regional cinemas and its art cinema. Because Indian cinema exemplifies an alternative type of hegemonic cinematic form, it presents an opportunity to defamiliarize the idea of Hollywood as the worldwide norm for mainstream cinema. But Indian commercial cinema's normativity for millions of viewers also points to the imbalance in curricular options. Most universities have no course on Indian cinema, and those that do usually offer only one or two courses. In contrast, Hollywood-related courses are generally divided under the headings of genre, auteur, and film history. The limited number of courses is the central problem in designing a course on Indian cinema in ways that go beyond a coverage model, and in a historical and formal survey of Indian films, one feels obliged to cover a fairly standardized and canonical set of films and topics. At the very least, any course on Indian cinema should aspire to contest the ideas of a singular Indian cinema, let alone the recently popularized term *Bollywood*, while also making some gesture toward the entirety of South Asian cinema both historically and geographically. This attempt would include not only the cinemas of India, Pakistan, Bangladesh, Nepal, and Sri Lanka but also cinemas in the numerous regional languages of India, such as Bengali, Marathi, Tamil, and Telugu.

An Indian Cinema Course

In designing Indian cinema courses, instructors face the competing claims of area studies and film studies approaches to the subject. In the United States and the United Kingdom most Indian cinema courses are still being offered primarily in a South Asian studies context. Such courses tend to emphasize recent films and sometimes make no distinction between films made in South Asia and those made in the diaspora. Within film studies, if one can imagine what it would be like to teach Hollywood cinema through a single course, it makes sense perhaps that most existing examples of Indian cinema syllabi follow a coverage model and want to be as inclusive as possible, even though there are obvious constraints to this approach, namely the relative unavailability of key films and the paucity of books and articles suitable for the undergraduate classroom. It is more common to find Indian cinema taught within the context of world cinema courses.

The first challenge of any Indian cinema course or even a week on Indian cinema in a general course would be to interrogate student expectations regarding the term *Bollywood*. This term is often assumed to be interchangeable with all Indian cinema, even though South Asia's long history of numerous regional cinemas in various languages and its alternative cinematic traditions are implicitly excluded by this term. Far from being a merely pedantic irritation in the way that Bollywood so blatantly echoes Hollywood, such an interrogation is necessary to point to both the term's recent provenance in popular discourse as well as its older history in cognates such as *Tollywood*, referring to the regional Bengali cinema produced in studios located in the Tollygunge neighborhood of Calcutta or *Nollywood* to refer to Nigerian cinema.[1] The popularity of *Bollywood* as a term, however, tends to obscure its inadequacy in designating the full historical and geographic scope of Indian cinema. Not least because of its enthusiastic adoption outside India and in the diaspora, the term *Bollywood* more appropriately signifies a particular form of post-1991 film that emerged with the shift in economic practices, modes of filmmaking, and audiences that came with the opening of India's markets.

Typically, an Indian cinema syllabus tends to spend one or two weeks, if that, on early Indian cinema from the silent period to the 1940s, dividing the rest of the course on the competing claims of periodization (e.g., the 1950s, 1970s, and post-1990s), film type or mode (e.g., melodrama, the courtesan film, and documentary), alternative cinemas (e.g., regional cinemas and art cinemas), stardom, and spectatorship. But how can one make the most of such a standardized course? One option is to use each week's material to work for more than one category so that a single film might introduce multiple concepts to a student. Both Raj Kapoor's *Awaara* (*The Vagabond*; 1951) and *Shree 420* (*Mr. 420*; 1955), for example, would not only allow discussion of postindependence Indian cinema in the 1950s but also address questions of a national cinema in India, the particular form of popular Bombay film, the functioning of stardom in the pairing of Raj Kapoor and Nargis, and issues of national and international spectatorship. Applying similar approaches to an earlier film such as Vishnupant Govind Damle and Sheikh Fattelal's *Sant Tukaram* (*Saint Tukaram*; 1936) enlarges the historical scope of the course, while also challenging students to attend to the different forms of spectatorship, stardom, and national cinema in South Asia.

In charting a course through the competing pressures of historical inclusion, film availability, and student predilections for only the most recent films, instructors may not be able to include only topics for which there are films and readings available. Important or popular films may be available but without any significant scholarly work to situate them for students, or scholarly work might analyze films that are not readily available. Instructors can now include a silent film in the syllabus, thanks to the British Film Institute's release of a DVD of Franz Osten and Himansu Rai's *A Throw of Dice* (*Prapancha Pash*; 1925), but they must be creative in assigning critical work related to the film, since there is no article that centers exclusively on it. Some readings mention it in discussing or surveying other silent films but do not address the full and immediate experience of watching the film. Certainly, one goal of teaching *A Throw of Dice* would be to counter the tendency among students to view such films as bitter pills to be swallowed before the real fun of recent (color and sound) films begins. The coverage model of Indian cinema courses can break down here if the imperative to have students experience as much of the full scope of Indian cinema as possible is further burdened with readings that function merely as surveys or summaries.[2] Often the absence of suitable readings can be made into a strength because articles that directly analyze a film end up doing all the work and leave very little room for students to do analyses, unless the reading is assigned after the film has been viewed and discussed.[3] Instead, articles or even short pieces that introduce useful concepts to students work better to generate discussion and active analysis. For *A Throw of Dice*, readings might include extracts from Suresh Chabria's *Light of Asia*,[4] a brief reading on orientalism, relevant entries from the *Encyclopaedia of Indian Cinema* (Rajadhyaksha and Willemen), an account of Germany's Universum-Film AG (UFA) studios,[5] and relevant segments from the interviews conducted by the Indian Cinematograph Committee in 1927.[6] I find it useful to give students a personal stake in the film by putting them to work in writing scene analyses or short responses to the film in relation to other orientalist fantasy films of the silent era, such as Fritz Lang's 1921 films *The Indian Tomb* and *The Tiger of Eschnapur*.

The burden of representation, or the weight of representational responsibility borne by the single-film text, lies heavy with national cinema courses, in which there is always the danger that each film may be taken to stand for much more than it actually does. Students may see each film as representative of certain issues and topics as signaled in the syllabus and readings; there is also the less obvious, involuntary tendency for students to regard unfamiliar cultural objects as ethnographic documents that are representative of whole cultures. To counter this tendency, instructors may find it helpful to emphasize the individuality of each film so that, for example, *Sant Tukaram* is not only a representative of the saint film, Prabhat Studios, or preindependent Indian cinema but also a very particular articulation of these (and other) categories. A common way to enlarge and complicate the representativeness of the chosen film is through a "clip fest" of other films, but I prefer to use that time instead to have students apply newly learned concepts to a close reading of the film. The more insidious forms of generalization that each film might encourage, such as how Indians practice religion from *Sant Tukaram*, might be held at bay if students spend time developing a personal and more focused relation to each film as a particular cultural and aesthetic object, through in-class discussion of clips and through written scene analyses. Half-baked cultural impressions might take second place to a knowledge grounded in the film's stylistic choices when students work, for example, on a shot breakdown and analysis of the scene that intercuts shots of Tukaram singing with shots of the statue of Vitthal and of multiplying Shivajis. Attention to the editing and cinematography in this scene helps anchor discussion of the film's particular forms of engaging a well-known biography at a particular historical juncture.

As the two examples of *Sant Tukaram* and *A Throw of Dice* demonstrate, each film used in the course might generate a different kind of student work, and the varying kinds of assignments can be divided among the students. Scene analysis assignments also function as a crash course in film studies for students in other fields. Yet close readings that merely focus on the text impoverish each film's complicated relation to historical realities. Rather than provide background historical and cultural information to students, I prefer to begin with their experience of viewing the film to generate questions on which the class can build an expanding range of critical work, starting with the ability to recognize a film's stylistic choices (cinematography, editing, mise-en-scène, and sound). To treat the Indian cinema course primarily as a film class rather than a culture course, the first step in initiating critical thinking is to insist on the visual specificity of cinema and to wean students away from analyzing a film as an unmediated cultural experience. Using students' stylistic analysis of clips as the starting point leads naturally into ever-expanding contexts, such as the film's historical context, its extratextual references, its spectators, and its theoretical implications. Attention to the theoretical implications of understanding film in different contexts allows students to place the specificities of Indian cinema, such as its modes of star circulation or its reliance on song and spectacle, in the larger context of debates within film studies.

Perhaps the most useful way of enlarging the scope of a standardized overview on Indian cinema is to draw on the strengths of the students in the classroom. Typically, an Indian cinema course attracts heritage students who might be from outside the humanities, film studies students, area studies students, and, recently, a diverse mix of students who identify themselves as fans of Bollywood films. The sharply differing degrees to which students are already acquainted with South Asian history or with film studies as a discipline present one challenge of designing and teaching such a course. To draw on the expertise each group brings into the classroom, I set aside a week's worth of class and screening time for a student-led workshop in which groups of students present to the class some aspect of Indian cinema that is not addressed in the syllabus. In courses that meet for a four-hour session once a week, all students present at the same time, so there is pressure to excel as well as a somewhat festive atmosphere. I find the workshop works best somewhere toward the end of the semester, though not in the last week. We generate the topics for these group research and presentation projects in class over the course of the first month through a discussion of student interests and of the syllabus as a text that constructs Indian cinema in a particular way. These short sessions at the start of each class also provide the opportunity to examine the competing historical, popular, and academic valences of terms such as *Bollywood*, *Bombay*, *South Asian*, *Hindi*, *art*, *popular*, *commercial*, and *Indian*. The workshop can also be the place to let students do the work of introducing basic cultural, historical, and geographic information. Topics have included censorship histories, regional cinemas, particular auteurs or star personae, film reception histories, industrial and production histories, global film exhibition histories, and paracinematic cultures (e.g., popular music, advertising, and fashion as they relate to film cultures). Certain parameters guide the research and presentations, such as the number and type of outside sources that must be used, the division of labor among the students, and the proportion of time spent outlining an argument and showing clips or providing background information. Most important, the presentation at the workshop, in which each student in the group must speak, is only one part of a longer process beginning with a group proposal and ending with individually written papers based on some aspect of the research project.

An alternative approach to designing a course on Indian cinema is to take the risk of eschewing the coverage model for a thematic model, which might organize the class around a topic such as gender, religion, or historical representation. In its worst form, the thematic model is ahistorical and appears to be arbitrary, but if it is designed with an eye to the coverage model, it can produce a refreshingly new, if uncanonical, view of South Asian cinema. One version of such a course might be structured around directors and producers who have had careers spanning multiple decades. A course on V. Shantaram, Mrinal Sen, and the Chopras (B. R. Chopra, Yash Chopra, and Aditya Chopra), for example, would span from the 1930s to the present, while also accommodating many of the other topics that might typically go into a traditional syllabus. Even though such a course might not include some canonical films like K. Asif's *Mother India* (1957), and *Mughal-e-Azam* (*The Great Mughal*; 1960) and Ramesh Sippy's *Sholay* (*Embers*; 1975), it would offer a way to address the problem of the world's largest film industry being represented by a single and increasingly standardized film course in most undergrauate film curricula.

A World Cinema Course

The tensions and compromises inherent in designing a single course on Indian cinema are further compounded in courses on world cinema, which might spend only one week on Indian cinema. Despite the best intentions, it is hard to avoid the "one-week/one-continent" mode of including non-Western cinema in world film courses. One problem is the implicit hierarchies in syllabi in which the pragmatics of instruction time and coverage of the field serve to ghettoize nonnormative texts. Another problem is tokenism or the interchangeability of non-Western films, in which the desired internationalization of the field might be considered satisfied equally by an Indian film, a Senegalese film, or a Hong Kong film. When approaching the single Indian (or other non-Western) film in a world cinema course, the burden of representation is even greater and the degree to which background cultural information is needed or desirable presents further pedagogical conflicts, such as the problems of close textual analysis as opposed to the pitfalls of oversimplified contextual analysis. Yet a complete absence of informational context might suggest the easy availability of other cinemas as interchangeable cultural consumables—a suggestion not far from the actual experience of today's film cultures in which DVDs, *YouTube*, and Internet downloads make an increasingly larger set of international films available to the casual viewer. Thus I prefer to foreground a theoretical concept, such as genre, reception, new screen technologies, or stardom, as the primary lens through which the film will be considered and use the particularities of geography and culture to complicate the meanings of such concepts. That is, cultural preparation and background need to be anchored in cinema-specific questions; otherwise, films from unfamiliar spaces take the path of least resistance and are read as anthropological representations of other cultures. These issues are related because no amount of background cultural information will resolve the burden of representation, especially in the case of non-Western films that depict poverty, such as Satyajit Ray's *Pather Panchali* (*The Song of the Road*; 1955) or Ritwik Ghatak's *Meghe Dhaka Tara* (*Cloud-Capped Star*; 1960). The experience of viewing hardship on screen, of course, may be usefully discussed in terms of the contested meanings attached to the act of watching suffering at a distance, be it war or poverty.[7]

In this context, there is also the temptation to find cultural specificity in the narrative forms and cinematic style of foreign films. Yet the quest for such specificities (like song and spectacle in Bollywood or oral storytelling modes in Senegalese films) needs to be tempered by consideration of the actual intercultural experience of film watching and filmmaking in most geographic contexts (see van der Heide). Even for an older film such as *Meghe Dhaka Tara*, a history of the film's critical reception and the means by which the film ended up in a classroom are worth discussing with students. For both the single course on Indian cinema and for other courses that seek to include one week on South Asia, many of these problems of pedagogy, which have no easy solution, are best approached through a practice of self-reflexivity of the kind we often laud in film texts. That is, for all of the kinds of courses discussed here, the syllabus might be offered as one of the course texts that students unpack for its assumptions, omissions, emphases, and struggles over meaning.

Notes

1. For a discussion of the history and circulation of the term *Bollywood*, see Prasad; Rajadhyaksha.

2. Barnouw and Krishnaswamy's book, for example, is an excellent resource for researchers but is too general for the undergraduate classroom.

3. In principle, this may be true of all film studies courses. Students may benefit from reading articles analyzing specific films only after having had the chance to discuss the films in the light of more conceptual readings.

4. This catalog accompanied the Indian silent cinema screenings at the Pordenone silent film festival in 1994.

5. See Jaikumar for the significance of UFA to early Indian cinema (*Cinema* 94–95). See also Jaikumar's useful review of the DVD of *A Throw of the Dice*.

6. This document is not yet widely available, but Jaikumar discusses it at length in *Cinema*.

7. Some recent examples are the debates surrounding the representation of poverty in Fernando Meirelles and Kátia Lund's *City of God* (2003) and Danny Boyle's *Slumdog Millionaire* (2008). Susan Sontag provides excellent conceptual frameworks for this topic.

Works Cited

Barnouw, Erik, and Subrahmanyam Krishnaswamy. *Indian Film*. New York: Columbia UP, 1963. Print.

Chabria, Suresh, ed. *Light of Asia: Indian Silent Cinema 1912–1934.* New Delhi: Wiley Eastern, 1994. Print.

Indian Cinematograph Committee. *Indian Cinematograph Committee, 1927–1928: Evidence.* Calcutta: Central Pub. Branch, 1928. Print.

Jaikumar, Priya. *Cinema at the End of Empire: A Politics of Transition in Britain and India.* Durham: Duke UP, 2006. Print.

———. "*A Throw of the Dice* (*Prapancha Pash*)." *Modernism/Modernity* 16.4 (2009): 845–48. Print.

Prasad, Madhava. "This Thing Called Bollywood." *Unsettling Cinema: A Symposium on the Place of Cinema in India. Seminar* 525 (2003): n. pag. Web. 16 May 2009.

Rajadhyaksha, Ashish. "The 'Bollywoodization' of the Indian Cinema: Cultural Nationalism in a Global Arena." *City Flicks: Indian Cinema and the Urban Experience.* Ed. Preben Kaarsholm. Calcutta: Seagull, 2004. 113–39. Print.

Rajadhyaksha, Ashish, and Paul Willemen, eds. *Encyclopaedia of Indian Cinema.* New rev. ed. London: British Film Inst.–Oxford UP, 1999. Print.

Sant Tukaram [*Saint Tukaram*]. Dir. Vishnupant Govind Damle and Sheikh Fattelal. Everest, 2008. DVD.

Sontag, Susan. *Regarding the Pain of Others.* New York: Farrar, 2003. Print.

A Throw of Dice [*Prapancha Pash*]. Dir. Franz Osten and Himansu Rai. 1925. Kino Intl., 2008. DVD.

van der Heide, William. *Malaysian Cinema, Asian Film: Border Crossings and National Film.* Amsterdam: Amsterdam UP, 2002. Print.

Cristina Venegas

Teaching Latin American and Caribbean Cinema

The strength of films coming from the new Latin American cinema (1962–84) catalyzed the teaching of Latin American and Caribbean cinema in the US academy. Focused on the pan-American reach of a movement that responded as much to censorship at the hands of authoritarian dictatorships as it did to imperialist interventions, university and college courses began to trace the characteristic heterogeneity of aesthetics and cultures and its transnational continuity and disruption. The emphasis on film culture as a social and political instrument helped define an ideological approach that coincided with independence movements in Africa and Asia, postcolonial writings, and counterculture wars stemming from exhausted imperialist paradigms. To place this cinema within the changing discipline of film history, theory, and criticism, instructors considered its formal contributions in the context of other aesthetic movements such as Italian neorealism and the political avant-garde. Key film manifestos such as Fernando Solanas and Octavio Getino's "Towards a Third Cinema," Julio García Espinosa's "For an Imperfect Cinema," and Glauber Rocha's "An Esthetic of Hunger," among others, framed a discussion about the relation between theory and cinematic practice and the necessity of formulating alternative intellectual and aesthetic positions. Films from Cuba, like Humberto Solás's *Lucía* (1968) and Tomás Gutiérrez Alea's *Memories of Underdevelopment* (1968); from Argentina, like Solanas and Getino's *Hour of the Furnaces* (1968); from Chile, like Patricio Guzmán's *Battle of Chile* (1975, 1977, 1979); and from Brazil, like Nelson Pereira dos Santos's *Barren Lives* (1963), along with important others from across the Americas, formed an incipient canon of internationally recognized films and filmmakers. Academic and pedagogical work necessarily focused on the historical and political confluence that brought about the formalization of the subject to university curricula in this era.

The development of this paradigm responded to shifts in the discipline of film studies as courses sought to engage with relevant contemporary issues (say, the neocolonial practices of dominant European and US cultural partnerships) and to expand interdisciplinary and transnational cooperation by film and literature scholars and practitioners. Subsequent turns toward psychoanalysis and feminist film analysis, cultural studies, and ethnic studies all brought a new emphasis beyond the importance of the initial historical turning point sustained by dynamic left politics of the early years of the Cuban revolution. Continued examination of these aspects has promoted, intensified, and renewed historical research in areas including early cinemas in the hemisphere, transnational exchanges in early and later collaborations, experimental cinemas, documentary, digital technologies, discourses of race and nationalism, and the meaning of a new global circulation for the future of the field. Transnationalism, a central quality of filmmaking in Latin America, continues, as posited by Marvin D'Lugo, to broaden the pedagogical path as "co-producing cultural identity" becomes increasingly identified with the work of global filmmakers (121).

These intellectual excursions have also interrogated the problem of subsuming Caribbean cultural production within the subject of Latin American cinema, further challenging the presumed unity under the regional nomenclature. While films from the Spanish-speaking Caribbean have typically formed part of Latin American cinema courses (especially Cuba and Puerto Rico), Caribbean cinema responds to several different cultural forces and politics produced by multilingual, multicultural, multiracial, and multihistorical territories; these forces, as Ileana Rodriguez contends, construct identities over time in an "American" space. Films like Perry Henzell's *The Harder They Come* (1973), from English-speaking Jamaica, and Euzhan Palcy's *Sugar Cane Alley* (1983), from French-speaking Martinique, respond to patterns of production that emerge from common cultural and linguistic zones, migrations, alliances, and exchanges that differ from those affecting Latin American filmmakers. Acknowledgment of shared characteristics (such as the size and scope of industries) and of divergent modes of signification and networks of Caribbean moving image production complicates our understanding of the idea of the transnational and the resulting exchanges (Burton, *Cinema*; Chanan; Burton, *Social Documentary*; López, "'Other' History"; Ďurovičová and Newman).

The revitalized Latin American and Caribbean cinema—operating at amateur and professional levels, under institutional agreements and changing media practices—has attracted greater visibility in the academy, including boosting enrollment in university courses and expanding scholarship. The dynamic exchanges begun in the 1970s have taken on new characteristics and levels of cooperation across the region, sometimes expressed in trade policies, signifying practices, and in personal cultural networks. For instance, the second annual Caribbean Cinema Traveling Exhibition in 2008 toured twenty-eight countries with forty films from locations such as Suriname, Trinidad and Tobago, Jamaica, Nicaragua, Curaçao, and Cuba ("Caribbean Cinema"). New research and teaching supports and extends continuities with earlier eras, the subsequent transformation of production strategies, and the variety of media interconnections of the twenty-first century.

The Pedagogical Landscape

The approach and scope of courses on the cinemas of Latin American and Caribbean regions vary, depending on a range of interrelated factors. While my analysis is informed by knowledge gained from teaching across several academic settings and international locations, the following draws on my experience in developing curricula in a media studies department with a humanities focus. The core curriculum of our undergraduate and graduate studies has a strong emphasis on historical, theoretical, and aesthetic inquiry of media enhanced by interdisciplinary collaboration related to postcolonial, industrial, global, or environmental issues. Fulfilling elective and general major and university requirements, survey courses such as Latin American Cinema serve a student population beyond film studies majors. Instructors thus face the challenge of balancing the provision of sufficient contextual introductory material, discipline-specific methods, and terminology—needed for depth of analytical training—and instruction in writing. In addition, at the undergraduate level, such courses remain introductory to the topic. The students' generational perspectives, cultural references, and patterns of media use demand an emphasis on "explaining" difficult texts and contexts, such as the peculiarities of *cinema novo* in Brazil, that differ significantly from American cinema as the tradition with which most students are familiar.

A transdisciplinary approach focuses on Latin American and Caribbean film as interrelated humanistic, aesthetic, economic, and industrial practices that are medium specific and overlapping with other media, such as satellite television. Through sweeping (and increasingly difficult to accommodate) surveys of cinematic production, the transnational is broken down into complex strands that work toward and against one another. Courses address trends, dominant genres, cultural and economic bonds, the emergence of digital technologies, political events, the development of media industries, the role of stars and celebrity, and changing audiences. To help students go beyond viewing historical texts, teachers must establish the conditions of technological exchange (e.g., patent or projection equipment ownership) and their links to later, unequal industrial and technological exchanges (López, "Early Cinema"; Paranaguá). This issue is key for students unfamiliar with how media institutions work outside their familiar environments of consumption. International political events such as the Mexican Revolution also provide students with a frame of reference for understanding transborder productions, the development of nationalist cultural policies, and battles against racist stereotyping.

Toward the end of the twentieth century, media industries in Latin America increasingly converged in response to the internationalization of film, television, and music industries. Local media conglomerates (like Grupo Cisneros in Venezuela) have created economic partnerships across media platforms to expand their markets, thereby fostering transnational patterns of consumption. Alliances may produce regional markets or regional associations to secure their national stakes and avoid being subsumed by transnational conglomerates. While markets expand, digital tools provide access to previously unavailable films and research materials. As a result, courses can cover larger and more intricate geopolitical and audiovisual territories now than in the past. Restoration of damaged prints, the result of international archival cooperation, opens up the history of lost or censored films to new students and scholars, thereby changing how we study media industries.[1] The increase in transnational and global cultural exchanges, financing, and distribution challenge and transform the teaching of cinemas by making available more teaching resources.

Inquiry into the cultural and geopolitical imagination of the cinemas of the region(s) has focused the problem of geopolitical specificity at the level of the nation-state, exploring the benefits and limitations of such an investigation. Approaches that critique national models, together with transnational and global perspectives, move us closer to identifying the set of interrelated forces that come together in the study of Latin American and Caribbean cinema.

Approaches: Regional Media

A regional view of the cinema of Latin America facilitates a shift in focus from the nation to the interconnections in historical, technological, political, and industrial development of the cinema. A course concerned with examining a particular national cinema might pursue various themes: it might chart a chronology of film production; examine key texts, filmmakers, and important events in industrial development; consider the relation of film to other arts and media; and investigate the effect of historical specificity on the national cinema's definition. Underlying this approach is the idea that the cinema produced within a particular geopolitical and cultural territory responds to and is determined by existing national characteristics. Yet not all groups and cultures within a geopolitical space determine their interests as national. Although national cinematic production still responds to specific national legislation, funding opportunities, and cultural and historical determinants, the idea of the national is not always a satisfying method for the study of cinematic production. It is important for teachers to have students consider the limits of this approach while helping them understand that nationalisms continue to form part of national imaginations across the globe, that moving image production within a national territory does not necessarily respond to national interests (as in Hollywood) or myths, and that other constructions of nations are possible (as with indigenous communities).

Changing national production models, emerging technologies, and increasing circulation of media products thus characterize twenty-first-century film industries. As the industries of the region respond to both local economic conditions and global markets, film education, training, and production are on the rise; filmmakers work, temporarily or permanently, outside their countries; and governments and investors pursue markets in novel ways and through different channels.

Yet the strategies needed to respond to these challenges are not entirely new. Today's cross-border economic and cultural exchanges have occurred since the arrival of cinema in Brazil in 1896. But now the multiplication of delivery systems beyond the movie theater that has accompanied globalization increases the flow of media products. This movement forces a move away from narrow, nationally based analyses to comprehensive readings of how transnational media industries function. To identify the fundamental mechanisms that drive them, scholarship has become increasingly attentive to transnational and local interactions as they occur within regional landscapes. The rise in coproductions exemplifies the new model of work. Multination funding agencies like Grupo Ibermedia (Latin America, Spain, and Portugal) and Cinergía (Central America and the Caribbean) were established to foment the production of film across national borders while taking advantage of the regional similarities of their markets. Students are gaining training across the region in schools or special courses. Prizes established at international film festivals introduce producers to new talent. American companies represented by the Motion Picture Association of America (e.g., Sony, Warner Bros.) are increasingly distributing Latin American films. National state funding policies have given way to a climate of mixed financing mechanisms that permit international capital. The variety and depth of sustained exchanges arising in the Latin American film industries exemplify the richness, scope, and complexity of what is studied under the heading of "regional."

Thinking regionally attends to the interconnection of cultures, languages, and markets that spill over into media consumption and production (in the case of Latin America, Spanish, Portuguese, and indigenous languages). It also addresses the proliferation of trade pacts with the concomitant issues raised by the establishment of cultural policies, integration, and exchange (e.g., Mercosur is a pact between Argentina, Uruguay, Brazil, Paraguay, and Venezuela). Finally, thinking regionally engages the increasing importance of a network of film festivals as premier sites of regional and international exhibition, marketing, and distribution (like those in Mexico, Argentina, Cuba, and Brazil).[2]

Guided by this three-way scope, the regional approach questions the implicit assumption of a coherent and interconnected set of production practices, ideas, and histories bound within regional categories like Latin America and Caribbean. It also investigates what this presumed unity cannot account for, including the interconnection of industries both locally and internationally, ideological and political differences, and how local and regional concerns relate to the global. This approach also involves understanding how the study of cinema and its practice has been institutionalized beyond the localities in question; in addition, it reveals the complexity of national perspectives and how legislative histories and the relations between the state and the private sector affect the view toward national financing of film industries.

Such a regional perspective is at work, for example, in a graduate course focused on media and trade within the North American Free Trade Agreement (NAFTA). Structured as a seminar, Post-NAFTA Media explores the role that film, television, the Internet, and other media play in configuring and altering the territorial landscape resulting from the 1993 agreement among Canada, Mexico, and the United States. The course explores a variety of perspectives and media, specifially how regional media considerations contribute to our field of study through topics such as cultural policy and agency, institutional frameworks, piracy, media activism, border culture, technological change facilitated by the trade pact, and democracy. NAFTA is one of many regional trade pacts throughout the world that scholars argue were triggered by the formation of the European Union. The relationship of culture to trade continues to be debated (see, e.g., Drucker; McAnany and Wilkinson). For some, it is a question of expanding markets under the banner of free trade, and for others it is also a question of cultural agency, political power, and global economics. The economic integration involved informs the construction of spatial dynamics, from borders to local cityscapes, from concrete institutional practices to virtual environments.

National Cinema in a Transnational Context

To deal productively with the concepts of national film culture, production, and imaging practices, scholars and teachers have approached the topic through such lenses as historical surveys of national production (e.g., the cinemas of Argentina and Brazil); defined periods (like Mexico's golden age); modern-day perspectives; the influence of transnational labor, cultural, and economic exchange; diasporas; the effect of other media; and political cinemas. The cinemas of Argentina, Mexico, Cuba, and Brazil play central roles within the historical record and available scholarly material and media artifacts. As home to the largest industries of the region, Mexico, Argentina, and Brazil are important centers of production—of film stars, music, films, and entrepreneurial bonds—and have strong production capabilities and constitutive markets. "New" cinemas have been coming from these industries since the mid-to-late 1990s, and particular films and filmmakers have garnered global attention (and box-office success) since the late 1990s. Such films as Alfonso Cuaron's *Y tu mamá también* (2001) and Fernando Meirelles and Kátia Lund's *City of God* (2002) have helped create a new category of analysis whereby different strategies for "facing up to Hollywood" (López, "Facing"), generated since the 1960s, translate into a Latin American Hollywood. Smaller industries, such as those of Chile, Colombia, and Peru, attract less curricular attention because of the size of their economies and the availability of materials. They are often productively addressed under thematic rubrics such as trauma and amnesia, the urban and the popular, and narratives of violence. Increasingly, secondary industries take part in coproduction agreements that make possible regional cooperation, problematizing the strict distinction of the national. The Uruguayan cinematographer turned director César Chalone's film *The Pope's Bathroom* (2007) is a Uruguay-Brazil-France coproduction distributed internationally. Inspired by real local events and set in the hamlet of Melo at the border between Uruguay and Brazil, the film is literally a cross-border exchange of contraband goods determined by global events like the pope's visit, small-town aspirations, and market interactions.

The transnational context of national cinema is evident in a course on Mexican cinema that deals with the history, politics, and culture of filmmaking in Mexico. The "national cinema" approach questions assumptions of what constitutes the national character of filmmaking in Mexico. Concurrently, it explores the strong nationalist cultural discourse that defined national identity. While viewing films produced in a specific territory (Mexico), discussion traces the transnational qualities that make up the culture of filmmaking, including those films made outside the national territory. The vast cultural, historical, and geographic landscape is covered through the lens of three historical markers: the pre- and postrevolutionary period (1910–30) and the project of nationalism; the 1968 student massacre in Mexico City and the rise of multiple national perspectives; and the political crisis of Mexico's long-ruling regime, the Partido Revolucionario Institucional (PRI), seen in the contested elections of 1988 and the subsequent emergent social movements such as the Zapatistas in Chiapas. Rather than efface the category of the national altogether, the goal is to explore the changing demands on the ideas of nation and nationalism, new categories used to define social practices and groupings, and how these issues are expressed through the cinema and in television. Of increasing importance is how these concepts contribute to the formation of a cultural policy and of Mexican cinema in a transnational context.

Revolutionary Media Cultures

Further integration of Latin American and Caribbean film into the culture of world cinema provokes the exploration of a particular thematic, revolutionary cinema and positions the study of political cinema, so central to the study and teaching of Latin American cinema, within the context of the cultures from which it drew influence and to which it responded. Latin American cinema in the 1970s served a social and political function. It informs as well a retrospective approach to the political cultures that produced a revolutionary imagination not only in Latin America but also in the former Soviet Union, China, Vietnam, Eastern Europe, Jamaica, Africa, and the United States. Specific to the history of Latin American and Caribbean cinematic culture and within a global mediascape, the retrospective approach considers the language of political cinema and the various ideologies and practices it generated globally.

Working with the concepts of utopia, social transformation, emancipation, revolution, and globalization can help students examine how these ideas coincide with cinema aesthetics to articulate a new cultural and political praxis. A comparison of socialist realism across nations, for instance, yields illuminating differences of gender politics and iconic cultures in revolutionary discourses. Focusing first on the cinema and later on digital media, students investigate the international and transnational ideological influence of Soviet, Chinese, and Cuban revolutionary cultures and the way that initially film and later virtual social networks contribute to the ideas of liberation from the 1920s to the present. We explore this theme through various lenses: philosophical and aesthetic perspectives such as modernism, postmodernism, and the avant-garde, as well as genres such as drama, documentary, manifestos, and virtual environments. The Cuban filmmaker Santiago Alvarez's documentary work for the Latin American Newsreel (e.g., *Now* [1965]) provides an important link to ideas of justice and racial equality circulating at the time of the US civil rights movement.

Finally, an appreciation of critical race scholarship, postcolonial investigations, and the sustained activism of indigenous groups throughout the Americas demands rigorous academic and curricular attention to indigenous networks of media production. Groups like the Latin American Film and Communication Coordination of Indigenous Peoples (CLACPI—an international grassroots network of indigenous media makers in Bolivia, Brazil, Chile, Colombia, Cuba, Guatemala, Mexico, and Peru) focus on community development, education, and social motivation, working both at the regional and community levels. Unlike commercial networks, CLACPI uses digital media to assist the poor, link communities, and preserve memories—all vital cultural and educational functions in a region where populations have endured long periods of economic turmoil, civil and political strife, urban growth, and rural degeneration. Whereas the issue of indigenous identity was of political importance in new Latin American cinema, today it extends beyond the earlier conflicts over representation to encompass the diverse use of digital tools, networks of activism, old and new media, and regional and global indigenous networks of distribution and exhibition.

The twenty-first-century curriculum of film and media topics related to Latin America and the Caribbean builds on past gains to address the complex web of transactions taking place through myriad spaces of use and production. Where once the study of these areas of production might have been limited to surveys of canonical films, courses today offer specialized topics, such as genre analyses (melodrama, road films, and so on), and attempt to train an increasingly diverse, decreasingly specialized, and growing number of students to theorize, decipher, and describe the complexity of transnational exchanges in the dynamic context of local and global cultural flows.

Notes

1. Archival restoration is taking on increasing importance throughout the hemisphere, as courses on the topic in Latin America are becoming more common. A summer 2008 seminar project at the Escuela Internacional de Cine y Television in San Antonio de los Baños, Cuba, for example, was dedicated to archival restoration.

2. Examples of such festivals include the Guadalajara International Film Festival, in Mexico; the Buenos Aires Festival de Cine Independiente, in Argentina; the Festival Internacional del Nuevo Cine Latinoamericano, in Havana; and the Festival do Rio, in Brazil.

Works Cited

Burton, Julianne, ed. *Cinema and Social Change in Latin America: Conversations with Filmmakers.* Austin: U of Texas P, 1986. Print.

———, ed. *The Social Documentary in Latin America.* Pittsburgh: U of Pittsburgh P, 1990. Print.

"Caribbean Cinema Will Travel to Twenty-Eight Countries." *ACN: Cuba News Agency.* ACN, 24 June 2008. Web. 3 Sept. 2008.

Chanan, Michael, ed. *Twenty-Five Years of Latin American Cinema.* London: British Film Inst., 1983. Print.

D'Lugo, Marvin. "Authorship, Globalization, and the New Identity of Latin American Cinema." *Rethinking Third Cinema.* Ed. Anthony R. Guneratne and Wimal Dissanayake. London: Routledge, 2003. 103–25. Print.

Drucker, Peter F. *Post-capitalist Society.* New York: Harper, 1993. Print.

Ďurovičová, Nataša, and Kathleen Newman, eds. *World Cinemas, Transnational Perspectives.* New York: Routledge, 2009. Print.

García Espinosa, Julio. "For an Imperfect Cinema." Martin 1: 71–82.

López, Ana M. "Early Cinema and Modernity in Latin America." *Cinema Journal* 40.1 (2000): 48–78. Print.

———. "Facing Up to Hollywood." *Reinventing Film Studies.* Ed. Christine Gledhill and Linda Williams. London: Arnold, 2000. 419–37. Print.

———. "An 'Other' History: The New Latin American Cinema." Martin 1: 135–56.

Martin, Michael T., ed. *New Latin American Cinema.* 2 vols. Detroit: Wayne State UP, 1997. Print.

McAnany, Emile G., and Kenton T. Wilkinson, eds. *Mass Media and Free Trade: NAFTA and the Cultural Industries.* Austin: U of Texas P, 1996. Print.

Paranaguá, Paulo Antonio. *Tradición y modernidad en el cine de América Latina.* Madrid: Fondo de Cultura Economica de España, 2003. Print.

Rocha, Glauber. "An Esthetic of Hunger." Martin 1: 59–61.

Rodriguez, Ileana. *Transatlantic Topographies: Islands, Highlands, Jungles.* Minneapolis: U of Minnesota P, 2004. Print.

Solanas, Fernando, and Octavio Getino. "Towards a Third Cinema: Notes and Experiences for the Development of a Cinema of Liberation in the Third World." Martin 1: 33–58.

Hamid Naficy

Teaching Accented Cinema as a Global Cinema

Cinema has always and everywhere been both a deeply local and a highly global industry and set of practices. Religious, ethnic, and national minorities, as well as émigrés, exiles, refugees, expatriates, and diasporic and transnational subjects, have contributed greatly to the rise of cinema and film industry in many countries and in the revival and redefinition of certain genres and national cinemas. Hollywood cinema, the most forceful in the world, was from the start both ethnic and global, and it has been renewed and revived by contributions of waves of new émigré, refugee, and ethnic filmmakers—from the Eastern European and Russian Jews of the early years to the German, Austrian, and British émigrés escaping the Nazi terror to the new ethnic directors such as Martin Scorsese, Francis Ford Coppola, and Woody Allen who helped create the new Hollywood cinema in the 1970s. The success of the Mexican filmmakers Alejandro González Iñárritu, Guillermo Arriaga, and Guillermo Del Toro; the Indian directors Mira Nair and Manoj Night Shyamalan; the Taiwanese director Ang Lee; and many other foreign, ethnic, and transnational directors working in Hollywood represents another transformation. By employing not just exilic, émigré, and ethnic directors but also transnational and diasporic directors, who make movies in their native languages, Hollywood has once again changed and rejuvenated itself to remain "on top of the world" cinema.

At the same time, in the postcolonial and post-Soviet eras, a fresh crop of exilic, émigré, diasporic, refugee, ethnic, and transnational filmmakers, working in the interstices of social formations and mainstream film and culture industries of the West, created a new transnational cinema that is at once global and local, a "glocal" or "accented" cinema (Naficy, *Accented Cinema*). If the dominant cinema is considered universal, neutral, value free, and without accent, the films of these transnationals are accented. Despite these filmmakers' key differences, their films share certain features—an accent—that emanates not so much from the accented speech of diegetic characters as from the displacement of the filmmakers, their interstitial and sometimes collective production practices, and the stylistic attributes of their films. These stylistic attributes include patterned uses of mise-en-scène, filming, narration, themes, characters, and structures of feeling. Specifically, in these works, mise-en-scène and filming are alternately claustrophobic or immense; time is fragmented and retrospective; space and place are split among a lost home, an uncertain elsewhere, and transitional places in between; narrative is broken up by memory, nostalgia, and the past and by fear of a future yet to come; characters are not whole, for they are haunted, doubled, split, and missing; and the integrity of native language is threatened by the intrusion of other languages. In short, multiplicity and fragmentation are dominant in accented films. The adoption of some of these strategies has led to the emergence of "multiplex films," which help rejuvenate mainstream cinema and give it a multiplex accent (Naficy, "From Accented Cinema" 4). Appropriated from the site of film exhibition where multiple movies are screened in one complex, the concept of multiplex films refers to films that are increasingly imbued with multiple industrial, technological, authorial, narrative, linguistic, or spectatorial formations (Naficy, "From Accented Cinema").

While sharing these attributes, accented films are far from homogeneous. I divide them in terms of place into exilic, diasporic, and postcolonial ethnic films and classify them in terms of style into feature fictional movies and experimental films. In addition, these films can be grouped together by overarching national, transnational, and regional affiliations, resulting in *beur* films and *banlieue* films in France (Bloom; Tarr),[1] black postcolonial workshop films in Britain (Eshun and Sagar; Diawara), Turkish films in Germany (Naficy, *Accented Cinema*), Iranian exile films in Europe and North America (Naficy, "Making"), and Asian American films in the United States (Feng). Some ethnic films (Friedman; Lourdeaux; Desser and Friedman) can also be taught fruitfully under the rubric of accented films, such as race movies (Stewart; Bowser, Gaines, and Musser), Chicano/Chicana films (Noriega; Fregoso), and Yiddish movies (Hoberman). The experimental accented films can also be discussed under the rubric of intercultural films (Marks).

In teaching accented cinema, instructors can use each of the stylistic attributes of the films and of the national, transnational, and ethnic classificatory schemas of accented films as appropriate topics. Since accented cinema theory is based partly on the social and cinematic location of the filmmakers, it also fits within the auteur cinema category. As a result, prolific accented filmmakers with an authorial signature can be taught under the auteur rubric as well. This approach might prove difficult since the standard printed biographical references may not deal with some of the filmmakers who naturally fall in the interstices of social and cinematic formations and are not recognized as national or international directors. Fortunately, the Internet is fast compensating for this shortcoming.

One pedagogical challenge accented filmmaking presents to teachers and students of cinema is the multilingualism of the films—the dialogue in some films is in over half a dozen languages, such as Atom Egoyan's *Calendar* (1993), Raúl Ruiz's *On Top of the Whale* (*Het dak van de Walvis* [1981]), and Alejandro González Iñárritu's *Babel* (2006), necessitating extensive on-screen translation and subtitling. Sometimes, however, as in *Calendar*, not all the dialogue is subtitled, creating illegibility as well as privileged communities of address among spectators who may have access to those languages. Other times, none of the dialogue is subtitled, a factor that limits the choices of films for class screening. Multilingual teachers and students have an advantage in such situations.

This restriction brings up the issue of cultural and linguistic competencies that are needed for researching, teaching, and writing about the accented cinema. Does working with accented films require multilingual and multicultural media teachers, or does it encourage narrowly defined niche studies, whereby each teacher engages with the cinema whose contexts she or he best understands? The same question would be relevant for students who might be asked to write about such films. Alternatively, accented cinema scholarship may encourage collaboration among scholars with specialized cultural and linguistic knowledge, the kind of collaboration not customary in humanities and film and media studies but routine in film and media productions and in sciences and medical fields. The formation of various minority caucuses within the Society for Cinema and Media Studies points to the emergence of such discursive niche formations within the discipline. But since most members are also members of more than one such formation, discursive multiplexing is at work as well.

Another challenge for teaching is the difficulty in accessing and affording some of the accented films. The rental or purchase price of these films tends to be high, since many of them are handled by small, nontheatrical, boutique distributors, such as Women Make Movies and Icarus Films, whose fee structures are based not on mass distribution but on small group viewers, such as classrooms. Because of limited distribution venues, some accented films do not travel beyond the borders of the producing nation, making access to them difficult. Some films can be obtained from non-English sources, such as La Médiathèque des Trois Mondes in Paris, but are generally not subtitled in English. The multiplicity of television standards worldwide (SECAM, PAL, NTSC, among them) creates additional access difficulties if multistandard players and television screens are not available to instructors at their university.

As the Internet increasingly becomes a film distribution and exhibition venue, accessibility and price may become less onerous in the near future. The Internet is also making access to the accented directors much easier; many maintain Web sites, from which serious scholars and teachers can obtain hard-to-find films, often at little cost. But that personal contact may create the expectation, or obligation, of easier critical treatment of the work. Film festivals are good sources of information about new accented films, particularly those that cater to independent and alternative film practices, such as the Toronto International Film Festival, the International Amsterdam Film Festival, and the International Film Festival Rotterdam, and special accented cinema festivals, such as Toronto's International Diaspora Film Festival, New York City's African Diaspora Film Festival, and the Exile Film Festival in Gothenburg, Sweden. The next best thing to attending these festivals is to refer to their Web sites, which usually provide technical and biographical information as well as film synopses and sometimes even print sources. Such Web sites as *Cinema without Borders* also provide useful information.

Another method for gaining access to the accented films while creating wide interest among students and the broad academic community is to organize with the university cinema or student film club a film festival or a film series with these films. This scheme usually provides teachers with additional funds far in excess of a single course's film rental or purchase budget. In fact, it may allow them to rent film prints on celluloid. Such events can be coordinated with a class so long as students sign up in advance for both the film series and the festival. In certain cities, it would be possible for teachers to tap into the services of foreign governments' cultural attachés to import through their diplomatic pouches, free of charge, the accented films produced in their countries. Instructors could enlist the assistance of undergraduate and graduate students in organizing such a festival or film series, providing them with a valuable film programming experience. Offering the event as a credit-bearing course in festival organizing gives students the opportunity to bolster their practice-based knowledge with theoretical and critical readings about the politics and poetics of festivals, to write the film notes, and to illustrate and design the accompanying brochure and Web site, further honing their professional skills.

To fully appreciate accented films, teachers and students need to understand not only the films' textual systems—their accents—but also their contextual worlds, an understanding that often requires research into the multiple cultures, politics, languages, ethnicities, religions, races, nationalities, demographies, and film industries involved. Some of this information can be found in established printed and audiovisual sources, which can take years to prepare and are therefore not very up-to-date. For more current sociopolitical information and maps, other dynamic sources should be sought. One readily available and reliable source is the Central Intelligence Agency, which offers country reports on its Web site *The World FactBook.* Teachers could ask students to dig up contextual information about a specific film to add to the authorial and production information gathered from elsewhere to fine-tune and enhance the film's stylistic analysis.

As studies of film become more technologically sophisticated, the need for technical competencies emerges in studying multidevice, multimedia, and multiplatform production and reception; these competencies far exceed both single-device familiarity and the traditional separation of film production from film studies. Increasingly, film and media studies and production areas are merging rapidly, paralleling the structural convergence within global media industries. Increasingly, job descriptions for new hires in film and media, particularly for small departments, include a preference for scholars competent in both critical studies and production. Finally, many of the challenges and issues teachers face in the classroom also arise in conference presentations and scholarly publications. Thus tackling these challenges in one situation may help resolve them in another. Guiding and mentoring the students about international conferences, periodicals, and publishers who have had a track record in dealing with accented cinema and its cognate fields—as well as about funders, distributors, and exhibitors of accented cinema products—both legitimize and expand the study and production of the films.

Note

1. *Beur* is French slang for Arab. *Beur* cinema and literature refer to films and writings produced by North Africans in France, many of which express the ambiguities and complexities of French multinational identity. *Banlieues* are neighborhoods and housing projects on the outskirts of large French cities in which racial and ethnic minorities live and which have been the sites of frequent immigrant demonstrations and protests. *Banlieue* films are akin to "hood films" in the United States.

Works Cited

Bloom, Peter. "Beur Cinema and the Politics of Location: French Immigration Politics and the Naming of a Film Movement." *Transnational Cinema, The Film Reader*. Ed. Elizabeth Ezra and Terry Rowden. London: Routledge, 2006. 131–42. Print.

Bowser, Pearl, Jane Gaines, and Charles Musser, eds. *Oscar Micheaux and His Circle: African-American Filmmaking and Race Cinema of the Silent Era*. Bloomington: Indiana UP, 2001. Print.

Desser, David, and Lester D. Friedman, eds. *American Jewish Filmmakers*. 2nd ed. Chicago: U of Illinois P, 2003. Print.

Diawara, Manthia. "Power and Territory: The Emergence of Black British Film Collectives." *Fires Were Started: British Cinema and Thatcherism*. Ed. Lester Friedman. Minneapolis: U of Minnesota P, 1993. 147–60. Print.

Eshun, Kodwo, and Anjalika Sagar, eds. *The Ghosts of Songs: The Art of the Black Audio Film Collective*. Liverpool: Liverpool UP, 2007. Print.

Feng, Peter. *Identities in Motion: Asian American Film and Video*. Durham: Duke UP, 2002. Print.

Fregoso, Rosa Linda. *The Bronze Screen: Chicana and Chicano Film Culture*. Minneapolis: U of Minnesota P, 1993. Print.

Friedman, Lester D., ed. *Unspeakable Images: Ethnicity and the American Cinema*. Chicago: U of Illinois P, 1991. Print.

Hoberman, J. *Bridge of Light: Yiddish Film between Two Worlds*. Philadelphia: Temple UP, 1995. Print.

Lourdeaux, Lee. *Italian and Irish Filmmakers in America: Ford, Capra, Coppola, and Scorsese*. Philadelphia: Temple UP, 1990. Print.

Marks, Laura. *The Skin of the Film: Intercultural Cinema, Embodiment, and the Senses*. Durham: Duke UP, 2000. Print.

Naficy, Hamid. *An Accented Cinema: Exilic and Diasporic Filmmaking*. Princeton: Princeton UP, 2001. Print.

———. "From Accented Cinema to Multiplex Cinema." *Convergence Media History*. Ed. Janet Staiger and Sabine Hake. New York: Routledge, 2009. 3–13. Print.

———. "Making Films with an Accent: Iranian Émigré Cinema." *Framework* 43.2 (2002): 15–41. Print.

Noriega, Chon A. *Shot in America: Television, the State, and the Rise of Chicano Cinema*. Minneapolis: U of Minnesota P, 2000. Print.

Stewart, Jacqueline. *Migrating to the Movies: Cinema and Black Urban Modernity*. Berkeley: U of California P, 2005. Print.

Tarr, Carrie. *Reframing Difference: Beur and Banlieue Filmmaking in France*. Manchester: Manchester UP, 2005. Print.

Eric Rentschler

Reconsidering New German Cinema

Two decades ago, most North American university and college courses on German film focused on the new German cinema, privileging the work of a select number of artist-auteurs (invariably the triumvirate Rainer Werner Fassbinder, Werner Herzog, and Wim Wenders, along with entries by Alexander Kluge, Volker Schlöndorff, Jean-Marie Straub and Danièle Huillet, and a precious few others) and celebrating their dramatic breakthrough and international prominence. Most of these offerings emanated from foreign language programs and often were cross-listed in film studies or communications departments, a practice that continues today. In the main they emphasized narrative features (not shorts or documentaries) made in the Federal Republic of Germany (FRG) between 1965 and 1985.

Indeed, after the addition of significant feminist films by Helke Sander, Helma Sanders-Brahms, and Margarethe von Trotta in the late 1970s, the canon of the new German cinema remained uncontested, the approach codified, and the chronology clearcut. The postwar period before the Oberhausen Manifesto in 1962 (in which twenty-six young filmmakers declared "the collapse of the conventional German film") would usually receive only passing mention as the disdained legacy of a Nazi-tainted "Papa's cinema" to which these rebellious activists took exception. In keeping with the dismissive perspectives of West German publicists like Joe Hembus and Walter Schmieding as well as of contributors to the influential journal *Filmkritik*, Anglo-American scholars considered the productions of the Adenauer era to be uninteresting, lifeless, and provincial. Beholden to the generic formulas of UFA and Hollywood, West German cinema of the 1950s, claimed its detractors, lacked critical volition, authorial élan, and experimental incentive. The festival successes of young German films in 1966 (Schlöndorff's *Young Törless* and Ulrich Schamoni's *Es* at Cannes, Kluge's *Yesterday Girl* at Venice) marked a radical point of departure and confirmed the Oberhauseners' resolve to "create the new German feature film."

Young German film and its extension, which would come to be known in the mid-1970s as new German cinema, confronted the aporias of the German past and in the process renewed German film, transforming bad history into a legitimate cinema. New German cinema gained renown for its resolutely personal voices, idiosyncratic visions, and formal alternatives. Putting into place the institutional means for a self-sufficient cinema of authors, the movement waged a logistic war against the established film industry and its classical patterns of recognition.

Three emphases figured in the initial academic constructions of the movement. First, it was seen as a countercinema that, for all the undeniable differences among a wide array of directors, maintained a collective sense of purpose and constituted a programmatic movement. With a heady blend of oedipal rage, antiauthoritarian initiative, and utopian fervor, new German filmmakers sought to free the flow of fantasy and combat the institutional forces that attempted to bind or direct it. Cinema, they claimed, should heighten cognition and expand experience; indeed, it should remap and redefine reality. Their deconstructive strategies (such as undernarrated stories, impure mixes of ingredients and materials, eccentric combinations of styles and sources, uncertain endings) meant to challenge the industrialized fantasy ware produced in Babelsberg and Hollywood, its seamless suture, formulaic shape, and ideological affirmation. This abiding disdain for the dominant cinema's spurious harmonizing went together with a belief in the positive power of the negative. As a counterpraxis (either as an art cinema or part of the international avant-garde), new German cinema fashioned itself as an *Autorenkino* (cinema of authors) that replaced the mass contrivances of the culture industry with personal and modestly budgeted (and sometimes imperfect and unprofessional, but for that reason all the more authentic) productions.

Second, as an oppositional national cinema, the movement had a political and a historical mission. New German directors examined the legacy of National Socialism as well as postwar Germany with a critical gaze, insisting on the uncompromising and painstaking look backward that the generation of their parents had eschewed. In place of what Alexander and Margarete Mitscherlich called an "inability to mourn"—an intense psychic attachment to Hitler and to the Nazi order—this collective of filmmakers endeavored, along the lines of the social theorist Theodor Adorno, to "work through" the past. Many key films sustained self-conscious works of mourning (e.g., *Our Hitler* [1977], *Germany in Autumn* [1978], *The Patriot* [1979], and *Germany, Pale Mother* [1980]), confronting the emotional and psychological life of a nation that caused and lost a catastrophic world war, surveying a traumatic past and its residue in the present, seeking to articulate and intervene against the precarious terms of postwar German reconstruction. In coming to grips with German history, these filmmakers were also conscious of their status within German film history, which had many lessons to offer about cinema's constructive possibilities—as well as its destructive powers.

Finally, the new German cinema functioned as part of a youth movement, enacting the desire of the 1968 generation to reconsider the German past in order to reinvent German identity. For some, filmmaking became a form of political agitation and overt intervention: shooting films, in this sense, served as a means of shooting back against an oppressive status quo. In the words of Fassbinder as quoted on the posters for the English-language release of *Die dritte Generation* (*The Third Generation*): "I don't throw bombs, I make films." In the speeding express train of history, the directors of the movement wanted to pull the emergency brake. To that end they probed different modes of address, alternative modes of spectatorship, other ways of telling stories and presenting images. Their films presented the political malaise of the FRG as experienced by the postwar generation. Some of the most revered efforts supplied poignant case studies of young people trying (and failing) to make their way in the world, dramatizing the vicissitudes of constituting oneself as a subject in a nation haunted by its past (Elsaesser), a historical difficulty with sexual, gendered, regional, racial, and ethnic ramifications.

A course today on postwar German cinema will want to take leave of the spirited partisanship from several decades ago and to reconsider the heady terms of its heroic master narrative. We will want to open the range of discourses; refine our critical tools; and, with the advantages of the present and the hindsight that it affords us, introduce new intertexts, historical constellations, and theoretical incentives that might help us review this body of work and reassess the dominant wisdom about it.

In that endeavor, let me suggest five possible points of departure:

1. To open up the films of this period to a more expansive range of intertexts beyond the once dominant discourses of anti-Americanism and postwar German guilt (and the inability to mourn), one might productively employ approaches to affect and shame as well as work done in cultural studies on fashion and self-styling. Performativity studies, likewise, offer many new avenues to films that "act out" at different levels. Rather than limiting discussions of new German cinema to its place in German film history and within attempts in the FRG to confront the past, one might explore its relation to influential postwar manifestations, such as the new music, the student movement, Fluxus, Action Art, the Situationist International, and other alternative projects. And as Caryl Flinn and Roger Hillman have convincingly demonstrated, the aural dimension of these endeavors (particularly in the way they orchestrate music and style) warrant more careful attention. It would also be useful to discuss not only how new German films negotiate time but how they use and represent space—in short, to explore their architectures, geographies, and topographies. Finally, one could extend the sampling of texts beyond a rarified ensemble of art films to consider shorts and nonfiction films, to factor in popular features as well as avant-garde undertakings (especially now that a diversity of materials is available in subtitled versions on DVD, such as the complete-work editions of Kluge, Sander, and Harun Farocki).

2. It is essential that we think of national cinema not just in terms of films that were produced in the FRG; in fact, the films of the new German cinema only constituted a small portion of the domestic market. A national cinema is not just the films made in a certain country at a certain time (Higson). What films circulated in West Germany at the same moment, and what importance did they assume? What is the relation between independent features of new German cinema and contemporaneous German commercial productions? Instead of focusing on the new German cinema's dialogue with American and Nazi cinema, one could compare West German films of the mid-1960s with the "rabbit films" that arose in the German Democratic Republic at the same time (Trumpener; Pinkert 179–202) or probe the influence of *cinema novo* on the critical *Heimat* films of the early 1970s. This expansive perspective, then, would nuance both the place of the movement at home as well as its place within an international context.

3. Using historical precision and an encompassing historical focus, we can complicate the master narrative that attended the movement and summarily shortchanged films made in the FRG before 1962 and after 1985. Our archive is much larger now: a more substantial selection of films is at our disposal, and the body of scholarship and information is far more considerable. With these resources, we might begin to conceptualize different chronologies and different narratives. The films of the Adenauer era, as monographs by Johannes von Moltke and Heide Fehrenbach bear out, figure within the larger dynamic of a postwar nation's process of modernization and normalization. If we want to comprehend the shape and substance of German dreams during the early postwar years, we can find no better resource than this contested sector of German film history. These films also returned in surprising ways during the 1980s (and well into the 1990s) after the demise of the movement, as objects of both affection and influence. Even today, some German filmmakers, wondering how they might create a popular cinema, look back with envy at features of the 1950s. Where we once found only objects of scorn and critique, we might look now for previously unacknowledged connections and continuities. In the same way, films made after the new German cinema, barring a few exceptions, were held to be a compromised and uninspiring site of popular incentives that rarely found audiences outside Germany. The decade between Doris Dörrie's *Men* (1985) and Sönke Wortmann's *Maybe . . . Maybe Not* (1994) was for many of us a down time, a "cinema of consensus" dominated by popular dictates and less inclined to formal experiment or stylistic innovation (Rentschler).[1] With the arrival of an exciting new generation of filmmakers (including Tom Tykwer, Romuald Karmakar, Christian Petzold, Fatih Akin, and representatives of the Berlin school), German cinema has found increasing attention both at home and on international circuits while in many ways still facing the same structural problems that have defined the cinema as an institution in Germany since the 1960s (Fisher and Prager). As we incorporate these new impulses into a larger picture, we need to rethink, fundamentally, the shape of postwar German film history.

4. New German cinema still abides as a good, if not unquestioned, object; the rhetoric used to discuss it remains one of admiration and celebration. Nonetheless, the limitations of the movement (especially the revisionist emphases of the later retro scenarios that emphasize the nation's suffering and martyrdom under both the Nazis and the Allied adversaries or occupiers) have become evident in ways that allow us to temper our previous enthusiasm while continuing to recognize the movement's historical

significance and cultural contribution (Kaes; Santner). We might think about how the movement's acts of mourning manifest decided incapacities. Indeed, we might even consider whether they are more aptly described as exercises in generational self-pity, attempts to forge a German identity decoupled from the burden of the past. Why did the new German cinema, for all its emphasis on acts of memory and the retrieval of history, so very rarely acknowledge the Holocaust? What accounts for this conspicuous oversight? Beyond a few notable exceptions (Fassbinder's *Katzelmacher* [1969], Christian Ziewer's *I See This Land from Afar* [1978], Sanders-Brahms's *Shirin's Wedding* [1976], and the work of Sohrab Shahid Saless and Peter Lilienthal), why did the movement focus on its historical problems and, outside its inimitable love-hatred of America, prove to be strikingly uncurious about foreign situations and the destinies of foreigners in Germany?

5. Postunification German productions compel us to think about national cinema in a changed nation confronted, more than ever, with questions of difference and diversity. Any updated understanding of German cinema will therefore want to address the function of transformations in an increasingly multicultural nation mindful of transnational and global determinants and the ways in which these incentives have (and have not) shaped recent German films and found (and not found) shape in them. For the students in our classes today, the notion of new German cinema has a host of new possibilities and meanings.

Note

1. The passing of the new German cinema and the dire state of German film culture during the late 1980s and most of the 1990s prompted many North American Germanists and film scholars to move back in history and study the Weimar cinema and the films of the Third Reich. Indeed, during the 1990s, classical German cinema and Nazi film arguably found a stronger presence in university course offerings than did new German cinema.

Works Cited

Adorno, Theodor. "The Meaning of Working through the Past." *Can One Live after Auschwitz: A Philosophical Reader.* Ed. Rolf Tiedemann. Stanford: Stanford UP, 2003. 3–18. Print.

Elsaesser, Thomas. *New German Cinema: A History.* New Brunswick: Rutgers UP, 1989. Print.

Fehrenbach, Heidi. *Cinema in Democratizing Germany: Reconstructing National Identity after Hitler.* Chapel Hill: U of North Carolina P, 1995. Print.

Fisher, Jaimey, and Brad Prager, eds. *The Collapse of the Conventional: German Film and Its Politics at the Turn of the New Century*. Detroit: Wayne State UP, 2009. Print.

Flinn, Caryl. *The New German Cinema: Music, History, and the Matter of Style*. Berkeley: U of California P, 2004. Print.

Hembus, Joe. *Der deutsche Film kann nicht besser sein*. Bremen: Schüneman, 1961. Print.

Higson, Andrew. "The Concept of National Cinema." *Screen* 30.4 (1989): 36–46. Print.

Hillman, Roger. *Unsettling Scores: German Film, Music, and Ideology*. Bloomington: Indiana UP, 2005. Print.

Kaes, Anton. *From Hitler to* Heimat*: The Return of History as Film*. Cambridge: Harvard UP, 1989. Print.

Mitscherlich, Alexander, and Margarete Mitscherlich. *The Inability to Mourn: Principles of Collective Behavior*. New York: Grove, 1975. Print.

Moltke, Johannes von. *No Place Like Home: Locations of* Heimat *in German Cinema*. Berkeley: U of California P, 2005. Print.

"The Oberhausen Manifesto (1962)." *West German Filmmakers on Film*. Trans. and ed. Eric Rentschler. New York: Holmes, 1988. 2. Print.

Pinkert, Anke. *Film and Memory in East Germany*. Bloomington: Indiana UP, 2008. Print.

Rentschler, Eric. "From New German Cinema to the Postwall Cinema of Consensus." *Cinema and Nation*. Ed. Mette Hjort and Scott MacKenzie. London: Routledge, 2000. 260–77. Print.

Santner, Eric. *Stranded Objects: Mourning, Memory, and Film in Postwar Germany*. Ithaca: Cornell UP, 1990. Print.

Schmieding, Walter. *Kunst oder Kasse: Der Ärger mit dem deutschen Film*. Hamburg: Rütten, 1961. Print.

Trumpener, Katie. "La guerre est finie: New Waves, Historical Contingency, and the GDR 'Rabbit Films.'" *The Power of Intellectuals in Contemporary Germany*. Ed. Michael Geyer. Chicago: U of Chicago P, 2001. 113–38. Print.

Zoran Samardzija

Teaching the Ends of Eastern European Cinema

Given that geopolitics has rendered the division of Europe into eastern and western spheres obsolete, how should one teach recent cinemas from the former eastern bloc? As a concept, Eastern European cinema no longer makes historical sense. In a course surveying the years 1945 to 1990, it works as a catchall for key national cinemas that emerged after World War II. It is commonplace in film history texts, for example, to discuss the Czech new wave in much the same way one discusses the French new wave, which serves as an introduction to the French filmmakers who gained international recognition during the 1950s and 1960s. In a corresponding sense, Eastern European cinema is a loose description of works by filmmakers who merge their ideological analyses of national histories with formal cinematic concerns. Both meanings are found in Mira and Antonin J. Liehm's *The Most Important Art: Eastern European Film after 1945*, one of the first book-length studies of post–World War II Eastern European cinema translated into English.

Today, designing a course on recent cinemas from the former eastern bloc poses its share of organizational problems. Among scholars, there is no consensus to what, if anything, should replace Eastern Europe as a catchall concept. In *Cinema of Flames: Balkan Film, Culture and the Media* and *Cinema of the Other Europe: The Industry and Artistry of East Central European Film*, Dina Iordanova argues for a predominantly regionalist approach, dividing the former Eastern European states into two distinct spheres of study: East Central Europe and the Balkans. Contrary to this approach, analyses of nationalist cinemas remain as prevalent as in the past, and book-length studies on Polish, Czech, and Hungarian cinema are continually being published. One should add that recent Romanian cinema has had a significant international impact; *The Death of Mr. Lazarescu* (2005) and *4 Months, 3 Weeks and 2 Days* (2007) won top prizes at Cannes.

The absence of a current equivalent to Eastern European cinema can nonetheless be turned into a critical advantage for students. The complex and evolving politics of European unification and integration demand that students be presented with multiple and contradictory perspectives on cinema from the former eastern bloc. At the very least, they should be made aware of regional cinematic identities and the persistence of national film industries. In addition, a course on this topic should address broad historical questions about postcommunist identity, the social and cultural legacies of the Yugoslav wars, and the increasing migration from the East to the West. Yet in foregrounding these questions, instructors should be sure to emphasize their transitory and ephemeral nature. If, after all, the goal of European unification evolves beyond the creation of a common market into the formation of a collective European identity, then ideally regions, nations, and even immigrants should cease to exist as we know them in a new Europe. This essay offers suggestions for introducing these complex issues to students and for organizing a course on recent East Central European and Balkan cinemas. Throughout, I highlight key films that dramatize these issues and that have, in my experience, invoked the most positive student responses.

Beginning at the End of Communism

A course on recent East Central European and Balkan cinema can begin by conveying to students how the end of communism and transition to free-market economies has produced indeterminate identities for many citizens. Entire courses could be devoted to the collapse of communist regimes, but the right films can convey some of the historical significance to students. *Gorilla Bathes at Noon* (1993) and *Good Bye Lenin!* (2003) are useful films in this regard. Moreover, screening the films together allows students to contemplate how radically different film styles can be used to represent history. In *Gorilla Bathes at Noon*, the director Dusan Makavejev returns to the dense associative montage style of his work from the 1960s and 1970s. With its eccentric use of footage from propaganda films and nonlinear editing, the film effectively presents students with the opportunity to discuss what it means for history to render an earlier ideological understanding of the world obsolete. It is important for instructors to establish this idea early on, since a survey of East Central European and Balkan cinema is, above all, an examination of nations and regions in transition.

Gorilla Bathes at Noon follows Viktor, a major in the former Soviet Union army whose entire unit has abandoned their posts after the unification of Berlin. Suddenly devoid of purpose, he decides to stay in the newly unified Berlin, avoiding arrest and resisting deportation. He wanders aimlessly, eats a lot of fruit, witnesses the dismantling of a large statue of Lenin, and subsequently hallucinates encounters with a transgendered Lenin who knits him a sock. Viktor also obsesses over a Soviet propaganda film about the Soviet liberation of Berlin because he fantasizes that his parents, brought together by an appearance of Stalin, met in the film. In a particularly humorous scene in *Gorilla*, Viktor visits a zoo and expresses his confusion that a Siberian tiger born in Germany can be called "Siberian." For Viktor, the world was only understandable when easily divisible between East and West, communist and capitalist, and designations of origin make little sense unless one was territorially bound to one's nation.

Like *Gorilla Bathes at Noon*, the popular German comedy *Good Bye Lenin!*, directed by Wolfgang Becker, also deals with historical obsolescence. Unlike Makavejev, however, Becker does not noticeably play with the stylistic conventions of narrative cinema, instead addressing historical obsolescence through narrative dramatizations. In the film, Alex's stridently communist mother has just awoken from a coma and does not know that Germany has unified. Afraid that the news would kill her, Alex works to shield her from learning that the wall has fallen. Instructors can use several of the highly comedic scenes from the film to lead students to question their assumptions about communism and capitalism. For example, one of the first things that Alex does with his newfound "western freedom" is to visit the porno shops that are now allowed to be open. Meanwhile, his sister, Maria, abandons school to work in a Burger King.

One of the most fascinating classroom discussions I recall having about the film arose from the largely satirical Burger King scenes, since many students were able to identify with having a menial job. Curiously, many of these same students failed to connect their identification with these scenes with the larger criticisms about capitalism that the film offers. Some even suggested that at least Maria now had the freedom to work in a Burger King. Rather than unsettle what I saw as the outright misreading these students gave, I took the opportunity to confront their assumptions, both positive and negative, about capitalism, freedom, communism, and what it means to transition from one system to the other.

Traveling East to West: Transforming the Travelogue

Asking students to confront their assumptions about capitalism and communism lays the groundwork for their exposure to more challenging and complex questions. Yet how should the course juggle historical questions about regionalism, migration, and the possibilities for an emergent European identity while offering a survey of key recent films? I have found that loosely presenting the material in the form of a travelogue provides students with the framework for engaging with these questions. To mirror the movements of peoples and histories for students, I begin with films about the unification of Berlin, move progressively southeast to the Balkans, and conclude with films set in the West about exiles, refugees, and laborers from the East.

It must be acknowledged that the travelogue carries much historical baggage, especially when dealing with Eastern Europe and the Balkans. Two influential historical studies, Larry Wolff's *Inventing Eastern Europe: The Map of Civilization on the Mind of the Enlightenment* and Maria Todorova's *Imagining the Balkans* argue that *Eastern Europe* and *the Balkans* are essentially discursive creations of travelogues. Wolff asserts that the division of Europe into eastern and western spheres originates in the numerous published travelogue diaries that were popular in the eighteenth century, creating an image of the East as the region of Europe saddled by barbarism and backwardness. Todorova exhibits a similar perspective and traces how the Balkans were discursively constructed in the western imaginary.

The travelogue can be transformed from a narrative that historically prescribes the division between civilization and barbarism into multiple narratives about differences in national and regional identities. It can also emphasize the diminishing role of borders, migration, and labor. In fact, several East Central European and Balkan films are travelogues or road movies that dramatize many of these issues. The German/Turkish romantic comedy *In July* (2000) follows its main characters, Daniel and Juli, as they decide to travel from Germany all the way to Turkey. The director, Fatih Akin, overloads his travelogue with homages to classic Hollywood road movies like *It Happened One Night* (1934), and the film has more in common with such classics than it does with its contemporary eastern travelogues. Despite its stylistic shortcomings, the film provides students with an opportunity to reflect on the different ways national identities are represented. They could be asked to respond to a prompt like the following: As Daniel and Juli travel farther away from the center of Europe toward Turkey, does the film highlight specific cultural differences among the various nations through which they journey?

In addition to narrative films like *In July*—or even *Ulysses' Gaze* (1995), which is set entirely in the Balkans—travelogue documentaries and experimental features have pedagogical value for students. *D'Est* (1993) is an experimental film from Chantal Akerman. Here, she records her travels through Russia and the former eastern bloc through a succession of meticulously composed shots of landscapes and people. The film aims to enact the transitions of history through camera placement, shot length, and framing. Less formally complex for students is the documentary *The Center* (2004), in which the director Stanislaw Mucha visits several sites that have at some point in history laid claim to being the exact geographic center of Europe. Both films ask students to attune themselves to see how historical changes are made visible in the spaces around them.

Disintegration and Reconciliation: Films about the Yugoslav Wars

Perhaps the most difficult historical subject to incorporate into a survey of recent films from the Balkans is the disintegration of Yugoslavia and the wars in Bosnia, Croatia, and Kosovo. Numerous films exist about the wars, but few will help students understand them in any but the most abstract moral and ethical terms. Even less helpful is a film like Emir Kusturica's infamous *Underground* (1995). Its aesthetic merits are undeniable—it incorporates so many divergent styles into its sprawling story that it serves as a summary of the different ways filmmakers from the Balkans and East

Central Europe have represented history in their works. It is so historically unreliable, however, that students need to be made aware of the political controversies that surrounded its release. Even then, students who are not already immersed in the entangled histories of the various nationalities of the former Yugoslavia find the controversies difficult to understand.

The Serbian film *Pretty Village, Pretty Flame* (1996) manages to be both accessible and complex in its diagnoses of the social and historical causes of the Bosnian war. While it relies heavily on male-bonding war-movie clichés and reflects the bias of its Serbian national origins, it invites students to think about images and the role they play in national mythologizing and warmongering. Moreover, the film presents students with multiple, contradictory perspectives on the historical functions of Serbian nationalism, alternately viewing Serbian nationalism as a democratic sentiment, a regression into barbaric forms of belonging, a creation of elitist propaganda, and a product of unresolved class tensions. In its unwillingness to offer a singular perspective on nationalism, it also opens up dialogue with films like *Good Bye Lenin!* and *Gorilla Bathes at Noon*. These films cannot imagine stable forms of social and political order to fill the vacuum left by the end of communism: chaos and disintegration seem the only short-term options.

Films that dramatize aftermaths of the Yugoslav wars tend to tell personal stories about displacement and emotional and physical trauma. It is debatable whether these films have the same moral obligation to offer intricate narratives and multiple perspectives about history as films about the onset of war do. Students tend to identify existentially and emotionally with films about reconciliation rather than treat them as dramatizations of historical conflicts. Ideally, students would see no distinction between the personal and the historical dimensions, but the right film is needed to help blur this line. The Bosnian film *Grbavica: The Land of My Dreams* (2006) effectively collapses the historical and the personal with its story of Esma trying to overcome the trauma of being repeatedly gang-raped in the war by Serbian soldiers. Living with her daughter in Sarajevo, Esma faces economic hardships. She also tries, unsuccessfully, to hide her past from her increasingly rebellious daughter, making up a story that her father was a Bosnian solider who heroically died in battle. Screened after *Pretty Village, Pretty Flame*, *Grbavica* offers a contrast to masculine fatalism and serves as a stark reminder that collapses in political order and warfare are often forcibly personalized for many women in the most horrifying and despicable ways.

The Ends of Eastern Europe and the World at Large

By concluding a course on recent cinema from East Central Europe and the Balkans with films that dramatize increases in migration and movements of people from the East to the West, instructors can prompt students to understand that European unification is an evolving historical process that will continue to alter how they and scholars will understand cinemas from the former eastern bloc. In particular, screening Western European films such as *Beautiful People* (1999) or *Code Unknown* (2001), both of which recount the lives of migrants from the East as well as globally, helps reinforce the idea that our understanding of regions, nations, and migrants will be transformed in the face of an emerging collective European identity. Such films, too, reflect on how far Europe is from achieving that ideal.

In many respects, the historical questions raised in this course extend far beyond Europe. Whether the focus is on migration, ethnic violence, or how to categorize cinemas in an era when regional and national identities are on the wane, the course maintains a global approach. One of the most intriguing final papers I received came from a student who was stationed in Iraq as a member of the National Guard. He was struck by the similarities between his firsthand experiences in Iraq and the violence depicted in two films we screened: *Cabaret Balkan* (1998), which deals with social disorder in postwar Serbia, and *No Man's Land* (2001), about the Bosnian war. He was deeply interested in thinking about representations of why societies collapse and descend into civil war, no doubt as a way to better understand what broader historical forces brought him to Iraq. In pedagogical terms, his comparison between Yugoslavia and post–Saddam Hussein Iraq is made possible because Eastern European cinema no longer exists. Europe can no longer be separated into East and West, and the globe is no longer geopolitically divisible into the First World, Second World, and nonaligned nations. Perhaps it is time to think about how to subsume existing cinemas under some cosmopolitan category of global cinema. Comparing the political and stylistic affinities among disparate nations and regions is a first step in this direction, which, in his own way, this student undertook.

Works Cited

Iordanova, Dina. *Cinema of Flames: Balkan Film, Culture and the Media*. London: British Film Inst., 2001. Print.

———. *Cinema of the Other Europe: The Industry and Artistry of East Central European Film*. London: Wallflower, 2003. Print.
Liehm, Mira, and Antonin J. Liehm. *The Most Important Art: Eastern European Film after 1945*. Berkeley: U of California P, 1977. Print.
Todorova, Maria. *Imagining the Balkans*. New York: Oxford, 1997. Print.
Wolff, Larry. *Inventing Eastern Europe: The Map of Civilization on the Mind of the Enlightenment*. Stanford: Stanford UP, 1994. Print.

David Desser

Teaching Japanese Cinema

The notion of "national cinema" has justifiably come under threat in recent years. Constructions of nations as impermeable, as pure expressions of unique cultural values, often with race as an unspoken undertone, simply are no longer viable. And it is not merely issues, broadly speaking, of globalization that have worked to undercut notions of the national. While globalization is an undeniable reality in the post–Cold War world, nations have always had transnational characteristics. The movement of ideas, not to mention people, across often arbitrarily constructed national boundaries has been a reality for generations upon generations. The cinema, in particular, has always been implicated in transnational movements; it was a globalized medium even before the term *globalization* came into vogue. Nevertheless, notions of the national had demonstrable consequences in the development of cinema(s) in the twentieth century and, in many ways, still have a force.

The cinema of Japan has been in the forefront of scholarly discourse surrounding the idea of national cinema, often with recourse to national characteristics to explain clearly visible differences in comparison to American and European cinemas. The pioneering work of Donald Richie, with Joseph L. Anderson and independently (*Hundred Years*; *Japanese Cinema*) has been largely concerned with explicating Japanese cinema by recourse to several paradigms of Japanese art and culture that come to define not only Japan's cinema but also Japan itself. The influential work of Noël Burch, though couched in a very different language—that of semiotics and neoformalism—was nevertheless rooted in cultural specificity as the foundation of Japan's evident national cinema style.

Attributions of Japan's cinema to its specific national characteristics are always in danger of playing into the hands of conservative forces in Japan, which throughout the twentieth century and into the twenty-first have claimed a cultural purity for the nation and used these ideas for pernicious ends. It is not inevitable, however, to fall into the trap of cultural essentialism to discuss a Japanese national cinema. Only the most willful postmodernist or academic careerist would deny what is apparent on the screen—Japanese cinema has films that are clearly differentiated from mainstream Western standards. To account for this evident difference, we may approach Japanese cinema through the traditions that Japanese filmmakers can mobilize at any particular moment. The idea of traditions requires some understanding of Japanese aesthetic modes that, attributable to national character or some other factors, have found their way into the cinema at different times and under the aegis of different filmmakers. Thus one can speak of the authorship of several Japanese directors—Kenji Mizoguchi's focus on the plight of women under patriarchy, feudalism, and capitalism; Yasujiro Ozu and his penchant for exploring the dissolution of the traditional Japanese family under the pressures of history and cultural change; Akira Kurosawa's concern with individual heroism amid institutional corruption—while acknowledging how their authorial characteristics are also inflected by their relation to a collective past. Industrial factors such as the studio system of Japan's classical era; the rise of independent filmmaking in the poststudio days; the centrality of anime, popular music, and video; along with shifts in market demographics complicate any simple notion of the mobilization of tradition, not to mention Japanese cinema's long love affair with foreign films, especially Hollywood's. Nevertheless, the rich cinematic legacy of Japan proved capable of producing a body of work of obvious artistic quality and of a certain character, however subtle.

A Visual Cinema

The influence of traditional visual modes of expression, especially painting, has a far-reaching influence on Japanese cinema. Certain aesthetic features of traditional painting are notable especially in standing screens (*byobu*), hanging scrolls (*kakejiku*)—which may be done in the so-called Chinese style, relying on colorful and detailed imagery, or the more subtle *sumi-e* (black-and-white ink painting) that emphasizes broad brush strokes—and the most famous of Japan's traditional visual mode, ukiyo-e (wood-block prints). All these visual modes are marked by similarities, in particular flatness. Depth and distance are indicated by height (objects at the bottom are read as near, at the top as more distant, rather than the use of receding lines and monocular perspective). Popular subjects of scrolls and screens include mountains, rivers, birds, and trees (human figures in landscape painting are invariably small and merely suggested). Seasonal markers are especially important and are linked to Japanese ideals of the cycle of life and the sense of transience and impermanence (see Sato 165–75). Landscapes are also a common motif in ukiyo-e, as are images of geisha, courtesans, and Kabuki actors. Though wood-block prints are prized for their appeal to more common tastes and were a mass-produced art, hanging scrolls and standing screens are common features in Japanese homes even today.

Mizoguchi's *Ugetsu* (1953) exemplifies how Japanese films may mobilize some of these long-standing aesthetic patterns. The film deliberately invokes several pictorial modes of expression and subject matter to tell its powerful story of war, the resultant corruption of family values, and its effect on women. Thus it is an especially resonant text to begin the study of Japanese cinema. A key moment in the film finds the primary couple—the potter Genjuro and his wife, Miyagi—separating (for what will actually be the last time) at a riverbank. The recollection of *sumi-e*-style ink painting is unmistakable: the rich black-and-white cinematography emphasizes the mist-shrouded riverbank, the trees sometimes occlude the view of the human subjects, and the scene invokes a sense of mystery (*yugen*) (see fig. 1). A kind of synthesis of many Japanese aesthetic modes may be found in the architecture, decor, and garden that comprise the mysterious mansion in which dwells the ghost-princess Wakasa. The interior of the mansion emphasizes both the use of shoji (sliding screens) and *byobu*; lacquer trays and earthenware pots recall traditional craftsmanship (it is no acci-

Figure 1. A scene from *Ugetsu*, invoking *sumi*-e-style ink painting

dent that Genjuro is a potter); and the elegant formal garden surrounded by the mansion is a marker of classical aristocratic dwellings.

The camera angles that Mizoguchi uses are also meant to invoke traditional pictorial modes. Mizoguchi's famous long-shot–long-take style emphasizes the flatness of the image, the distance from human figures, and the often partial views. This influence is not only apparent in the riverside parting scene but also in the bird's-eye view of Genjuro and Wakasa that Mizoguchi provides, looking from the garden into the mansion at a forty-five-degree angle that seems to strip away part of the wall and roof. One can lay a still from this scene alongside any number of images derived from another traditional Japanese pictorial mode, the *emaki-mono* (narrative picture scroll). It is even possible to link Mizoguchi's flowing camera movements to the kind of unrolling of a picture scroll (Richie, "Influence" 160–62; Sato 170–71).

None of these highlights need detract from the historical moment in which the film was produced. Indeed, one could argue that the invocation of older Japanese pictorial modes is owed precisely to the needs of the film's production. For instance, Daiei, the production studio, desired to make films for export in the wake of the success of *Rashomon* (1950) at the Venice Film Festival in 1951. They favored films that emphasized the exotic appeal of the Japanese period film. *Ugetsu*, in fact, like *Rashomon*, became a prizewinner at Venice. It is also possible to postulate a desire to return to some sort of Japanese national feeling in the wake of the massive changes brought about by the defeat in World War II and the postwar occupation. (*Ugetsu* was released the year after the occupation came to an end.) It may also be useful to see this tale of medieval civil war and its effects on the innocent as an allegory for the disastrous militaristic adventurism of World War II.

A Narrated Cinema

Storytelling is a universal characteristic of culture and civilization, and perhaps early cinema struck chords of familiarity with audiences everywhere not just for its magical illusion of life captured on the move but also for its ability to convey narrative. Among the Japanese storytelling modes are oral tales, written accounts (*The Tale of Genji*, which appeared in the eleventh century, is often cited as the world's first novel), and cinema. Many of these artistic media combine multiple strands of narrative devices, what Anderson has described as "commingled media," different modes of discourse within the same work—for example, images and written text in medieval narrative picture scrolls, often claimed as the precursor to Japan's most popular commingled medium, manga (comic books and graphic novels) (261–65). Whether focusing on the heroic exploits of samurai warriors, the lovelorn fate of poor merchants, or the comic mishaps of ordinary people, modern modes of storytelling in Japan have clear roots in the past. In addition, many of these older styles, such as the comic forms of *rakugo* (humorous storytelling narrated by a lone figure seated on a bare stage) and *manzai* (breakneck wordplay with two comedians) continue their popularity today, not only in theatrical venues but also on television. Thus it is no surprise to find continuities in the cinema of many traditional narrative modes.

The cinema of Ozu, long prized in Japan for its ability to capture the essence of Japanese daily life (and for that reason held back from much Western distribution for many years after the likes of Mizoguchi and Kurosawa were already well-known overseas), participates thematically in certain Japanese aesthetic traditions, as well as many narrative ones. Like the Japanese novel of the late nineteenth through mid twentieth centuries, Ozu's cinema relies less on narrative drive than on episodes intended to reveal feelings rather than plot. His cinema has been compared to the haiku, a compressed and constrained mode of expression capable of producing sudden flashes of insight and poignancy. There is a poetic quality to his films, especially in his use of still-life transitions between scenes, such as clothes hanging on a line, empty hallways or corridors, landscapes,

Figure 2. A typical "pillow shot" for Ozu

trains moving down the track—images that have sometimes been called "pillow shots," after the poetic term "pillow words" (*makura kotoba*) (see fig. 2). The associativeness of his titles, including *Banshun* (*Late Spring* [1949]), *Bakushu* (*Early Summer* [1951]), *Higanbana* (*Equinox Flower* [1958]), and *Ukigusa* (*Floating Weeds* [1959]), seems deliberately to recall the seasonal markers so common in Japanese pictorial and poetic traditions (despite the fact that, as Shigehiko Hasumi has pointed out in his essay "Sunny Skies," it always seems to be summer in Ozu's films).

Besides oft-noted aspects of Ozu's late style—such as a still camera, low-level (or tatami-level) shooting, and the use of 360-degree space—Ozu's narrative style is highly elliptical. The filmmaker will often eliminate not just less dramatic transitional scenes but also potentially moving and climactic ones. In *Tokyo Story* (1953), for example, when the old parents discuss leaving for Tokyo, we next see them not on the train, not at Tokyo Station, not even in the car coming from the station, but walking into their son's home (see Desser, "*Tokyo Story*"). In Ozu's films about marrying off a twenty-something daughter, we never see the wedding and often typically not even the groom. By the strategic use of elided action, Ozu makes demands on his audience atypical of mainstream cinema, while also allowing the audience to fill in the emotions that take place off screen.

As different as he is in virtually every way from Ozu, Kurosawa is also a deceptive traditionalist, even in his early and middle films. The foregrounding of narrative, per se, in the form of demonstrating how cinema is a commingled medium is one of the less-remarked-on authorial characteristics of Japan's supposedly most Western director. From unassigned voice-over narration in *Stray Dog* (1949) and *Ikiru* (1952), to the famous multiple narrations that complicate *Rashomon*, to the veritable compendium of narration and narrating devices in *High and Low* (1963)—telephones, tape recorders, motion picture film, drawings, maps, voice-over with flashbacks—Kurosawa is as much concerned with narration and its multiple possibilities as he is with his mixture of dynamic montage and long takes.

A Theatrical Cinema

The influence of classical Japanese theater on its cinema cannot be overstated. More than a pictorial or narrative mode, the cinema in Japan arose as a theatrical form, with numerous direct borrowings from the theater, ranging from actors to stories to famous scenes from well-known plays to the use of *onnagata* (male actors playing female roles) and the omnipresence of the *katsuben*, or *benshi* (the film narrator who notoriously was often more popular than any actor, director, or film). Though one can find many films to illustrate this influence (such as the famous Noh-inflected Shakespearean *Throne of Blood* [1957] and the innovative *Ballad of Narayama* [1958], which uses Kabuki techniques, including a narrator, painted backdrops, and flat framing), the "theatrical signifier," as Burch called it, may be found throughout a host of nonrealistic, highly formal films (see Keiko McDonald for a survey of the links between film and theater and close readings of theatrical adaptations). The filmmaker Seijun Suzuki, who works in genres such as the *yakuza* (organized crime), youth, and war films, nicely illustrates the way highly theatricalized moments appear in otherwise seemingly commercial films. The opening scene of *Story of a Prostitute* (1965), for instance, takes place in front of a flat, painted screen, and the lighting of the set interposes spotlights into deep shadows. The climax of both *One Generation of Tattoos* (1965) and *Tokyo Drifter* (1966) sees the frame burst into an array of primary colors, and the scenes are filmed in what are deliberately indicated as stage sets. *Gate of Flesh* (1964), a film in no way derived from or overtly invested in traditional Japanese theater (it is a critique of many elements of Japanese culture, including its postwar shift to a vehemently American-style capitalism), is replete with highly stylized moments, from the Kabuki-like visage and performance of Jo Shishido to the color-coordinated associations that mark the four prostitutes.

One can also point to Kon Ichikawa's *An Actor's Revenge* (1963), which plays with theatrical conventions in a highly self-conscious manner to tell the story of a famous Kabuki *onnagata* seeking vengeance on the men who drove his parents to death. All the tools of the cinema, such as wide-screen framing, rich colors, trick photography, and deft editing, can be used to explore how cinema liberally, and often deliberately, borrows from traditional Japanese drama. Similarly, a film like *Double Suicide* (1969) uses the aesthetics of the highly stylized Bunraku (puppet or doll) theater to make pointed commentaries on the stultifying and sometimes dehumanizing nature of conventional Japanese culture. Thus tradition can be put to the service of cultural critique in very modern ways.

A Generic Cinema

For serious filmgoers, the Japanese cinema of the 1950s and 1960s meant the art films of Mizoguchi, Kurosawa, and Hiroshi Teshigahara, but for most viewers it meant, in a word, Godzilla. The *kaiju-eiga*, or monster movie, in usually poorly dubbed and often edited formats, shown in drive-in theaters or on television, stood in for Japanese cinema in the minds of those unfamiliar with the more serious, or at least less giant-monster-driven, films that had become festival favorites. Though the special effects in the *kaiju-eiga* are often impressive (and subtitled formats lend a gravitas to the films lacking in dubbed versions) there is no getting around the fact that Godzilla is, basically, a man in a rubber suit. Despite the interesting allegorical and cultural dimensions to these films, teaching them presents problems for a Western cultural context in which special effects and computer-generated imagery aspire to ever-greater realism in contradistinction to Japanese aesthetic preferences. Still, the Japanese cinema is one highly based in genre; even Kurosawa's auteur masterpieces *Seven Samurai* (1954), *Yojimbo* (1961), and *Sanjuro* (1962) have their roots in a decades-old cinematic mode. Since there is a danger in reifying Japanese tradition through recourse to period films—even those that are highly critical of feudal values and the samurai code, such as Masaki Kobayashi's

Seppuku (1962) and *Samurai Rebellion* (1967)—a turn to the modern-day melodrama provides an interesting demonstration of commercial imperatives and the sociocultural context of genre production.

For melodrama in Japan, as throughout the world, the primary subject and audience are women. Japanese cinema of the 1920s and 1930s drew heavily on the *shimpa* theater to tell stories of romances doomed by class differences, familial obligations, and other social forces. Mizoguchi, Heinosuke Gosho, and Mikio Naruse created a first golden age of Japanese cinema by producing timely films examining changing social mores and the pressures of modernization. In the 1950s, a host of melodramatic cycles arose to examine the ever-increasing toll postwar economic growth was taking on the Japanese family, especially women. As in the samurai film, one of the primary structuring devices is the culturally derived conflict between duty (*giri*) and natural, human inclinations (*ninjo*). But instead of being subjected to the whims of a feudal lord, the put-upon women in the melodrama are torn by obligations—to parents, siblings, even larger social forces—in the new postwar reality.

One such film is Naruse's elegant *When a Woman Ascends the Stairs* (1960). Focusing on a bar hostess in the famous Ginza area of Tokyo, the film critiques the emphasis put on money in the economy of sexuality that hostess bars represent. A widow who has turned to the bars to support her family refuses the sexual advances of her businessmen clients and longs only to marry a decent man. This being a melodrama, marriage proves elusive, and she betrays her code only to be left exactly in the same situation in which she began—ascending the stairs to a bar to begin her unpleasant evening's work, pasting a smile on her face, and gulping down the liquor that makes her sick.

A Postmodernist Cinema

This survey has relied on canonical films and filmmakers and is thus in danger of seeming old-fashioned and, worse, ignoring the recent Japanese films that have garnered a significant and active fan base. Instead of conceptualizing what has come before as retrograde, however, we may see classical Japanese cinema as constituting its own tradition, possessing its own modes and practices. This way, subsequent filmmakers can take a stand toward a cinematic tradition, much like earlier directors interposed themselves with prior aesthetic modes. Any understanding, for instance, of the so-called Japanese new-wave cinema must take into account the response of directors like Nagisa Oshima, Masahiro Shinoda, and Shohei Imamura to their cinematic elders (see Desser, *Eros*). In more recent years, directors like Shinji Aoyama (*Eureka* [2000]), Shunji Iwai (*Love Letter* [1995], *All About Lily Chou-chou* [2001]), and Isao Yukisada (*Go* [2001]) have extended the style of Mizoguchi and Ozu to explore issues like alienation, the plight of youth, and the state of race relations in today's Japan.

It is perhaps no accident that the best known and respected of Japan's directors of the 1990s and into the new millennium is one who consciously draws on stylistic, thematic, and generic dimensions of traditional Japanese cinema. Kitano "Beat" Takeshi, who has a background as a *manzai* performer on television and has worked as an actor with legendary directors like Oshima and Kinji Fukasaku, creates films with unmistakable references to genre (*Zatoichi* [2003], to the samurai film; *Boiling Point* [1990] and *Sonatine* [1993], to the *yakuza* movie). Perhaps more surprising, some of the style and themes of Ozu are also apparent. A sense of quietude, acceptance, and loss pervades *Hana-bi* (1997). Shots of Nishi and his wife show them sitting on tatami silently eating cake; there is a pair of shoes and a child's tricycle in an otherwise empty hallway; there is a marked preference for frontal framing and a lack of emotionality throughout the film. These are hardly the traits of a taut thriller about a policeman on the run from both criminals and cops. Yet it is precisely those gestures toward Japanese tradition—to Ozu's cinema and to other icons of Japanese culture (Zen temples, Mount Fuji, cherry blossoms [see Gerow 146–52])—that Kitano can both participate in the stream of Japanese cinema and advance it.

Anime and J-Horror

The complexities and sheer volume of anime (Japanese animation, much of it derived from the massive manga production that dominates Japanese publishing) make it difficult to encapsulate in a week or two in a class on Japanese cinema. A more interesting strategy would be to base such a course on a prerequisite of (live-action) Japanese cinema. The continuities and discontinuities between anime and nonanimated cinema would be revealing, as would the continuities with precinematic aesthetic practices. The vast range of anime—science fiction, samurai, and youth dramas—certainly allow for comparisons with live-action genres, including horror. And as for "J-horror"—contemporary Japanese horror films—it, too, should be seen in both contrast and continuity with earlier cinema.

The cultural specificities of the form are notable—especially the omnipresence of ghosts and the way they are imaged—as are its derivations from Hollywood. The most popular of Japanese forms in the West since the *kaiju-eiga*, anime and J-horror certainly deserve some consideration. Still, to approach them in terms of their distinctively Japanese origins and dimensions, instead of their cult or mainstream appeal outside Japan, is best done with a foundation in the Japanese cinema based solidly in the range of practices and forms that gave it its flavor and specificity.

Works Cited

Anderson, Joseph L. "Spoken Silents in the Japanese Cinema; or, Talking to Pictures: Essaying the *Katsuben*, Contextualizing the Texts." *Reframing Japanese Cinema: Authorship, Genre, History*. Ed. Arthur Nolletti, Jr., and David Desser. Bloomington: Indiana UP, 1992. 259–311. Print.

Anderson, Joseph L., and Donald Richie. *Japanese Film: Art and Industry*. Expanded ed. Princeton: Princeton UP, 1982. Print.

Burch, Noël. *To the Distant Observer*. Berkeley: U of California P, 1979. Print.

Desser, David. *Eros Plus Massacre: An Introduction to the Japanese New Wave Cinema*. Bloomington: Indiana UP, 1988. Print.

———. "*Tokyo Story:* The Space of Ambivalence." *Film Analysis: A Norton Reader*. Ed. Jeffrey Geiger and R. L. Rutsky. New York: Norton, 2005. 456–72. Print.

Erlich, Linda C., and David Desser, eds. *Cinematic Landscapes: Observations on the Visual Arts and Cinema of China and Japan*. Austin: U of Texas P, 1994. Print.

Gerow, Aaron. *Kitano Takeshi*. London: British Film Inst., 2007. Print. World Directors ser.

Hasumi, Shigehiko. "Sunny Skies." *Ozu's Tokyo Story*. Ed. David Desser. New York: Cambridge UP, 1997. 118–29. Print.

McDonald, Keiko. *Japanese Classical Theater in Films*. Cranbury: Assoc. UP, 1994. Print.

Richie, Donald. *A Hundred Years of Japanese Film*. Tokyo: Kodansha, 2001. Print.

———. "The Influence of Traditional Aesthetics on the Japanese Film." Ehrlich and Desser 155–64.

———. *Japanese Cinema: Film Style and National Character*. Garden City: Anchor, 1971. Print.

Sato, Tadao. "Japanese Cinema and the Traditional Arts: Imagery, Technique and Cultural Context." Ehrlich and Desser 165–86.

Dudley Andrew

Teaching World Cinema

The name *world cinema* has not always been with us. When I began teaching in 1969, many schools frankly divided their film offerings into American and foreign. At the University of Iowa, I inherited Survey of Film, which touched on Hollywood for a couple weeks and then looked abroad for the rest of the term. But when I moved to Yale in 2000, recognizing that thirty years had brought new perspectives on a much wider landscape, I refashioned the course, baptizing it World Cinema. This title was welcomed, even solicited, by the Department of Comparative Literature, which sponsored it as part of its high-profile initiative in world literature, aiming to renew a famous and well-subscribed undergraduate major. I was glad to stamp my place in comp lit with World Cinema, and I wanted to give a highly international cast to the Film Studies Program, where I was appointed codirector.

The adjective *world* counts for a lot, especially if one considers the alternatives. *Global* sounds more aggressive and too often precedes the noun *Hollywood*, where it refers either to the master strategies of the studio conglomerates or to the style and ambition of blockbusters muscling for all-out distribution. The James Bond series, with its British veneer, is an amiable example. I have not been above screening *Tomorrow Never Dies*

(1997) in my course just to give the students the satisfaction of following out a text that effectively analyzes itself as an allegory of global entertainment. Situated in the South China Sea, it has an advantage over, say, *Independence Day* (1996), which literally burrows into the soil of one nation-state (guess which one) that becomes the center of a united globe under attack from intergalactic forces. Global films like these entice students and provide empowering experiences whereby the readymade analysis of such elements as plot, characters, mise-en-scène, locations, and point of view leads to the equally obvious analysis of the political economy and ideology responsible for their look, their values, and indeed for the money and effort that brought them into existence. In the context of this course, such films can be treated as self-parodies, samples of something to step across or even to step on as one progresses to increasingly complicated films and situations.

The swagger and self-promotion of anything going by the name "global" hardly characterizes "the cinema of small nations"[1] or many of the great auteurs who have given luster to the art, and so I prefer International Cinema or The International Art Film as a second alternative course title, one that identifies a classier class of movies, buoyant enough to float above and then beyond their place of origin, so that they can address savvy viewers elsewhere. If global cinema gets written about in the business section of the *New York Times*, international films are taken up in the arts section. The former aims to dominate several screens at every multiplex through saturation booking, while the latter can be found at more selective theaters. More in tune with the humanities approach to literature and art history, International Cinema offers students complex and diverse works, paying only secondary attention to the economic and political structures in which these films incubate and survive. A "masterpieces" approach lets each film preen center-stage for a week, or, to change the metaphor, walks students through a garden of flowers. If appreciation and discrimination be the first (as well as the final) goal here, it is greatly aided by a botanical investigation of stylistic and thematic trends; students can learn to track migration patterns of personnel (actors, directors, cameramen) and of fashions or ideas from great film to great film and from nation to nation. In short, they can look for the results of general processes within the patterns of each singular, distinctive work.

I also prefer the adjective *international* to *global* as a counterweight to student and industry pressure that would have us concentrate solely on what is recent, immediate, and most in the news. For a course called International Film invites the examination of historical periods as well as the current one, introducing a healthy variety of films and providing a clearer view of cultural dynamics. In fact internationalism is often the best way to characterize post–World War II cinematic modernism, which was, I have argued, a pan-European strategy designed to counter Hollywood. While nations remain crucial in identifying types and qualities of movies even after the classical era, from 1945 until at least 1975 an international community of critics evaluated and interpreted what would be remembered. Luis Buñuel and Ingmar Bergman could become international figures, and Michelangelo Antonioni would strive to be the international artist par excellence in his films from *Blow-Up* (1966) on. Material covered in Global Cinema, on the other hand, would not pick up until the 1970s, right after modernism collapses, which it does in large part because Hollywood reasserted itself through the muscular new distribution patterns that made *Jaws* (1975) and *Star Wars* (1977) so important in the history of the medium. The modernist period from neorealism through the multiple new waves contains cinema's brashest claims for cultural significance; films were thought to be on a par and in dialogue with novels and plays, yet commanded vaster audiences than these parallel expressions. Films were thus capable of potent political critique and of energizing the social movement of the times, at least until 1968, perhaps their highpoint and turning point. Several excellent recent textbooks manage to get their arms around this era, showing the general conditions after the "year zero" of 1945 that led to the hopes of a new cinema capable of contributing to a new European society.[2] While the politics of the Cold War brought disappointment to the social aspirations, vigorous new types of films did challenge and overthrow many classical structures. An ocean of modernism touched shores around the world. Although each new wave arose out of specific and distinct national conditions (in France, Japan, Great Britain, Czechoslovakia, Brazil, the USSR, and Yugoslavia), each encouraged and influenced the others, thanks to a flourishing festival circuit, magazines, and film schools. My students read one of these textbooks, and we screen and discuss a few examples. I also assemble clips from a score of 1960s films (none more than six minutes long) so students can sample the variety of fresh voices from that decade. I pick two of these clips for them to comment on during an in-class midterm. They digest the general upheaval of this decade while sensing how differently it was experienced in Prague, London, Tokyo, Paris, and Rio de Janeiro. Students can enumerate a litany of new-wave techniques while understanding to what very different uses they had been put. And students can recognize the double dialogue filmmakers kept up: with members of their national community (other filmmakers, writers, painters, and musicians) and with filmmakers elsewhere whom they encountered at festivals and through magazines.

A course title need not be its destiny. International Film may have responded to the dynamics of the modernist era while Global Cinema came along to deal with image traffic after the digital era had arrived, but courses bearing these titles can both plant their feet far back in the medium's past. That other postwar, the one beginning in 1918, produced an international art cinema that thrived in the 1920s until sound (and the language issue that accompanied this new technology) combined with strident politics to make of cinema primarily "la projection nationale," as Jean-Michel Frodon has termed it. But even during high nationalism one can profitably examine stylistic migrations like the one from German expressionism to French poetic realism in the 1930s and then to the film noir of 1940s Hollywood. Or one can trace the path of an idea of political cinema from the USSR of the late 1920s to Italy in the 1930s, where neorealism incubated despite a fascist state, and from there to Latin America in the 1960s. As for Global Cinema, should such a course not begin with the brothers Auguste and Louis Lumière sending their cameramen far and wide to both capture images of distant places and project images there that were captured elsewhere to serve as an emporium of exotic pictures? Or take the case of the novelist Jun'ichirō Tanizaki, who turned to scriptwriting around 1920, because, he claimed, film made him feel more cosmopolitan than did literature. It took several years for his works to be translated into Western languages, and he had to wait years for Japanese translations of Thomas Mann, André Gide, and Jack London. With the cinema, however, he knew that in Tokyo he was watching works of D. W. Griffith, Thomas Harper Ince, and Paul Wegener that were playing simultaneously—or nearly so—in London and Buenos Aires. Cinema made him a citizen of the world, a member of a cosmopolitan elite. And he surmised correctly that, beyond this elite, a huge percentage of the earth's population knew about, and laughed at, Charlie Chaplin.

Picking up many concerns from these alternatives, the course World Cinema means to project the situation and role of cinema across several sorts of maps while taking into account the different phases at play in what I call its "time zones."[3] Spreading out geographically and historically, this course presents an array of samples that together suggest the diversity of cultural values and of the cinematic imagination while exploring the ecology that permits or threatens such diversity. For this project, we must measure the economic and cultural infrastructure that allows films to make their way here and there, sometimes examining the interdependencies and movements among films, personnel, and motifs from place to place, with an eye to establishing the growth pattern of the art. At the same time, World Cinema stays alert to the different roles cinema plays in specific locations, roles established by the state, by popular audiences, and by the culture industry.

Cinema requires such shifts of attention from film to system, from global to specific audience, because it is a constitutionally dialectical medium, especially when seen against the far more monological discourse of television. Of course every technology can be put to use in various ways (films have been watched on television for decades, for instance); still there do exist technological predispositions that have tended to form distinct, even opposite, social functions. Television, emerging out of radio broadcasting, addresses its audience directly, often frontally as in news programs, advertising, and MTV. And it brings the truth or the illusion of being present with and to the audience, in real time. We attend live to the news, sports events, the Oscars, ongoing disasters, presidential debates, and so on. Even when it displays something prerecorded, television maintains its potential for being present. At any minute someone may break into the broadcast—the president, say, or the weatherman—to speak to us in our living rooms, imploring us or giving us directions. The television is part of our living room (or bedroom), coexisting with us as furniture, our equipment for living. It shares much with the telephone and for a long while was treated as an extension of the telecommunications industry, an arrangement that cable has recovered and a dream of copresence that Skype has fulfilled.

For better or worse, we constantly live alongside television, whereas we choose to go out to the movies, leaving home and paying to enter an alternative space through a series of frames: the posters and marquee, the box office and vestibule, the curtains or soundproof doors, and finally the darkened interior where, as André Bazin says, we are led by the flashlight of the usher "to the night of our waking dream" (*What* 107). The film begins, and we enter the world of the screen that exists very well without us. In classical cinema, no one addresses us directly; we encounter images taken in the past, haunting the room for the duration of the projection. The cinema is foreign to us even as we strive to digest it, to incorporate what we take in through our eyes.

Cinema has not always promoted its otherness, and many spectators today are tuned into popular cinema the way they are tuned into television. In the period of classical cinema people would say, "Let's go to the movies," in the same tone a later generation would say, "Let's watch TV." Indeed, one part of the term *classical* celebrates the harmony that unites audience and producer in a feedback loop. Bazin compared Hollywood to French classical theater, suggesting that the success of both had less to do with the authors whose names we all know (John Ford, Howard Hawks, Jean Racine, Pierre Corneille) than with the "genius of the system," a system that included society's vigilant attention and feedback (Bazin, "On the *Politique*" 258). In the Hollywood of Bazin's time, it was hard to make a bad film, just as minor playwrights in Louis XIV's court never really fell down, whereas a few generations later, a writer as gifted as Voltaire wrote tragedies that were abysmal failures because the era had changed; tragedies were no longer so "natural" as they had been.

Classical cinema was most natural, so to speak, during the period of high nationalism between the world wars when Americans felt right at home in the movie theater no matter where the film might take them (to Oz with Dorothy or to Washington with Mr. Smith). A national audience huddled within picture palaces and corner theaters around the country to watch on the big screen what the studios sent them each week. And what they sent them was largely familiar because of the star and genre systems. While this feeling for the movies persists (e.g., in *Forrest Gump* [1994]), it does so under a variety of viewing conditions (television, computer downloads) and alongside other attitudes that films and audiences adopt. The classical-national function may come first to mind when one speaks of the movies in general, but it constitutes just a single phase of world cinema; moreover, it might even serve an aberrant function, given that cinema seems born to emphasize dislocation and discomfort. From the outset films surprised and even shocked audiences with alien images, as in 1898 when the Japanese gaped at Russian landscapes, Turkish faces, and quaint Spanish customs. World Cinema seizes on such moments, emphasizing everyone's attraction to and fear of the foreign, the different, the elsewhere and otherwise. In the United States, *foreign film* has always been a code word for deep realism, daring or difficult narratives, and taboo topics.

Of course, "[e]very film is a foreign film . . . somewhere," even classic Hollywood productions (qtd. in Scott).[4] World Cinema can challenge students to examine the films they feel most at home with but from the perspective of someone the films do not immediately address. How did

Flying Down to Rio appear to Brazilian audiences in 1933, or *Morocco* to North Africans in 1930? Some Hollywood films dare to introduce this other perspective so as to unsettle their home audience. In the dramatic center of *Three Kings* (1999), while Mark Wahlberg is being tortured by an Iraqi soldier, the director George Russell uses conventional cutaways to Wahlberg's wife and child in Arizona to heighten the scene's pathos and our identification with the victim. But then Russell matches these images in a flashback to the Iraqi torturer's child killed by American bombs. Our sympathies and perspective become troubled. I press the advantage of this disturbance by screening *Marooned in Iraq*, the 2002 film by the Kurdish director Bahman Ghobadi because it literally reverses the direction of *Three Kings.* Where the latter ends happily with a group of Iraqi dissidents successfully crossing into Iran, the former follows beleaguered Kurds trying to cross the same border, but this time from Iran into Iraq. The same landscape (though *Three Kings* was shot in Arizona) looks and means something very different in these two films, both of which are comedic adventure stories. Students are forced to look at Iraq from two distinct perspectives, that of adventurers who become knights errant in a foreign land and that of a migrating and abject people, aiming to survive as near foreigners in their own country. *Three Kings*'s technological overkill stands in ironic opposition to the makeshift Kurdish production, with its clever and engaging guerrilla style. George Clooney's attraction is matched by the Kurdish singer who evidently is every bit as famous in Iran. Both films profit from the comparison, because the opposition between them points up oppositions internal to each.

Film studies has always promised to open seemingly unified texts until they expose their internal tensions. The films we study in World Cinema fulfill this promise almost from the outset. Since education is so much a matter of assimilating the foreign, we need only exploit what foreign films initiate as a way to develop the requisite skills and reflexes to understand them. Why not begin by interrogating the viewing experience a class has just undergone, ideally on a large screen? Discounting for a minute what a classroom screening means, the distinction between our watching a Brazilian or an Iranian film in the United States and the experience it provided its first audiences leads to the recognition of a series of differences that can be put into play dialectically.

The friction that heats up arguments about what a film signifies is constitutional of all but the most local or most universal of films. Films that travel nowhere (like the video films made in Kenya, seen only by Kenyans and a few anthropologists) operate as I suggest television does, self-present to the culture they represent. At the other end of the scale, global films like *Star Wars* expect to make everyone feel at home with them wherever they are watched.

Cinema's ambition to be universal set against its obvious local inflections has fueled one valuable debate to have enlivened film studies since 2000, the so-called vernacular modernism debate initiated by Miriam Hansen, where *modernism* stands for a worldwide phenomenon that took place (is still taking place) in phases and lurches, while *vernacular* refers both to the organic, grass-roots engine driving (cinematic) modernism and to the local ways in which, à la Michel de Certeau, the strategies of the entertainment industry are reworked into the tactics of ordinary urban viewers as they read and respond to movies in unauthorized and idiosyncratic ways. In the first years of the studio system, Hollywood gambled that its immense lead in technology, capital investment, the manufacture of films, and sheer product (stories, stars, spectacle) could overcome any fragmentation brought about by the introduction into movies of literal language. Hollywood's vaunted ubiquity overcame obvious language barriers, Hansen argues, by appealing to a preverbal sensorial language understood wherever modernity was underway. Hollywood believed it had united the globe after discovering a common entertainment quotient for America's diverse immigrant audience, through which it could confidently cut across local languages and mores everywhere. In this sense Hollywood played a decisive role in the incubation of mass culture in Shanghai, Tokyo, and Berlin. But Hansen insists that it did not play the same role in each place. Each site processed these films in its own way, triggering three peculiar, though related, versions of melodrama from home producers. The specific features of cinematic production and reception in the three cities prevented them from being mere spokes radiating from the racing wheel of a mechanized modernist machine or outposts of the imperial reach of image capitalism. But neither are they isolated monads of modernization, for they are all subject to similar technological constants and a body of rules covering production, distribution, and exhibition. Moreover, there could be secants that link, say, Berlin to Tokyo, bypassing Los Angeles altogether. In fact, a rapport between Japan and Europe can be felt in the Taisho era (1915–25) and then again during the Japanese new wave of the 1960s. Moreover, Tokyo constituted a smaller version of Hollywood between the wars, as Michael Baskett has recently demonstrated in his book *The Attractive Empire: Transnational Film Culture in Imperial Japan*. While Taisho modernism may have been affected by what Hollywood purveyed, by the 1930s Japanese cinema competed against Hollywood for the Asian market. Taiwan and Korea (and soon Manchuria) were fed a diet of Japanese-style films by their colonizers; other contested places on the Pacific Rim, like Shanghai, for a while had a choice between two types of foreign films (Hollywood and Japanese), which they would process in their own Chinese manner, as evidenced by the touching melodramas produced there in the 1930s.

The inevitable duality of something made in one place to be seen both at home and abroad stands out in every film that is subtitled or dubbed. It stands out, that is, in most films, since virtually everywhere—except in America—cinema's otherness is continually and unmistakably present at the bottom of the screen. Subtitles redouble the foreignness of the image, letting us know that we are witnessing a spectacle produced by (and presumably for) others elsewhere, one that is part of a discourse we must decipher. Reading subtitles, or adjusting to the gap between face and voice in a dubbed print, we confront the cinema's bifurcated nature as image and text, spectacle and signification.[5] Did anyone ever believe Jacques Rivette when he proclaimed that it does not matter that the dialogue of Kenji Mizoguchi's films is incomprehensible to most of us and that his tales treat topics utterly alien to us, because Mizoguchi speaks "the only language a filmmaker need know, the language of mise-en-scène"? On the contrary, in watching *Ugetsu* (1953), as our eyes flick from subtitles to image every few seconds, we imagine a Japanese audience capable of following what the characters' lips pronounce, able to understand references to places, costume, and local conventions. *Ugetsu* makes for a great example, since it won the Venice Festival competition in 1953 and placed near the top of the Japanese film magazine *Kinema Junpo*'s list in Japan that same year. I challenge my students to imagine those qualities that appealed to both audiences (its universal humanism) and those that most likely appealed to one audience and not the other. The story, featuring an Asian ghost appearing in various guises since the eighteenth century, might have echoed a familiar theme that touched the Japanese audiences but left Western audiences to relish an eerie tale from a distant culture.

Using Mizoguchi's film in World Cinema allows the class to encounter many of the most important problems and possibilities in film studies. Mizoguchi has been termed the most Japanese of filmmakers, especially in comparison with Akira Kurosawa; indeed the Kurosawa-Mizoguchi debate that raged at *Cahiers du cinéma* in the 1950s dramatized something crucial: that national and ethnic background always interacts with forces and realities beyond the nation. Kurosawa may be an ideal exemplar of postwar

Japan, which, since the American occupation, has not been able to ignore the West. His adaptations of Fyodor Dostoyevsky, Maksim Gorky, and William Shakespeare remain Japanese for all that. Meanwhile, Mizoguchi adapted several classic Japanese authors (Chikamatsu Monzaemon, for instance, known as the Japanese Shakespeare), but perhaps with a Western audience partly in mind.

With the possible exception of France, no other nation has maintained itself as so powerful an alternative to Hollywood for so long a period as Japan has.[6] Yet from the outset, unlike Hollywood, Japanese cinema has faced up to—and exploited the possibilities of—cinema's duality. Two exhibition chains divided all theaters in the country into those that screened only Japanese-language works and those that screened foreign films. Some spectators might never enter a foreign-film theater, content to think of the movies as delivering home-grown entertainment. Other spectators, aesthetes and cosmopolitans, might never attend a Japanese-film theater, convinced that Japanese films were behind those produced elsewhere and wanting to be in touch with whatever advertised itself as modern.

In the silent era, which lasted until 1936 in Japan, the Japanese watched films while listening to a *benshi*, a kind of lecturer posted to the side of the screen. For foreign films, he would give the Japanese translations of the intertitles and clarify geographical and cultural points to aid the comprehension of the film. For Japanese films, he would voice the dialogue (adopting the appropriate intonation for female or child characters) and elaborate on the plot and themes. Thus the Japanese spectator of those early years seemingly never was drawn into the screen as a unitary site of identification, for the *benshi*'s voice and physical presence countered the image, even when reinforcing the sentiments expressed on screen.

While the course's name tempts the instructor to change location every week so as to survey as much of the world as possible, I find it important to spend several weeks in one place so that the key concerns of the course can take shape and so that a given national cinema can be shown to fluctuate over time. Debates about whether the striking quality of Japanese cinema in the 1930s (derived from a feudal aesthetic or part of American-style modernization?) arise in different terms in the late 1950s with the coming of the Japanese new wave. Many students can sense this tension today, in the popularity of anime, of cult directors like Takashi Miike, and of a certain cool Japanese sensibility that strikes some as participating in universal postmodernity. Others would underscore Japan's idiosyncratic image culture. With this duality in mind, one can follow out the fate of the ghost genre after *Ugetsu* to discover if Japanese ideas about the spirit world are portable. The fact that *Ringu* (1998) was remade in Hollywood might make one believe that the differences between the cultures and their films had narrowed. But other Japanese ghost films have not made their way to the West, instead floating down the Pacific Rim where they encounter an accessible, indeed welcoming audience sensibility.[7]

Japanese image trade with the rest of Asia reminds us how crude the local/global distinction can be. After looking at the shifting nature and function of film in Japan from the silent age to the postwar, new wave, and postmodern posture, my course World Cinema does not take up another nation. Rather it looks at a particular phase across a geographic expanse (the new waves of the 1960s) or examines regions, such as the Balkans, West Africa, or East Asia. Each film selected invites an investigation into its national situation, but the nation is only one of several lenses employed. Switching powers of magnification brings other aspects of the film and of cinema as a whole into focus. Take Edward Yang's *YiYi* (2000)—this Cannes Film Festival winner may be the densest cinematic representation of modern Taipei ever made, but it has yet to be screened in that city. It stands as an exclusively international film even though it is tied to a particular city. The lead character, however, does talk on the phone to a former lover in Chicago, and he meets up with her in Tokyo, where he, like so many other of his countrymen, travels on business. I like to suggest that Taiwan's cinema can only be described the way a surveyor might, by triangulating it according to three reference points: Japan (its longtime colonizer), China (its imaginary other) and the United States (the financial and political ally that put it on its feet). Taiwanese filmmakers like Yang or Hou Hsiao-Hsien have been masterfully sensitive to the particularities of Taiwanese culture and language yet increasingly attentive to the regional and cross-Pacific ties tangible and visible (e.g., television or on the Internet) everywhere on that island.

A similar configuration holds in Ireland, where filmmakers often choose either to go back to the roots of Irish lore (occasionally even using Gaelic) or to follow an emigrant populace to Britain or America. Neil Jordan has managed to do both, and so he may be considered the most representative Irish director, since the island of his birth, just like Taiwan, looks out on an expansive horizon that includes a former colonizer (England), a place of emigration and imagination (the United States), and a financial and political ally that has let it achieve a good measure of autonomy (the European Union). Such regional relations are normally far more operative than the facile idea of the global, and they do not obliterate the role of the nation that continues to be central in cinema. As Markus Nornes reiterates in

Cinema Babel, nation-states, even those that share borders, foster, block, and regulate movies in distinct ways. Nowhere is this more evident than along the Pacific Rim, where actors and genres may travel with relative ease, but where business practices, government policies, antipiracy laws, and outright censorship make each national site an island with a distinctive cinematic coastline. Korea, Hong Kong, Japan, the Philippines, China, Taiwan, Thailand, Singapore, and Vietnam may share genres, talent, and a varying degree of cultural references, but highly local situations govern how each production comes about and then how each film reaches its audience. *Pan-Asian* has become a useful term, but it describes no spectator. Every spectator is in place and every place has its rules, conventions, and history. Producers and distributors must be sensitive to these commonalities and differences. So too must the student of World Cinema.

After a dozen weeks addressing films with such concerns in mind, students should have the chance and the ability to choose as the domain of a final paper a group of films coming from some circumscribed area. Watching a handful of films related by auteur, genre, star, and theme and reading about several others, after having surveyed the cultural-political-economic situation within which these films were formed, students can explore one or two rich examples in the dialectical manner the course foregrounds. That is, they can place the films and track their cultural work while finding themselves displaced by their experience, rethinking their conventions in relation to the obtuse difference posed by images coming from elsewhere. Text/context, here/there: these are the dialectical pairs that operate unmistakably throughout World Cinema and that make it such a supremely valuable addition to the humanities.

Notes

1. This phrase is the title of a fine anthology edited by Mette Hjort and Duncan Petrie.

2. See, e.g., Cowie; Nowell-Smith; Kovács.

3. I have tried to clarify these dimensions of cinema's world geography and its time zones in two articles, "An Atlas of World Cinema" and "Time Zones and Jetlag: The Flows and Phases of World Cinema."

4. A. O. Scott attributes this formula to Atom Egoyan and Ian Balfour, in the introduction to their anthology *Subtitles* (2004).

5. For an overview of the many world cinema elements tied to the hurdle of language see Ďurovičová.

6. Since the 1920s Japan has turned out on average well over three hundred films a year.

7. Taiwan's second most popular film, after *Crouching Tiger, Hidden Dragon* (2000), has been *Double Vision* (directed by Chen Kuo-fu [2002]), which was backed by Columbia Pictures and featured a recognizable American actor, David Morse, to grab a worldwide audience. But while a hit in Asia, the film did not travel well to the West, where audiences could not credit the Taoist basis and cultural references crucial to its premise.

Works Cited

Andrew, Dudley. "An Atlas of World Cinema." *Remapping World Cinema: Identity, Culture and Politics in Film.* Ed. Stephanie Dennison and Song Hwee Lim. London: Wallflower, 2006. 19–29. Print.

———. "Times Zones and Jetlag: The Flows and Phases of World Cinema." Ďurovičová and Newman 59–89.

Baskett, Michael. *The Attractive Empire: Transnational Film Culture in Imperial Japan.* Honolulu: U of Hawai'i P, 2008. Print.

Bazin, André. "On the *Politique des Auters.*" Hiller 251–58.

———. *What Is Cinema?* Berkeley: U of California P, 1967. Print.

Cowie, Peter. *Revolution! The Explosion of World Cinema in the Sixties.* London: Faber, 2004. Print.

Ďurovičová, Nataša. "Vector, Flow, Zone: Towards a History of Cinematic *Translation.*" Ďurovičová and Newman 90–120.

Ďurovičová, Nataša, and Kathleen Newman, eds. *World Cinema, Transnational Perspectives.* New York: Routledge, 2010. Print.

Frodon, Jean-Michel. *La projection nationale: Cinéma et nation.* Paris: Jacob, 1998. Print.

Hansen, Miriam. "Vernacular Modernism: Tracking Cinema on a Global Scale." Ďurovičová and Newman 287–314.

Hillier, Jim, ed. Cahiers du cinéma*: The 1950s: Neo-realism, Hollywood, New Wave.* Cambridge: Harvard UP, 1985. Print.

Hjort, Mette, and Duncan Petrie, eds. *The Cinema of Small Nations.* Edinburgh: Edinburgh UP, 2007. Print.

Kovács, András Bálint. *Screening Modernism: European Art Cinema, 1950–1980.* Chicago: U of Chicago P, 2007. Print.

Nornes, Mark. Introduction. *Cinema Babel: Translating Global Cinema.* Minneapolis: U of Minnesota P, 2007. 1–28. Print.

Nowell-Smith, Geoffrey. *Making Waves: New Cinemas of the 1960s.* London: Continuum, 2008. Print.

Rivette, Jacques. "Mizoguchi Viewed from Here." Hiller 264.

Scott, A. O. "What Is a Foreign Film Now?" *New York Times.* New York Times, 14 Nov. 2004. Web. 18 Mar. 2011.

Part III

Interdisciplinarities

Introduction to Part 3

In one of his earliest articles on film, "On the Impression of Reality in the Cinema," published in *Cahiers du cinéma* in 1965, the renowned film theorist Christian Metz wrote:

> Cinema is a vast subject, and there are more ways than one to enter it. Taken as a whole, it is first of all a fact, and as such it raises problems of aesthetics, of sociology and of semiotics as well as the psychologies of perception and intellection. (3)

The interdisciplinary approach that Metz describes—involving aesthetics, sociology, semiotics, and psychology—was drawn directly from his engagement with the work of filmology. Filmology was a movement organized initially by the French intellectual and academic community, and then it expanded to an international arena in an effort to arrive at a comprehensive, pluralistic approach to the study of film.[1] It originated in Paris in 1946 with the publication of Gilbert Cohen-Seat's *Essai sur les principes d'une philosophie du cinéma* ("Essay on the Principles of a Philosophy of Cinema"). Cohen-Seat put forth a project whose purpose was twofold. First, he aimed to draw attention to the necessity of film study and its relevance to the concerns of existing academic disciplines; second, he endeavored to establish a methodology based on a dichotomy of phenomena: the filmic fact (the phenomena of film, as stimulus, as art object, as message, as text) and the cinematic fact, which involved those phenomena bearing on cinema as an institution, including economic, cultural, as well as sociohistorical factors. Filmology quickly became institutionalized, forming an association in 1946 and establishing a journal in 1947. Both were meant as international forums for scholars to discuss the cinema from a variety of perspectives and disciplinary approaches.

Filmology is important to remember today because it was a first attempt to organize cinema studies across disciplinary divides between the humanities and social sciences, encompassing literature, art history, sociology, psychology, and history. It also had a direct impact on the formation of the Society for Cinema and Media Studies (SCMS) in the United States. Established in New York in 1959, the Society of Cinematologists (the forerunner to SCMS) likewise aimed to give the scholarly study of film visibility and academic credibility. Its first president, Robert Gessner (of New York University), had traveled to Paris, where he met with Cohen-Seat and other scholars. When he returned to New York, Gessner explicitly modeled the constitution of the Society of Cinematologists on that of the French organization.

Hence, interdisciplinarity has defined the scholarly study of film in both the United States and abroad for decades. As noted in our introduction, several books have further traced the institutional and intellectual foundations of US cinema studies, expanding the boundaries of interdisciplinarity beyond the academy to include the government, museums, and the publishing industry (see Wasson; Decherney; Polan; Grieveson and Wasson). Each of these recent books provides ample evidence of the rich history of interdisciplinarity within film and media studies, which the essays in this section further elaborate and explore.

Indeed, whether analyzing the relation of film and literature or film and language, showing how legal history affects every aspect of cinema (including questions of copyright, intellectual property, censorship, subsidy, monopoly, tax, and trade), or examining how historical and psychological analysis contributes to the study of film, the essays in this section offer a range of ideas for organizing courses on multiple interdisciplinary topics and themes. In the tradition of filmology, the essays gathered here also explore the aesthetic shapes and political directions of film and media studies in our own time and endeavor to open up dialogue across the humanities and social sciences so as to engage with students and scholars across traditional disciplinary divides. Nowhere does this interdisciplinary impulse show more promise than in the writing of film history. Given the online availability of newspaper databases, census records, and genealogical resources, undergraduates can now conduct new original film research while gaining an appreciation for narrative craft and historical method. Thus do aesthetic concerns overlap with those regarding history, society, and law, reminding us, once again, what Metz underscored more than fifty years ago; namely, that the cinema is a vast subject, that there are more ways than one to enter it, and that interdisciplinarity is at the center of the discipline of film and media studies.

Note

1. For a detailed history of filmology, see Lowry.

Works Cited

Cohen-Seat, Gilbert. *Essai sur les principes d'une philosophie du cinéma*. 1946. Paris: PUF, 1958. Print.

Decherney, Peter. *Hollywood and the Culture Elite: How the Movies Became American*. New York: Columbia UP, 2005. Print.

Grieveson, Lee, and Haidee Wasson. *Inventing Film Studies*. Durham: Duke UP, 2008. Print.

Lowry, Edward. *The Filmology Movement and Film Study in France*. Michigan: UMI Research, 1985. Print.

Metz, Christian. "On the Impression of Reality in the Cinema." *Film Language: A Semiotics of the Cinema*. Trans. Michael Taylor. Chicago: U of Chicago P, 1990. 3–15. Print.

Polan, Dana. *Scenes of Instruction: The Beginnings of the U.S. Study of Film*. Berkeley: U of California P, 2006. Print.

Wasson, Haidee. *Museum Movies: The Museum of Modern Art and the Birth of Art Cinema*. Berkeley: U of California P, 2005. Print.

Garrett Stewart

Literature and Film—Not Literature on Film

I address here the teaching of film and literature, not separately, as often happens with the mixed menu of a single undergraduate class, but pertinently together. In which case everything depends on the *and*, the point of conjunction between media. In the courses I describe, including the most recent exhibit from my classroom experiments in this vein over three decades, the yoking *and* is not simply a convenient pedagogic link. Instead, it marks the apex of a sustained triangulation, rethinking novel and film in relation to their narrative common denominators and in the light of the axioms, challenges, and implications of narrative structure per se and its induced responses.

Topics in Fiction and Film: Mediation and Surveillance, like many of the narratives it convenes and investigates with students, has a backstory. After a decade's worth of strictly literary instruction, I began teaching film at the University of California, Santa Barbara, in the early 1980s, under a familiar twin imperative, academic and bureaucratic alike—to capture the first wave of 1980s interdisciplinary interest in narratology and to offer larger-enrollment courses for the English department. Once launched, Narrative Form typically enrolled from 150 to 200 students, with separate screenings and meetings with teaching assistants, and was often focused on a given genre like science fiction. Whatever the thematic profile, the point was to "read" each medium for the linguistic, ocular, and aural contours of its narrative structure.

In this regard, the effort was explicitly to break from the pattern of *Wuthering Heights* on page and screen, or, in other words, to forego adaptation studies and their tendency to prefer one version of a classic over another and to probe instead the shared narrative purposes of certain structural or stylistic choices. Thus the embedded narratives of Emily Brontë's *Wuthering Heights* were compared not to the 1930s film but to the structure of Orson Welles's *Citizen Kane*, with its refracted or prismatic mix of biographical perspectives. In other segments of the course, the flashbacks and "superimpositions" of Joseph Conrad's *Heart of Darkness* came into the orbit of similar effects in Federico Fellini's *8½*. Prose ellipsis called out for comparison with the freeze frame, rhythmic caesuras with jump cuts. From week to week, discussion took seriously David Bordwell's sense of technique or style (even when underplayed in his own examples) as part of the equation by which, in his influential definition of narrative, "syuzhet and style interact in the course of cueing and channeling the viewer's construction of the fabula" (53). It was, in short, a course about how structure (or plot) and its medium-specific manifestations (not just inflections) generate story.

When I moved to the University of Iowa in the mid-1990s, two contingencies helped reshape and downscale the lecture format of that initial sectioned course: a departmental building with few big classrooms (nothing resembling the auditorium I taught in at UCSB, with its professionally staffed rear-projection facilities) and a resulting tradition of small-enrollment, writing-intensive courses. In addition, a rubric already on the books had lain dormant for a few years: Topics in Fiction and Film. Just add "as narrative" to the title, and I was ready to jump-start the course again, which I have taught regularly now for over fifteen years with DVD materials and a mixed undergraduate clientele typically half from the English department, half from film studies. Never mind that the prepackaged rubric was illogical, given that many films (and all of those I would be screening) are fictions in themselves. This formulation allowed me to explain on day 1 that the course would put not just the prose back in fiction but also the filmstrip back in screen narrative (and since then, the digital scan—at the production rather than just the distribution end of things) by concentrating on the material ingredients of each medium separately. In comparing lexigraphic with cinematographic devices, we would make sure that the operable features and underlying constituents of each medium were closely monitored in their recruitment to narrative form.

Until 2010, I had most often taught that evolved and mutated course under the thematic subheading of Modes of Fantasy in Fiction and Film, beginning with Tzvetan Todorov's account (using his book *The Fantastic* chapter by chapter, week by week), stressing as Todorov does the undecidable vacillation in the genre between psychological and supernatural explanations for destabilizing events, the "uncanny" versus the "marvelous." The one thing this course, like its California predecessor, was never designed to follow was the point-by-point comparative model, as with Shakespeare Goes to the Movies or Victorian Fiction on Screen, retaining instead the traces of its origin in the heyday of general narrative theory. Here, then, is the catalog description, with two discussion meetings per week and a separate screening time set aside between them:

> Under the general heading of narrative structure in prose and film, this term's course will focus on the two distinct media in their deployment of "uncanny" form and content. What special technical powers of the cinematic medium make film particularly good at maximizing devices and themes developed earlier in fantastic prose narrative? How are we made aware of the film medium's own "spooky" powers, as compared with the hallucinatory evocations of literary writing? How do narrative framings and secondary transmissions tend to enhance even while distancing the effects of their core narratives? These are the kinds of questions we will pursue from week to week, braced by theoretical readings and discussion. In both our screenings and our fiction reading, we will move between "genre fiction" (avowed tales and films of gothic horror, fantasy, or science fiction) and the more muted forms of these motifs in melodrama, psychological thrillers, avant-garde cinema, etc. ("English 172")

Again, there was no wholesale comparison of Mary Shelley's *Frankenstein* and James Whale's film version, just a clip from the frame tale of the 1935 Whale sequel, *Bride of Frankenstein*, with Mary Shelley, Byron, and Percy Shelley in discussion over her feverish inventive imagination, a prologue brought into comparison with the prefatory apparatus of the novel. Rather than book versus movie deliberations, then, the course began with a reading of the epistolary bracket of *Frankenstein* and the harrowing episodes it gives itself over to. Our conversation about the novel was usually paced out over the first three weeks alongside such other framed narratives as Robert Wiene's *The Cabinet of Doctor Caligari* (1920), Buster Keaton's

Sherlock Jr. (1924), and Max Ophüls's *Letter from an Unknown Woman* (1948). This unit was typically followed by another venture in literary framing in a purer form of the fantastic, Henry James's *The Turn of the Screw*, with its plot of sexual obsession and repetition compulsion getting aligned with similar thematic stress in *Vertigo* (1958) and the anthology film *Dead of Night* from 1945. Robert Louis Stevenson's *Dr. Jekyll and Mr. Hyde* and Oscar Wilde's *The Picture of Dorian Gray* were then paired up with films involving less blatant and gothic, but still potent, motifs of the doppelgänger—as structuring principle of a recursive narrative—from Ingmar Bergman's *Persona* (1966) through Krzysztof Kieślowski's *The Double Life of Veronique* (1991).

I used some specific tactics to bolster this analytic strategy. From week to week, the second discussion session following the film screening—and often involving clips from that film or brief excerpts from other relevant titles—began with the students breaking up into smaller discussion groups of five or six members to discuss issues raised in the e-mails I required each of them to send to me the day after the weekly screening, from which I would select out the most intriguing observations (or questions) for follow-up. As sensitivity training (or limbering-up exercises) in the rigors of close analysis expected for the longer papers, these e-mails called for quoting and analyzing, in terms of both technique and theme, a single sentence from a novel or a single shot from a film. In the most recent versions of that course on the textual fantastic and its uncanny residues, this inculcated habit of close, medium-specific apprehension met its ultimate test case in a final week's comparison between the spectral return of the political repressed in Conrad's *Heart of Darkness* and a later variant of this pattern in Michael Haneke's 2005 masterwork *Caché*.

It was students' spirited reaction to the Haneke film and the way it tapped directly into their generation's visual literacy—and their willingness to fend off frustration and suspend disbelief in regard to its enigmatic ending—that encouraged me to revamp the cross-disciplinary emphasis of the course to concentrate, within a broader survey of this theme, on a timely contemporary issue: the new global culture of surveillance. This topic, I hoped, would allow some serious attention to the spate of Middle Eastern war films (see Stewart) as well as comparison with certain post-9/11 Homeland Security fables like *Eagle Eye* (2008) or *State of Play* (2009).

Under the adjusted thematic umbrella (and catalog subtitle) Mediation and Surveillance, the course still attends primarily to the narrative armatures that underlie such plots, with consideration of competing narratological accounts (from Bordwell to Peter Brooks) introduced mostly in minilectures rather than through extensive secondary reading. I emphasize instead reading the films and novels as micromanaged textual systems. The course catalog summarizes as follows:

> This is an interdisciplinary course in both the formal and the thematic dimension of mediation and surveillance in certain exemplary film and literary texts, the weekly screenings anchored by a classic dystopian novel of the last century, George Orwell's *1984*, a high-tech espionage novel of the post-9/11 era, John le Carré's *A Most Wanted Man*, and, in between, that Victorian classic of textual counter-surveillance, Bram Stoker's *Dracula*. ("English 175")

Beginning with the surveillance and manhunt films of Fritz Lang from the 1920s and early 1930s, including *M* and *The Testament of Dr. Mabuse*, and their 1960 Cold War update in *The 1000 Eyes of Dr. Mabuse*, we move forward within the same tradition to the unmanned eyes of Middle Eastern surveillance satellites in Ridley Scott's *Body of Lies* (2008) and the early minutes of point-of-view reconnaissance through the digital eye of the robot drone that opens *The Hurt Locker* (2009). Along a different but related trajectory, we return to various treatments of mediated spying and its links to voyeurism in films from Alfred Hitchcock's 1954 *Rear Window* and Michael Powell's 1960 *Peeping Tom* (where the syndrome is called out as "scoptophilia") to the "precog" clairvoyance of Steven Spielberg's *Minority Report* (2002) and on to the virtual reconstruction of the past through surveillance, its erotic lure included, in Tony Scott's *Deja Vu* (2006). In another unit we track aural surveillance from Francis Ford Coppola's 1974 *The Conversation* on through Brian De Palma's audio reworking, in 1981's *Blow Out*, of the evidentiary photographic theme from Michelangelo Antonioni's 1966 *Blow-Up* down to Florian Henckel von Donnersmarck's 2006 *The Lives of Others.*

I indicate below in abbreviated form some of the final paper topics, pursuant to this diverse but overlapping body of thematic material, that have emerged from our class conversations, with an expectation in each case that the essay writer do close technical analysis (of editing, shot patterns, camera angles, lighting, sound, and so on) or the prose equivalent (diction, syntax, metaphor, simile) and put into boldface at least three sentences of commentary at different points in the analysis at which such observed details are linked directly and explicitly to theme and its ironies—where the work of interpretation has thus detected the conversion, under local narrative pressure, of form into content. In anticipation of this requirement, I stress repeatedly that, just as one cannot write effectively on a novel without going back to highlighted paragraphs for rereading and citation, so one cannot write on a film without looking at key scenes again in the Media Reserve Room and "quoting" their most arresting details. Beyond a general question on "closure" as distinct from "end" in the finalizing of plot vectors, these are among the other areas of consideration that have suggested themselves:

Free Indirect Discourse under Conditions of Covert Operations

For those wishing to hone their skills of close verbal analysis, compare the ways in which free indirect discourse (FID) is used in *1984* and *A Most Wanted Man* to enter the consciousness of a character within a broader thematic of spying and coercion. How does the disclosure of private thought operate in these plots of monitored lives and state "invigilation" (the word for the German mode of surveillance in Le Carré). Choose climactic episodes in which some shift in verbal/subjective register in the treatment of FID or its variant as internal monologue is keyed to an irony of the plot.

Crossing the Line: Objectivity vs. Intervention

Compare the intersubjective nature of optical or aural surveillance in the collapsed distinction between spy and spied upon—or, in other words, the breached border between the subject and the object of such secret scrutiny. In *Rear Window*, *The Conversation*, *The Final Cut*, *Minority Report*, *A Most Wanted Man*, or *Body of Lies*, what ironies gather round the moment when the policing or transcribing agent tries to enter or alter the world he spies upon? How might this same set of ironic reversals apply to the explicitly erotic camcorder voyeurism in *American Beauty* or *Benny's Video*?

Machines of Detection

Explore technologies of information gathering and surveillance from the telegram and dictograph cylinders of *Dracula* through the satellite feeds and simultaneous translation monitors of *A Most Wanted Man*, including tape recorders, biochips, and precog virtuality. In films we've screened since *The Lives of Others*, including *The Final Cut*, *Minority Report*, and *Deja Vu*, how has the nature of digital imaging, satellite targeting, and electronic virtuality become central in the narratives, whether as part of a state bureaucracy or a commercializing of surveillance? Or explore how broadcast and espionage, mass media and covert record, coincide in the "telescreens" of *1984*.

Films within Films

From the propaganda cinema in *1984* through trumped-up sexual assault footage in *Seconds* and on to the laser holograms of the dead son in *Minority Report* or the invasive VHS tapes of *Caché*, how does the canonical movie-within-the-movie format (or its high-tech upgrade) comment on the mediation of the film we are watching, including perhaps the "zoe chip" of *The Final Cut* or the "surveillance window" of *Deja Vu*?

Plot/Complot/Counterplot

Compare the deceits of international espionage in the sting operation of A *Most Wanted Man* and the false terrorist plot in *Body of Lies*. How do these devices function as metanarratives (fictions within the fiction)?

Parallel Montage

How is intercutting between simultaneous streams of action used as a function of omniscience or surveillance in a novel like *A Most Wanted Man* or in such screen narratives as *The Conversation*, *Minority Report*, *Deja Vu*, *Syriana*, or *Body of Lies*?

Ghost Agency

An off-campus option for those who want to carry the course's themes right down to the minute and out into the multiplex: Just in time for a paper, *The Ghost Writer*, a Hitchcockian thriller by Roman Polanski, has opened locally, a Le Carré–style "intelligence agency" mystery turning on covert operations, surveillance, encryption, double agents, and delivering the mandatory trick ending (twice over, in fact). Compare the "extreme rendition" accusations against the British prime minister in this new film with the counterterrorist themes of *A Most Wanted Man*, closing in on a crucial episode or two for details. But if you write on this, be prepared to sit through the commercial screening twice and take notes, since it won't be available on DVD.

From about twice this many possible topics, the students are expected to choose one for their final five-to-seven-page essay (after a shorter four-to-five-page paper earlier in the term). And on the take-home final exam, they are invited to choose from among the same list of topics for briefer answers to several of the questions not taken up in their full papers. As it happened, I had committed to writing this essay just a week before the exam answers for that semester's course were due, and it occurred to me to dig in my heels early on for my own writing (rather than grading) obligation. Instead of letting the good and bad analyses wash over me in alternating waves of elation and chagrin, gratification and resignation—business as usual—I decided to log in the interesting responses for possible illustration here. In the language of many an administrator lately, I would thus render up, albeit spottily, an output assessment of the course. Suffice it to say that I read the exams with redoubled interest, and I give here two examples each from closely observed comments on narrative devices in literature and in film that succeeded especially well in offering formal leverage on broad arguments.

In the pair of examples on prose fiction, the first is hypernuanced, the second hyperintuitive, yet each is linked effectively to the overarching logic of remediation we had been discussing. As with the pair of film examples, I reproduce these responses, for economy's sake, in a mix of paraphrase, compression, and actual quotation. Moving beyond more obvious instances in *1984*, one student picked up on the idea of free indirect discourse as we had sampled it in class, its deployment so deft and unnerving in its invasion of mental privacy that narrative omniscience and Big Brotherhood come to seem like two sides of the same coin. But his treatment of this stylistic function was something new and unexpected, resulting from a high-magnification lens trained on individual sentences. He actually brought the inferences of such an oblique discursive register to bear on a scene of film screening within the novel—and not the famous propaganda montage so well translated to a parody of Soviet realism in the precredit sequence to the Michael Radford film version from the year 1984 (from which we had seen a clip). The student's commentary zeroed in, rather, on an actual theatrical war film screened in the novel, as reported by italics in the hero's first illicit and breathless diary entry and submitted to his own shot analysis. As the show-stopping, crowd-pleasing carnage is described in jolting syntactic fractures and quick-cut iterations, the reader is, through the hero's removed and ironic witness, folded into the collective mind of the hyped-up, war-addicted audience, seeing through their eyes the cinematic fireworks—as these are filtered in turn through an aerial optics of surveillance and targeting familiar from films screened in our course and thus tightening the link between war and cinema advanced by such theorists as Paul Virilio and Friedrich Kittler.

Here is how the scene offers itself for analysis: "*Last night to the flicks. All war films. Audience much amused by shot of a great huge fat man . . . you saw him through the helicopters gunsights, then he was full of holes and the sea around him turned pink*" (Orwell 8). Sighting through gunsights is one of the most frequently motivated point-of-view shots in our semester's collective backlog of surveillance narratives, exactly what Virilio means in his subtitle by the safe (but often incriminating) remove of cinema's "logistics of perception" at the intersection between militarism and mimesis. And, with the helicopter still aloft, the response itself takes off in the diarist-hero's unpunctuated venting:

> *Then the helicopter planted a 20 kilo bomb in among them terrific flash and the boat went all to matchwood. Then there was a wonderful shot of a childs arm going up up up right up into the air a helicopter with a camera in its nose must have followed it up and there was a lot of applause from the party seats.* (Orwell 9)

As the student saw at once, narrative film is assimilated to a "propaganda mentality" in the vicinity of the hate broadcasts, with callous vicarious thrills replacing empathy. Further, what is being captured in a phrase like "going up up up right up" is the visceral response of the mass—as mob—audience, so that "terrific" can be mindlessly celebratory, like "wonderful" later, as well as a more neutral modifier for the extremity of the "flash." And when "the boat went all to matchwood," this image is more than a metaphor for splintering, invoking as well the miniaturizing special effects of such scenes when staged for fictional film, "the typical wooden model blasted to smithereens."

Another response to prose fiction as prose, in an exam answer on closural moments by the same student, quoted the last sentence of Le Carré's *A Most Wanted Man*. In Hamburg, a leftist female lawyer and a much older conservative banker smitten with her (over the course of their attempted rescue of an innocent Arab youth from extradition as a terrorist suspect) are left desolate in the aftermath of a brutal American intervention from behind the scenes of the relatively benign German secret service (and, in terms of audiovisual surveillance technology, from over their shoulders as well, including hidden directional microphones, fish-eye lenses, and satellite feeds). As had been pointed out in class discussion, the novel's last paragraph opens in allusion to the modus vivendi for the American involvement in the Arab world, displaced here to the stench of Western commerce near the Hamburg docks: "A crisp night wind was whisking off the lake, bringing a smell of oil from the harbor" (322). What took me by surprise was this student's intuitive finding in the last sentence of that same last paragraph, innocuous enough at first glance—even in its prevented sentimentality between banker and lawyer, representatives of a cultural establishment rendered powerless by covert operations. The prose trails off this way: "Brue put his arm round her shoulders where he had always wanted to put it, but he doubted whether she knew it was there" (322). This fizzled epistemology of desire had for the student essay a further and finer irony, however. It distills "the whole nature of her manipulation throughout the book by forces outside her awareness,"[1] as if to remind us that for chapters on end she has not known what was going on behind her back. In this last moment not just the essence of mutual uncertainty in espionage fiction but the heroine's particular obliviousness is "symbolized by the final phrase," so that nonrecognition has become a summarizing gesture in a novel characterized by so bitter a geopolitical trick ending and its withering double cross (extreme rendition for the hero at the hands of the CIA, rather than legalized immigrant status granted by the Germans).

Closure is indeed a topic that frequently brings out the best in student analysis, in part because it is the textual site where form and content cannot be missed to coincide at their vanishing point. Or to put it in the terms of Bordwell's definition, here is where the last move of the *syuzhet* has done its structuring work simultaneously with the viewer's cogeneration of the fabula, leaving us nothing to respond to but their productive convergence—as well as the frequent stylistic flourish that has secured it. In another essay on the issue of closure (in ironic resonance, again, with the theme of surveillance), which incorporated notions of diegetic (in-scene) versus nondiegetic sound in their special complication here, an adventurous student examined how, in *The Lives of Others*, a Stasi secret agent eavesdropping on a dissident theater artist in the former East Berlin meets his symbolic comeuppance by poetic justice and "dramatic irony." For long stretches at a time the agent is seen listening through secret attic earphones to the sounds of everything from conversation or piano playing to lovemaking—sounds transposed to the ambient space of the spy's hideout. Noting this eavesdropping as one filmic variant of free indirect discourse, whereby we seem to inhabit that other space reframed as if it were the spy's own, the student saw plot taking its revenge in the long run. The East German agent ends up being demoted for his sympathetic intervention in the artist's secret and anonymous publication in the West.

He is punished by a routine basement job steaming open and resealing correspondence among a row of similar clerical lackeys, "listening only to the public radio that all can hear," as the student observed, rather than being any longer "wired into privileged information"—even as this broadcast outlet interrupts their labors, once and for all, by announcing the fall of the Berlin Wall.

Mediation and surveillance converge in another example of ironic closure from the same student, who, unprompted by anything we had considered in class (beyond some general remarks on suture theory and our frequent attention to the shot/countershot pattern), probes cinema's unique means for the construction of subjectivity. The film discussed was the mutliplot Middle Eastern political thriller *Syriana* (dir. Stephen Gaghan [2005]). Briefly tracking its story lines across alternating geopolitical locales, the exam paper was drawn finally to the frantic parallel montage of the penultimate episode, where a rogue CIA agent (George Clooney) rushes to rescue a Saudi prince from an assassination attempt—all the while monitored by the CIA drone satellite poised to take him out on command. When the two men converge at the cross-hairs of this aerial missile grid, and thus at the final double cross of the plot, the cut to a "shot/reverse shot pattern at ground zero" (fig. 1, fig. 2)—a technique that usually "makes for interpersonal space in film" (as the student also put it)—is interrupted by a flashback, like a retroactive déjà vu, in which the student notes further that we see, as if through the eyes of each character simultaneously, an inset reprise of their met glances earlier in an elevator where the CIA agent was mistaken by the prince as a Canadian envoy. "The Canadian?" he now asks when they are face to face again in the desert. Worse, an American—and this exchange occurs just a split second before the moment of flaming impact and obliteration.

In my experience, student observation—student thinking—seldom gets any better than this:

> Their looming death becomes all the more tragic because not only are we implicitly aware of their bodies from the satellite POV, but also of their subjectivity from the flashback. Thus before the narrative chooses to kill the character, it fully constructs "the person" as a body and mind within the cinematic apparatus and the viewer's internalization of the narrative, a narrative which can persist now only by shifting at this moment to an external point of view, [first from] a car just beyond the kill zone (fig. 3) [and then once again] from the omniscience of the satellite scan (fig. 4) [just before annihilation].

Figure 1. Warning shot

Figure 2. (Mis)recognition

Figure 3. Last sighting

Figure 4. Final shooting

Let me seek closure for my remarks on this emblematic note. The kind of writing such a course is designed to elicit has, ideally, just this mix of intense closeup and aerial purview, its finely calibrated details locked down within the bigger thematic picture.

Note

1. All student work is quoted with permission.

Works Cited

Bordwell, David. *Narration and the Fiction Film.* Madison: U of Wisconsin P, 1985. Print.

Brooks, Peter. *Reading for the Plot: Design and Intention in Narrative.* New York: Knopf, 1984. Print.

"English 172: Narrative and the Cinema: Modes of Fantasy in Fiction and Film." Fall 2010. *ISIS: The University of Iowa Courses.* ISIS, n.d. Web. 30 Aug. 2011.

"English 175: Topics in Film and Literature: Mediation and Surveillance." Spring 2010. *ISIS: The University of Iowa Courses.* ISIS, n.d. Web. 30 Aug. 2011.

Kittler, Friedrich. *Optical Media.* 2002. Trans. Anthony Enns. London: Polity, 2010. Print.

Le Carré, John. *A Most Wanted Man.* New York: Scribner, 2008. Print.

Orwell, George. *1984.* 1949. New York: New Amer. Lib., 1977. Print.

Stewart, Garrett. "Digital Fatigue: Imaging War in Current American Film." *Film Quarterly* 62.4 (2009): 45–55. Print.

Syriana. Dir. Stephen Gaghan. Warner Bros., 2005. Warner Home Video, 2006. DVD.

Todorov, Tzvetan. *The Fantastic: A Structural Approach to a Literary Genre.* 1970. Ithaca: Cornell UP, 1975. Print.

Virilio, Paul. *War and Cinema: The Logistics of Perception.* 1984. Trans. Patrick Camiller. London: Verso, 1989. Print.

Nataša Ďurovičová

Teaching Cinema across Languages

Overview of Issues

Rare are the undergraduate film studies classes in the United States in which the first screening of a subtitled film, likely preceded by the instructor's justificatory comment, does not bring up a groan from the auditorium. Opting for a film with a dubbed track might meet less initial resistance but would drastically reduce the repertoire of films or DVDs available to the instructor (at least, again, in the United States). Like medicine, film in translation may be good for you, anglophone film students know, but it requires some effort to take in.

But what if the affect were reversed and the process of translation, instead of being viewed as a regrettable if unavoidable disturbance, could be tackled as an integral element of the film studies curriculum? The premise of this essay is that studying the general history of cinema is fundamentally incomplete without attending to the matter of films' global circulation, a process inextricably involved with translation and spanning the silent and the sound eras. The topic can be introduced either in a stand-alone class or as a reiterated perspective inflecting a variety of other courses (on film theory or world film history, on genres such as action films or musicals, as well as any course focused on a national cinema). In either case, however, its relevance rests on some general theoretical assumptions:

1. Attending to a film's language under the sign of translation *redirects the standard historiographical paradigm from cinema as a national project toward cinema as transnational practice* (see Ďurovičová, "Vector"). The assumption that a film can circulate beyond national borders has been a factor in all phases of production, from cinema's very first years. Thus in the silent period the work of title translation complemented other forms of adaptation (most often through editing) in the postproduction for foreign-release prints. And it became clear in the earliest years of the sound era that a regional or an acoustically complex sound track would make a film more difficult to export than the single-channel, carefully synchronized and redundant dialogue and sound effects, combined with an illustrative music track now known as the classical model.[1] More generally, dramas of translation and its failure—that is, dramas of geopolitical miscommunication—have recently become common enough through polylingual films like *Babel* or *The Cuckoo* or *Letters from Iwo Jima* to suggest the emergence of a distinct transnational subgenre (see Wahl).

2. In a medium with a precarious relation to "the original," *focus on translation draws attention to the general matter of textual variants and cinematic textuality along philological lines.* Films have always been modified to adapt to geographically, politically, historically, and technologically changing environments, through reediting, retitling, colorization, and other processes. In this sense the work of translation is comparable to the work of censorship, in that both factor cinema's fundamentally heteroglossic character, with its range of coexistent and competing (discursive) voices (see Stam and Shohat). Similarly, the inevitable traces inflicted by dubbing or subtitling present a challenge to critical approaches resting on assumptions of textual unity, such as authorship, or of the normative status of the classical style. For while the graphemic or acoustic supplement of subtitling or dubbing is meant to be considered functionally equivalent and thus invisible with respect to the original, its blatant difference cannot be denied and obviously influences a film's reception (see Ďurovičová, "Local Ghosts"). Extending this logic of difference, as relayed by recent translation theory, Mark Nornes has made a forceful argument "for an abusive subtitling" (155), that is, for an attitude toward subtitling that would admit and even stress as supplementary translation by formal devices of estrangement (see esp. ch. 5).

3. If language is what ties texts to their geopolitical origin, *translation is the work of loosening these ties to the point of rendering them arbitrary: only then can globalization* (in its general sense of extreme space compression) *proceed*. As cinema adapts to its contract with digital remediation (presently in the form of the DVD and direct downloads), the traditional processes of dialogue translating are being upgraded to a more thoroughgoing process of *localization* in which not only language but also other key markers of provenance (such as code and all other metadata making the DVD playable in a given region) must be rewritten for the local environment (see Cronin, *Translation and Globalization*).

Depending on the course, time limits, and the institution's resources, the unit on translation and cinema could be organized in two distinct directions. It could study the basic ground rules and practices involved with a film's crossing (or failing to cross) linguistic barriers (e.g., any national film history course). Alternatively, it could be a gateway to a broader discussion in which translation is only one, variable element in the modular system of filmmaking and thus points to the mutable life of film as print, circulating across space and time in different versions, including its current, digitally remediated format (e.g., courses on narrative theory as well as any history-driven courses, including documentary and experimental cinema).

In addition, the knowledge of a foreign language, though a student would benefit from it, is not a prerequisite for either understanding the problematic or doing serious work on this topic. A comparison of two versions of a film—an original and a translated version—yields an obvious difference in the basic viewing experience, which can be described semiotically (on the level of the signifier—extra graphemes, sounds, asynchronicity) or phenomenologically (different perceptual experiences of immediacy, of reading versus seeing, etc.).

The Practices of Translation

Disciplinary Boundaries

Over the last decade film studies has had an energetic, if latent, partner in translation studies proper (which is in turn organically interconnected with language fields, as well as with work in general linguistics and semiotics—bringing film studies back to the discipline's roots in a side-by-side study of film and language). And from the early 1990s on, roughly coinciding with the surging consciousness of globalization that the World Wide Web brought about, a growing wing of translation studies has been devoted to the subfield of audiovisual translation (generally studying film and television; see Gambier and Gottlieb). While translation certainly does not equal foreign language acquisition, it is inevitably a component in the process of learning a language. Literature on audiovisual translation thus commonly tackles the disciplinary verso, as it were, of the kinds of questions foreign language teachers may be asking themselves as they decide whether or how to use a film in their classes: How close or faithful are the subtitles to the foreign language dialogue? Which aspects of speech do they highlight, and which do they suppress? What is the perceptual loss and gain of a spectator listening, watching, and reading simultaneously and comparatively?

To demonstrate for students what is at issue in these processes, teachers can present a comparison of clips from "home language" films in which the baseline of English is dramatized in confrontation with the varied uses of "foreign speech." Taking for instance recent Hollywood productions such as *Lost in Translation*, *Spanglish*, *Hidalgo*, or *Letters from Iwo Jima*, a class discussion about what gets translated and how is an easy warm-up exercise, letting students discover and discuss scenes when non-English dialogue offers simply acoustic mise-en-scène (i.e., when it remains, in effect, noise). This exercise gives them an immediate opportunity to think about the linguistic investment, the semantic stakes, the politics, and the perils—even the narrative mysteries—of translation without any knowledge of a second language. The discussion can instead lead to questions about how these films would be adapted for distribution (theatrical, digital) in the corresponding "symmetrical" linguistic region—in the cases cited, Japanese and Spanish.[2]

Studying Translation Procedures

Comparing multiple-language versions. The foreign language versions of films produced mainly from the transition-to-sound period through the 1930s (i.e., between the 1929 crash and the start of World War II) demonstrate the staggering amount of linguistic and cultural reinterpretation deemed necessary for successful international distribution and exhibition once sync sound came in. They also instructively highlight the genealogy of sound norms, some of which remain central to our understanding of the representation of the body.[3]

Many DVDs now collate such versions into what might be called an original edition. Some examples include the German- and the English-language release of UFA's 1930 *Der blaue Engel / The Blue Angel*, MGM's 1930/31 German- and English-language *Anna Christie*, a collated English and Spanish version of Stan Laurel and Oliver Hardy features, and G. W. Pabst's adaptation of Bertolt Brecht's *Three Penny Opera* as *Dreigroschenoper* as well as *Opéra de quat'sous*. Playing both versions in their entirety (with the foreign language version's English subtitles on, when necessary) and then running two selected corresponding scenes simultaneously on side-by-side monitors (the foreign language version with the subtitles now off and the volume up a bit, the better to register differences and nuances of voice) is an approach that never fails to generate a good class discussion. Such straightforward comparison may then open up to a discussion of possible cultural connotations and formal distinctions latently sorting under the rubric "national cinema features": How to make sense of a slightly faster editing pace in the French as opposed to the German version of the Pabst film? How to interpret—or whether to interpret—the difference in what Garbo is wearing in the German version and the American version of *Anna Christie*?

Polyglot films and subtitles. Running deliberately counter to the paradigm of a national cinema is a world cinema current that seeks to embody the cinematic institution's inherent cosmopolitanism. In this distinct current, films are polyglot, geopolitically decentered, speaking in more than one language, and using this tension as both a form of expression and of substance: the clashes of the various languages and the characters' mutual comprehensibility, or lack thereof, are here essential to the plot.

Historically this practice was an exception. The 1931 bilingual *Kameradschaft* stands as a thematic and political touchstone of the left-wing internationalist policies virtually demanding such use of film language; the famous four-language, cross-talking projection room scene in Jean-Luc Godard's 1964 *Le mépris* was clearly intended as a parable for the total schism modernism brought to cinema. But today, as themes of migration, exile, and diaspora become pervasive in movies (partly reflecting the cultural and economic realities of new transnational state formations such as the European Union) and as blockbusters look to maximize global revenue by courting a transnational rather than a national market as their baseline (e.g., Warner's "poly-Asian" *Memoirs of a Geisha*), the clash of languages is becoming a recurrent trope.[4] Three excellent recent examples among many are *The Cuckoo*, from Russia (dir. Aleksandr Rogozhkin [2002]); *Le grand voyage* (dir. Ismaël Ferrouki [2004]), from France; and *Divine Intervention* (dir. Elie Suleiman [2002]), from France, Morocco, Germany, and Palestine, each built around the basic premise of people dependent on one another without being able to speak one another's language. This discursive structure renders subtitles, of course, as moot as they are indispensible, for their work is precisely to level and so effectively to undo the gap in comprehension.

Dubbing. It is only by teaching dubbing as a topic (rather than lapsing back onto the commonplace that it is a painful but inevitable semiobstruction of the original dialogue) that we can directly address the peculiar and potent asymmetry known as the American exception and its profound consequences.

As in most matters of film sound, the ground rules of the global translation were put into place during the transition-to-sound years (1927–31). Though the cost of subtitles was generally only about a tenth of that of a dubbed version, the insertion of a text over the image was tainted by its link to the just outdated silents; even more importantly, distributors deemed that dialogue as mediated by writing presented an absolute obstacle to reaching the often incompletely literate world audience. Only countries at once too small to recoup the cost of dubbing and with a very high level of literacy were thought to be suitable for subtitles: the first instances were Scandinavia and the Netherlands (France was next, giving in to pressure by a mix of domestic and foreign distributors by only allowing the so-called *versions originales* with subtitles in a dozen or so *art et essai* cinemas nationwide).

Whether that decision was driven by the audiences or by the distributors' *fiat* remains open to debate. In effect, however, dubbing became the principal mediating channel for the mass distribution of imported films in most of the world's big markets (e.g., Italy, Germany, Japan, France, China, USSR/Russia, India); in the United States, meanwhile, this translation strategy has been accepted as aesthetically off-limits by the critics as well as the trade press. Whatever the formal merit of this stance, it has since the 1930s performed the job of a stylistic fig leaf for the monopoly grip of Hollywood's vertically integrated industry on US theater screens. With the dubbing-equals-bad axiom as a foundation,[5] imported films have almost always been practically excluded from the US mass market. In turn, however, the material elements of the imports (plot, characters, music) were often quite well received in the United States in the form of (nontranslated) "originals" known as remakes: examples range from virtual shot-by-shot replications such as the Swedish *Intermezzo* (1936) and the US *Intermezzo: A Love Story* (1939), the French *Pépé le Moko* (1937) and the US *Algiers* (1938), and the French *À bout de souffle* (1960) and the US *Breathless* (1983) to looser calques like the Japanese *Ringu* (1998) and the US *The Ring* (2002). Meanwhile, the minoritizing effect of subtitles—the literal mark of difference in US imports—only confirms the central and fixed bias in favor of the American cultural product as the norm (see Mowitt).

Discussion of the dubbing difference can be started off with the basic estrangement exercise of showing a DVD edition of a classical Hollywood film in a dubbed version (accompanied by English subtitles if needed). John Ford's *How Green Was My Valley* (1941), screened with Spanish-language dialogue, for instance, at once invites a comparison of the acoustic remixing of the two versions, prompts a discussion of the corporeal aura a particular voice and a given language perform for the human figure and for a fictional character, and can also open up on a comparison of (the English) subtitles as compared with the original dialogue track. In other words, the questions to the students become: What is it the audiences in dubbing countries have been watching and listening to for these past eight decades if not the original sound track of imported films? Does it matter? And if not, why is it so impossible for US audiences to tolerate dubbed films?

Alternatively, most Italian films, whose unique sound aesthetic is characterized by a sound track generated entirely in postproduction, are fundamentally amenable to and compatible with dubbing. Replaying the same scene of, say, *Amarcord* (1973) with its original sound track and its English dubbing makes apparent how relatively similar they are in their equidistant reverb and thus postsynced quality. It is this detachable sound track that made possible the wild hybridity—and thereby exportability—of spaghetti westerns, a strategy sharing some features with Bollywood's heightened stylization through postproduction sound.

Remediation: Film Translation in Digital Environments

Finally, translation opens up yet another path of inquiry inside film studies, one that stretches beyond the concerns of language narrowly defined. For language also functions as a way to track the vagaries and politics of remediation in the service of making a film go global. What changes occur, in other words, when the images and sounds previously stored on acetate and on reels have been replaced—remediated—by digitized discs with their plethora of new functions, huge capacities of extra storage, and near infinite reproducibility?[6]

A first ready way of investigating these mutations is to chart the addition of languages as they follow or deviate from the region codes regulating the global release patterns of DVDs: What are the pathways and the language supplements of an American film when a distributor releases it on a region 2 DVD, for instance, given that this region is made up of at least a dozen nation-states?[7] Does every country get its own language? And when a film is released on DVD accompanied by one or several translation tracks, how deep does its translation scheme reach—that is, does it include director comments or bonus materials? How would the reception of, say, a Brazilian film in the United States be affected if all the extra materials remain in Portuguese? Inversely, what are the decisions involved in translating or not translating the complex supplement of materials on the "special edition" Hollywood blockbusters released in several dozens of world markets on the same day? These questions aim less at translation in the sense of a process for achieving comprehension than at translation as a caliper of sorts, a way of gauging the degree of a film's localization—or, measuring just how noticeable the cultural distance between a film's provenance and its reception remains. A film (like other kinds of software such as video games) is said to be fully localized when the viewer-consumer does not perceive the text as in any sense foreign, alien, or marked by translation.

But the latent global distribution network that the World Wide Web provides for cinema in its digitized version also provides an infrastructure that is distinct and separate from the physical DVD. Though a film may not have been translated for the commercial exhibition circuit, it can nonetheless be possible to find downloadable, often "homemade" full-length translations in the form of peer-to-peer file sharing sites, offering a kind of paralegal linguistic companion for the film—a protocol that in turn may allow a multitude of local receptions much more comprehensive than any multiplex ever would. Similarly, the "fan-subbing" (subtitling done by fans) flourishing in conjunction with Japanese anime has spawned technologies and software that make it possible for anyone to subtitle an anime (clip) and post it on *YouTube*. As the various automated translation sites proliferate, ranging from generic cut-and-paste windows inside search engines like *Google* and *Yahoo* to somewhat more specialized sites like *Animelab*, so do the prospects grow of "dragging" almost any film across any linguistic boundary. Locating and studying this culture of film appropriation through a linguistic tool may be among the more popular class assignments.

The unique hieroglyphic mix of image, sound, and word that characterizes cinema has in effect been a stealth translator machine for many decades in the service of an easy and pervasive anglophony. A thought experiment in which one imagines that the bulk of the world's cinema for the last eighty years has been in, say, Chinese, instantly illuminates the far-reaching and profound consequences of this moving hieroglyph's effect and the many reasons for studying it.

Notes

1. For a meticulous study of silent-to-sound transition with emphasis on translation, see Rossholm.

2. The pervasive thematization of translation in recent cinema is the major concern of Michel Cronin in *Translation Goes to the Movies*.

3. See three special issues of the journal *Cinema and Cie*, 4 (2004), 6 (2005), and 7 (2005), on this topic.

4. Mark Betz proposes subtitled polyligualіty as a central feature of "European art cinema." See also Rossholm.

5. The traditional audience opinion is supposedly that noticing lip-synch destroys the illusion of reality, while the basic cinephile argument is that by replacing the performer's voice, dubbing makes it impossible to experience the film as it would be by the domestic spectator.

6. Lev Manovich offers one gloss of remediation: "If we want to describe what new media does to old media with a single term, 'mapping' is a good candidate. Software allows us to remap old media objects into new structures—turning media into 'meta-media.' . . . In contrast to media, meta-media acquires three new properties. First, with software, data can be translated into another domain—time into 2D space, 2D image into 3D space, sound into 2D image, and so on. . . . Second, media objects can be manipulated using GUI (graphical user interface) techniques such as: move, transform, zoom, multiple views, filter, summarize. . . . And third, media objects can now be 'processed' using standard techniques of computerized data processing; search, sort, replace, etc. media objects can now be 'processed.' "

7. See "DVD Region Code." For a discussion of this aspect of digitalization see Kayahara.

Works Cited

À bout de souffle. Dir. Jean-Luc Godard. Beauregard/SNC, 1960. Film.

Algiers. Dir. John Cromwell. MGM, 1938. Film.

Amarcord. Dir. Federico Fellini. PIC Distribuzione, 1973. Film.

Anna Christie. Dir. Jacques Feyder. MGM, 1930. Warner Home Video, 2005 DVD.

Babel. Dir. Alejander Gonzalez Iñárritu. Paramount, 2006. Film.

Betz, Mark. *Beyond the Subtitle: Remapping European Art Cinema*. Minneapolis: U of Minnesota P, 2009. Print.

Der blaue Engel / The Blue Angel. Dir. Josef von Sternberg. UFA, 1930. Kino on Video, 2001. DVD.

Breathless. Dir. Jim McBride. Paramount, 1983. Film.
Cronin, Michael. *Translation and Globalization*. New York: Routledge, 2005. Print.
———. *Translation Goes to the Movies*. New York: Routledge, 2008. Print.
The Cuckoo. Dir. Aleksandr Rogozhkin. Kinokompania STV, 2002. Film.
Divine Intervention. Dir. Elie Suleiman. Pyramide, 2002. Film.
Dreigroschenoper / Opéra de quat'sous. Dir. G. W. Pabst. Nero Films, 1931. Criterion Collection, 2007. DVD.
Ďurovičová, Nataša. "Local Ghosts: Dubbing Bodies in Early Sound Cinema." *Il film e i suoi multipli / Film and Its Multiples*. Ed. Anna Antonini. Udine: Forum, 2003. 83–98. Rpt. in *Moveast* 9 (2003): n. pag. Web. 29 Mar. 2011.
———. "Vector, Flow, Zone: Towards a History of Cinematic Translatio." *World Cinemas, Transnational Practices*. Ed. Ďurovičová and Kathleen Newman. New York: Routledge, 2009. 90–120. Print.
"DVD Region Code." *Wikipedia*. Wikimedia, 25 Mar. 2011. Web. 30 Mar. 2011.
Gambier, Yves, and Henrik Gottlieb, eds. *(Multi)Media Translation*. Amsterdam: Benjamins, 2001. Print.
Le grand voyage. Dir. Ismaël Ferrouki. Pyramide, 2004. Film.
Hidalgo. Dir. Joe Johnston. Touchstone Pictures, 2004. Film.
How Green Was My Valley. Dir. John Ford. Twentieth Century–Fox, 1941. Twentieth Century Fox Home Entertainment, 2001. DVD.
Intermezzo. Dir. Gustaf Molander. Svensk Filmindustri, 1936. Film.
Intermezzo: A Love Story. Dir. George Ratoff. United Artists, 1939. Film.
Kayahara, Matthew. "The Digital Revolution: DVD Technology and the Possibilities for Audio-visual Translation." *Journal of Specialized Translation* 3 (2005): n. pag. Web. 29 Mar. 2011.
Letters from Iwo Jima. Dir. Clint Eastwood. Warner Bros., 2006. Film.
Lost in Translation. Dir. Sofia Coppola. Universal Pictures, 2003. Film.
Manovich, Lev. "Understanding Meta-Media." *CTheoryNet*. Ed. Arthur Kroker and Marilouise Kroker. CTheory, 26 Oct. 2005. Web. 29 Mar. 2011.
Memoirs of a Geisha. Dir. Rob Marshall. Warner Bros., 2005. Film.
Le mépris. Dir. Jean-Luc Godard. Embassy, 1964. Film.
Mowitt, John. "The Hollywood Sound Tract." *Subtitles: On the Foreignness of Film*. Ed. Ian Balfour and Atom Egoyan. Cambridge: MIT P, 2005. 381–401. Print.
Nornes, Mark. *Cinema Babel: Translating Global Cinema*. Minneapolis: U of Minnesota P, 2007. Print.
Pépé le Moko. Dir. Julien Duvivier. DisCina, 1937. Film.
The Ring. Dir. Gore Verbinski. Dreamworks, 2002. Film.
Ringu. Dir. Hideo Nakata. Toho, 1998. Film.
Rossholm, Anna Sofia. *Reproducing Languages, Translating Bodies: Approaches to Speech, Translation and Cultural Identity in Early European Sound Film*. Stockholm: Almkvist, 2006. Print.
Spanglish. Dir. James L. Brooks. Columbia Pictures, 2004. Film.
Stam, Robert, and Ella Shohat. "The Cinema after Babel: Language, Difference, Power." *Screen* 26.3–4 (1985): 35–58. Print.
Wahl, Christoph. "Discovering a Genre: The Polyglot Film." *CinemaScope* 1 (2005): n. pag. Web. 5 Sept. 2011.

Adam Lowenstein

Teaching Film and Trauma

To teach filmic representations of events such as the Holocaust, Hiroshima, or the Vietnam War is to face several theoretical and practical dilemmas. On the one hand, these instances of what I refer to as historical trauma cry out for committed pedagogical engagement. How else will we uphold the promises of "never again" if our students do not learn about these horrific moments in history that predate their lifetimes? On the other hand, is there not a risk that teaching historical trauma on film may violate certain notions of respect for the overwhelming aspects of events that some label "unrepresentable"?[1]

In this essay I reflect on my attempts to implement in the classroom what I have written about elsewhere as those "allegorical moments" in cinema that transpire in relation to historical trauma. An *allegorical moment* is "a shocking collision between film, spectator, and history where registers of bodily space and historical time are disrupted, confronted, and intertwined" (Lowenstein 2). In my research, I strive to identify allegorical moments where they are not usually assumed to exist: in "low" cultural forms such as the horror film. In my teaching, I aim to provoke encounters with the allegorical moment for students, whether we are examining implicit or explicit representations of historical trauma. I stage what Miriam

Bratu Hansen calls issues of "competing representations and competing modes of representation" (85). Hansen focuses on a particular case of competition between popular and art house films about the Holocaust by turning to their critical reception among intellectuals. She describes how these critics tended to perceive Steven Spielberg's popular Hollywood film *Schindler's List* (1993) and Claude Lanzmann's art house documentary *Shoah* (1985) as "two mutually exclusive paradigms of cinematically representing or not-representing the Holocaust" (78). For Hansen, opposing the two films in this manner erases what is so potentially productive about considering them together as competing modes of representation: to "take all aspects—omissions and distortions, displacements and possibilities—of public, mass-mediated memory culture seriously" (99).

Film and Literature: Representing the Vietnam War

What, then, does it mean to teach historical trauma on film through the allegorical moment and the notion of competing representations? First of all, it means raising the issue of whether historical trauma can ever be relegated to a past that appears safely removed from our present. In the fall semester of 2001, I taught for the first time an undergraduate film studies course called Film and Literature: Representing the Vietnam War. The unit that opened the class was "Is the Vietnam War Past or Present?" To pursue this question, I distributed to the students an article from *Time* magazine covering the then recent controversy surrounding the former senator and decorated veteran Bob Kerrey (see McGeary and Tumulty). Kerrey had just admitted that he participated in a massacre of unarmed civilians during his tour of duty in Vietnam thirty-two years earlier. The opportunity to discuss such a timely article might seem to be an unusual stroke of good luck that instructors can hardly count on, but my experience with teaching historical trauma suggests that such current articles are usually not very difficult to find. Memorials, anniversaries, public debates, and of course new books and films dedicated to the events tend to make such news material fairly accessible. The sad but inevitable fact that contemporary historical events often mirror previous ones, such as today's wars in Afghanistan and Iraq echoing yesterday's Vietnam War, also provides pedagogical opportunities of this kind.

I screened in class that first day the documentary *Dear America: Letters Home from Vietnam* (dir. Bill Couturie [1987]), based on actual letters written during the war and collected in a 1985 book of the same name edited by Bernard Edelman. In the film, several famous actors read the letters, accompanied by archival and home movie footage from the era. By juxtaposing the *Time* article and the film, I hoped to highlight different ways in which it is not so easy to locate the Vietnam War solely in the past. The Kerrey article illustrates how decisions made decades ago can still reverberate in the present, particularly when those decisions were made by an individual who went on to become a major political figure. But *Dear America* stages another version of the past living in the present, one where everyday people who have not received national attention can still have voices that speak to us now. The fact that these voices in the film are performed by recognizable actors indicates that current fame remains a factor when legitimating who may speak in public, but the film's sense of a living Vietnam War diverges notably from the article's presentation.

Beginning the course with *Dear America* also allowed me to foreground the theme "Voices from Vietnam" that I would return to throughout the semester. The shock of the allegorical moment stems not only from blurring distinctions between past and present but also from addressing the film spectator in particularly confrontational ways. Is it more disturbing to hear the voice of a prowar veteran or an antiwar veteran? What if the veteran's voice is conveyed through a documentary rather than a fiction film? What if that voice is channeled through a film that refers to the war only in implicit ways, rather than explicit ones? What if that veteran is African American? or a woman? or Vietnamese? or someone devastated by the war who is not a veteran at all? I assembled the course's films and readings around such questions, reminding the students of the possibility that for every voice from Vietnam that we hear, many others are likely silenced or forgotten.

For example, pairing Ron Kovic's 1976 autobiography *Born on the Fourth of July*, a written account of his experiences as a Vietnam veteran, with Martin Scorsese's *Taxi Driver* (1976), a fiction film that features the troubled Vietnam veteran Travis Bickle (Robert De Niro), invites students to grapple with very different versions of this figure. This unit, like all the others in the course, also included an assigned critical essay geared toward opening up discussion of that week's film. In the essay I chose for this unit, Cynthia J. Fuchs argues that *Taxi Driver* "reveals the disordering effects and the disordered foundations of Vietnam, representing not the war, but its dispersion" (34). By foregrounding this sense of "dispersion," where the war occurs in America as well as in Vietnam, I asked students to search for moments where the figure of Kovic collides with that of Bickle. How does Kovic's desire to direct his anger toward political action illuminate or depart from Bickle's decision to express his anger through what he delusionally perceives to be righteous violence? And even if this anger is managed in deeply contrasting ways, is there evidence that it can reveal shades of Kovic in Bickle or Bickle in Kovic? It is this sort of recognition, where the comfort of a "good" Kovic and an "evil" Bickle falls away, that leads to the allegorical moment.

The combination of Kovic's *Born on the Fourth of July* and Scorsese's *Taxi Driver* not only fulfills the course's general rubric as Film and Literature but also highlights the goal of approaching the Vietnam War through competing modes of representation. I decided against pairing Kovic's autobiography with Oliver Stone's powerful 1989 film adaptation because of certain dangers that often arise when values of fidelity motivate discussion of literature adapted to film. Debates about whether the literary source or the film adaptation is better or worse usually rest on reductive assumptions about how a film should be faithful to its source material. Such debates rarely acknowledge fully (if at all) the status of film and literature as media so strikingly dissimilar in many of their aesthetic, technological, and cultural aspects that the whole notion of a faithful adaptation risks becoming more of a dead end than anything else. Indeed, a number of scholars have recently attempted to inject new life into the area of film adaptation studies by calling for alternatives to conventional ideas about fidelity in adaptation (see Elliott; Leitch; MacCabe, Warner, and Murray; Naremore; Stam). Ultimately, I felt that the questions I wanted students to consider when film and literature emerge as competing modes of representing the Vietnam War present themselves more challengingly in the spaces between Kovic's literary and Scorsese's filmic works, rather than those between Kovic and Stone. I opted for questions connected to how Scorsese's "nightmare" version of the veteran can speak cinematically to those dimensions of Kovic's experience, as well as the Vietnam experience more broadly, that we might miss or avoid otherwise.

Of course, all teachers know that no matter how thoughtfully and carefully they plan a course beforehand, the reality of how a class unfolds will almost always differ significantly from the teacher's original vision. One major variable that I could not have foreseen during my initial preparations for Film and Literature: Representing the Vietnam War was how the events of September 11, 2001, would alter the tenor of the course. Since 9/11 fell during the third week of the semester, the first film I taught post-9/11 happened to be *The Green Berets* (dir. John Wayne and Ray Kellogg

[1968]). Most critics dismiss this film as ridiculous, with its turgid pacing, cardboard characters, and absurd mapping of World War II film formulas onto Vietnam to occupy a staunchly prowar position. But it is also a film of considerable historical interest in that it was the rare Hollywood film produced during the war (rather than afterward) that referred explicitly to the conflict, a circumstance made possible largely through the presence of the film's star and codirector, John Wayne. As the essay I assigned that week by Michael Anderegg notes, "What is particularly unsettling about *The Green Berets*, however, is the extent to which the John Wayne persona has been reduced to a simpleminded parody of itself . . . the simplistic icon of mindless heroism" ("Hollywood" 25).

My original prediction that students would easily dissect and critique the hollow heroism of *The Green Berets* suddenly seemed quite naive in the immediate wake of 9/11, when fear and anger were running high in the national consciousness. As it turned out, our discussion of *The Green Berets* was characterized by tensions associated with 9/11 that would structure the rest of the course. Some students felt that speaking about Vietnam and 9/11 at the same time was a pointless exercise, since then we were "wrong" and now we were "right." Others welcomed the opportunity to explore Vietnam as a context for some of the volatile debates wracking the country after 9/11, especially prowar versus antiwar sentiments and questions about how an enemy is constructed ideologically by news media, literature, and film. Even though the impact of 9/11 made our discussion of *The Green Berets* and all the film and literature covered subsequently something quite unlike what I had imagined initially, the discussions often accessed the contentious qualities of the representations I had hoped to examine along the lines of the allegorical moment. But the route had changed, as had the affect of the students involved.

Cinema and Trauma

In Film and Literature: Representing the Vietnam War, I used the differences between literature and film to teach historical trauma as a matter of competing modes of representation. But this strategy is not the only one available to achieve this pedagogical goal. Another is juxtaposing more than one instance of historical trauma within a single course. In Cinema and Trauma, a graduate seminar I taught during the fall semester of 2000, I devoted the first half of the course to films concerning the Holocaust and the second half to films addressing the atomic bombings of Hiroshima and

Nagasaki. My aim was to take what I saw as the productive aspects of the theoretical debates organized around the Holocaust as an issue related to "the limits of representation" (Friedlander; see also Hirsch and Kacandes; Levi and Rothberg; Postone and Santner) and distance them from the less productive claims that the Holocaust must always stand alone in history, that it was an absolutely singular event without precedents or antecedents.

I was aware that this pedagogical move encompassed a significant amount of risk. The risk was different from the kind I encountered in Film and Literature: Representing the Vietnam War, that is, the issue of "faithful" film adaptations drawn from literary materials. In Cinema and Trauma, the danger was that by speaking about the Holocaust and Hiroshima together, the two events would end up becoming equated and losing their specificity. Even worse, this loss of specificity could lead to minimizing or banalizing both events, rather than illuminating each through the other. But my decision to move forward was influenced by the German Jewish philosopher Walter Benjamin, who reminds us that for historical materialism to honor a sense of "*Jetztzeit*," or "time filled by the presence of the now" (261), it must "seize hold of a memory as it flashes up at a moment of danger" (255). I interpret Benjamin's *Jetztzeit* as an allegorical moment, "an instant in which an image of the past sparks a flash of unexpected recognition in the present" (Lowenstein 14). As such, "the allegorical moment of *Jetztzeit* is not only disruptive, unpredictable, and open to revision, but also potentially dangerous" (14). In other words, I finally felt that the potential benefits of defamiliarizing the Holocaust and Hiroshima to achieve a sense of recognition in the present outweighed (and, in certain ways, necessitated) the risk of juxtaposing these two instances of historical trauma.

I began Cinema and Trauma by discussing the changing definitions of post-traumatic stress disorder (PTSD) in the three most recent editions of the American Psychiatric Association's *Diagnostic and Statistical Manual of Mental Disorders* (*DSM*). I accompanied this discussion with a screening of Atom Egoyan's *The Sweet Hereafter* (1997), an adaptation of the 1991 novel by Russell Banks that depicts the individual, familial, and communal reactions to trauma after a small town loses many of its children in a tragic school bus accident. By opening the course with the *DSM* and *The Sweet Hereafter*, I wanted to install some self-consciousness about the difficulties of transposing formulations of personal, psychic trauma onto national or international events of historical trauma. If we cannot diagnose and treat historical trauma at the level of the collective the same way we do with an individual afflicted with PTSD, then how do we approach cinematic representations of personal or historical trauma? How useful are clinical psychological terms or conceptual frameworks when it comes to trauma and film? In *The Sweet Hereafter*, Egoyan skillfully applies cinema's capacities to present time continuously but nonchronologically, point of view as a matter of multiple perspectives not always located with particular characters, and sound as atmospheric device as well as narrative commentary. All these cinematic strategies (among others) lend the film ways of representing trauma without necessarily serving as a clinical case study.

Reading Sigmund Freud's *Beyond the Pleasure Principle* during the second week of the course acted as a bridge between the psychological and the historical. Freud's landmark 1920 meditation on the psychological phenomena we now file under the heading of trauma was clearly influenced by World War I. The second week's screening was Alain Resnais's *Night and Fog* (*Nuit et brouillard*; 1955), a French documentary focusing on the Nazi concentration camps of World War II. *Night and Fog* could also be understood as traversing personal and historical trauma by pioneering some of the technical and thematic approaches to disjunctive memory contained in *The Sweet Hereafter*, but Resnais incorporates archival footage from the war as well. The result is a complex, demanding film in terms of both intellect and affect—its very form intimates how challenging and important it is to find means of interweaving the personal and the historical.

I returned to Resnais several weeks later, using his 1959 film *Hiroshima, mon amour* (written by Marguerite Duras) to mark the course's transition from the Holocaust to Hiroshima. This choice naturally had the benefit of encouraging students to connect the Holocaust and Hiroshima through the lens provided by Resnais's authorship. But the film also highlighted one of the course's key conceptual frames: national cinema and its discontents. *Hiroshima, mon amour* is commonly regarded as a French film, but it is actually a French-Japanese coproduction, and Japan within the film (from actors to settings) is crucial if often curiously abstracted. By following screenings in the course of Holocaust-related films from France (*Night and Fog*; *Shoah*), Germany (*Germany, Pale Mother* [*Deutschland, bleiche Mutter*]; *Heimat*), Italy (*Life Is Beautiful* [*La vita è bella*]), and the United States (*Schindler's List*), *Hiroshima, mon amour* helped foreground our previous discussions of national cinema. Part of the point of these discussions was to use the concept of national cinema so that historical trauma on film could be approached as a matter of competing representations. A French film about the Holocaust is not likely to imagine the event the same way a German film does, for example. But at the same time, one cannot assume that a French film will be any more or less "true" to the Holocaust than a German film, just as the Holocaust itself, like so many instances of historical trauma, certainly affects particular nations in particular ways without ever being solely national. In this sense, *Hiroshima, mon amour* opened a space where the Holocaust films in the course that preceded it could speak to the Hiroshima films to come, such as *Akira* (dir. Katsuhiro Otomo [1988]) and *Black Rain* (*Kuroi ame*; dir. Shohei Imamura [1989]). This space made use of the national without ever reducing historical trauma to the exclusive property of any one nation or the representation of historical trauma to any single cinematic mode (whether realism, fantasy, Hollywood, art film, documentary, or animation).

My account of teaching historical trauma on film has outlined some of the risks and rewards involved with tackling this subject in the classroom. I have suggested that the notions of the allegorical moment and competing representations, in several different pedagogical contexts, are important for managing these potential risks and rewards. No matter how daunting the challenges presented by teaching historical trauma in relation to cinema, I have always found that grappling with these films along with my students can make the traumatic past live for us now in shocking, worthwhile ways. I hope that others can find some value in my reflections as they attempt to make rewards out of the risks.

Note

1. Such questions resonate with a wide range of scholarship across contemporary media, literary, and cultural studies, often referred to under banners such as trauma studies or memory studies. See, for example, Caruth; Kaplan; Kaplan and Wang; LaCapra; Landy; Radstone and Schwarz; Rothberg.

Works Cited

Akira. Dir. Katsuhiro Otomo. Akira Committee, 1988. Film.

Anderegg, Michael. "Hollywood and Vietnam: John Wayne and Jane Fonda as Discourse." Anderegg, *Inventing* 15–32.

———, ed. *Inventing Vietnam: The War in Film and Television*. Philadelphia: Temple UP, 1991. Print.

Benjamin, Walter. "Theses on the Philosophy of History." *Illuminations*. Ed. Hannah Arendt. Trans. Harry Zohn. New York: Schocken, 1969. 253–64. Print.

Black Rain [*Kuroi ame*]. Dir. Shohei Imamura. Hayashibara Group, 1989. Film.

Born on the Fourth of July. Dir. Oliver Stone. Ixtlan, 1989. Film.

Caruth, Cathy, ed. *Trauma: Explorations in Memory*. Baltimore: Johns Hopkins UP, 1995. Print.

Dear America: Letters Home from Vietnam. Dir. Bill Couturie. HBO, 1987. Film.

Edelman, Bernard, ed. *Dear America: Letters Home from Vietnam.* New York: Norton, 1985. Print.

Elliott, Kamilla. *Rethinking the Novel/Film Debate.* Cambridge: Cambridge UP, 2003. Print.

Freud, Sigmund. *Beyond the Pleasure Principle.* 1920. Ed. and trans. James Strachey. New York: Norton, 1961. Print.

Friedlander, Saul, ed. *Probing the Limits of Representation: Nazism and the "Final Solution."* Cambridge: Harvard UP, 1992. Print.

Fuchs, Cynthia J. "'All the Animals Come Out at Night': Vietnam Meets *Noir* in *Taxi Driver.*" Anderegg, *Inventing* 33–55.

Germany, Pale Mother [*Deutschland, bleiche Mutter*]. Dir. Helma Sanders-Brahms. Helma Sanders-Brahms Filmproduktion, 1979. Film.

The Green Berets. Dir. John Wayne and Ray Kellogg. Warner Bros., 1968. Film.

Hansen, Miriam Bratu. "*Schindler's List* Is Not *Shoah*: Second Commandment, Popular Modernism, and Public Memory." *Spielberg's Holocaust: Critical Perspectives on* Schindler's List. Ed. Yosefa Loshitzky. Bloomington: Indiana UP, 1997. 77–103. Print.

Heimat. Dir. Edgar Reitz. Edgar Reitz Film, 1984. Film.

Hiroshima, mon amour. Dir. Alain Resnais. Argos, 1959. Film.

Hirsch, Marianne, and Irene Kacandes, eds. *Teaching the Representation of the Holocaust.* New York: MLA, 2005. Print.

Kaplan, E. Ann. *Trauma Culture: The Politics of Terror and Loss in Media and Literature.* New Brunswick: Rutgers UP, 2005. Print.

Kaplan, E. Ann, and Ban Wang, eds. *Trauma and Cinema: Cross-Cultural Explorations.* Hong Kong: Hong Kong UP, 2004. Print.

Kovic, Ron. *Born on the Fourth of July.* New York: McGraw, 1976. Print.

LaCapra, Dominick. *Writing History, Writing Trauma.* Baltimore: Johns Hopkins UP, 2001. Print.

Landy, Marcia, ed. *The Historical Film: History and Memory in Media.* New Brunswick: Rutgers UP, 2001. Print.

Leitch, Thomas. *Film Adaptation and Its Discontents: From* Gone with the Wind *to* The Passion of the Christ. Baltimore: Johns Hopkins UP, 2009. Print.

Levi, Neil, and Michael Rothberg, eds. *The Holocaust: Theoretical Readings.* New Brunswick: Rutgers UP, 2003. Print.

Life Is Beautiful [*La vita è bella*]. Dir. Roberto Benigni. Cecchi Gori Group, 1997. Film.

Lowenstein, Adam. *Shocking Representation: Historical Trauma, National Cinema, and the Modern Horror Film.* New York: Columbia UP, 2005. Print.

MacCabe, Colin, Rick Warner, and Kathleen Murray, eds. *True to the Spirit: Film Adaptation and the Question of Fidelity.* New York: Oxford UP, 2010. Print.

McGeary, Johanna, and Karen Tumulty. "The Fog of War." *Time* 7 May 2001: 25–33. Print.

Naremore, James, ed. *Film Adaptation.* New Brunswick: Rutgers UP, 2000. Print.

Night and Fog [*Nuit et brouillard*]. Dir. Alain Resnais. Argos, 1955. Film.

Postone, Moishe, and Eric Santner, eds. *Catastrophe and Meaning: The Holocaust and the Twentieth Century*. Chicago: U of Chicago P, 2003. Print.
Radstone, Susannah, and Bill Schwarz, eds. *Memory: Histories, Theories, Debates*. New York: Fordham UP, 2010. Print.
Rothberg, Michael. *Multidirectional Memory: Remembering the Holocaust in the Age of Decolonization*. Stanford: Stanford UP, 2009. Print.
Schindler's List. Dir. Steven Spielberg. Universal, 1993. Film.
Shoah. Dir. Claude Lanzmann. Historia, 1985. Film.
Stam, Robert. *Literature through Film: Realism, Magic, and the Art of Adaptation*. Oxford: Blackwell, 2004. Print.
The Sweet Hereafter. Dir. Atom Egoyan. Alliance, 1997. Film.
Taxi Driver. Dir. Martin Scorsese. Columbia, 1976. Film.

Mark Lynn Anderson

Teaching Film Historiography

The only textbook published in the United States and entirely devoted to film historiography appeared over a quarter of a century ago, in 1985. *Film History: Theory and Practice*, by Robert C. Allen and Douglas Gomery, is a key document in what quickly became known in film studies as "revisionist history," a fairly widespread if not always coherent disciplinary call for increased evidentiary rigor and explanatory power in the writing of film history.[1] Allen and Gomery sought to move film history away from a preoccupation with films and toward a concern with providing descriptions of the "generative mechanisms" that could account for the appearance, endurance, and disappearance of various forms and practices related to the cinema (Gomery, "Film History"). By arguing for a "reformulation of aesthetic film history" that would explain the historically specific conditions of the production and reception of motion pictures (Allen, "Aesthetic Film History" 78), the authors also attempted to diminish the prominence of the great work of art within film history. Close analyses of film form and style were to be subordinated to discussions of the promotional, critical, and popular discourses that established the historical backgrounds against which films appeared and became meaningful. Allen and Gomery proposed that contextual evidence garnered from trade publications, newspaper reviews, and advertising was no way supplemental to a historical understanding of motion pictures and that such resources were, in effect, equally important objects of study for the new film history.[2]

Not coincidentally, the same year saw the publication of *The Classical Hollywood Cinema: Film Style and the Mode of Production to 1960*, a hefty five-hundred-page tome by David Bordwell, Janet Staiger, and Kristin Thompson that made extensive use of studio records and trade publications to describe the historical organization and global dominance of the studio system as a product of rational industrial and business practices.[3] The "mode of production" of the book's subtitle signaled within film studies a decisive move away from the sort of poststructuralist political economy that had underwritten various semiotic interpretations of film texts. Bordwell, Staiger, and Thompson sought to document minutely the history of studio organization and its relation to film style so as to explain the endurance of the classical style as an institutional system whose generative mechanisms were principally economic, not ideological. *Classical Hollywood Cinema* thus served as a rather daunting model for the sort of film historical practice being called for by Allen and Gomery—its detailed comprehensiveness and enormity proposed that film historical research should be valued only to the extent that it might ultimately contribute to this expansive project. For those of us who grew up in the shadow of the book, let alone for undergraduates encountering questions of film history for the first time, the ideal of a complete history of the cinema, even as it provided us with concrete methods and resources for research, served to marginalize important film historical works with either smaller or quite different aspirations. It is important to know, though, that revisionism was only a moment in an older and more enduring discourse about the poverty of film history.

Sixty-one years ago, the film archivist James Card lamented the dearth of reliable film histories: "The student turns to film histories and there finds confusion, gossip, and the wildest sort of speculation. He quickly sees that scholarship is no prerequisite to the writing of motion picture history" (279). Citing Card ten years later, the film studies professor Robert Gessner concluded that the wretched state of film history had "not diminished appreciably by the passing parade of publications" (74). In the mid-1970s, Thomas Cripps complained that the appearance of film histories in "cheap, easily made formats" brought out by those commercial publishers of coffee-table books

> has denied us a half a lifetime of scholarly study and criticism which has been papered over by a recent rash of "interpretive history," which lacks the annotation, bibliography, fully quoted documents and expository footnotes which form the foundation of true interpretive history. (43)

By 1985, however, Gomery would claim the small victory that several of the newer film historical surveys were "advances over older works—inaccuracies have been corrected and new research has been incorporated" ("Researching" 28). Even so, he concludes that the "demand for film history books has far outrun the pace of original research in film history." And despite the so-called historical turn within film studies that was to have begun with Allen and Gomery in the 1980s, Sumiko Higashi noted in 2004 that conference panels, journal articles, and published monographs on film history represented a rather small and apparently diminishing proportion of film studies work, and she suggested part of the problem was "that most academics who train students in Film Studies have not themselves been trained to do empirical research" (94). Of course, while empirical research may or may not be a necessary condition for film history, it certainly is not its sufficient condition. The apparent waning interest in film historical work may stem from issues other than a lack of proper training in research methods.

In part, then, the history of film history in the United States over the last half century has been a history of complaint about the lack of reliable and rigorously researched historical work. While obviously the repetition of such a complaint justifies the need for more film historical writing, as well as the production of more film historians, it also has two largely unintended consequences for the teaching of film historiography. First, it unfairly characterizes the work of earlier or pioneering film historians as lacking any substantive value for either the contemporary film historian or the student of film history. The bugaboos of gossip, speculation, and commercialism are used to pose both older and popular film histories as of historical interest only. Second, and more damagingly, the persistent call for increasing rigor has produced a distinct footnote fetish, a particularly intense attachment to referring readers to unique and hard-to-get-at archival records and document collections. So if film historiography defines both an appreciation of film historical work and a practical familiarity with its methods, what is an undergraduate instructor to do in the face of this demand that film history always be new and elaborately supported by primary research? For both undergraduates and graduate students, undertaking original historical research is, of course, one of the most important ways of coming to understand the work of the historian.

With the increasing availability of newspaper databases, census records, and genealogical resources online, having undergraduates conduct original film historical research has never been easier. Significantly, Gomery provided models for conducting various types of primary research in his chapter on the writing of film history, and he makes a special plea for conducting local studies of film exhibition, censorship, and reception since such research can "make a contribution to the state of film historical knowledge," particularly in small towns and rural areas where the practices of film business and culture are likely to have departed from the industry-endorsed urban model of the downtown, first-run picture palace that has so often been privileged in traditional accounts of the American cinema ("Writing" 193). Several important studies of local exhibition have appeared since, of which Gregory A. Waller's *Main Street Amusements* and Kathryn H. Fuller-Seeley's *At the Picture Show* are the most influential. Fuller-Seeley's collection of work on local film reception, *Hollywood in the Neighborhood*, provides useful examples of particular cases studies, as well as essays on the historiography of local film exhibition and reception. Against traditional revisionism, this anthology also functions as a working demonstration of how film historical research might productively proceed without the cover of a reigning paradigm. Creating a class project around questions of local research is a relatively simple and effective means of involving students in the practices of historical research and writing.

A good place to start is with the local newspaper. Almost every town has a run of a town or regional paper available on microfilm at the local library. When teaching at a small liberal arts college in the Finger Lakes of New York State, I asked the thirty students enrolled in my course on silent cinema to conduct a historical survey of theaters showing motion pictures in the college's town. I assigned each student a year from 1896 through 1926. For the first week, each student was to examine every issue of the local and college newspapers published in the month of April during the assigned year, reporting back to the class each and every mention of motion pictures in the life of the town or college. Predictably, students assigned to the earlier years had less to report back than students with later years. At the next class meeting, we recorded the findings on the board and then repeated the assignment for the month of November. This exercise produced all sorts of information about special screenings at a local labor hall, film lectures at the opera house, the appearance and disappearance of several nickelodeons and an exchange, the eventual appearance of an eight-hundred-seat house for vaudeville and motion pictures in early 1912, the arrival of the first picture palace three years later, the demonstration of Edison talking pictures at the opera house in 1913, and the eventual control of the opera house by a film theatrical chain. We were also able to determine when the local newspaper began reviewing film on a regular basis.

Since I had already envisioned a project on local exhibition, I divided the class up into groups of four to six students and asked each group to continue researching one of the nickelodeons or theaters identified in our preliminary newspaper research. I instructed the groups to consult city directories at the local library to ascertain exact locations of theaters and, if possible, the names and residences of the owners and operators (also determining what had occupied the same location before and after it became a site for film shows). Students then visited the local history museum to inspect fire insurance maps, as well as to inquire if the museum had clippings files or had collected any additional materials on these first movie theaters. Subsequent work included writing letters to the city clerk to determine if licensing, censorship, or tax documents still existed for any of these theaters; attempting to locate descendants of earlier theater owners still living in the area; talking with the current managers of the two theaters still in operation; searching *eBay* for postcards that might feature local street scenes depicting one of the town's theaters or nickelodeons; visiting and photographing any existing buildings that had once been theaters; as well as continuing with further, directed newspaper research. Eventually, we decided that each group would collectively write a short history of their respective theater, discussing its size, dates of operation, the sorts of pictures screened there, pricing, seating policies, and any other interesting information about the business and its place in the community. Since the town was very small and all but one of the original buildings were still standing, we decided that these histories could be combined and edited into a guided walking tour that would take the form of a tourist pamphlet. While this final step never came to completion, the histories that emerged from the class were deposited with the local history museum and would have formed the basis of subsequent student research, if I had taught the course again.

While this sort of ongoing research project provided students with an opportunity to produce original historical work, with an eventual audience in mind, it also worked in tandem with the rest of the course as a means of particularizing some of the grand narratives of film history. For example, the group working on the motion pictures at the opera house could immediately report on the special pricing and local promotion of Giovanni Pastrone's *Cabiria* (1914), the internationally celebrated historical epic from Italy. This information led to a rather animated and extended discussion of how and why cultural prestige was increasingly becoming a means to control the local exhibition market and attract publicity in this college and summer resort town during the mid-1910s. For the first time, I experienced a classroom discussion about a historical topic where the students had a far higher level of expertise than I.

As far as I am concerned, then, the most important task in teaching film historiography to both graduates and undergraduates is to radically demystify the archive by expanding it and dislocating it. In 1985, Allen and Gomery felt they could announce the dawning of a new film historical practice because of the increasing availability of business records and personnel papers at various archives. While they insisted that no documents or collections had intrinsic worth, being valuable only within the context of a particular research project, most revisionist historians clearly privileged corporate and government records as having greater relevance and authority than other documents (such as scrapbooks or oral histories) in answering the most central questions of American film history. Yet, since 1990 there has appeared in the discipline a rather dizzying array of film historical work on everything from amateur filmmaking clubs in the 1930s to the development and deployment of X-ray cinematography, with seemingly little in the way of a widely shared disciplinary paradigm or research method. While the revisionists' proposal of a consensus model of film historical research has not come to pass, the (still only partial) turn away from the film text as the central concern of film history made possible the consideration of previously unacknowledged, unrecognized, and unavailable primary sources for writing film history: fan magazines, government documents, local newspapers, memoirs, letters, business records, oral histories, buildings, postcards, census records, scrapbooks, advertising, patent records, medical files, insurance maps, travel guides, recipe books, and telephone directories. By expanding the parameters of the archival, revisionist film history opened the doors to its own undoing; in a very real sense, the devil was in the details. While this situation creates challenges for the teaching of film historiography, the broadening of what might count as sources for film history, coupled with an enormous increase in electronic data storage and retrieval capacities, makes it easy to have students undertake all sorts of original film historical research independently. Archival experience is one of the most effective means of teaching an appreciation of current film historical practices and problems. Perhaps, then, the central question of film historiography today is, What is an archive?

One approach to answering this question is to have undergraduate students create archives of their own, charging each of them with forming and managing a unique collection of artifacts and documents. The only requirements would be that the collection must have some relation to film culture or history, no matter how tangential, and that the archivist should begin the collection and select items for inclusion out of some personal interest in the items or their subjects. Unlike traditional research, such collections are formed without an articulated research question; instead, they are determined by an individual's interest in a subject and a desire to collect and preserve materials relevant to the contemplation and continuation of that interest. Like all archives, the future uses of these collections remain relatively unspecified. If each student then presents her or his archive to the rest of the class and discusses its development, the contingency of the personal archive becomes glaringly apparent; it becomes even more so if you ask students to write short histories that are limited solely to the resources of another student's archive. I have successfully used such an assignment in an undergraduate course on the "star system," where I required students to keep scrapbooks on film stars of their choosing. The scrapbooks then served as the principal resources for the writing of critical star biographies. One can imagine establishing various sorts of collection policies in the constitution of classroom archives.

There are several important lessons about the archive to be learned from such an assignment. After the presentations, students see that all collections have a history and are mediated by the contingencies of various interests that privilege certain subjects and artifacts over others. Many film historians never inquire into the provenance of the collections they use, and those that do rarely make those stories a part of the story they are telling. If students are asked to write histories that make use of one another's personal archives, they gain a further appreciation of the ways that collections both limit and enable the construction of particular histories. The authority that the small archive seemingly grants to the written history is then shown to be principally an effect of the prior existence of the archive as an entity separate from and supporting that history. In other words, the credibility that the historian gains from having consulted the archive is a result of that consultation, not, despite impressions to the contrary, of the archive's geographic distance, exclusivity, or venerability.

Another means of domesticating the archive is to present students with a limited number of artifacts and ask each of them to write a short history that cites only those artifacts as supporting evidence. One could, for example, create an "archive" of only three items: a newspaper account of an event; a photograph of a person referred to in the news article, but taken at a far earlier moment; and an advertisement from a magazine fairly contemporaneous with the newspaper report. I would allow students to spend some time with these artifacts so as to contemplate how they might be made to tell something about the past. Then I would distribute the collected histories for all students to read and eventually discuss. While such an exercise could demonstrate that a limited number of primary sources can support a vast number of different historical accounts, often with widely differing subjects, such an assignment also might increase student confidence in working with a paucity of surviving evidence and help students develop an ability to make nuanced claims that respect the limited record without diminishing the significance of a historical interpretation. Combined with the careful and thorough reading of the endnotes attached to some of the most esteemed works of recent film history, this sort of assignment can be used to fight against the fantasy of a "complete archive" that subtends so many students' feelings of inadequacy as historians. All histories make use of extremely finite resources, and while the search for additional primary material relevant to a research project remains important, the devaluation of historical work because of its perceived lack of concomitant and corroborative evidence often distracts us from the principal task of the historian: interpreting the evidence of the past in narrative form.

Such historical interpretation, though, is precisely what revisionist historians wished to diminish; Allen cautioned that historical work is deeply compromised when "the conventions of traditional fictional narrative are allowed to take precedent over solid historical analysis" ("Reading" 44). The distrust of narrative has been a lingering symptom of an enduring empirical historicism that seeks scientific rigor by privileging historical process (description) over events (narration). While philosophers of history have long observed the contributions that narrative necessarily makes to any understanding of the past, only recently have theorists such as Jacques Rancière and cultural historians such as Carolyn Steedman argued in direct response to the ascendant authority of the archive that fiction is inextricable from any recounting of the past and that storytelling must be not only acknowledged but also pursued as the special task of the historian.

Historiography is interested in the means by which a story about the past gets told, and it proposes that all stories are open to both factual and narrative revisions. A long-standing method of teaching film historiography is through the comparative reading of film histories. One can, for instance, require students to read several different accounts of the emergence of feature-length motion pictures in the United States by assigning the relevant chapters from, say, Terry Ramsaye's *A Million and One Nights*, Benjamin Hampton's *A History of the Movies*, Lewis Jacobs's *The Rise of the American Film*, and Eileen Bowser's *The Transformation of Cinema, 1907–1915*. In directing students to evaluate these accounts, one has several options that are not mutually exclusive but are nevertheless often in tension.

First, students can be asked to evaluate critically each account on its explanatory merits, including the quality of its supporting evidence, the historian's apparent understanding of historical change or stasis, and the relative plausibility of the account offered. Such a reading ultimately aims at ranking the various accounts in terms of their evidence, logic, and elegance and deems "best" the account that offers the most relevant and verifiable data to explain more phenomena, more convincingly, according to a rational logic of historical causation and determination. The results are rarely surprising. Second, one can use this comparative work to highlight the establishment of film historical facts and their function, by posing questions for discussion such as, "Why might it be problematic to credit the emergence of the feature film to the rise of the independents?" These sorts of critical readings are promoted by Allen, who also demonstrates another way of reading film histories in his case studies of Ramsaye and of Robert Grau's *Theatre of Science* ("Reading"). Allen describes the conditions of both books' production through a discussion of each author's biography, his occasions for writing film history, and the state of the publishing market at the time of writing. Such a contextual reading obviously requires additional research, but one can usually find evidence of the "situatedness" of any published history in, for example, the author's acknowledgements, his or her self-presentation, or even the credited sources of the book's images. Providing such a production context can give students an appreciation of how history is tied to and grows out of the life of the historian, though Allen promotes this reading only to demonstrate the complex mediation that any historical account undergoes, the highly regrettable but necessary condition of film history for him.

Yet instead of seeing the historical context of film history as something to be identified and quarantined, one can look to the circumstances of the historian as a constitutive part of that history and what it tells us. Students who have already practiced writing history from an archive they devised will be familiar with the contiguities between the place of the historian and the perspectives of the history told. This difference marks more than emphasis; it is a completely different conception of historical practice. While Allen shows how an earlier crediting of Thomas Edison with the development of the cinema was tied to prevalent ideologies of entrepreneurial invention and, in the case of Ramsaye, to the marketing situation of *A Million and One Nights*, he does so only to pronounce such attributions as unfortunate distortions of fact that have since been corrected by more careful research and by a more complete historical record ("Reading" 58). As Allen describes this process of reading, "historical works might be 'opened up' and their cultural determinations *read out*" (51; my emphasis). Yet it is also possible to countenance the errors of a historian such as Ramsaye while treating *A Million and One Nights* as a specific way of remembering the film historical past; in other words, the book is a historical *work* that asks us to know the past from a historical point of view that is itself historical. Parsing out what is true and what is false is not as important here as determining what such a way of seeing the past makes visible and what it might exclude.

Sustaining its reliance on the trope of magic and on the story of Scheherazade, *A Million and One Nights* is an avowedly mythic history, one that posits the cinema as tied to the primordial wish to overcome the alienation of language. Ramsaye seeks to account for the cinema's development through organic models of growth that explain how the progressive development of ever larger and more complex forms (whether social, technological, or economic) results from the strivings of a human collective. Indeed, Ramsaye ends his history with Adolph Zukor, "a Caliph Haroun Alrashid in a new Baghdad-on-the Hudson," contemplating not his economic empire but a bronze cast of his grandson's first shoes (2: 834). The cinema is a product of generations, not a wholly unfamiliar idea in the history of film theory, with heroes such as Edison and Zukor only geniuses of the system. Even with all its Orientalist trappings, Ramsaye's idea that the captains of the industry are subject to a logic that precedes them and determines their actions in predictable ways is not appreciably different from the assumptions a film historian such as Gomery makes, in his various accounts of the transition to synchronized sound, about the sheer rationality of business practices in the 1920s. The idea, though, is not to evaluate film histories only in terms of their persuasiveness or the soundness of their assumptions but to attend to the poetics of each history, ascertaining how its representations make visible or felt certain peoples, events, and conditions of existence in the past and, furthermore, to determine with whose interests such a story lies. Having students read first and last chapters of film histories can be useful for discussing how a particular history seeks to represent the past, so long as their attention is directed to the story told and not only to the adequacy of the questions raised or the validity of the conclusions reached. One can begin such a process by asking students the rather startling question, "How did this history make you feel?" "Feeling" here is more than emotional affect; it names the various sorts of alliances that the historian forms with the people of the past. Ultimately, the aim is for students to consider the real social contexts of film historical practice so that they might determine—even before the collection of historical facts and their placement in the telling of a story about the past—just how they wish readers of their historical writing to feel about the world as it is and as it is imagined to have been.

Notes

My thanks go to Mark Garrett Cooper for his enormously helpful criticism and insights.

1. Because of the volume's rejection of specialized theoretical terminology, one thing revisionist history has going for it, pedagogically speaking, is its clarity of expression, and *Film History: Theory and Practice* is still a very serviceable textbook in the undergraduate classroom, as is its model of dividing film history into recognizable subfields: aesthetic film history, technological film history, economic film history, and social film history. Unfortunately, McGraw-Hill has allowed this title to go out of print for the first time since its initial publication.

2. Despite alarms in some quarters that scholarly attention to the films themselves might disappear from film historical practice, Eric Smoodin has argued that close textual analysis has remained a tenacious academic requirement for even those histories most exclusively interested in institutional questions.

3. Mark Betz describes the tumescence of *Classical Hollywood Cinema* as instantiating "the thorough specialization of film study within the academy [as well as] the demands for those who reach terminal degrees to publish work of a certain size and length for a certain audience—themselves" (336).

Works Cited

Allen, Robert C. "Aesthetic Film History." Allen and Gomery 67–108.

———. "Reading Film History." Allen and Gomery 43–64.

Allen, Robert C., and Douglas Gomery. *Film History: Theory and Practice*. New York: McGraw, 1985. Print.

Betz, Mark. "Little Books." *Inventing Film Studies*. Ed. Lee Grieveson and Haidee Wasson. Durham: Duke UP, 2008. 319–49. Print.

Bordwell, David, Janet Staiger, and Kristin Thompson. *The Classical Hollywood Cinema: Film Style and the Mode of Production to 1960.* New York: Columbia UP, 1985. Print.

Bowser, Eileen. *The Transformation of Cinema, 1907–1915.* New York: Scribner, 1990. Print. History of the American Cinema 2.

Card, James. "The Problems of Film History." *Hollywood Quarterly* 4.3 (1950): 279–88. Print.

Cripps, Thomas. "The Future Film Historian: Less Art and More Craft." *Cinema Journal* 14.2 (1974–75): 42–46. Print.

Fuller-Seeley, Kathryn H. *At the Picture Show: Small Town Audiences and the Creation of Movie Fan Culture.* 1996. Charlottesville: U of Virginia P, 2001. Print.

———, ed. *Hollywood in the Neighborhood: Historical Case Studies of Local Moviegoing.* Berkeley: U of California P, 2008. Print.

Gessner, Robert. "Cinema and Scholarship." *Journal of the Society of Cinematologists* 3 (1963): 73–80. Print.

Gomery, Douglas. "Film History as History." Allen and Gomery 3–23.

———. "Researching Film History." Allen and Gomery 25–42.

———. "Writing Film History." Allen and Gomery 193–212.

Grau, Robert. *The Theatre of Science.* New York: Broadway, 1914. Print.

Hampton, Benjamin B. *A History of the Movies.* New York: Covici, 1931. Print.

Higashi, Sumiko. "Film History, or a Baedeker Guide to the Historical Turn." *Cinema Journal* 44.1 (2004): 94–100. Print.

Jacobs, Lewis. *The Rise of the American Film: A Critical History.* New York: Harcourt, 1939. Print.

Ramsaye, Terry. *A Million and One Nights: The History of the Motion Picture.* 2 vols. New York: Simon, 1926. Print.

Rancière, Jacques. *The Names of History: On the Poetics of Knowledge.* Trans. Hassan Melehy. Minneapolis: U of Minnesota P, 1994. Print.

Smoodin, Eric. "The History of Film History." *Looking Past the Screen: Case Studies in American Film History and Method.* Ed. Jon Lewis and Smoodin. Durham: Duke UP, 2008. 1–33. Print.

Steedman, Carolyn. *Dust: The Archive and Cultural History.* New Brunswick: Rutgers UP, 2002. Print.

Waller, Gregory A. *Main Street Amusements: Movies and Commercial Entertainment in a Southern City, 1896–1930.* Washington: Smithsonian, 1995. Print.

Peter Decherney

Teaching Film Law and Policy

Just about every element of film and media history has a legal or regulatory dimension. A course on sex or politics in cinema, for example, might include discussions of obscenity or sedition laws. A course on film authorship might include readings about how copyright law underpins both industry practices and cultural assumptions about originality and attribution. Considering a course on globalization? Trade policy has always controlled the international circulation of film, and it has often been a prime determinant of film style from the French new wave to fifth-generation Chinese cinema.

No course on Hollywood would be complete without a discussion of the *Mutual Film Corporation v. Industrial Commission of Ohio*, *United States v. Paramount Pictures* (the Paramount Decree), and the Motion Picture Production Code. And courses on convergence and new media would be remiss not to include at least a mention of the Digital Millennium Copyright Act or the Supreme Court's *Metro-Goldwyn-Mayer Studios v. Grokster* decision (about file-sharing software) or the Federal Communications Commission's wireless spectrum auction.

While some of the landmark events in film's legal and regulatory history are staples of course syllabi, there are many reasons to include a broader range of legal material. The law is often a major factor in determining film industry practice and audience behavior. Court cases and policy debates can give tangible and material form to abstract issues. And students and faculty members often find it revelatory that policy makers and judges struggle with the same theoretical concerns as scholars: How are new media like old media? Who is the author of a film? (Decherney). This essay considers some approaches to incorporating film law and policy into courses. Other approaches to film and law not discussed here might look at film as evidence in courts or the representation of courts and government in film.

Resources

Doing social science research may be daunting to the humanist. But, in many ways, the tools for doing this kind of research are more advanced than those available for doing research in the humanities: the databases of both scholarship and primary material are extremely rich and well developed. When researching law and policy, you need to leave your chair and computer even less frequently than when researching film history or theory.

Many works of film history mention key pieces of legislation or landmark court decisions. There is a smaller body of work that focuses directly on film law and policy. The scholars Thomas Guback, Dallas Smythe, Douglas Gomery, Kristin Thompson, Ian Jarvie, Patricia Aufderheide, Albert Moran, and Toby Miller, among others, have written and edited significant books that look at national or global film policy. Many more books look at the impact of policy on national film industries, largely because, since the late 1930s, the film industries of all but a few countries have relied on direct government subsidies.

Much more research on film and related policies exist beyond the usual boundaries of the field. The *Social Science Research Network* (*SSRN*) is an online repository that scholars use to upload work on law and policy, among other subjects. *SSRN* and its contents are freely available on the Web, and authors often post working drafts as well as preprint versions of their work. *LexisNexis* is a one-stop venue for legal scholarship, news, and primary documents that allows users to search law review articles and legal and policy news items and retrieve cases by party name, citation, or keywords. The *Westlaw Database* also has cases and secondary literature, including many valuable legal treatises. Several databases contain a wealth of material on the history of film and media policy and law. *JSTOR* is a terrific resource for historical law journal articles, and *HeinOnline* collects a wide range of historical legal scholarship and documents. The less widely available *The Making of Modern Law* collects British and US treatises from 1800 to 1926 as well as US Supreme Court records from 1832 to 1978.

Not every institution will give every library patron access to every legal database. Court decisions, in particular, can be hard to find, despite the fact that they are government works and part of the public domain. Fortunately, many legal resources are freely available, and more and more court decisions are being made freely available on the Web as well. Yale Law School's *Curiae* hosts US Supreme Court cases and briefs. *Oyez* also collects recordings of recent Supreme Court arguments. Listening to the dizzying barrage of questions from the justices often reveals the key issues at stake in a case, and the audio can be a welcome addition to text-heavy syllabi. *FindLaw* is not as comprehensive or easy to use as *LexisNexis* or *Westlaw*, but it does make some cases and articles available for free. *AltLaw* is also working to bring all US case law to the Web for free. The Library of Congress's *Thomas* database is an invaluable resource that makes legislative material freely available. You can use *Thomas*, for example, to look up pending legislation and see which members of the House of Representatives or Senate are supporting it. The White House Web site and the Web sites of individual members of Congress can also have useful collections of speeches, news coverage, and, increasingly, video material.

There are no one-stop databases for international policy. But policy documents and descriptions can usually be found through the organizations that oversee international agreements and treaties. If you are interested in copyright policy, for example, you can turn to the World Intellectual Property Organization's site. Helpful Web sites for trade policies include the World Trade Organization's, the United Nations's, and UNESCO's.

Several public interest organizations provide updates on current media, telecommunications and Internet legislation, and significant court cases. The activist organizations Electronic Frontier Foundation, Public Knowledge, and Free Press all offer regular e-mail updates, blogs, and Web sites. They take strong positions on the issues and, in general, serve as correctives to the corporate interests of media conglomerates. For other positions, you can turn to the sites of the libertarian Cato Institute or the right-wing, "market-oriented" Progress and Freedom Foundation. The Motion Picture Association of America also offers on its Web site regular position statements, news releases, speeches, attempts at consumer education, and antipiracy tools. Google has become a significant force in the creation of media policy, and the company's public policy blog offers updates on Google's policy positions and litigation.

Most major newspapers, including the *New York Times* and the *Wall Street Journal*, and many specialized periodicals also cover national and international media law and policy. *Ars Technica* and the expensive *Warren's Washington Internet Daily* are useful and accessible sources for staying on top of policy developments.

Reading material from the activist and trade organizations is often a good entry into policy and legal issues and debates. In many cases, this material may be sufficient to understand the stakes and general terms of the issues. Having students follow the Electronic Frontier Foundation or Google blogs throughout a semester can show them that censorship, privacy, and intellectual property are current and highly contested issues. But there is really no substitute for going to original cases and legislation. In my experience, with enough context and a legal dictionary, undergraduates as well as graduate students and faculty members without much law and policy experience can examine and learn from original legal documents. Inevitably, humanities faculty members and students bring valuable cultural and critical perspectives to the analyses of these documents.

Industry Structure and Development

There are many approaches that lend themselves to the use of film policy and law in the classroom. The most common approach to teaching film policy and law is to incorporate it into courses on the structure of the film industry. Policy is central to the development of national film industries from quotas and trade restrictions to government subsidies and tax incentives to antitrust regulations. In the study of many national cinemas, policy becomes especially relevant during times of military or economic crisis. In the United States, for example, World War I sedition laws constrained both film content and the flow of films into and out of the country. During the New Deal, the National Recovery Administration allowed Hollywood to act as a monopoly until the Supreme Court declared the policy unconstitutional.

If law and policy can help explain the development of national film industries, there is also much that educators trained in the humanities and culture can bring to the study of policy, because policy and culture always influence each other. The study of Chinese piracy is a fascinating example that might be relevant to courses on new technologies or reception studies as well as courses on Hollywood and Chinese cinema. Legal scholars invariably use a developmental model to explain the rampant video piracy in China. The People's Republic of China, the theory goes, is developing toward a legal system that resembles those in the United States and other developed countries. As China produces more intellectual property that it wants to protect in the global market, its government will take steps to enforce its antipiracy laws. This is a model that has great currency with students as well as scholars.

But many Chinese policies that stem from cultural differences with the West foster rather than deter piracy. Censorship and trade restrictions combined with a weak antipiracy infrastructure clearly encourage piracy. The strong censorship of films in China and the lack of a rating system ensure that many films that cannot get official distribution will find alternative routes to reach viewers. In addition, China only imports approximately twenty foreign films a year to be distributed in the country. The dearth of foreign films leaves many mainstream Hollywood and other releases to find underground methods of distribution.

The vast and unchecked circulation of pirated material has also led to a culture of piracy. As Laikwan Pang, Shujen Wang, and others have shown, the culture of piracy has implications for production and viewing alike. Chinese filmmakers, for example, are willing to make films about taboo subjects, because they know that the pirate network will ensure domestic distribution even if their films are officially censored. And the quick and dirty methods of subtitling, dubbing, and reproducing films for pirate distribution have led to particular aesthetic norms and expectations. Often, the new pirated versions either intentionally or inadvertently subvert the ideological messages of the original text.

As scholars of culture have given valuable context to the question of Chinese antipiracy policy, it is in the humanities classroom that questions of policy and culture can come together to inform each other in teaching the development and structure of film industries.

Film Analysis

Film law and policy might also be introduced into the classroom in the service of film analysis. Filmmakers regularly have to contend with either government censorship or internal, industry content regulation—and usually both. An enormous body of scholarship has analyzed the impact of censorship and film content, an impact that goes beyond straightforward limits on expression. As Richard Maltby, Stephen Prince, and others have shown, the Production Code Administration did not just remove salacious, violent, and heterodox scenes from American films; it also created a multivalent system for reading film imagery. In another example of the influence of policy on content, many films have either explained or critiqued specific government policies. Examples include Dziga Vertov's Soviet newsreels, *Kino-Pravda* (1922–25); Pare Lorentz's government-funded New Deal documentaries, *The Plow That Broke the Plains* (1936) and *The River* (1938); and Michael Moore's attack on the US health-care system, *Sicko* (2007).

The impact of policy on content can be difficult to discern and is usually controversial. An exploration of it can prompt methodologically complex and politically important questions. How, for example, has media deregulation and the resultant conglomeration of the US film industry changed the subject matter and style of American film? To what extent can we use media ownership policies to explain the rise of the blockbuster, the global reach of Hollywood, and the emergence of what Henry Jenkins calls "transmedia storytelling" (293)?

One significant way that policy contributes to film is by determining what cannot be expressed and represented. Policy, in other words, points to the lacunae in film history as well as the roads taken. Censorship is a clear mechanism for silencing expression. In postrevolutionary Iranian cinema, for example, many political subjects are taboo, and women on screen must wear traditional Islamic head scarves, even in private scenes. The filmmaker Tahmineh Milani was imprisoned in 2001 for fomenting counterrevolutionary ideas in her film *The Hidden Half* made the same year, and many Iranian films have been banned from domestic distribution and filmmakers have been denied visas to travel abroad. As often happens, the limits on expression have led to creative alternatives. The new Iranian cinema's enormously successful and influential allegorical style of filmmaking arose, in part, because filmmakers could not address political issues directly (Dabashi; Phillips).

There are subtler forms of suppression as well, such as the government's using subsidies to help determine which films are made and which projects are eliminated at the proposal stage. In the United States, the National Endowment for the Humanities is one of the leading funders of documentary films. Its rigorous and tightly controlled system of review and support determines the types of documentary films that reach theater and television screens.

"Untold Stories," a report by the film and media scholar Patricia Aufderheide and the legal scholar Peter Jaszi, uncovered another method through which the law has silenced documentary filmmakers. The unpredictability of the fair use legal doctrine led insurance companies to require documentary filmmakers to clear the rights to every trace of copyrighted material in their films. Documentary filmmakers could not rely on fair use to justify the interpolation of copyrighted material into their films. Entire genres, such as history documentaries, became prohibitively expensive for any film wishing to find a distributor. Thus law and economics worked together to determine the field of documentary production. Aufderheide and Jaszi addressed the situation by developing a code of best practices for documentary filmmakers. Their code has since changed the policies of many insurance companies, distributors, and broadcasters, clearing the path for the creation and distribution of documentary films (see *Documentary Filmmakers' Statement*).

From copyright law to censorship to tax incentives for independent production, the law contributes to what can be expressed on film and how viewers read films. Because law is an essential element of film artistry and spectatorship, it belongs on syllabi that cover film style and analysis.

Teaching, Scholarship, and Preservation

An instructor might also bring film law and policy to the classroom by examining their influence on the development of film and media studies. Media professors filed an amicus curiae, or friend-of-the-court, brief in the US Supreme Court's 2005 case on file sharing (*MGM v. Grokster*). The brief explained that the court's 1984 Sony Betamax decision allowed the VCR to be exploited and, in turn, provided a foundation for the growth of media education:

> Media education and scholarship never would have developed as an important field in college and university curricula and an increasingly important element of secondary education in the United States without [home video] technology. (Brief 7)

Law and policy control how media is used in the classroom, and it is important for faculty members and students to think reflexively about the influence of law and policy on the development of the field of film and media studies.

The Society for Cinema and Media Studies (SCMS) has been an active voice in policy debates for several decades. In the 1980s, when Congress was considering the legal status of film authorship—and authorship more generally—in the light of the new technology of film colorization, SCMS (then SCS) sent a statement to the Senate subcommittee considering new legislation and had a society representative, John Belton, a professor at Rutgers University, testify before the US Copyright Office (Belton, "SCS Statement"; Belton, "Comments"). The society then gained a position on the National Film Preservation Board (NFPB), the organization that Congress created as a result of those hearings. The NFPB is responsible for annually selecting films to be protected and preserved.

When film scholars became frustrated by publishers' refusal to accept a fair use defense for publishing film stills in textbooks and monographs, SCMS (again, SCS at the time) issued its own statement of fair use best practices. Many academic publishers adopted the statement as internal policy, and books and journal articles have since been much better illustrated and argued than they might have been without the statement (Thompson, "Report").

In 2006, three professors from the University of Pennsylvania (myself among them) sought an exemption to the Digital Millennium Copyright Act that would allow media professors to make digital clips from DVDs and other digital media. SCMS supported the request, and the exemption was eventually granted. Without it, film and media teachers either had to break the law to capture clips for class or use low-resolution analog images (see Sender and Decherney). In 2009, the Copyright Office expanded the exemption to include all professors, media students, noncommercial filmmakers, and many others.

In 2006, SCMS built on its earlier fair use statement and on the best practices movement started in the wake of Aufderheide and Jaszi's report. The society's "Statement of Best Practices for Fair Use in Teaching for Film and Media Educators" asserted and clarified the broad range of educational uses that copyright law allowed either through specific exemptions or under the fair use defense. Following the SCMS statement, the Film Studies Association of Canada released its "Statement on Copyright," a statement of practices it believed to be protected by Canada's fair dealing exemption.

The reflexive approach to teaching film law and policy may be the most immediate and provoke the most visceral responses from faculty members and students alike. As a result of new video production technologies and Web 2.0 sites like *YouTube*, law and policy reach deeper into academic and pedagogical uses of media than ever. Thinking about the impact of law and policy on film education not only encourages comparisons with commercial media production but also leads to reflection on the state of film education and on its future.

Works Cited

Aufderheide, Patricia. *Communications Policy and the Public Interest: The Telecommunications Act of 1996.* New York: Guilford, 1999. Print.

Aufderheide, Patricia, and Peter Jaszi. "Untold Stories: Creative Consequences of the Rights Clearance Culture." *Center for Social Media.* Center for Social Media, 2004. Web. 16 Aug. 2011.

Belton, John. "Comments of Professor John Belton on Behalf of the Society for Cinema Studies, Hearing on New Technology and Audiovisual Works." *Technological Alterations to Motion Pictures and other Audiovisual Works: Implications for Creators, Copyright Owners and Consumers.* Washington: US Copyright Office, 1989. Note 279. Print.

———. "SCS Statement on Creative Rights." *Cinema Journal* 27.2 (1988): 5–7. Print.

Brief of Media Studies Professors as *Amici Curiae* in Support of Respondents. Metro-Goldwyn-Mayer Studios, Inc., et al. v. Grokster, Ltd., et al. 545 US 913. (No. 04-480.) Supreme Court of the US. 2005. Print.

Dabashi, Hamid. *Close Up: Iranian Cinema, Past, Present, and Future.* London: Verso, 2001. Print.

Decherney, Peter. *Hollywood's Copyright Wars: From Edison to the Internet.* New York: Columbia UP, 2012. Print.

Documentary Filmmakers' Statement of Best Practices in Fair Use. Center for Social Media. Center for Social Media, 2005. Web. 16 Aug. 2011.

Film Studies Association of Canada. "Statement on Copyright." *Film Studies Association of Canada.* Film Studies Assn. of Canada, 2008. Web. 20 Jun. 2008.

Gomery, Douglas. *The Coming of Sound: A History.* New York: Routledge, 2005. Print.

Guback, Thomas. *The International Film Industry: Western Europe and America since 1945.* Bloomington: U of Indiana P, 1969. Print.

Jarvie, Ian. *Hollywood's Overseas Campaigns: The North Atlantic Movie Trade, 1920–1950.* New York: Cambridge UP, 1992. Print.

Jenkins, Henry. *Convergence Culture: Where Old and New Media Collide.* New York: New York UP, 2006. Print.

Maltby, Richard. *Harmless Entertainment: Hollywood and the Ideology of Consensus.* New York: Scarecrow, 1983. Print.

Miller, Toby, Nitin Govil, John McMurria, Richard Maxwell, and Ting Wang. *Global Hollywood 2.* London: British Film Inst., 2005. Print.

Moran, Albert, ed. *Film Policy: International, National, and Regional Perspectives.* London: Routledge, 1996. Print.

Pang, Laikwan. *Cultural Control and Globalization in Asia: Copyright, Piracy, and Cinema.* New York: Routledge, 2006. Print.

Phillips, Richard. "Iranian Director Tahmineh Milani Speaks with WSWS." *World Socialist Web Site.* World Socialist Web Site, 29 Sept. 2006. Web. 16 Aug. 2011.

Prince, Stephen. *Classical Film Violence: Designing and Regulating Brutality in Hollywood, 1930–1968.* New Brunswick: Rutgers UP, 2003. Print.

Sender, Katherine, and Peter Decherney. "Defending Fair Use in the Age of the Digital Millennium Copyright Act." *International Journal of Communication* 1 (2007): n. pag. Web. 16 Aug. 2011.

Smythe, Dallas. *Dependency Road: Communication, Capitalism, Consciousness and Canada.* Norwood: Ablex, 1981. Print.

Society for Cinema and Media Studies. "The Society for Cinema and Media Studies' Statement of Best Practices for Fair Use in Teaching for Film and Media Educators." *Cinema Journal* 47.2 (2008): 155–62. Print.

Thompson, Kristin. *Exporting Entertainment: America in the World Film Market, 1907–1934.* London: British Film Inst., 1985. Print.

———. "Report of the Ad Hoc Committee of the Society for Cinema Studies, 'Fair Usage Publication of Film Stills.'" *Cinema Journal* 32.2 (1993): 3–20. Print.

Wang, Shujen. *Framing Piracy: Globalization and Film Distribution in Greater China.* Latham: Rowman, 2003. Print.

Part IV

Genre and Mode

Introduction to Part 4

When the typical undergraduate thinks about movies, he or she often thinks in terms of film genre. In fact, much of the work in early Anglo-American film criticism focused on genre, including *Horizons West*, by Jim Kitses, which analyzed the western; *The Comic Mind*, by Gerald Mast, which considered film comedy; and *Underworld USA*, by Colin McArthur, which examined the crime film. In later years, this research was followed up by volumes on such genres as the musical (*The American Film Musical*, by Rick Altman) or science fiction (*Screening Space*, by Vivian Sobchack). With the rise of feminist studies, it was noted that many of the genres considered previously had a male bias. Thus work began on more female-oriented genres like melodrama and the woman's film in particular (e.g., *The Desire to Desire*, by Mary Ann Doane). As film studies took a decidedly political turn in the 1980s, work on genre (like Thomas Schatz's *Hollywood Genres*) also focused on the manner in which a genre bespeaks and addresses cultural malaise—be it war, the dissolution of family, or economic crisis.

In film studies, when one speaks of genre, one generally invokes the category of fiction or dramatic film that is further divided according to certain story types—ones that involve particular settings (e.g., the urban locale of the crime film), character types (e.g., the theatrical ingenue of the musical), or stylistic tropes (e.g., the wide-screen panorama of the historical spectacle). While early writing in film studies was largely descriptive, recent work has tackled sophisticated genre theory. Here one thinks of *Film/Genre*, in which Altman makes a distinction between "semantic" and "syntactic" elements. By the former he means a genre's common traits, attitudes, characters, shots, sets; by the latter, the textual bonds established between those elements. The essays in this section discuss teaching genre theory as well as specific traditional forms. Beyond that, one essay examines the process by which new genres (or cycles) are fashioned in response to pressing social issues.

The title of this section mentions genres and modes. The use of *modes* is meant to differentiate the kinds of story type discussed above (associated with the fiction/dramatic/live-action cinema) from far broader categories of production and organization. From the earliest days of cinema history (with the short actualities shot by Thomas Edison in the United States or by the brothers Auguste and Louis Lumière in France), the documentary (also known as the nonfiction film) has been a crucial mode. In fact, for many early theorists, including Siegfried Kracauer and André Bazin, nonfiction was a preferred type of production—one that allegedly took advantage of specific properties of the cinema. For Bazin, for instance, the photographic image was a kind of "decal" or "transfer" from the material world. As he notes, "the photographic image is the object itself . . . it shares by the virtue of its very becoming, the being of the model of which it is the reproduction" (14). Courses on documentary film have become requisite in the film studies curriculum at the same time that their nonfiction status has been widely and aggressively interrogated.

Another broad mode of cinematic production is animation, which is frequently counterpoised to live-action cinema. All attempts to narrowly define the mode tend to fail, however, since many scholars include in this category pixilation, by which live-action images are photographed frame by frame and later revivified to look artificial. Furthermore, since all cinema involves setting into motion static shots, the entire medium is considered by some to be a form of animation. This type of film also has historical roots in the turn of the twentieth century, in the cartoons by Winsor McCay and Émile Cohl and the pixilated comedies by Ferdinand Zecca. Traditional animation was, of course, achieved through drawings. But, in recent years, computer-generated imagery has taken over the field, not only creating more three-dimensional figures but infiltrating live-action cinema with invisible special effects so that the distinction between it and animation becomes even fuzzier.

Finally, one can consider experimental or avant-garde film another broad mode, although it is one that might use live-action, animation, or both—and include a host of photographic methods (e.g., X-ray, solarization, or negative photography). Like the other modes, experimental film dates back to early film history, with 1920s works like *The Fall of the House of Usher* in the United States, *Rétour à la raison* in France, *Rain* in the Netherlands, and *Uberfall* in Germany. While fewer courses in the academy tend to focus on animation and experimental cinema than on traditional genre films, these modes are crucial to comprehend and more upper-level classes have begun to address them.

Works Cited

Altman, Rick. *The American Film Musical.* Bloomington: Indiana UP, 1987. Print.

———. *Film/Genre.* London: British Film Inst., 1999. Print.

Bazin, André. *What Is Cinema?* Trans. Hugh Gray. Berkeley: U of California P, 1968. Print.

Doane, Mary Ann. *The Desire to Desire: The Woman's Film of the 1940s.* Bloomington: Indiana UP, 1987. Print.

Kitses, Jim. *Horizons West: Directing the Western from John Ford to Clint Eastwood.* London: British Film Inst., 2004. Print.

Kracauer, Siegfried. *Theory of Film: The Redemption of Physical Reality.* New York: Oxford UP, 1960. Print.

Mast, Gerald. *The Comic Mind: Comedy and the Movies.* Chicago: U of Chicago P, 1979. Print.

McArthur, Colin. *Underworld USA.* New York: Viking, 1972. Print.

Schatz, Thomas. *Hollywood Genres: Formulas, Filmmaking, and the Studio System.* Philadelphia: Temple UP, 1981. Print.

Sobchack, Vivian. *Screening Space: The American Science Fiction Film.* New Brunswick: Rutgers UP, 1997. Print.

Steven Cohan

Teaching Film Genre(s)

Some preliminary institutional background to what I shall be discussing in this chapter may help frame my comments about teaching genres since, at least from a curricular perspective, my situation is probably not all that commonplace. Although film courses are a regular offering of the English department at Syracuse University, where I teach—we have several faculty members and graduate students specializing in film studies, and lecture courses on film and popular culture serve as the primary training ground for most new teaching assistants in the PhD program regardless of their declared fields—we do not require let alone offer the standard building blocks of a film major or minor: courses in the medium's histories before and after sound, major directors, national cinemas, or genres. Rather, our curriculum organizes courses according to their specific methodological approaches, or "modes of inquiry"; almost all upper-division courses have a main title (the "generic" name) and a subtitle identifying a section's topic (its textual objects and mediating critical lens), and these subtitles vary from section to section and from semester to semester.

Given this somewhat open-ended curricular structure, an informing sense of methodological purpose gets built into my film courses as I design a syllabus. When I teach film noir, for example, I offer it under the course name Reading Gender and Sexualities: The Sexual Politics of Film Noir. Insofar as this course is also cross-listed with the women's and gender studies department and can count toward the minor in gay and lesbian studies, the matter of genre seems quite secondary in its instruction. Feminism and queer theory motivate my teaching of this course, determining the films I select to represent noir as a historically tense representation of gender (ab)normality and ambivalent sexualities and the critical readings I assign to direct class discussions. This course places film noir in a context that does not immediately draw on, and so seems to jar with, the terms in which film buffs and academics usually view noir as a genre having a distinctive form and self-defining canon.

All that said, having taught in this curriculum for nearly two decades, I must also confess that I usually find myself discounting the frequency with which I do teach through genre regardless of the methodological approach I take. In addition to the course on film noir, I regularly teach Theorizing Forms and Genres: The Hollywood Musical, and I offer a survey of American film melodrama at the graduate level. Genre is also an inevitable topic in another course I sometimes teach on film and narrative theory. Genre, finally, inaugurates the second half of my lower-division course Interpretation of Film, a popular gateway to the English major.

In that gateway course I use genre as the hinge point in the syllabus to move out of strictly formalist concerns—cinematography, mise-en-scène, editing, sound, narrative structure, classical spectatorship theory—and toward the wider social contexts of production and reception. How I achieve this transition exemplifies my pedagogical approach to genre in all my courses. To start the lesson, I give students some background on the narrative and stylistic constitution of genres as exemplified by film noir, with which many are already familiar, and the woman's film, which I ask them to think about as an antecedent of today's "chick flick." For visual illustration of the differences, I show the segments on the glamour lighting of female stars and noir lighting from the documentary *Visions of Light: The Art of Cinematography* (1993). The students then view *Mildred Pierce* (1945) and, before the next class meeting, write a two-page paper making their case for how this film addresses a viewer through genre. In the next class we discuss what they have argued about *Mildred Pierce* in their papers. Then we watch its trailer.

The trailer always intrigues students, very quickly rousing them into lively conversation, because it conceals the mother-daughter melodrama and, through the careful reediting of certain scenes and the addition of new material featuring male characters describing Mildred as temptress and she-devil, it characterizes her as a dangerous femme fatale. As a result, the trailer foregrounds for the class how industry and audiences alike rely on genre as a selective interpretative strategy, as the students' arguments about this film's generic address had already begun to make evident. During the ensuing discussion some students (typically but not exclusively male) see the trailer more or less as an accurate condensation of the narrative, revealing how they watched *Mildred Pierce* primarily as noir, oftentimes going on to confess that they felt indifferent to the melodrama except as the backstory for the murder mystery. Other and usually more vocal students (typically but not exclusively female) protest the trailer's exclusions, what they call its "dishonesty," revealing how they concentrated much more on Mildred's labor and motherhood and consequently viewed the murder mystery simply as a framing device. I do not consider either response to be right or wrong, since my intent is to use *Mildred Pierce* and its trailer to illustrate how genre can look like the famous rabbit-duck drawing (their realization that the film may be a hybrid of both genres readily emerges from their disagreements). In addition, at some point during the discussion I show a variety of US and international posters for the film, each selling it through different genres or even historically distant contexts (as in the famous one bringing GIs home to Mildred). The point of this lesson, then, is to make vivid how and why, despite the biological paradigm that inspired classic definitions of *genre* as a term akin to *species*, genres do not reside within film texts as their DNA; rather, viewing through genre is a valuable and sense-making but far from totalizing reading strategy brought to a film and thus not literally organizing it from the inside out.

Rick Altman and Steve Neale, who have both written extensively on genre throughout their careers, openly question the extent to which it ought to be understood solely as a formal narrative structure that gets codified and so internalized in an individual text through convention. To be sure, film studies has a long tradition of formal analysis of genres (see Altman, "American Film Musical" and *Film/Genre*), which drew on many of its premises about aesthetic forms from literary models. And many critical studies and academic courses still benefit from their understanding of genre as sets of formal properties and aesthetic conventions that groups of film share. Nonetheless, in a revision of his earlier structuralist theorization of genre, Altman concludes:

> I never awakened to the fact that Hollywood itself harbours many divergent interests, and that these multiple genre practitioners use genres and generic terminology in differing and potentially contradictory ways. . . . Each genre is simultaneously defined by multiple codes, corresponding to the multiple groups who, by helping to define the genre, may be said to "speak" the genre. (*Film/Genre* 208)

Neale likewise points out that "genre as a term has been used in different ways in different fields," so its function has never been governed entirely "by logic or conceptual consistency" (28). Thus he posits:

> Genres do not consist solely of films. They consist also of specific systems of expectation and hypothesis which spectators bring with them to the cinema and which interact with films themselves during the course of the viewing process. (31)

In their books, Altman and Neale ask who create genres: filmmakers? the studios? reviewers and critics? audiences? The audience members' expectations certainly derive from their familiarity with such conventionalized forms as film noir (or the western or romantic comedy), but, as in the *Mildred Pierce* trailer, such expectations—arising from while also creating the genre being perceived when watching or analyzing a film—are also conditioned by advertising and promotion. As crucially, viewer expectations are historically influenced by the discourses about films that circulate outside the cinema auditorium but that nonetheless inform the experience of watching a film. Further complicating matters, industrial and critical discourses often use different terms when naming the generic form to which a given film or popular cycle belongs. In the 1940s the US film industry informally called "the red meat crime cycle" what became, after the fact and through French criticism, "film noir" (Biesen 2, 96–97). On the other hand, as Neale documents, trade reviewers labeled these same crime films "melodramas" (3), a term film scholars in the 1980s equated almost exclusively with the woman's film, a label rarely used during the studio era, according to Altman (*Film/Genre* 70–77).

Genre, in sum, is most usefully understood as a critical, industrial, affective, and formal template for locating the shared likenesses of certain films in their histories of production, canonization, and reception. Yet interrogating a genre's stability by no means dismisses entirely the utility of formal analysis, which is why I typically begin with matters of form when organizing my courses around a genre. The course on film noir begins with critical readings discussing the genre as a recurring narrative pattern that is motivated by character types (the hard-boiled investigator or working-class outsider and the femme fatale who seduces him, thereby jeopardizing his professionalism or foiling his ambitions), mediated by a male subject (as epitomized by the frequent combination of flashback structure and voice-over narration), and visually rendered through a discernible cinematic style that defines urban and psychological spaces in very concrete if enigmatic ways (starting with how it refracts the characters' sexualities, anxieties and guilt, and moral ambiguities). This pattern is immediately evident to students in the first films we watch: *Double Indemnity* (1944), *Laura* (1944), *Detour* (1945), and *Out of the Past* (1947). Yet such formal elements may sufficiently characterize what noir looks like but fail to determine with exactness whether it ought to be categorized as a cycle, a style, a mode, or a bona fide genre on a par with the western and romantic comedy. After all, these same American "red meat" crime films and melodramatic thrillers from the 1940s share their narrative structures, character types, flashback narrations, and visual style with other genres, other eras, and other national cinemas. Even so, film noir today signifies as a major genre, whether viewed in formal, academic, or (prompted by the self-consciousness of the noir revival starting in the mid-1970s) industrial terms.

Despite that generic slipperiness, I begin by approaching film noir as a coherent and discernible form to accustom students to paying heed to textual details and, more important, to give them a valuable analytic vocabulary for their close readings. I also begin to emphasize for them how the textuality of noir helps locate it in its cultural production as a distinctive artifact of the postwar era. I therefore conclude this first unit with *The Big Sleep* (1946) as a case study of the Production Code Administration's role in shaping the texture and subtexts of film noir. Following upon this vivid instance of institutional authorship, I ask students to consider further how historically specific cultural anxieties about gender, sexuality, race, class, labor, and nationalism motivated the emergence of film noir as a postwar phenomenon. Toward this goal, I devote the middle portion of the semester to studying some films alongside documentaries about postwar concerns (*The Life and Times of Rosie the Riveter* [1980], *Coming Out under Fire* [1994], *Hollywood on Trial* [1976]). Viewing films such as *Mildred Pierce*, *Crossfire* (1947), and *In a Lonely Place* (1950) in tandem with accounts of their era better enables students to see and hear in film noir the historical moment that produced (the conditions of) film noir and its sexual politics.

The final third of my course jumps several decades to look at neo-noir as both a reflexive rereading of the genre's postwar historicity and as a postmodern reimagining of the genre's sylistics and narrative conventions. Sustaining the specific focus of my course on sexual politics, I emphasize how neo-noir likewise pivots on anxieties about the instabilities of gendered norms and sexual identities that characterize its historical moment, including the feminist rereadings of noir in the 1980s (see Kaplan). Even while taking the syllabus toward the present day, I still resist viewing the genre's history as a survey sampling one or two exemplary films from each decade. Rather, experience with this course has convinced me that historicizing a genre in its social as well as industrial moment(s) of production challenges students to think complexly about its dense and oftentimes contradictory textual and historical materiality.

On the other hand, my course on the Hollywood musical more consciously studies a film genre from a predominantly formalist perspective. In fact, on paper this course seems to refute the conviction that I just proclaimed—my syllabus looks like a conventional genre survey, with the 1930s, 1940s, 1950s, and poststudio era each represented by three or four films—although here too appearances are a bit misleading. Since the musical differs from other genres by virtue of its production numbers (they are, after all, what make a musical a recognizable genre), it seems counterintuitive not to approach this genre through its formal elements. The genre's scholarly touchstones are well represented in my own edited collection, which began as a course reader and serves as the spine of this course. The volume's essays reiterate how the musical is inseparable from its formal elements: whether because of the utopian sensibility signified by its numbers (Dyer), the dual focus structure underlying its formation of the romantic couple as a synthesis of opposing cultural values (Altman, "American Film Musical"), or the self-reflexivity with which it celebrates popular entertainment (Feuer, "Self-Reflective Musical" and *Hollywood Musical* 1–47).

Having taught this course many times during the past dozen years, I find that my students, many of them declared and devoted fans of the musical, base their interest on the contemporary stage musical and its cinematic transfers. Accordingly, the initial thrust of my syllabus is aimed to teach them how to watch a film musical formally, which is also to say "cinematically"—and thus differently from its more plot-heavy theatrical cousin and from how commercial movies and television have trained students to watch films for linear plotting alone.

On the second day of class and before I have screened a full-length feature musical, I show just the musical numbers of *Easter Parade* (1948) in sequence, asking the class to fill in the narrative gaps and to reflect on the basis of their inferences and expectations about what is to happen and who is to be coupled. (If any students have seen the film, I use them as secondary commentators who can amplify or even correct the conclusions or guesses of classmates later on in the discussion.) This exercise indicates how the numbers structure the unfolding of a plot while also directing the class's attention to performance and spectacle as central elements of a musical even when perceived as being excessive and hence irrelevant to or in contradiction with the plotting of the interrelated fates of the couple and the show. Admittedly a well-constructed, integrated musical from the Arthur Freed unit at MGM at the height of its aesthetic dominance of the genre, *Easter Parade* actually stacks the deck in favor of this introductory lesson; counting reprises and a song montage, the film has twenty numbers, some quite neatly outlining the narrative action and some not as neatly stalling or interrupting it. So my excision of the plot portions—and I never do show this musical in its entirety—easily makes my point that numbers are not simply amplifications of or digressions from the plot but work together as a principle of structuration, an organization of meanings and pleasures for an audience. This exercise thus reverses the accepted wisdom about musicals, derived from filmmakers and critics taking the integrated musical as their aesthetic touchstone, that numbers serve the main narrative in a formally subordinate relation as opposed to the other way around.

Although a formalist orientation inspires my course overall, there are several ways in which the design pulls against it, my understanding of genre here dovetailing with my pedagogical approach to film noir. Despite the surveying of decades, I do not teach the musicals in chronological order. Instead, I begin in earnest with the 1950s musical and the integrated musical from Freed and MGM, since these amply illustrate the students' initial reading assignments about the genre's conventions; only afterward do I move back to the 1930s to show (through Fred Astaire and Ginger Rogers) the antecedents of the genre's aesthetic template of formal integration while also interrogating it (through Busby Berkeley and the aggregate format of even most Freed musicals); then I shuffle the chronology before concluding with the genre's deconstruction much later in the century. I pair *Gold Diggers of 1933* with *Gentlemen Prefer Blondes* (1953), for instance, followed by a pairing of *The Gang's All Here* (1943) with *The Pirate* (1948), to interrogate the genre's formal conventions, expose the heterocentric bias of its dual focus, examine industrial practices such as stardom and collaborative authorship, raise the problematic of reception through feminism and camp, and ultimately foreground the contrasting stature of the genre for the studio era, when it was mainstream entertainment and bankable product, and for today's film culture, when its fandom is highly marginalized according to gender, sexuality, and generation. In addition, I frequently introduce a film at a screening by showing thirty to forty-five minutes of clips. These can include excerpts from related musicals, documentaries, cable television biographies, and compilations, and their purpose is to establish industrial and cultural contexts for, depending on the particular film, the screen persona and career of a star, a show-business tradition such as vaudeville or drag, the transition to sound, the knotted history of blackface, the dismantling of MGM, and so forth.

I have concentrated on my film noir and musical courses both to illustrate some pedagogical strategies I have found useful and to indicate some of the complex issues that teaching through genre raises for the study of commercial films in the classroom, especially those that seem outmoded or contrived to students. I also try to incorporate this sense of historical distance into my teaching of a genre when I begin, asking in the musicals course, for example, where (Turner Classic Movies? DVD? museums? *YouTube*?) and with whom (parents? grandparents? friends or roommates?) students have acquired their generic literacy. As I continue to develop these courses, finally, new media resources (such as fan Web sites devoted to podcasting or blogging about a genre) amplify my resources for a genre study. Ultimately, I have no particular investment in determining absolutely what constitutes genre as a singular and coherent object. To my mind, asking whether genre is a form, an industrial practice, an aesthetic tradition, or a reception strategy demands the reply, "all of the above." That response always turns out to be the most productive one for my teaching.

Works Cited

Altman, Rick. "The American Film Musical as Dual-Focus Narrative." 1989. Cohan 41–51.

———. *Film/Genre*. London: British Film Inst., 1991. Print.

Biesen, Sheri Chinen. *Blackout: World War II and the Origins of Film Noir*. Baltimore: Johns Hopkins UP, 2005. Print.

The Big Sleep. Dir. Howard Hawks. Perf. Humphrey Bogart and Lauren Bacall. Warner Bros., 1946. Warner Home Video, 2000. DVD.

Cohan, Steven, ed. *Hollywood Musicals, the Film Reader*. London: Routledge, 2002. Print.

Coming Out under Fire. Dir. Arthur Dong. New Video, 1994. Film.
Crossfire. Dir. Edward Dmytryk. Perf. Robert Mitchum, Robert Ryan, and Robert Young. RKO, 1947. Warner Home Video, 2005. DVD.
Detour. Dir. Edward G. Ulmer. Perf. Tom Neal and Ann Savage. Producers Releasing Corp., 1945. Image Entertainment, 2000. DVD.
Double Indemnity. Dir. Billy Wilder. Perf. Barbara Stanwyck, Fred MacMurray, and Edward G. Robinson. Paramount, 1944. Universal Home Entertainment, 2004. DVD.
Dyer, Richard. "Entertainment and Utopia." 1977. Cohan 19–30.
Easter Parade. Dir. Charles Walters. Perf. Judy Garland and Fred Astaire. MGM, 1948. Warner Home Video, 2005. DVD.
Feuer, Jane. *The Hollywood Musical*. 2nd ed. Bloomington: Indiana UP, 1993. Print.
———. "The Self-Reflective Musical and the Myth of Entertainment." 1977. Cohan 31–40.
The Gang's All Here. Dir. Busby Berkeley. Perf. Alice Faye and Carmen Miranda. Twentieth Century–Fox, 1943. Twentieth Century Fox Home Entertainment, 2007. DVD.
Gentlemen Prefer Blondes. Dir. Howard Hawks. Perf. Jane Russell and Marilyn Monroe. Twentieth Century–Fox, 1953. Twentieth Century Fox Home Entertainment, 2001. DVD.
Gold Diggers of 1933. Dir. Mervyn LeRoy. Perf. Dick Powell, Ruby Keeler, Aline MacMahon, and Joan Blondell. Warner Bros., 1933. Warner Home Video, 2006. DVD.
Hollywood on Trial. Dir. David Halperin. Cinema Associates–October Films, 1976. Image Laserdisc, 2006. DVD.
In a Lonely Place. Dir. Nicholas Ray. Perf. Humphrey Bogart and Gloria Grahame. Columbia, 1950. Columbia TriStar Home Video, 2003. DVD.
Kaplan, E. Ann, ed. *Women in Film Noir*. Rev. and expanded ed. London: British Film Inst., 1998. Print.
Laura. Dir. Otto Preminger. Perf. Dana Andrews, Gene Tierney, and Clifton Webb. Twentieth Century–Fox, 1944. Twentieth Century Fox Home Entertainment, 2005. DVD.
The Life and Times of Rosie the Riveter. Dir. Connie Fields. First Run Features, 1980. Film.
Mildred Pierce. Dir. Michael Curtiz. Perf. Joan Crawford, Ann Blyth, Zachary Scott, Jack Carson, and Eve Arden. Warner Bros., 1945. Warner Home Video, 2003. DVD.
Neale, Steve. *Genre and Hollywood*. London: Routledge, 2000. Print.
Out of the Past. Dir. Jacques Tourner. Perf. Robert Mitchum and Jane Greer. RKO, 1947. Warner Home Video, 2004. DVD.
The Pirate. Dir. Vincente Minnelli. Perf. Judy Garland and Gene Kelly. MGM, 1948. Warner Home Video, 2007. DVD.
Visions of Light: The Art of Cinematography. Dir. Stuart Samuels. Image, 1992. Image Entertainment, 2000. DVD.

E. Ann Kaplan

Teaching Futurist Dystopian Cinema

Students have always been fascinated with science fiction film and literature, and courses in this area are of long standing. However, in the post-9/11 world, the rapid increase in production of a certain form of disaster film led me to differentiate certain movies from the plethora of films about catastrophe and especially from the genre science fiction as such. I call this new genre the "futurist dystopian film." A course on this invented film genre is timely and reflects increasing interest on the part of students in understanding the meanings and global implications of disaster.

In this essay, then, I discuss my course on the futurist dystopian cinema that is increasingly evident in the post-9/11 era. The aims of the course are first to define and elaborate characteristics of the new genre, paying attention to an oscillation I find between utopian and dystopian thinking in the history of Western thought that is repeated in these films; second to tease out the meanings (including politics) of the stories told in the selected films, especially regarding gender and race; third to theorize what the increasing prevalence of the dystopian genre today tells us about fears for the future in global perspective; finally, in the light of what we have learned, to analyze the emotional work the genre performs in the public sphere.

But before students can appreciate the new genre or the process of inventing a genre, they need help with understanding genre in cinema in general. One cannot spend much time on genre theory in film as such, but a couple of sessions in part 1 of the course, laying out the basics regarding film and genre, are necessary before dealing with futurist dystopian films and fiction. I turn briefly in these sessions to classic work by Rick Altman and Christine Gledhill on film genre.

I begin by asking students to discuss what they already know about genre and film. Often they do not have much to say, although with prompting one student usually mentions the western or the gangster genre, perhaps drawing on previous film courses. But if I ask for current examples, no one can find a film that fits what they know of the classic film type. This line of questioning allows me to comment that indeed we have today a situation in which many Hollywood studios regularly collapse traditional genres into one another, and filmmakers do not confine their work within a specific genre as in the days of classical Hollywood cinema. In support of this view, Gledhill notes postmodern practices of "picking and mixing" that enable "film-makers to take inspiration from critical as well as studio categories" (223).

But this practice does not mean that genre is waning as a critical and production category. In *Film/Genre*, Altman notes the irony of "producers . . . actively destroying genres by creating new cycles, some of which will eventually be genrified," while film scholars "are regularly trying to fold the cyclical differences back into genre, thus authorizing continued use of a familiar, broad-based, sanctioned and therefore powerful term" (71). Genre is still mentioned in trade journals like *Variety*, even if in terms often different from classical categories.[1] And as Gledhill has argued, with the waning of auteurism and "grand theories" of cinema, genre criticism has become a mechanism for remapping Hollywood (223). "Genre analysis," Gledhill notes, "tells us not just about kinds of films, but about the cultural work of producing and knowing them" (222).

It is as part of the "cultural work of producing and knowing" cinema that critics invent genres that Hollywood and independent producers may not be aware of. That is, film scholars may select from very broad-based Hollywood genre categories (such as, in my case, sci-fi) subgroupings that suggest shifts in cultural values, anxieties and perceptions that are illuminated by the new genre. One example of such inventing within a broad Hollywood category is that of 1970s academic feminist critics, who, freed from the business of marketing film, invented the genre of the woman's film, conceived as a subset of an already contested category, the melodrama, to address neglected aspects of classic films (see Kaplan). The new genre enabled feminists to distinguish oppressive from more progressive images of women on film and to illuminate the complexity of female representation resulting from male culture's anxieties and confusions about gender. "Woman" in cinema, feminists showed, was not a reflection of society on film but an imaginary construct. The invented genre revealed previously hidden social biases and cultural concerns.

Once I have established with students that genres are flexible and multivalent and yet essential for understanding the cultural work that classic and invented genres perform, I can move on to the case study, my new genre, futurist dystopian films, for the purposes of exploring cultural change and political (as well as aesthetic and discursive) analysis. But first we need to consider the differences between the new genre and two other genres related to it, namely science fiction (with its long literary and film tradition) and nuclear disaster cinema. What is it that distinguishes the new futurist dystopian genre? Since the distinction between science fiction film and the new subset is easy to see, in an undergraduate class I start with that contrast by juxtaposing Roland Emmerich's 1996 *Independence Day* (or Steven Spielberg's 2005 remake of the 1953 *War of the Worlds*) and Albert and Allen Hughes's *The Book of Eli* (2010).[2] Students gain a much better idea about genre if they do the work of figuring out structures, visual repetition, tropes, and politics in the films for themselves. Such a stark contrast between the films easily makes its point: students see not only how *Independence Day* seemed to anticipate 9/11 in envisaging the destruction of New York City but also that the agents of catastrophe in the film are aliens not human beings (Žižek, *Welcome*). The film is set in the director's present (1996) with a commensurate everyday world. By contrast, *The Book of Eli* is set in a futurist postholocaust United States, in which all social institutions as we know them have collapsed. While the structure of the world remains in place (there are roads, houses, nature), it is destroyed: houses have been looted and abandoned, bodies lie in the woods, stores have been torn apart by scavengers, the natural world is baked by endless harsh sun. Eli (played by Denzel Washington), having somehow escaped death, struggles to survive in this utterly depleted world as he walks west on dangerous roads (scavengers will kill for a morsel of food) on a mission to bring his "book" to an outpost he's heard of in San Francisco. On the way he endures many traumatic situations, including near capture by a violent warlord hoarding scant resources for himself and a favored few.

This scenario contrasts dramatically with classical sci-fi, which involves alien creatures or machines arriving from outer space into a usually peaceful (at least normal) human world; it also contrasts with technological or cyberspace cinema, like *The Matrix*, which is often celebratory and full of action even as protagonists struggle against the cyberspace computers.

Turning briefly to nuclear disaster cinema, I note that there are enough American films about such disaster to constitute a subset of the futurist dystopian genre.[3] While these films more closely approach the dystopian genre than do regular science fiction cinema, there are significant differences between nuclear films and the new genre. First, in contrast to the futurist dystopian films, this subset relates to a specific technology that is an ongoing threat to human life and (in the original series of films) to a specific political context—namely the Cold War between the United States and the Soviet Union (*On the Beach* [1959] and *Fail-Safe* [1964] are classics of this well-represented subset). Few films in the futurist dystopian genre have such specific threats at the core of the narrative, and with the Cold War over, any specific political context is usually missing. Instead, depending on the film, there are either veiled suggestions about climate change, terrorism, immigration, or projections of future catastrophes, such as infertility or deadly viruses, or genetic mutation making human beings into monsters; none of these situations come about in the context of any specific international war.

Second, very few nuclear disaster films deal with the postholocaust experience or show human beings surviving at all in the wake of a nuclear catastrophe (but see exceptions noted below). Many films deal with a nuclear power plant or other sites of accidental or near nuclear disasters, often focusing on the heroes who try to prevent leakage or to save people once a leakage has happened (see *The Peacemaker* [1977], *The China Syndrome* [1979], *Atomic Train* [1999]). Since most films do not focus on the devastation following a nuclear holocaust but follow the heroic struggles of individuals involved to prevent catastrophe, some films in the genre are closer to science fiction, where, as we saw, the aliens are generally safely eliminated or returned to where they came from.

One might find time to show the prototype for the nuclear genre, namely the first version of *On the Beach*, made in 1959 fairly close to the Hiroshima catastrophe, to clarify the differences. Students will readily see that the film focuses only for a few minutes on post–nuclear holocaust San Francisco. For the most part, the narrative deals with relationships and romances among Australians in Melbourne waiting for the radiation from the United States to reach them. Made in the midst of the Cold War, the film focused on the specific (and realistic) danger of nuclear war set either by the United States or the Soviet Union. *On the Beach* (like *Fail-Safe*) was remade as a television series in 2000 in a very different global era, significantly just before 9/11. The nuclear issue was temporarily muted at the time, and 9/11 had not yet had its global psychological impact.[4] The series is closely modeled on the 1959 film, rather than on the original 1957 novel, by Nevil Shute, and again does not deal with the kind of postholocaust world discussed above in relation to *The Book of Eli* and that is typical of the new futurist dystopian genre.

Depending on how much time one wants to spend on the nuclear theme, I would suggest screening one of three films, *The War Game* (1965), *The Day After* (1983), or *Threads* (1984). All three have similar scenarios regarding the impact of a nuclear bomb and anticipate the post-9/11 futurist dystopian genre in their graphic depiction of destruction and loss of life. All three were also controversial because of their explicit and realistic dramatization of a worst-case scenario of a nuclear holocaust. While the unflinching realism of the impact on ordinary people of a nuclear explosion prevented *The War Game* from being aired on the BBC in 1964, it was later released as a feature film. *The Day After* aired on television but was controversial for the same reasons. *Threads* follows the narrative of *The Day After* closely but is far more detailed about the medical, biological, and agricultural aspects of radiation and the devastating impact over many years on Britain and on the community. In this sense, it comes very close to the futurist dystopian film.

With the exception of *Threads*, then, these films need to be distinguished from the futurist dystopian genre for at least two reasons. First, there is a difference in narrative time: in the nuclear drama case, there is usually a sudden disturbance of normal family or work life by nuclear war; in the futurist dystopian genre the films most often begin with a world that has long suffered deprivation and has slowly been declining over long (but unspecified) time, so that people are worn out with trying to survive. Second, in the nuclear holocaust settings people help one another, whereas in the futurist dystopian scenario, the long deprivation has produced humans scavenging for the last morsels of food or so depressed and alienated by authoritarian control and hardship that they are no longer able to empathize with others.

The contrast, then, if obvious, is striking, since aliens no longer destroy human worlds, nor is the catastrophe occasioned by international war with deadly bombs. Human beings deplete the planet. An increasing number of films with themes and tropes similar to those in *The Book of Eli* have emerged in the wake of 9/11, such as *28 Days* (2002), *The Day after Tomorrow* (2004), *Children of Men* (2006), *I Am Legend* (2008), *Blindness* (2008), *Wall-E* (2008), *District 9* (2009), *2012* (2009), and *The Road* (2010). As we look at some of these films in a preliminary way, I ask students to note common plot characteristics and character types, tropes, and cinematic techniques that recur across the body of films. In addition to the cause of catastrophe being humanity not aliens, students see that the films are set in a future not that distant from our own (many films in the genre are set in specific near-future dates, such as 2012 or 2027); the films typically start with the world already destroyed, all systems and coherent life gone; the plot is usually about a white male trying to save Western civilization by saving a woman or child or both (*Eli* and *I Am Legend* are unusual in that the protagonist is black, but other films often include African American characters in ways the class will analyze later); and usually there is hope for the world's surviving at the end. Variations in the genre include the world being destroyed a bit later in the film (as in *The Day after Tomorrow*); animated characters (but not aliens) appearing along with or replacing human beings; and with climate change, immigration, and terrorism often implied if not directly involved as the causes of catastrophe. These differences from classic sci-fi say much about deepening imaginaries of disaster.

At this point in the course, students have an idea about genre in film, know something about what it means to invent a genre, and have a sense of how the futurist dystopian filmic world compares with that of classic sci-fi, and so we move to part 2 of the course, where we probe more deeply and address harder questions. One such question has to do with the Western tradition of utopian/dystopian thought, a tradition that might illuminate the film (and related literary) genre. Thus I start part 2 with a brief history of utopian thought and the varied uses that have traditionally been made of this form of thinking. Again, I begin by asking students to discuss what they know about utopias and dystopias, with examples from film or fiction. I then refer to the long history of utopian thought and its inevitable dystopian underside so as to prepare students for exploring how, in most of the films in the genre, dystopia seems to give birth to utopian thought, although we know that utopian visions in turn spiral down back to dystopia. We spend time thinking about the utopian endings of the films—or their seeming utopianism. Why do the films end this way? Are these really utopian endings? By the end of the course, we will begin to critique the modality of a binary utopia/dystopia structure and think about alternatives. But for now, students learn to recognize the pattern.

Once students are oriented to the theoretical underpinnings of the course, we move to part 3 and start looking at select films in depth and undertaking the more usual treatment of cinematic texts. I juxtapose two films again to show students the contrast between sensationalizing disaster and looking critically at what human beings are doing to human beings. I pit *The Day after Tomorrow* against *Blindness* and *I Am Legend* against *Children of Men*. An interesting aspect of dystopian films emerges—the prevalence of foreign directors (Mexican, Brazilian) in the genre—which I address as the class begins to examine what directors are trying to show in their varied scenarios. We think about some of the following questions: How are gender and race depicted in each film? Does the director simply carry to the envisaged future the race and gender relations of today? Or does he or she predict changes in such relationships? What about the race or class of the action hero? Films like *District 9*, *2012*, *I Am Legend*, and even *Avatar* (really outside the new genre) will provide lots to talk about in class. Other questions concern issues of ethics, citizenship, reproductive politics, and immigration: What is the director saying about sociality, political organization, and freedom in the film? What ideologies of the heteronormative family prevail? Why are so many of the films set in large international cities? Here readings include research by feminist scholars on bioethics in select films (especially *Children of Men*) and on masculinity in the films. We also read Slavoj Žižek (*Violence*) and Giorgio Agamben, since some films in this genre highlight capitalism as we know it as having failed and as being replaced by new kinds of political (nondemocratic) structure, such as that described by Agamben.

Part 4 of the course picks up some of these themes when we start to theorize what the prevalence of the dystopian genre means in terms of cultural consciousness and perhaps a paradigm shift. With the background of films and discussions in the past weeks, I now ask students to begin thinking about possible reasons for the dystopian genre's popularity. As appropriate, I suggest links to the trauma of the sudden destruction of the Twin Towers in New York, together with related worries about immigration (the foreign terrorists moved freely about the United States as they planned their crimes) and the increasing international crisis of climate change (in turn affecting immigration), and ask whether it is appropriate to call films with such themes *futurist*. Do these scenarios really depict the future, or is this future actually a projection of the present pushed to an extreme? Questions about the future and the possibility of knowing as against imagining it appropriately arise here.

While one has to beware (and teach students to beware) too glibly attributing paradigm shifts to specific events, nevertheless instinctively many people are experiencing a new cultural consciousness in the wake of 9/11—at least in the West (Europe, the United States, Latin America, Canada). It is important for teachers to keep in mind that today's students were very young when 9/11 happened and that the post-9/11 world is their norm. To help them experience such a shift, teachers can show a rare precursor of the dystopian genre, namely Richard Fleischer's 1973 *Soylent Green*, made from Harry Harrison's short story "Make Room! Make Room!" This film, like the post-9/11 films, is set in a major Western city (New York), deals with a catastrophe (overpopulation), and addresses how the powerful people hoard scant resources for themselves. Yet the ambience of the film remains if not lighthearted at least somewhat distanced from the crisis. It does not seem to take the catastrophe seriously enough, even though it is clearly a crisis brought on by human beings, not aliens. Even the scene of George C. Scott's euthanasia is not made disturbing (although there is a shock for viewers when we find out old people's bodies are the source of the crackers others are living on), and sequences of rioting people being scooped up by huge cranes on trucks appear slightly comical. I ask students to think about the different experience of watching *Soylent Green* and *The Book of Eli* and to ponder the extent to which the post-9/11 climate in the United States might partly account for it.

Finally, we turn to the complex question about the emotional work these films do in the public sphere. What is the appeal of the genre? To whom are the movies addressed? Do they allay fears for the future (unlikely) or provide relief for guilt about what human beings are doing to one another? Who watches the films and why? (I have students check online reviews and Internet commentaries to search for some possible answers.) How far might Sigmund Freud's theory of the death drive or at least the urge for aggression and destruction be part of the picture? We read Freud's 1930 dystopia *Civilization and Its Discontents* at the end of the course so as to bring us back to where we started, thinking about the circularity of dystopia and utopia that Freud suggests here and in his war essays ("Thoughts"; see also de Lauretis). In concluding sessions, I encourage students to think beyond this circularity and to envisage other, ethical kinds of thought to help human beings move beyond catastrophe.

Notes

1. Reviews in the 3 September 2007 issue of *Variety* labeled a new Sydney Lumet film "tragedy," a term not frequently used; a new version of *3:10 to Yuma* a "Western remake" but also "R-rated Oater"; *Shoot 'Em Up* an "actioner"; *Atonement* a "romancer"; *Romance and Cigarettes* "an Indie Musical Comedy"; and *Hatchet* a "Horror Film." The reviews still use "Bio-pic" but call only one film, *Hunting Party*, "drama" (rather than melodrama). Notation of gender is interesting: *3:10 to Yuma* is "male-centric," and *Shoot 'Em Up* is aimed at "younger males." Sundance films are listed under "the specialty side."

2. In general, students usually view DVDs of the films outside class, but I prepare short clips or (most effective I think) *PowerPoint* presentations from frame grabs. This way, we can then focus on the single image and discuss how meaning is expressed through cinematic techniques and choices the director makes.

3. I leave aside here international examples of the nuclear disaster film. Given the vast international impact of nuclear bombs and nuclear power stations, it is not surprising that this subset of films about catastrophe is made in more nations than the other genres being considered here.

4. In the wake of the 2011 nuclear catastrophe in Fukushima, Japan, produced by an earthquake, I imagine the nuclear disaster genre will be revitalized.

Works Cited

Agamben, Giorgio. *Homo Sacer: Sovereign Power and Bare Life.* Trans. Daniel Heller-Roazen. Stanford: Meridien, 1998. Print.

Altman, Rick. *Film/Genre.* London: British Film Inst., 2000. Print.

de Lauretis, Teresa. *Freud's Drive.* London: Palgrave, 2009. Print.

Freud, Sigmund. *Civilization and Its Discontents.* Trans. and ed. James Strachey. Introd. Christopher Hitchens. Afterword by Peter Gay. New York: Norton, 2010. Print.

———. "Thoughts for the Times on War and Death." *Collected Papers.* Ed. Joan Riviere. Vol. 4. London: Hogarth, 1949. 288–317. Print.

Gledhill, Christine. "Rethinking Genre." *Reinventing Film Studies.* Ed. Gledhill and Linda Williams. London: Arnold, 2000. 221–43. Print.

Kaplan, E. Ann. "Troubling Genre / Reconstructing Gender." *Genre and Gender.* Ed. Christine Gledhill. Urbana: U of Illinois P, forthcoming.

Žižek, Slavoj. *Violence.* New York: Picador, 2008. Print.

———. *Welcome to the Desert of the Real: Five Essays on September 11 and Related Dates.* London: Verso, 2002. Print.

Michael Renov

Teaching the Documentary Film

This essay focuses on documentary teaching practices and perspectives that are broadly framed and practical, having to do with perceptions of how the developing field of documentary studies plays out in the classroom: What films are most useful? What impediments exist with regard to distribution? How important is a global purview for teaching the documentary?

But first I feel obliged to offer a brief autobiographical aside, since what I have to say here is primarily based on my personal experience. I began teaching documentary in the 1980s, when I was first hired at the University of California, Santa Barbara, in a class on post–World War II documentary film, the follow-up to a course taught by Chuck Wolfe on the classic documentary works of the 1920s, 1930s, and 1940s. Despite having had Steve Mamber (author of *Cinema Verité in America*) as my dissertation adviser, I had never taken a class on documentary, because none were being offered. Like other documentary scholars of my generation, I got my training on the job, by screening and reading and teaching and discussing. With few papers and fewer panels on documentary topics at the Society for Cinema Studies conference (the precursor to the Society for Cinema and Media Studies), the classroom was the principal laboratory for testing ideas about documentary.[1]

I offer the following list of goals to which the documentary pedagogue may profitably aspire:

To provide local knowledge
To facilitate a grasp of the film-historical context
To promote historical understanding
To model political activism
To engage with the semiotics and aesthetics of cinema
To showcase documentary's global reach
To offer lessons in truth telling and epistemology
To effect practice
To provide an ethical showcase

These goals articulate with the discrete elements of the well-known fourfold query (the who, what, why, and how of pedagogy) in varying ways. Most of us tend to foreground certain of these goals in our teaching of documentary; it is neither possible nor desirable to hold them in equipoise. Of necessity, my account of each of them here will be telegraphic rather than comprehensive.

To Provide Local Knowledge

By *local knowledge* I mean something like information, the delivery of fact, inflected or lowercase knowledge, that which satisfies the underlying epistephilic urge. Local knowledge is a phrase derived from the anthropologist Clifford Geertz, whose examination of the relations between fact and law across diverse cultures traced out a web of interconnection between the general and the particular, the construction of legal norms on the one hand and the happenings or "fact-configurations" of everyday life on the other. Law, he concluded, is local knowledge, "local not just as to place, time, class, and variety of issue, but as to accent—vernacular characterizations of what happens connected to vernacular imaginings of what can" (215). The documentary film is typically a storehouse of nuanced and localized knowledge, fact-configurations packaged into meaningful structures calculated to stimulate then satisfy the innate curiosity of audiences.

One motivation for teaching documentary is to offer experiences that satisfy the human appetite for local knowledge. I see this as a fundamental pedagogical aim yet one that rarely stands alone. I watch *Planet Earth* (2006) to be amazed and to sample the natural wonders of the world, but I do not often choose to teach such work without other supporting motives. This most elementary pedagogical goal reminds me of an apocryphal tale, namely that one of the most successful documentaries of all time, based on sales, was an educational film for fire fighters on how to coil a fire hose. We teach the documentary film to supply local knowledge.

To Facilitate a Grasp of the Film-Historical Context

No one who teaches documentary film, even those who eschew the historical survey, can afford to remain blind to the film-historical dimension. I am a firm believer that teachers do not have to show an Auguste and Louis Lumière *actualité* or *Nanook of the North* (1922) the first week of class, but they had best attend to history in some measure. Otherwise students are apt to conclude that Jean Vigo's *À propos de Nice* (1930) is a brilliant example of *cinema verité*, a term that does not become meaningful for three more decades.

Regarding this pedagogical goal, the "to whom" question is deeply relevant. I am far less likely to foreground the film-historical for a class of nonmajors. But I think everyone should know that the documentary impulse is as old as cinema even if the documentary as a filmic type does not get established until much later. I do not feel obliged to follow a simple chronology or stick to canonical texts. But I am grateful for the recently available collection *Unseen Cinema: Early American Avant-Garde Film, 1894–1941*, since it allows me to show the very brief *24 Dollar Island* (1926), by Robert Flaherty, in lieu of *Nanook*. I can offer a more concise introduction to Flaherty's epic romanticism while leaving room for a more varied introductory week.

Encouraging students to grapple with historical questions in the emergence and development of the documentary film is not the same as teaching films in chronological order. Historical understanding can be approached through a thematic or special-topics orientation just as it can be through a survey. I feel obliged to remind the class that documentary has always developed in relation to the formats, technologies, and apparatuses of particular moments so that Jean Rouch's or Richard Leacock's tinkering with the 16mm camera in the early 1960s shaped specific films while facilitating the evolution of documentary film style on two continents. American guerrilla television of the 1970s is important in part for its forceful introduction of a cheap and portable format—video—which changed documentary history yet again and in so doing presaged the arrival of

YouTube. The pedagogical challenge is not to force-feed names and dates but to usher students into thinking historically about a complex cultural formation, the documentary film.

To Promote Historical Understanding

I am often critical of historians or other nonspecialists who use documentary films purely illustratively, inattentive to the specificities of cinematic language. But the documentary form does furnish ample opportunity for enlivening history for today's students. It is tempting to teach the civil rights era through the *Eyes on the Prize* series (1987) or World War II by way of Ken Burns and Lynn Novick's *The War* (2007). Documentary films function particularly well as occasions for discussing matters of historiography, the methods used for the writing or production of historical narratives. Accounts of the past are always authored and presented from specific perspectives, but the neutrality of prose can obscure that fact. Music, voice-over narration, reenactment, and interviews are some of the tools that documentary filmmakers use to represent historical events, and they can all be shown to bear ideological effects. Teaching documentary can be the occasion for asking how history gets written, what process of selection is entailed to carve out a particular view of the past. This topic may end up overshadowing the content of any given historical documentary.

In recent documentary practice, the home movie has functioned as a dramatic portal to past experience, source of a private history that can be made to narrate the broader social field. Peter Forgacs's *The Maelstrom* (1997) is composed primarily of home movie footage shot by a young Dutch Jew over the course of a perilous decade. The Peereboom family becomes the locus of our understanding, their private chronicle narrating a tragic spiral toward destruction at the hands of national socialism that mirrors the plight of millions. Home movies can be treasure troves of memory, indexes of an irretrievable past that can be nimbly repurposed and overlaid with reflective text or narration in the hands of such filmmakers as Jonas Mekas, Michelle Citron, Rea Tajiri, Richard Fung, Alan Berliner, Jay Rosenblatt, and Jonathan Caouette. World historical events get scaled down and turned inside out to reveal the private suffering that lies within. These works offer opportunities for engaging students in an open-ended dialogue about history as lived experience rather than as public event.

To Model Political Activism

Many of us came to the teaching of documentary through our interest in social change and our recognition that the documentary wields a power of engagement for young audiences. It would be difficult for any pedagogue to avoid documentary's historical convergence with political activism. Among the noteworthy moments and documentary makers are Dziga Vertov, with his Kinoki during the silent film era; Joris Ivens, Ralph Bond, and the Workers Film and Photo League in the 1930s; Santiago Alvarez, Fernando Solanas and Octavio Getino, and the Newsreel Collective in the 1960s; the guerrilla television collectives of the 1970s; the feminist and queer activists whose efforts began in the 1970s and continue today; Eastern European, Korean, and Chinese makers documenting popular movements of resistance in the 1980s and 1990s; and the viral media activists of the current moment. Michael Moore's *Fahrenheit 9/11* (2004) shattered box office records during the summer of an American presidential campaign when, for a moment, it seemed a movie might alter the fortunes of a nation. Some students think *An Inconvenient Truth* (2006) might mark a sea change in American public opinion toward climate change. Documentary's political engagements exert a powerful attraction for audiences and help explain why many of us teach this work.

I have found Jane Gaines's essay on political mimesis to be a valuable classroom tool for its attention to the visceral dimension of documentary film reception, the ways that the textures of images, the rhythms of sound and editing can induce us to "body back" what we are shown and in so doing perhaps induce agency. I love the conversations this essay inspires among my students. It offers a great opportunity for a mutualist, experientially driven rather than top-down approach to pedagogy. If I show Alvarez's short film *Now* (1965), a music video precursor that matches Lena Horne's inspired vocals to briskly edited, high-energy archival footage of civil rights protestors, and ask students if the message gets under their skin, they are all likely to have an opinion. I might then choose to complement that discussion with an exposition of Aristotle's forms of rhetorical proof to suggest some concrete tactics for persuasion that have functioned effectively for millennia. For the teacher of documentary film, nothing quite equals the thrill of observing how the genre can reach the hearts and minds of students in every era.

To Engage with the Semiotics and Aesthetics of Cinema

All of us who teach the documentary are obliged to ask our students not just "What does this mean?" but "How does this mean?" Although I do not always utter the words *semiotics* or *aesthetics*, many important works of the 1920s, what Bill Nichols has called the films of "poetic exposition," as well as more current experimental documentaries are textbooks for teaching the fundamentals of cinematic language. I cannot show *À propos de Nice* without talking about Soviet-style intellectual montage, the only way to explain why images of the leisured classes sunning themselves in the South of France are intercut with brief shots of ostriches or crocodiles.

The cinepoem and the city symphony help ground the documentary enterprise in the modernist moment. The career of Joris Ivens, bookended by *Rain* (1929) and *A Tale of the Wind* (1989), is an exemplary one, reminding us that political advocacy derives its power from the maker's control of his medium. As I argue in "Toward a Poetics of Documentary," persuasion, far from being opposed to aesthetics, depends on expressivity for its instantiation. I may choose to show the work of Stan Brakhage or James Benning in a documentary context, in part because they push at nonfiction's discursive boundaries, but canonical texts such as *Tongues Untied* (1990) or *79 Springtimes of Ho Chi Minh* (1969) will also suffice to demonstrate that documentary is the *creative* treatment of actuality and that aesthetic innovation can induce heightened audience response.

To Showcase Documentary's Global Reach

Nowadays I insist on introducing students to documentary films and filmmakers from six or eight countries. I am deeply grateful to Jane Balfour for introducing me to Sergei Dvortsevoy, a Kazakhstani filmmaker whose *Bread Day* (1998) has reinvigorated my teaching of the observational mode. After decades of teaching *Primary* (1960) and *Titicut Follies* (1967), I am relieved to be able to illustrate the tenets of direct cinema while also introducing the class to the realm of post-Soviet Russian cinema. More than ever, documentary is a global phenomenon; remarkable work is being produced in Brazil, Finland, China, Australia, and throughout Africa, as well as countless other locations not previously featured in standard documentary histories. The recently released *Encyclopedia of the Documentary Film*, edited by Ian Aitken, has helped redress the dearth of resources for studying global documentary culture.

Visible Evidence, an annual conference on documentary film, is an international event that will only achieve its full potential when it has been staged on every continent where documentary filmmaking thrives—that is, everywhere but Antarctica. The Flaherty Seminar, formerly held once a year exclusively in upstate New York, has begun to organize occasional gatherings in international locations and always reaches out to makers from around the world.

My preliminary efforts to poll others (through the Visible Evidence Listserv) tells me that most teachers of documentary are ever in search of the means to broaden their geopolitical horizons. Access is always a stumbling block. At least for Latin American documentary, which has experienced a dramatic resurgence in recent decades, there is a resource that will make possible the screening of many hundreds of films, old and new. Docfera is an organization that, as stated on its Web site, aims to become "the first web platform and the largest digital archive for Latin American documentaries in the world." Under the direction of Andrea Hirsch, Docfera plans to attract institutional subscribers who will be given online access to a huge, highly searchable cache of Latin American documentary films.

One final observation on the importance of teaching documentary in a global frame: one can never fully anticipate the cross-cultural resonances of documentary spectatorship. I recently had the experience of showing *London Can Take It* (1940) to a group of Jordanian, Palestinian, and Lebanese students in Amman. I was amazed by the immediacy of that film for these young people who have lived with bombs and bloodshed all their lives. The postscreening conversation focused on the film's construction of national character, the assertion of British resolve, toughness, and resiliency. The students, it seemed, had no comparable national stereotypes to draw on for their own survival narratives. That teaching experience has forever changed my reception of the film.

To Offer Lessons in Truth Telling and Epistemology

Jerome Bruner has written of the necessity of an enlightened educational policy that, in addition to encouraging young people "to honor the culture's traditions of sensibility or cultivatedness—its past," will "seek to equip them with 'flexibility' and 'resilience'" (208). These attributes are moral and intellectual, less learned than practiced or modeled, developed over time to the point of competence and even self-sufficiency. Students may have the technical facility to navigate and even intervene in the contemporary mediasphere, but, in the face of myriad truth claims attached to political campaigns, advertising, and news coverage, they have far less competency for calibrating their responses more finely than indifference, acceptance, or undifferentiated skepticism.

If knowledge is justified belief, our job is to help students analyze the ways that claims for truth get justified in the works we screen. I begin my course by positing the truth claim as the defining condition of the documentary; we then work to ferret out those claims and decipher the rhetorical ploys and aesthetic practices that render them convincing for audiences. Despite the disparagement from philosophers such as Noël Carroll who see film scholars ill-suited to the task, I think all educators must be in the business of training our pupils as epistemologists as well as learners. Why shy away from "going meta" in our teaching, when offering models for political and intellectual critique can help students construe their experience well beyond the classroom?

I even think some filmic texts can make vital contributions to spawning clarity of mind and judgment. Although one must be prepared to complement the screening with lots of historical context, including an Emile de Antonio film such as *In the Year of the Pig* (1969) or *Millhouse: A White Comedy* (1971) on the syllabus can have tonic effects. As described by critics such as Tom Waugh, Doug Kellner, and Dan Streible, de Antonio's collagist approach requires the audience's active engagement and powers of judgment. Frequently, archival footage is pitted against an interview so that the personal testimony calls into question or undercuts the historical record seemingly established by the archival material. As with the work of Errol Morris, viewers are forced to remain vigilant—to sift evidence, evaluate credibility, and extract authorial point of view—throughout the experience. Tutelage in both visual and epistemological literacy is among our most vital tasks as educators.

To Effect Practice

This pedagogical goal may not apply to all teachers of documentary in all settings. I have a strong commitment to working at the intersection of theory and practice. I love having production students in my classes and observing them gleaning ideas and inspiration from the films and books they encounter. Filmmakers bring a kind of pragmatism to their study of documentary that is useful for the scholar. They want to know how things are made, what works and why. Nothing makes me happier than seeing production students begin to reevaluate their preconceptions and rethink their projects because of what they encounter in the classroom. I take special pleasure in assigning the writings of practitioners from Vertov to Rouch to David MacDougall since they tend to recover the moment when idea becomes action.

The University of Southern California's School of Cinematic Arts is consulting on the creation of a new film school to serve the Middle East to be based in Aqaba, Jordan. I have already had the opportunity to teach a documentary workshop to students learning the production ropes, a tremendously gratifying experience. I observe their responses to Rouch and Edgar Morin's *Chronicle of a Summer* (1960), Humphrey Jennings's *Listen to Britain* (1942), Jon Alpert's *Hard Metals Disease* (1984), or Brian Hill's *Songbirds* (2005). New horizons open up for them as they think through their personal stories, relationships, and agendas for change. When theory and practice meet in this way, the results are enormously rewarding for all.

To Provide an Ethical Showcase

I conclude with ethics. I was very pleased to discover that Nichols's recent *Introduction to Documentary* begins with an account of the ethical issues encountered in the study or production of the documentary film. I share Nichols's view that ethics is the place to begin—and end—the study of the documentary. In recent years, I have included a screening of Werner Herzog's *Grizzly Man* (2005) on the first day of my documentary class. It is a remarkable film in many respects—gripping, repugnant, ecstatic—and it raises many questions that resonate throughout the term. Whose film is it? one may ask. Is the creator Herzog or his subject, Timothy Treadwell, whose footage commands a sizable proportion of screen time? The question of authorship plays out across future screenings of TVTV's *Four More Years* (1972), Tom Joslin and Peter Friedman's *Silverlake Life: The View from Here* (1993), Forgacs's *The Maelstrom*, and Alain Resnais's *Night and Fog* (1955). In some cases, the thorniest problems arising from shared authorship are ethical. Can one ever fully decide the "rightness" of Herzog's construction of Treadwell, *Grizzly Man*'s filmmaker savant, or reconcile the gap between Treadwell's efforts toward self-construction and the version of the man offered us by the film? Do we not feel a little queasy when Forgacs takes over for Max Peereboom, *The*

Maelstrom's doomed amateur filmmaker? Would Joslin have approved of his protégée Friedman's choices in depicting both Joslin's and his partner Mark Massi's deaths?

Likewise, what are we to make of Albert and David Maysles's rendition of Big and Little Edie Beale in *Grey Gardens* (1975)? My students never tire of arguing about who is exploiting whom in that film, of trying to untangle voyeurism from exhibitionism or find a comfortable angle of reception for themselves. Student responses have been amped up recently by the success of the Broadway version of the film, the countless fan Web sites, and the feature film version. What does one say when Angelo gets fired from his factory job in *Chronicle of a Summer* or Alpert's aggressive tracking of corporate crimes in *Hard Metals Disease* leaves his worker-informants jobless? Should the public's right to know or the filmmaker's will to point a finger at social injustice trump privacy or a steady paycheck for his subjects? When Fred Wiseman filmed at the Massachusetts Institution for the Criminally Insane at Bridgewater in *Titicut Follies*, did those inmates ridiculed and demeaned on camera for all eternity really exercise informed consent? Is informed consent even possible in such circumstances, and how much does that matter?

What all these films and our responses to them have in common is a tendency to jam the moral compass, to jostle us out of our comfort zone as we strive to decide the rightness of the representation. As the documentary teacher must train epistemologists, so we are duty bound to make moral philosophers of our students. Emanuel Levinas and others have written weighty tomes that help us comprehend and come to grips with the obligations self owes other. These books are demanding reads and require a background in the history of ideas. The documentary films we show our students are invaluable training grounds for the exercise of moral judgment. The ethical stakes are high for nonfiction, far beyond those of fiction, because these documentary representations entail human subjects and potentially life-changing consequences. As we struggle to decide where we stand and test our responses to these films, we ready ourselves for making the difficult choices life demands.

The goal of our teaching in matters of ethical judgment should not be to offer definitive answers so much as to offer occasions for testing our moral reflexes. If we share Bruner's sense that flexibility and resilience are the best aids to survival and full citizenship for our students, we would do well to accord the ethical domain a privileged place in our teaching.

Note

1. When I applied for what was described as an explicitly documentary job at the University of Southern California in 1985, I did so on the basis not of my publications but of my teaching experience. I'd come to love my documentary class and regarded the prospect of a tenure-track job teaching what I liked best as too good to be true. My job talk became the essay "Re-thinking Documentary: Toward a Taxonomy of Mediation"; my career as a documentary scholar had begun, but it was teaching that led the way.

Works Cited

Aitken, Ian, ed. *Encyclopedia of the Documentary Film.* New York: Routledge, 2006. Print.

Bruner, Jerome. *In Search of Pedagogy: The Selected Works of Jerome Bruner, 1979–2006.* New York: Routledge, 2006. Print.

Gaines, Jane M. "Political Mimesis." *Collecting Visible Evidence.* Ed. Gaines and Michael Renov. Minneapolis: U of Minnesota P, 1999. 84–102. Print.

Geertz, Clifford. *Local Knowledge: Further Essays in Interpretative Anthropology.* New York: Basic, 1983. Print.

Nichols, Bill. *Introduction to Documentary.* 2nd ed. Bloomington: Indiana UP, 2010. Print.

Renov, Michael. "Re-thinking Documentary: Toward a Taxonomy of Mediation." *Wide Angle* 8.3-4 (1986): 71–77. Print.

———. "Toward a Poetics of Documentary." *Theorizing Documentary.* Ed. Renov. New York: Routledge, 1993. 12–36. Print.

Mark Langer

Teaching Animation

Teaching animation is in many respects unlike teaching any other kind of film course, in terms of its student constituency, its traditional place in the curriculum, and the academic opportunities it offers. In regard to this first aspect, animation comes with a peculiar set of expectations from students. It is not unusual for an instructor to deal with extremes—some students dismiss animation as something that they outgrew with puberty, while others are rabid fans of, say, Warner Bros. cartoons or Japanese anime and show up to lectures bringing action figures and intense obsessions. In such cases, student preconceptions constitute hurdles to academic examination of the subject. Student fans in particular may have an amazingly detailed empirical knowledge of the subject (often more than their instructor) but may lack, and may even be hostile to, critical or theoretical perspectives. Thus teaching animation, unlike a course focusing on Ingmar Bergman, requires the instructor to overcome preexisting attitudes of students who either deem the subject unworthy of serious consideration or resist theory as antithetical to their viewing pleasure.

Animation has had a spotty history within the academy. During the 1960s, when film became institutionalized as a form of intellectual discourse with academic journals and university programs, expressions of interest in mainstream Hollywood animation were at best ignored. At worst, these expressions were dismissed on both intellectual and aesthetic grounds. Affected by widespread tendencies among arbiters of film culture to disregard all but highbrow forms of humor, animation was relegated to reaches of a cultural limbo even beyond those occupied by other film genres, such as the musical or comedy. Popular cultural discourse joined with intellectual discourse in a rejection of animation as incoherent with highbrow or even middlebrow thought. Within mainstream culture and its organs of legitimation, animation was thought to be devoid of cultural capital.

This characterization applied only to commercial animation and did not encompass the experimental or independent animation of filmmakers like Viking Eggeling or Jan Svankmajer. While books such as Ralph Stephenson's *Animation in the Cinema* castigated most commercial animation, it praised the work of independent artists internationally. Independent animation, however, tended to be marginalized as a minor subclassification of experimental filmmaking, a branch of production that was ignored by critics and the general public.

Views began to change around the mid-1970s, following such events as the New York Lincoln Center Disney retrospective in 1973, Jay Cocks's 1973 article on Chuck Jones in *Time*, the animation issue of *Film Comment* edited by Greg Ford in 1975, and the Whitney Museum Disney show in 1981. In this period, institutions of higher learning began to introduce animation as part of general scholarly film curricula, rather than as ghettoized craft courses or programs in the fine arts. In New York, the New School for Social Research introduced a course on the history of animation in 1973, taught by Leonard Maltin. By 1975, I taught a similar course at the Graduate School of Arts at Columbia University. Now, courses that are either exclusively devoted to animation or have a strong animation component are no longer unusual in university curricula. Consecutive editions of a standard introductory text demonstrate this increased emphasis on animation within the broader discipline of film studies. In 1979, David Bordwell and Kristin Thompson's *Film Art: An Introduction* mentioned animation in a scant three pages. By 1993, the fourth edition contained thirty-six pages with references to animation and included a section devoted to analyses of animated films. Concurrent with this movement in academia, film journals such as *Cinema Journal*, *Screen*, and *Film History* began routinely publishing articles on topics previously covered only in such underground animation periodicals or fan magazines as *Funnyworld*, *Film Fan Monthly*, or *Mindrot*. Animation is now served by its own blind peer-reviewed journals, such as *Animation Journal* or *Animation: An Interdisciplinary Journal.* In addition, several textbooks offer general introductions to the subject, such as Maureen Furniss's *Art in Motion: Animation Aesthetics.*

Animation is often regarded as a tiny subset of the larger discipline of cinema, although the animation theorist Alan Cholodenko suggests that since live-action cinema is a series of still images brought to life by the projection process, it is actually a subset of the larger field of animation (Introd. 20). Regardless of one's point of view, animation is a huge topic, the study of which is complicated by the fact that there is no commonly accepted definition of *animation.* A course trying to give an overview of the vast range of the field would have to stretch wide to include the disparate relevant material within the limits of an academic term. Such material includes both shorts and features and varies from children's entertainment to instructional or educational films to the most avant-garde experimental works. It covers almost every national cinema in the world. Animation involves the use of a broader range of media platforms than those encountered in more traditional film studies courses, since animated films are produced not only for theatrical exhibition, television, and computer games but also for Internet viewing through computers and other personal electronics.

Central to the study of animation are problems that one may not encounter in many other areas of the film studies curriculum, including time period, media forms and platforms, critical discourses and literatures, and availability of visual sources. With respect to time period, it should be noted that animation has a longer history than film, beginning with such optical toys as the magic lantern, the 1832 phenakistoscope, or the 1867 zoetrope. Actual theatrical presentation of projected animated works originated with slides of moving magic lanterns in Étienne-Gaspard Robert's phantasmagoria in 1794 and continued with the charming, hand-drawn images of Charles-Émile Reynaud's projecting praxinoscope in 1882. Not only does animation's genesis anticipate the rise of photographic cinema, it remains at the forefront of motion picture expression today. Animation is of paramount importance to cutting-edge technologies in today's moving-image media, with the development of computer-generated images (CGI) and various Web-based productions.

With respect to media forms and platforms, animation is also anomalous. While the study of the feature-length film predominates in film studies, the short film, the abstract film, and works produced for other media platforms (such as the Internet or television) have a much more central role to play in the study of animation. And since animation includes special effects, many films that are not marketed specifically as animated films, such as Steven Spielberg's *War of the Worlds* (2005), are largely done through computer animation and indeed are hardly imaginable without it. In terms of course design, this overlap can lead to a need to present a vast array of media in class and to discuss a far less coherent body of work than demanded in other types of film studies courses.

And while critical discourses surrounding feature-length films, such as those regarding ideology, gender, genre, and nation, tend to revolve around issues related to narrative, animation tends to give greater focus to formal qualities, such as color, composition, and motion. Addressing form involves training students who may already be conversant with the intelligent viewing of live-action cinema to pay attention to visual analysis and such concepts as synesthesia. While some general theoretical works on cinema apply to animation, there is also a literature that treats animation specifically. This ever-growing body of theoretical work on animation—such as that of Andrew Darley, Esther Leslie, and Cholodenko, among others—is not well-known within film studies. This problem is compounded by the relatively short period of time in which a critical and theoretical literature on animation has existed. Much of it is in out-of-print books or in scholarly journals devoted to animation that may not be readily available either in university libraries or to the instructor wishing to scan a journal article or book chapter for electronic course reserves. Finally, while canonical live-action films are for the most part readily obtainable, the same is not generally true of animation. But conditions in recent years have improved markedly, as the availability of films on DVD has increased rapidly.

The broad scope of animation offers equally broad possibilities for course design. Survey courses are possible, using organizational models such as chronological or technological. A variety of texts such as Giannalberto Bendazzi's *Cartoons: One Hundred Years of Cinema Animation* or Paul Wells's *Understanding Animation* are available to support courses. For the reasons outlined above, however, I would discourage mounting such broad courses, since their format encourages "a mile wide and an inch deep" type of scholarship. This approach might have been justified when the limited availability of both animated films and published scholarship provided narrow boundaries for a survey course, but in the current circumstances, it is inadvisable.

More focused courses dealing with national traditions, either comparing different cultural approaches to the animated film or dealing with a specific national context, are also possible. Student interest in Japanese anime, for example, is matched by the availability of films by Osamu Tezuka, Mamoru Oshi, or Hayao Miyazaki and well supported by an extensive literature, including Susan J. Napier's *Anime from* Akira *to* Howl's Moving Castle. Such a course could deal with critical debates about "Japaneseness," global distribution and consumption, the influences of European and American models, the effect of other Japanese media (such as manga) or cultural practices on anime aesthetics, the relation of narrative themes and the Japanese historical experience, *otaku* ("techno-nerd") culture, *kawaii* ("cuteness") in anime, genres like *mecha*-anime, and so on. Similarly, the vast array of American animation is easily obtainable on DVD and covered by scholars like Michael Barrier, in *Hollywood Cartoons: American Animation in Its Golden Age*, or Wells, in *Animation and America*.

Another possibility would be for an instructor to organize a course around a traditional film studies topic like authorship and examine great animation directors, including Tex Avery, Chuck Jones, Lotte Reiniger, and Oskar Fischinger. Granted, such a course could be limited by the availability of certain bodies of work and literature—for example, it would be far less challenging for an instructor to mount a course on the Warner Bros. animator Chuck Jones, around whose work a sizable body of literature has developed, than it would be to organize one on the equally prolific work of fellow Warner Bros. animator Friz Freleng, about whom little exists in the way of scholarly publications. Oskar Fischinger, Lotte Reiniger, Len Lye, Caroline Leaf, and a host of other avant-garde animators produced much smaller bodies of work, not always available on DVD or accompanied by a large literature, yet they are worthy of study, perhaps in a course devoted to the avant-garde.

Animation lends itself to courses on gender studies, either using animated materials exclusively or in conjunction with live-action films. One thinks of such animated personae as Snow White, Prince Charming, Preston Blair's Red, Bugs Bunny in drag, and so on. While there is a literature dealing with this in particular reference to animation, like Kevin Sandler's "Gendered Evasion: Bugs Bunny in Drag" or Amy M. Davis's *Good Girls and Wicked Witches: Women in Disney's Feature Animation*, much literature from the broader field of gender studies applies.

Genre studies approaches also apply to animation, with such genres as superhero cartoons, jazz cartoons, science-fiction animated films, and animation noir. As with authorship, gender, and other approaches, these films can be taught in an exclusively animation film course or together with live-action films. For example, among the earliest film noirs were the Max and Dave Fleischer *Superman* series of 1940–41, which, along with CGI-intensive films like Frank Miller's *Sin City* (2005), would make an interesting inclusion to a course on noir.

Because of the diversity of the field, animation lends itself well to specialized examination. A course on Disney might offer rich opportunities to examine the notion of authorship through the blurred distinction between Walt Disney and the products of the corporation that bears his name, including a consideration of subauteurs like Dick Huemer, David Hand, Al Hurter, Norm Ferguson, Ub Iwerks, or Joe Grant. Such a course could also look at the interactions of cinema, commerce, and the state, since Disney frequently cooperated with the US government in the creation of propaganda films or through expressions of the World War II and Cold War zeitgeist, as explored in Steven Watts's *The Magic Kingdom: Walt Disney and the American Way of Life*. In addition, the Disney strike and its aftermath was a key event in the blacklist period in Hollywood; Walt Disney was even a friendly witness giving House Committee on Un-American Activities testimony. Several books, from Ariel Dorfman and Armand Mattelart's *How to Read Donald Duck* to Carten Laqua's *Mickey Mouse, Hitler and Nazi Germany: How Disney's Characters Conquered the Third Reich*, examine Disney in the context of other countries. The course could also address the relations among amusement parks, television, Internet, publishing, and such ancillary products as toys and clothing, as explored by Stephen M. Fjellman in *Vinyl Leaves: Walt Disney World and America*. And since no other company is so closely identified with America as Disney, one could approach the production and consumption of Disney films in the light of American culture, both within the country and overseas.

Animation offers the possibility of a course organized around the body in cinema, from the early-twentieth-century Ko-Ko the Clown cartoons to current CGI efforts like *Final Fantasy: The Spirits Within* (2001) and *The Spirit* (2009). A course organized around the body might examine technology from the rotoscope to motion capture, where the human body is used as a guide to animation. Motion capture results in the copresence of the biological and the technological, opening up discussion of this phenomenon in terms of Sigmund Freud's idea of the uncanny. The anomalous bodies of animated characters, often fusing animal, mechanical, and human elements in their design and behavior, lend themselves to a discussion of freaks, cyborgs, and the violations of the boundaries that separate different classifications of being. Works like Rosemarie Garland Thomson's edition *Freakery: Cultural Spectacles of the Extraordinary Body* or Joanna Bouldin's "Bodacious Bodies and the Voluptuous Gaze: A Phenomenology of Animation Spectatorship" could support such a course, as could less animation-focused work by scholars like Vivian Sobchack.

Since so much animation is devoted to children's entertainment, an animation course analogous to one on children's literature could easily draw on existing scholarship such as Nicholas Sammond's *Babes in Tomorrowland: Walt Disney and the Making of the American Child, 1930–1960*, Joseph Tobin's collection *Pikachu's Global Adventure: The Rise and Fall of Pokémon*, or Heather Hendershot's anthology *Nickelodeon Nation: The History, Politics, and Economics of America's Only TV Channel for Kids*. Such a course might trace how childhood has been constituted as a stage in life, in terms of gender or consumption patterns, in a variety of historical and national contexts through animated film and television.

In recent years, a body of literature has developed on the interaction between animation and leading theorists in the twentieth century. A course dealing with the work of aesthetic, cultural, and political theorists and animation could include books like Jay Leyda's *Eisenstein on Disney* or Esther Leslie's *Hollywood Flatlands: Animation, Critical Theory and the Avant-Garde*. Since CGI and photo-real "synthespians" (hybridized characters such as those generated through motion-capture processes in films like *Beowulf* [2007]) pose challenges to concepts of indexicality, another possibility is the reevaluation of earlier theorists such as André Bazin and Charles Peirce in the light of more recent examinations of indexicality, like Michele Pierson's *Special Effects: Still in Search of Wonder* or Andrew Darley's *Visual Digital Culture: Surface Play and Spectacle in New Media Genres*, as well as Cholodenko's edited collection *The Illusion of Life II*.

This list is not exhaustive, but it points to the kinds of topics that can be investigated under the rubric of animation. Animation exists in so many forms and in so many ways that challenge our understanding of cinema. It is a fertile field for instructors to investigate and a source of intellectual pleasure, development, and insight for students.

Works Cited

Barrier, Michael. *Hollywood Cartoons: American Animation in Its Golden Age*. New York: Oxford UP, 1999. Print.

Bendazzi, Giannalberto. *Cartoons: One Hundred Years of Cinema Animation*. Trans. Anna Taraboletti-Segre. Bloomington: Indiana UP, 1994. Print.

Bordwell, David, and Kristin Thompson, eds. *Film Art: An Introduction*. 4th ed. New York: McGraw, 1993. Print.

Bouldin, Joanna. "Bodacious Bodies and the Voluptuous Gaze: A Phenomenology of Animation Spectatorship." *Animation Journal* 8.2 (2000): 56–67. Print.
Cholodenko, Alan, ed. *The Illusion of Life II: More Essays on Animation.* Sydney: Power, 2007. Print.
———. Introduction. Cholodenko, *Illusion* 13–95.
Cocks, Jay. "Show Business: The World that Jones Made." *Time* 17 Dec. 1973: n. pag. Web. 25 Apr. 2011.
Darley, Andrew. *Visual Digital Culture: Surface Play and Spectacle in New Media Genres.* London: Routledge, 2000. Print.
Davis, Amy M. *Good Girls and Wicked Witches: Women in Disney's Feature Animation.* Eastleigh: Libbey, 2006. Print.
Dorfman, Ariel, and Armand Mattelart. *How to Read Donald Duck: Imperialist Ideology in the Disney Comic.* Trans. David Kunzle. New York: Intl. Gen., 1975. Print.
Fjellman, Stephen M. *Vinyl Leaves: Walt Disney World and America.* Boulder: Westview, 1992. Print.
Ford, Greg, ed. Spec. issue of *Film Comment* 11.1 (1975): 1–96. Print.
Furniss, Maureen, ed. *Art in Motion: Animation Aesthetics.* Rev. ed. Eastleigh: Libbey, 2007. Print.
Hendershot, Heather, ed. *Nickelodeon Nation: The History, Politics, and Economics of America's Only TV Channel for Kids.* New York: New York UP, 2004. Print.
Laqua, Carten. *Mickey Mouse, Hitler and Nazi Germany: How Disney's Characters Conquered the Third Reich.* London: Hermes, 2009. Print.
Leslie, Esther. *Hollywood Flatlands: Animation, Critical Theory and the Avant-Garde.* London: Verso, 2002. Print.
Leyda, Jay. ed. *Eisenstein on Disney.* By Sergei Eisenstein. Trans. Alan Upchurch. Kolkata: Seagull, 1986. Print.
Napier, Susan J., ed. *Anime from* Akira *to* Howl's Moving Castle*: Experiencing Contemporary Japanese Animation.* Rev. ed. New York: Palgrave, 2005. Print.
Pierson, Michele. *Special Effects: Still in Search of Wonder.* New York: Columbia UP, 2002. Print.
Sammond, Nicholas. *Babes in Tomorrowland: Walt Disney and the Making of the American Child, 1930–1960.* Durham: Duke UP, 2005. Print.
Sandler, Kevin S. "Gendered Evasion: Bugs Bunny in Drag." *Reading the Rabbit: Explorations in Warner Bros. Animation.* Ed. Sandler. New Brunswick: Rutgers UP, 1998. 154–71. Print.
Stephenson, Ralph. *Animation in the Cinema.* London: Zwemmer, 1967. Print.
Thomson, Rosemarie Garland, ed. *Freakery: Cultural Spectacles of the Extraordinary Body.* New York: New York UP, 1996. Print.
Tobin, Joseph, ed. *Pickachu's Global Adventure: The Rise and Fall of Pokémon.* Durham: Duke UP, 2004. Print.
Watts, Steven. *The Magic Kingdom: Walt Disney and the American Way of Life.* Boston: Houghton, 1997. Print.
Wells, Paul. *Animation and America.* Edinburgh: Edinburgh UP, 2002. Print.
———. *Understanding Animation.* London: Routledge, 1998. Print.

Scott Nygren

Teaching the Avant-Garde Film

The challenge in teaching avant-garde film is to construct a course that remains open to the unpredictable invention of the materials being studied. This course cannot be classically defined in terms of a straightforward object of study or hierarchical structure of ideas; instead it considers a dynamic project that continually questions all categories and structures. Its only protocol is the rule of no rules.

Yet this conception of such a course does not mean that the materials cannot be recognized or taught. In retrospect, many films can be grouped as part of historical avant-gardes and others considered as contemporary currents and activities. Historical and theoretical books have proliferated especially in recent decades, and many of the films and videos are becoming available on DVD. However, the boundaries of study remain fluid, the elements unstable, and the values contested. Even the name of this area of activity remains in dispute: avant-garde? experimental? independent? An effective course will invite students to develop sea legs and adapt to a field where the ground is continually shifting and to learn how to improvise new strategies in response to the unexpected.

Accordingly, there is no single correct way to teach the avant-garde, although certain parameters of the field can be established. Perhaps the best way to approach the material is to consider these parameters and then reinvent the course according to the situation in which it is taught.

Zones

First, several areas or zones of activity, perhaps three or four depending on how one counts, can be recognized within a history of alternative film. The historical avant-garde can be identified with Europe, especially Paris, in the 1920s, although important films were also produced in Germany, the United States, and Japan, and some activities extend into the 1930s and 1940s. Since these activities cannot be simply located in a single decade or nation, the concept of a region of filmmaking activities, or zone, can be helpful.

From Fernand Braudel's *longue durée* to Michel Foucault's epistemological break, historiographical methods since 1945 have often spatialized time to foreground complex reciprocal causality among multiple factors within a cultural context. An organizing concept that cuts across classical categories of time and space can be productive, since the Dada movement that begins avant-garde film was a fundamentally international art practice that has been continually revived ever since and thereby escapes the familiar categories of nation or period. At the same time, history after Foucault considers multiple practices and discourses outside of any teleological narrative that assumes unitary origins and goals. Reference to periods such as the 1920s can remain as a convenience to identify a series of practices that emerge at a specific moment, but only in the context of a zone of activities that extends past any single decade or place. Avant-garde work and a contemporary theorization of history intersect and can be introduced to students through the practical concept of zones.

A second region or zone of activities then emerges in the United States in the 1940s, expands dramatically in the 1950s and 1960s, and continues into the 1970s and 1980s, when important work was also produced in Europe. Based in part on the interests of avant-garde filmmakers, a question then develops whether to include early film as another region of activity, since all film produced from 1895 to 1915, before the consolidation of major studios, can in retrospect be considered experimental. A third or fourth zone would then include work that has emerged in a world context since the 1990s. This new work is often intercultural in both principle and in exhibition sites and continues to expand into the twenty-first century.

Shifts in format contribute to the segmentation of avant-garde film history in these terms. The 1920s marked the first moment when artists active in avant-garde art gained access to 35mm film equipment and could initiate films outside commercial conventions. Small-format film and video, specifically 16mm, 8mm, and later Super 8 film and VHS, made it possible for a new generation of filmmakers to gain access to the medium of moving images during and after World War II. Digital video and computer editing have characterized the most recent wave of avant-garde activity and again has made it possible for filmmakers to produce work outside corporate and business constraints.

In all these cases, the key to avant-garde activity has been access to media where new work can be produced for little or no money, to avoid the strings attached to business financing. An industrial business model requires a system of institutional production, mass marketing, and mass audience, in turn dependent on large-scale investment, specialized job roles, and standardized conventions for efficient operation. The problem here is not that managers of film industries are unimaginative, since some at least are open to innovation, but that the logic of large-scale capital investment necessarily requires predictable formulas and conventions for commercial films to maximize the chance of a return on investment.

In contrast, the budget of an avant-garde film is ideally zero, so that no preconditions exist prior to filming. When budgets are involved, the no-strings-attached premise is part of what characterizes an avant-garde approach. Experimental filmmaking in the 1940s made use of army surplus 16mm cameras that were then cheaply available. After the cost of film soared in the 1970s, because of the escalating price of silver as an essential ingredient in the silver halides of photographic emulsion, small-format film, video, and digital media became important for their low cost. In the same way, avant-garde activity presupposes an antisystem, or alternative models of distribution and exhibition, independent of audience demand. A significant new work tends to create an audience rather than fulfill expectations. One fundamental characteristic of avant-garde work is that it remains irretrievably antieconomic.

Different generations of filmmakers also distinguish these different zones. Hans Richter, Viking Eggeling, Man Ray, Fernand Léger, Marcel Duchamp, Germaine Dulac, Luis Buñuel, and Jean Cocteau are among those associated with the first historical avant-garde of the 1920s. Maya Deren, Kenneth Anger, Stan Brakhage, Bruce Conner, Jonas Mekas, Nam

June Paik, Yvonne Rainer, Su Friedrich and many others helped renew the avant-garde in the United States from the 1940s to the 1980s. Most recently, Tracey Moffat, Wu Ming, Marlon Fuentes, Yael Bartana, Pierre Huyghe, Renee Green, and Elja-Liisa Ahtila represent a new generation of world production and invention. Any grouping of names unavoidably implies other names, sometimes in very productive ways. For example, Len Lye continues the work of the 1920s avant-garde into the 1930s through his work in the British documentary movement, and Kinugasa Teinosuke's *Kurutta ippêji* (1926; *Crazy Page*) is among the most important avant-garde films ever made, although the film received no recognition outside Japan until the 1960s. European filmmakers such as Kurt Kren, Malcolm LeGrice, Yann Beauvais, and Valie Export renewed the international character of the avant-garde in the 1960s and 1970s. Any listing of names necessarily combines well-known figures with underrecognized or unknown producers, and this process continually destabilizes any tendency toward a restrictive canonization.

Concepts

Immediately, however, once zones, media, and names are set out, questions arise that make these initially clear groupings less clear and more interesting. A history of the avant-garde is inseparable from theoretical questions that problematize the categories and narratives through which "history" is understood. Early cinema, for example, may seem avant-garde to us today since it operates outside dominant studio conventions, but it certainly was not understood in that way at the time. The surrealists first retrieved some early fantasy films by reconsidering them as precursors of their surrealist project, so that Georges Méliès and Louis Feuillade came to be seen as significant. Minimalist and conceptualist filmmakers in the 1960s valued different early films,[1] consistent with their concerns, and their interest contributed to Tom Gunning's 1986 essay "The Cinema of Attraction: Early Film, Its Spectator and the Avant-Garde." Where, then, does one place early cinema in a chronology of the avant-garde? At the beginning, when it was not recognized as such, or retrospectively in the 1920s and 1960s as recontextualized precursors?

Germaine Dulac represents another case of volatile chronology. Dulac's 1926 film *La coquille et le clergyman* (*The Seashell and the Clergyman*) is arguably the first surrealist film produced, followed by Man Ray's *L'étoile de mer* (1928) and Luis Buñuel's *Un chien andalou* (1929). Histories of this period often privilege *Un chien andalou* as the most important surrealist film and dismiss *La coquille et le clergyman* as a betrayal of the Antonin Artaud screenplay on which it is based. Popular and critical response today often repeats this valuation. After Sandy Flitterman-Lewis's 1987 "The Image and the Spark: Dulac and Artaud Reviewed," however, Dulac's position in this historical narrative has become open to reconsideration.[2] When histories of the avant-garde began to be written after World War II,[3] stories of surrealist riots against Dulac and for Artaud and Buñuel were cited as the basis for valuing the latter over the former. Yet more recent research suggests that the stories reporting the riots are conflicted and that Dulac invented many of the cinematic strategies that Buñuel pursued. Further, Buñuel's film today seems transparently oedipal in its narrative, despite its initial reception as chaotic, and its violence against the traditional viewer can be seen as generated from misogynist assumptions—the eye slashed at the beginning, for example, is a woman's. In contrast, Dulac's film is characterized by strategies of repetition that Gilles Deleuze associates with the avant-garde in *Difference and Repetition*. In a feminist and Deleuzian reading, Dulac emerges as a remarkably interesting figure.

Teaching surrealist film then raises the question, Does *La coquille et le clergyman* logically come before or after *Un chien andalou*? Either way, the goal is to help students recognize the instability and retrospective narratives that unavoidably frame our access to the past. At the same time, teaching the avant-garde can help students learn to consider films not as static objects but as events, material traces that continually develop and transform meanings over time and that always remain open to yet other unanticipated readings.

The case of Dulac can lead to other questions of theoretical framing. Critical writing about the avant-garde before the 1980s often derives from classical, Romantic, and phenomonological premises. As a result, most writing considers the avant-garde in terms of heroic artists (usually male) and seeks to descriptively explicate the films in terms of classical aesthetics.[4] This approach applies to writing about avant-garde literature, art, music, and theater, as well as film. Only after the 1970s did writing question earlier critical assumptions and reconsider the avant-garde through poststructuralist, feminist, and other theoretical frameworks.

The transformation of the avant-garde filmmaker into a heroic artist coincides with the collecting of avant-garde materials by museums and archives.[5] The canonization of selected works becomes critically recognized as modernism, which is arguably a distinct and separate phenomenon from the avant-garde yet today frames our access to it. In this sense, modernism can be considered an institutional and critical reception of the historical avant-garde that seeks to translate its project into classical individualism and aesthetics. In contrast, the avant-garde in practice radically decentered or eliminated the individual from its position in classical narrative and actively challenged established institutions of government, the military, religion, and art. There is, in other words, a contradiction between the avant-garde as an active project and its critical reception and preservation in museums.[6] This contradiction is usually framed by a critique of museums and academic institutionalization, but it could also be debated as a paradoxical archiving of works that remain ready to explode in the imagination of an active viewer.

In addition, the emergence of a new avant-garde film movement in the United States in the 1950s and 1960s coincides chronologically with the emergence of structuralism and poststructuralism in France, yet these two movements remained largely unaware of each other. Often these projects are considered unrelated, yet they have increasingly been reconsidered as operating from parallel principles in different contexts. P. Adams Sitney initiated a connection when he argued that a specific body of late 1960s films in the United States were "structuralist," although these films are better understood as minimalist and conceptualist projects that invite poststructuralist theorization. In contrast, the structuralist movement historically coincides with the work of the late 1950s and early 1960s US avant-garde, preceding the work that Sitney then somewhat arbitrarily named "structuralist film." Teaching this problem can then be framed as a debate about how or whether these projects can be related. On the one hand, poststructuralism can generate new insights into avant-garde films, yet, on the other, a phenomological insistence on the films in their own terms can help resist the reduction of the avant-garde into an illustration of theories.

At some point, the term *avant-garde* needs to be questioned, either in an introduction to the class or later, in the context of critical theorization. All available names for this body of work are misleading and remain provisional. The term *avant-garde* was originally borrowed by nineteenth-century artists from the military context of troops on the front lines and suggests shock troops in advance of society at large. This term has become widely used to delineate a specific body of films and practices that remain outside commercial systems of mass production and distribution, although the militarism and futurity implied by the term are no longer viable. *Experimental* is another common term for this body of work, to evoke experimental science as a cutting edge of research and knowledge, but it can wrongly imply that such films are unfinished, preliminary, or mere trial and error. *Underground* became a popular designation during the 1950s and 1960s, both as a parallel to underground resistance movements during World War II and because some New York theaters were located in basements, but the term can misleadingly imply that these films are narrowly oppositional to a dominant industry rather than autonomous. *New American cinema* and *independent film* have been appropriated by the Hollywood industry. *Expanded* and *alternative* are other possibilities but also seem to describe some films better than others—minimalist films work by reducing rather than expanding, and *alternative* again seems to beg the question of a mainstream model. In other words, no term can adequately represent the multiplicity and unpredictability of practices in these films, so *avant-garde* or *experimental* are terms often used by default, despite their known inadequacy.

Boundaries remain unsettled. Debates can be distributed throughout the course to destabilize any sense that history has become fixed in place. What is the relation between avant-garde practices in literature, art, music, and theater beginning in the mid-nineteenth century and avant-garde film beginning in the 1920s? In this context, it is noteworthy that *avant-garde* continues to be used in the field of film to designate a specific area of work but has disappeared from the art world, where all work is assumed to be derived from principles that were historically avant-garde. What is the relation between the French new wave and US avant-garde film? Do these form two avant-gardes, as Peter Wollen once argued, or do they represent different kinds of invention separated by commercial and independent contexts? Is *The Cabinet of Dr. Caligari* (Germany, 1919) an avant-garde film, as Richard Murphy claims, a foundational film of German narrative cinema, or something in between? How do we understand the work of Dziga Vertov, who used what we would today call avant-garde techniques to create what later became known as documentary film? Where can a horizon of contemporary avant-garde work be located? What is the significance of sequences by avant-garde filmmakers in feature films, often used to represent dreams, psychosis, or subjective states, from Salvador Dalí in *Spellbound* (United States, 1945) to Klaus Wyborny in *Every Man for Himself and God against All* (West Germany, 1974)? How does feminist theory relate to work by such film- and video makers as Holly Fisher, Steina Vasulka, and Abigail Child, whose important work has often remained unrecognized by feminist critics? Beyond the work in art galleries, film festivals, and on the Web, does the avant-garde intersect with music videos or digital techniques in narrative films?

Practical Problems

In some respects, the practical problems of teaching avant-garde film have become similar to those of teaching any film course. The availability of films varies, whether in 16mm, videotape, or DVD, and books may be out of print. The films that are easily available on the Internet may not be the most important materials to study, and the quality of digital video may not provide an adequate experience of the film. For better or worse, teaching film must always navigate among the distortions, significant absences, and reconfigurations of the field produced by the conditions of availability and access to materials.

Many of these problems tend to be compounded in the field of the avant-garde. Although it was the medium for most avant-garde work from the 1940s through the 1980s, 16mm film has virtually disappeared from the media environment. Canyon Cinema and the New York Filmmakers' Cooperative (NYFC) are among the few who still distribute 16mm, and NYFC was in jeopardy of losing its space during the financial crisis of 2009. Students today often gain access to avant-garde film and video through DVDs and *YouTube*, despite their problematic visual quality.

Because many avant-garde films specifically engage the materiality of film as a medium, the possibility of a DVD version raises many questions. From Man Ray's *Retour à la raison* (France, 1923) to Stan Brakhage's *Mothlight* (United States, 1963), Morgan Fisher's *Cue Rolls* (United States, 1974), and many others, the viewing of the film implies an ability to pick up the film strip and see the frames in relation to the experience of projection. What does it mean to release such a film in a digital format that eliminates the material strip and frames? Arguably the ability to watch a DVD one frame at a time can never be the same, because the location of the frame in a series along the strip remains invisible. One response to this problem has been a reluctance among some filmmakers to release their films in a video format, but this decision can make their work invisible in an increasingly digital environment.

Another problem specific to teaching avant-garde film is that the sites and contexts of avant-garde activity are often significant but disappear in the classroom. Beginning with fairground cinemas and Dadaist theatrical events and continuing through film festivals, Super 8 cafés, cine clubs, and museums and galleries, avant-garde work often participates in a context larger than the individual screen. As one example, film and video installations are now playing an increasingly important role in a contemporary intercultural avant-garde. How can students study materials that are only available in a select number of galleries and museums, usually restricted to a small number of major metropolitan areas? At best, a student can usually see a very small number of such installations. Yet installations often raise interesting questions about the number, location, and shape of screens that cannot be represented in a single-screen format. At present, photo documentation often represents the only access most students will have to these important but elusive materials.

Practical Teaching Strategies

Since there is not and cannot be any single correct way to teach avant-garde film, the random availability of films and books can be used to generate productive limits on the teaching of a course. The procedure can be borrowed from the filmmaking practice of setting an arbitrary restraint, such as shooting only in close-up or eliminating the sound track, to provoke an inventive solution to making a film. In teaching, such limits can lead to a continual reinvention of the material and the foregrounding of debates and limits to organize the course, creating a teaching model of fluidity and reinvention parallel to the materials being studied.

A syllabus can be organized according to either of two basic approaches. One begins with the historical materials, presented in a broadly chronological sequence combined with movements backward and forward in time when necessary to recognize the retrospective revaluation of specific films. Michael O'Pray's *Avant-Garde Film: Forms, Themes and Passions* is a rare example of a current book that tries to include the entire history of avant-garde film, although its judgments are problematic and it narrows to British work in the contemporary era consistent with its purpose. Rudolf Kuenzli's anthology *Dada and Surrealist Film*; Lauren Rabinovitz's *Points of Resistance: Women, Power, and Politics in the New York Avant-Garde Cinema, 1943–71*; and Holly Willis's *New Digital Cinema: Reinventing the Moving Image* are examples of books that contribute to a historical approach. Kuenzli's anthology is a model of incisive contemporary work that reconsiders and intensifies our understanding of past events, particularly those of the 1920s. Rabinovitz takes up the position and initiative of women filmmakers at a moment when historical marginalization was increasingly colliding with the importance of new work. Willis considers digital video in the multiple contexts of the avant-garde, music videos, and commercial film.

The other approach begins with concepts through which avant-garde films can be understood, organized around contestations and debates. Jeffrey Skoller's *Shadows, Spectors, Shards: Making History in Avant-Garde Film*; Scott MacDonald's anthology *Screen Writings: Scripts and Texts from Independent Filmmakers*; and Laura Marks's *The Skin of the Film: Intercultural Cinema, Embodiment, and the Senses* can contribute to this strategy. Skoller considers how avant-garde film engages and transforms the representation of history. MacDonald collects writing from filmmakers to foreground a multiplicity of concepts and practices. Marks takes a Deleuzian approach to contemporary avant-garde film in a world context. Another possibility here would be George E. Marcus's "The Modernist Sensibility in Recent Ethnographic Writing and the Cinematic Metaphor of Montage." Marcus argues that modernist strategies of simultaneity and multiple causality are crucial to address current problems in ethnographic filmmaking.

The texts mentioned above are either currently in print or recently published and available in libraries and are useful for teaching a broad introductory course. Many other important books are available as e-books or through libraries for further research into either a historical or a conceptual approach. Malte Hagener's *Moving Forward, Looking Back: The European Avant-Garde and the Invention of Film Culture, 1919–1939* and Jan-Christopher Horak's *Lovers of Cinema: The First American Film Avant-Garde, 1919–1945* consider the European or American contexts of the historical avant-garde. Among edited volumes, Wheeler Winston Dixon and Gwendolyn Audrey Foster's *Experimental Cinema: The Film Reader* and Doug Hall and Sally Jo Fifer's *Illuminating Video: An Essential Guide to Video Art* are important collections of essays on avant-garde film and video, respectively. Scott MacDonald's *Avant-Garde Film: Motion Studies* considers fifteen specific films as an approach to the avant-garde field; his *A Critical Cinema: Interviews with Independent Filmmakers* gathers interviews with avant-garde filmmakers in five volumes.

The question of how to proceed depends on the circumstances of and participants in any specific course. At the same time, the different models of teaching are not mutually exclusive, since the problems are connected. At their best, the two approaches can lead into one another, since a history of concepts and practices is bound up with concepts and practices of history.

Notes

1. Ken Jacobs's *Tom, Tom, The Piper's Son* (United States, 1969) is an early example of this revaluation, which continued with Ernie Gehr's *Eureka* (United States, 1974), Hollis Frampton's *Gloria!* (United States, 1979), and other work.

2. The process of rethinking Dulac's position in avant-garde film history both precedes and follows this essay. Flitterman-Lewis is cited here because her work is concise and easily available to beginning students in Rudolf Kuenzli's anthology *Dada and Surrealist Film.*

3. The legend of the riot at the premiere of *La coquille et le clergyman* occurs in texts as disparate as Georges Sadoul's *Dictionary of Films* and David Curtis's *Experimental Cinema: A Fifty-Year Evolution.*

4. For example, P. Adams Sitney's pivotal 1974 book, *Visionary Film: The American Avant-Garde,* is primarily organized as a series of essays about individual filmmakers, evaluated through such classical models as "lyrical" and "epic," within the Romantic framework of the artist as "visionary." At the time, Sitney was making a deliberate gesture to legitimize experimental film by linking new works to established aesthetic philosophies, but its categories and procedures have been repeated ever since. Noting the limitations of these approaches does not delegitimize Sitney's invaluable work nor those of subsequent writers, but it does open up opportunities for productive reconsideration.

5. The Museum of Modern Art in New York City was founded in 1929 and added its film library in 1935. MoMA has been a determinative influence on the worldwide organization and exhibition of modern art throughout the world ever since, in no small part because of the destruction of Europe in World War II.

6. The contradiction continues to have force even when the artist willingly collaborates in the role of heroic artist, because the social role required for institutional recognition is not the same as the figure in representation. Artists as different as Pablo Picasso and Stan Brakhage were willing to play the role of heroic artist to gain public recognition. In their artistic work, however, the human figure is transformed, marginalized, or eliminated.

Works Cited

Curtis, David. *Experimental Cinema: A Fifty-Year Evolution.* London: Studio Vista, 1971. Print.

Deleuze, Gilles. *Difference and Repetition.* Trans. Paul Patton. New York: Columbia, 1994. Print.

Dixon, Wheeler Winston, and Gwendolyn Audrey Foster. *Experimental Cinema: The Film Reader.* New York: Routledge, 2002. Print.

Flitterman-Lewis, Sandy. "The Image and the Spark: Dulac and Artaud Reviewed." Kuenzli 110–27.

Gunning, Tom. "The Cinema Attraction: Early Film, Its Spectator, and the Avant-Garde." *Film and Theory: An Anthology.* Ed. Robert Stam and Toby Miller. Malden: Blackwell, 2000. 229–35. Print.

Hagener, Malte. *Moving Forward, Looking Back: The European Avant-Garde and the Invention of Film Culture, 1919–1939.* Amsterdam: Amsterdam UP, 2007. Print.

Hall, Doug, and Sally Jo Fifer. *Illuminating Video: An Essential Guide to Video Art.* New York: Aperture, 2005. Print.

Horak, Jan-Christopher. *Lovers of Cinema: The First American Film Avant-Garde, 1919–1945.* Madison: U of Wisconsin P, 1995. Print.

Kuenzli, Rudolf E., ed. *Dada and Surrealist Film.* Boston: MIT P, 1996. Print.

MacDonald, Scott. *Avant-Garde Film: Motion Studies.* Cambridge: Cambridge UP, 1993. Print.

———. *A Critical Cinema: Interviews with Independent Filmmakers.* 5 vols. Berkeley: U of California P, 1988–2006. Print.

———, ed. *Screen Writings: Scripts and Texts from Independent Filmmakers.* Berkeley: U of California P, 1995. Print.

Marcus, George E. "The Modernist Sensibility in Recent Ethnographic Writing and the Cinematic Metaphor of Montage." *Visualizing Theory: Selected Essays from V. A. R., 1990–94.* Ed. Lucien Taylor. New York: Routledge, 1994. 37–53. Print.

Marks, Laura U. *The Skin of the Film: Intercultural Cinema, Embodiment, and the Senses.* Durham: Duke UP, 2000. Print.

Murphy, Richard. *Theorizing the Avant-Garde: Modernism, Expressionism, and the Problem of Postmodernity.* Cambridge: Cambridge UP, 1999. Print.

O'Pray, Michael. *Avant-Garde Film: Forms, Themes and Passions.* London: Wallflower, 2003. Print.

Rabinovitz, Lauren. *Points of Resistance: Women, Power, and Politics in the New York Avant-Garde Cinema, 1943–71.* Urbana: U of Illinois P, 1991. Print.

Sadoul, Georges. *Dictionary of Films.* 1965. Trans. Peter Morris. Berkeley: U of California P, 1972. Print.

Sitney, P. Adams. *Visionary Film: The American Avant-Garde.* New York: Oxford UP, 1974. Print.

Skoller, Jeffrey. *Shadows, Spectors, Shards: Making History in Avant-Garde Film.* Minneapolis: U of Minnesota P, 2005. Print.

Willis, Holly. *New Digital Cinema: Reinventing the Moving Image.* London: Wallflower, 2005. Print.

Wollen, Peter. "The Two Avant-Gardes." *Studio International* 190.978 (1975): 171–75. Print.

Part V

Style and Craft

Introduction to Part 5

If, as stated earlier in this volume, the study of the cinema is a highly interdisciplinary project, one might say that film is a stylistically intermedial form since it draws on numerous other arts, such as painting, orchestral music, opera, drama, sculpture, dance, and even architecture. Ingmar Bergman once likened film directing to building a cathedral; Maya Deren treated cinema as choreography; and Robert Breer approached the medium like drawing. While formally multifarious, however, the cinema has its particular elements and structures—for instance, merging audio and visual components or juxtaposing images through shot-to-shot montage. Thus it is crucial for teachers to comprehend the particularities of the medium's formal elements, since they are the building blocks of a work's overall style. While the topic is covered in broad strokes in basic classes like Film Analysis or Introduction to Film (often using David Bordwell and Kristin Thompson's *Film Art*), some upper-level or topics classes examine a stylistic component in depth, such as film sound, music, or mise-en-scène, the elements discussed in three of the essays that follow.

Film sound, of course, constitutes one half of cinematic practice, at least since 1926. But, as we know (but some of our students do not), even during the silent era, sound was a crucial aspect of film exhibition, often involving both noise and music. Sound cinema also began to entail dialogue, carefully miked and synchronized to the lips of the actors speaking on-screen. While much of film criticism has taken a basically visual perspective (elevating the image to the primary element of film form), recent years have seen the burgeoning of sound theory by which such issues as acoustics and the body, the spatiality of sound, and the use of voice-over narration (and its gendered implications) have come to the fore, making it a highly resonant topic for classroom teaching.

Music is a primary sound component that has links to other arts: popular song, classical orchestration, opera, and the stage musical. But it has a particular history and valence in the cinema that must be acknowledged. Interestingly, Thomas Edison first saw the future of cinema as tied to his earlier invention of the phonograph and in the late 1890s produced works for his Kinetophone (a sound-enabled peep show machine) that often involved one-minute movies of people singing. In recent decades, film studies has seen a spate of publications on music and cinema (see, e.g., Gorbman; Prendergast; Buhler; Burt), proving that the subject is of interest both to musicologists and film scholars.

Similarly, mise-en-scène relates to another art, namely theater (from which the term is derived); but the specifics of cinema (involving variable camera distance and movement, the use of real locales, particular codes of lighting) make its screen articulation very different from stage and worthy of attention. Also relevant to dramatic precedents is the question of film acting—another central component of film style, and, over the course of film history, much has been written about silent and sound screen performance by such critics as Roberta Pearson, Charles Affron, Virginia Wexman, and James Naremore. Beyond acting (whether based on the Method or, in earlier generations, on Delsartean postures), cinema's status as a mass art raises the question of how performance has merged with the phenomenon of stardom—another popular topic for film courses. Based on theoretical work by Richard Dyer, Richard deCordova, and Edgar Morin, among others, star studies has come to include not only analyses of performers' on-screen personae but also their broader star texts that circulate offscreen (through newspapers, fan magazines, television, photographs, and gossip).

The final essays in this section confront certain crafts involved in making films. While this volume is addressed primarily to professors in the humanities, often their students are majoring in film production and only taking critical studies classes as a small segment of their curriculum. Because of this split within the discipline, production students often do not see the relevance of studying history and theory. It is crucial, however, that the issue be confronted and the gap bridged, making it clear to students that they will be creatively hampered if they do not comprehend the broad history of cinema (silent and sound, commercial and experimental, documentary and fiction, American and "foreign"). It is for this reason that great filmmakers like Martin Scorsese support earlier cineastes like Akira Kurosawa and are dedicated to film preservation. In a similar fashion, the art of screenwriting can be taught in a way that transcends an instrumental how-to model or an exclusive focus on what sells. (After all, Jean-Luc Godard once said, "A story should have a beginning, a middle, and an end . . . but not necessarily in that order" ["Jean-Luc Godard Quotes"].) Rather, a class on the topic can broadly confront questions of narrative analysis, involving exploration of plots and subplots, cinematic principles of character development, act structuration, variations on storytelling, and cinematic modes of making meaning. In this manner, a humanities approach can inform a screenwriting course, making it not only a practicum in craft but a class on film theory and form.

Works Cited

Affron, Charles. *Star Acting: Gish, Garbo, Davis.* New York: Dutton, 1977. Print.

Bordwell, David, and Kristin Thompson. *Film Art: An Introduction.* Boston: McGraw, 2009. Print.

Buhler, James. *Hearing the Movies: Music and Sound in Film History.* New York: Oxford UP, 2010. Print.

Burt, George. *The Art of Film Music.* Boston: Northeastern UP, 1994. Print.

deCordova, Richard. *Picture Personalities: The Emergence of the Star System in America.* Urbana: U of Illinois P, 1990. Print.

Dyer, Richard. *Heavenly Bodies: Film Stars and Society.* Basingstoke: Macmillan, 1986. Print.

Gorbman, Claudia. *Unheard Melodies: Narrative Film Music.* Bloomington: Indiana UP, 1987. Print.

"Jean-Luc Godard Quotes." *BrainyQuote.* BrainyQuote, 2011. Web. 3 May 2011.

Morin, Edgar. *Stars.* Trans. Richard Howard. Paris: Seuil, 1972. Print.

Naremore, James. *Acting in the Cinema.* Berkeley: U of California P, 1988. Print.

Pearson, Roberta. *Eloquent Gestures: The Transformation of Performance Style in the Griffith Biograph Films.* Berkeley: U of California P, 1992. Print.

Prendergast, Roy. *Film Music: A Neglected Art.* New York: Norton, 1992. Print.

Wexman, Virginia. *Creating the Couple: Love, Marriage, and Hollywood Performance.* Princeton: Princeton UP, 1993. Print.

Caryl Flinn

Teaching Film Music

Because music lacks the clear-cut referentiality of language, it poses certain challenges to the teaching of film. Conventionally it has been used to establish mood, but it also helps identify genre and cultural and historical location (not always with accuracy: one Hollywood director instructed the composer to use French horns "since the movie was about France"); it identifies people, objects, or themes (Bernard Herrmann's score for *Citizen Kane* [1941] provides strong clues about "Rosebud" to observant listeners); it offers ideological critique or commentary (Francis Ford Coppola banked on the kitschy militarism of Richard Wagner's "Ride of the Valkyrie" in *Apocalypse Now* [1979]); or it incites consumers to purchase downloads, sound tracks, and other products.

To illustrate music's role in shaping film interpretation in introductory classes, I adapt Lev Kuleshov's famous experiment in which the same shot of an actor's face was edited alongside three other images to create three vastly divergent perceptions and readings. Using a clip from an unidentified silent film, I play it three times with different musical extracts (I have used pieces from *Mars Attacks!* [1996], *Monsieur Hulot's Holiday* [1953], and music by Aaron Copland). Suddenly the unidentified clip becomes a scene from a thriller or horror film, a jaunty comedy, or a study in Americana.

Critics and practitioners have studied the relation of music and the moving image even before the advent of sound cinema. Publications as early as the 1910s recommended particular musical cues for would-be piano players and exhibitors to accompany their screenings. By the advent of sound film, however, most discussion of film music quickly centered on the practice of underscoring, background music played under dialogue to enhance emotional or other attributes, as in the clichéd swell of violins in love scenes or the boisterous brass of battle scenes. While not synonymous with nondiegetic music, underscoring is often understood to characterize it.

In 1936, Kurt London delineated some of the dominant characteristics of underscoring and other early Hollywood practices in his study *Film Music.* Despite London's criticism of many of those tendencies, he helped define what came to be understood as classical scoring conventions at the beginning of Hollywood's golden age of film music, an era that spanned roughly from the mid-1930s to the early 1950s. London noted, for instance, that the presence of film music must be motivated to serve its "illustrative" purpose (125) and that, in contrast to concert music, film music was "apprehended . . . unconsciously . . . [and] that good film music remained unnoticed" (37).

To make music less noticed, underscoring relied on an arsenal of techniques that are important to identify and investigate. Working alongside other cinematic elements to ensure narrative clarity, music's task was to appear as transparent as possible to avoid distracting attention away from the story line and the illusion of a unified film. Music was so subordinate that composers were rarely brought in to begin work until after the film was shot and edited. (This "unnoticeability" is clearly less applicable to music not used as underscoring, such as a song performed in the film.)

Motifs and leitmotifs identified themes, characters, or places, such as Max Steiner's "Tara's Theme" in *Gone with the Wind* (1939). The leitmotif was one of many principles from Wagnerian opera subtending the practice and discussion of film composing during the classical studio era; also influential was Wagner's concept of the "total artwork," or *Gestamtkunstwerk*, which Wagner attributed to opera in the nineteenth century and critics attributed to the cinema in the first decades of the twentieth century. This is not to say that Wagner's ideas were imported wholesale without modification or discussion, but they nonetheless helped shape the discourse on film scoring of the time.

The practice of "Mickey Mousing," as the name suggests, was used often in animation work and in comedies. Here music appears to mimic the movement of on-screen action, such as a descending scale accompanying a character descending a staircase. (Mickey Mouse's star turn as the sorcerer's apprentice in Disney's *Fantasia* [1940] is a celebrated example of this practice.) Other animators found different ways to put music into their films: in the 1920s and 1930s, New York's innovative brothers Max and Dave Fleischer mixed live-action footage of popular performers such as Cab Calloway or Ethel Merman singing alongside animated stars such as Betty Boop.

When teaching cinema music, it is important to stress that despite its dominance, the classical paradigm of scoring, along with its conventions of film listening—passive listeners, unconscious of the music—was never monolithic. To assert otherwise gives short shrift to nonunderscoring aspects of film scores (e.g., the presence of songs and popular music, experimental music, jazz, or music from beyond Anglo and Western cultures); it also downplays the diversity of film music practices within industrial film production (documentaries and experimental films, early "race films," etc.) and among film consumers (assuming homogenous audiences with homogenous responses), much less tending to scoring traditions outside Hollywood.

An established counterexample to Hollywood scoring practice is the work of the Soviet film director Sergei Eisenstein. Eisenstein's conception and use of film music was part of his larger critique of Hollywood cinema. He dissented against its use of transparent, analytical editing; its star system; and its focus on individual-centric stories. Although Eisenstein worked primarily during the silent era, he was acutely attentive to the relation of music and the moving image and used musical metaphors to describe many aspects of the cinema, notably its rhythm. He argued that all of film's formal elements worked on equal footing and advocated for conflict among those elements; indeed, the notion of collision grounds his famous conception of dialectical montage or editing. Thus, in contrast to its "unnoticed" subservience in Hollywood, music for Eisenstein was an element to deploy actively. Many cite his film *Alexander Nevsky* (1938), with a score by Sergei Prokofiev, as an example of this practice, finding music, character placement, and visual composition as mutual complements.

The prominent Frankfurt school theorist Theodor Adorno wrote often on music, frequently to condemn its diminishment under mass reproduction and capitalism; he was also an occasional composer. Hanns Eisler was a composer and music essayist (London thanks him in his prefatory remarks to *Film Music*). A committed Communist, Eisler began as a working-class modernist in Germany, where he collaborated with the radical playwright Bertolt Brecht, but after the rise of Hitler, Adorno and Eisler spent several years working in Hollywood as refugees. To call their experience an unhappy one is an understatement: in 1948, Eisler was actually deported, a victim of McCarthyism. Their polemical *Composing for Film* was a result of these experiences and took dead aim at the classical paradigm of cinema music.

For Adorno and Eisler, music in Hollywood veiled the contradictions and heterogeneity of cinema, recalling the critique of Eisenstein (whom Eisler and Adorno challenge for believing that a direct relation between music and image was possible). They argued that Hollywood's scoring conventions produced coddled, compliant, unthinking listeners. To change this convention, Eisler and Adorno advocated for practices that defied the fiction of music's fusion and unity with the image. Reading their work while viewing Fritz Lang's *Hangmen Also Die* (1943) can generate interesting debates about whether Eisler's score produces the kinds of effects advocated in his writing. Eisler and Adorno demanded that cinema music discourage passive, immersive audience involvement and solicit active, critical listening and reflection. Such a change would obviously necessitate changes in the production process, such as not waiting until postproduction to bring composers on board. *Composing for Film* is a useful teaching tool for combining aesthetic, industrial, and ideological approaches to music in the cinema; it also elaborates the political and economic stakes behind film music in general and the classical model in particular.

Adorno and Eisler, Eisenstein, and others articulated an influential concept that belongs in every film music class. This understanding proposes that film music works either in parallel relation to the image (a relationship of resemblance) or in counterpoint to it (a relationship of contradiction). Hollywood scoring is said to elaborate the former, since music standardly reinforces actions or moods established by the image; non- or postclassical practices are usually associated with the latter. Illustrations are bountiful: for parallelism, Joan Crawford in a love scene underscored with Isaac Stern's violin from *Humoresque* (1946); for counterpoint, "Stuck in the Middle with You" in the torture scene of *Pulp Fiction* (1994).

Like Eisenstein in the late 1920s, film theorists in the 1980s often argued that the practice of counterpoint could encourage oppositional effects and potential political critique, in part because it broke the illusion of unity upheld by Hollywood. While not without its value, the argument seems somewhat unnuanced and essentialist by current standards. It is worth stressing that almost every film music scholar has commented on the restrictiveness of this parallel-counterpoint binarism (Claudia Gorbman calls it "curiously primitive" [15]), considering it a false and simplifying dichotomy.

Screening a mainstream narrative film, such as *Pennies from Heaven* (1981), can provoke useful questions about such assumptions. *Pennies from Heaven* follows an American sheet music salesman in the Great Depression who literally breaks into song (in staged numbers) to escape his impoverished life. Steve Martin and the rest of the cast lip-synch to prerecorded songs of the era. The songs clearly serve a utopian function, and, although it is a brutally false one, its escapism brings joy not just to the diegetic characters but also to listeners, who can appreciate its commentary on social and economic inequities.

Richard Dyer influentially theorizes this dimension of film music's function in his "Entertainment and Utopia." Although Dyer is concerned with musicals, his argument has proved useful to film music studies. Dyer posits that music, color, movement, and other "non-representational signs" can generate the impression of "what utopia would feel like" in the cinema (177). He adds that the contours of such utopias are always socially and materially founded, so that, for instance, in America during the Depression—a period marked by scarcity—the experience of watching the excess of a Busby Berkeley musical would be potent indeed. A punning illustration of it is offered in the opening number of *Gold Diggers of 1933*, "We're in the Money," in which the penniless chorines are clad, literally, in coins. Dyer's concept of music and utopia works well in the classroom and is equally effective with postclassical and nonmusical cinema. The driving techno of *Run Lola Run* (1998), for instance, intimates an energy that, while matching the rhythmic gallop of its protagonist, was arguably at odds for contemporary audiences discouraged by the disappointments of postunification Germany.

Since the romantic era, critics have notoriously inscribed music with transcendental, nonhistorical, and universalizing powers. Film music offers instructors ways to unmask and then problematize that belief. For instance, it's important to note that the demise of Hollywood's golden age of film scoring loosely coincided with the disintegration of the studio system. By the 1950s, a wide range of scoring practices made their way into mainstream US cinema: rock and roll appeared in movies such as *Rock Around the Clock* (1956); compilation scores with pieces by multiple artists emerged, violating underscoring's ideal of unity; the use of jazz increased dramatically (e.g., *Walk on the Wild Side* [1962] and *The Sweet Smell of Success* [1957]); and art music not composed in a neoromantic vein, such as Leonard Rosenmann's score for *The Cobweb* (1955), openly flirted with atonality. Nonmusical factors accompanied the movement away from neoromantic underscoring, especially in the United States: shifting demographics, the rise of youth culture as a social and consumer force, the early work of civil rights and social protest.

By this time, music had shifted from always already "unconscious" in Hollywood film practice to something the industry wanted to bank on, consciously. With increasingly aggregate industries of postwar media production and distribution, the lucrative business of releasing sound track LPs and hit theme songs left the sheet music of yesteryear in the dust. Classroom research projects on the shifting strategies of film music merchandising work well for this topic. Nonclassic practices merit extensive coverage: French new wave films like *Breathless* (1959) deliberately interrupted and fragmented the music that periodically underscored them; Toru Takemitsu's work for Akira Kurosawa is exciting to share with students for combining Western music with traditional Japanese forms and instruments; the new German cinema often reworked existing music, using scratched recordings of high art classics like Ludwig van Beethoven's Ninth Symphony in Rainer Werner Fassbinder's *The Marriage of Maria Braun* (1979) to disrupt the myth of untainted, "pure" German culture; in the United Kingdom, the violent, futuristic *Clockwork Orange* (1971) not only also used Beethoven but forever altered the joy and exuberance of "Singin' in the Rain" by featuring it during a gruesome attack scene. The transnational circuits of music are nicely illustrated in the Korean film *Like a Virgin* (2006), which follows the experiences and fantasies of a transgendered youth, linking his yearning and the film's title to the pop song by Madonna. These examples show students ways to explore how music produces particular meanings, positions, and feelings in numerous and distinctly nonclassical ways.

In 1987, Claudia Gorbman's *Unheard Melodies* was published, and many consider it the tutor text of contemporary film music studies; it remains essential reading for any serious student of film music. She takes the title from Keats's "Ode to a Grecian Urn," clearly invoking music's classic function, as well as hinting at its relative neglect in cinema scholarship of the time. Privileging neither musicology nor film studies but exploring their interactions, Gorbman uses semiotic theory to consider how music can produce meaning in narrative film, how it can anchor an image, how it can immerse auditors. Building on Adorno and Eisler, Gorbman adds psychoanalysis to elaborate how narrative film music has been overwhelmingly used to "render the individual an untroublesome subject: less critical, less 'awake'" (5). Her close readings of several texts can be taught alongside those films in class.

Film music scholarship quickly developed as a legitimate field within cinema studies. It took a little longer to take root in musicology, where music's movement into cultural studies, popular culture, and critical theory encountered more resistance. Studies from this period include Royal Brown's *Overtones and Undertones*, Caryl Flinn's *Strains of Utopia*, Krin Gabbard's *Jammin' at the Margins*, Russell Lack's *Twenty Four Frames Under*, Martin Marks's *Music and the Silent Film*, and Kathryn Kalinak's *Settling the Score*, which offers an excellent introduction to musical terminology. Most of this scholarship concentrated on classical film scoring. In the ensuing decades, scholars have diversified that focus, and a fuller array of film music practices now garner their attention. Monographs and anthologies have appeared on film music of Australia (Coyle), Germany (Flinn, *New German Cinema*; Hillman), global cinema (Slobin), and on international composers such as Takemitsu (Burt) and Arvo Part (Maimets-Volt), all of which are useful in courses dealing with particular national cinemas and cultures or with transnational culture and global cinemas.

Film music has become a more inclusive field at the beginning of the twenty-first century, encompassing work in folk, popular, and ethnic music; music of particular geographic regions (see Creekmur on songs in Bollywood film); and specific genres and directors (see Kalinak, *How*, on Ford's westerns). Various approaches and methodologies characterize the field. In the 1970s, the French politician Jacques Attali wrote *Noise: The Political Economy of Music*, elaborating music's shifting social functions over historical and economic phases; I have found this to be an effective text in upper-level undergraduate or beginning graduate classes. Attali's too-neat periodization of music merits critique. But because the book ends with the late 1970s, students can be asked to identify contemporary configurations among social and material conditions and the function and circulation of music.

Jeff Smith's *The Sounds of Commerce* examines Hollywood's postwar film music through a marketing perspective, concentrating on popular songs and music, and is useful in classrooms exploring the institutional underpinnings of cinema music. Scholars such as Nicholas Cook and John Richardson consider the relationship of music and multimedia phenomena including new media technologies and video games; studies on elevator music, lounge music, and jukebox tunes further highlight the shifting parameters of the field's object of study. Anahid Kassabian has developed theories of film music reception differentiated by gender, ethnicity, and age and prefers to consider the affiliations film music prompts over the narrower parameters of identification. Frequently, students find her framing more useful and flexible than older, often exclusively psychoanalytic paradigms. Here, movies like *Nick and Norah's Infinite Playlist* (2008) and *High Fidelity* (2000) elaborate concepts of affiliative listening at narrative and musical levels; the films' deeply conventional treatment of gender would be equally interesting to investigate.

Teaching film music works well in courses outside media studies departments. The subject can be used as an effective tool to explore constructions of class, ethnicity, gender, sexuality, and other identity markers. If there are any doubts about how film music is gendered, I show a film noir: femmes fatales get their overwhelming share of jazz motifs. Queer studies is another rewarding approach, as is exploring film music as an alternative camp aesthetic (see, e.g., Lumby). Affect theory is equally rewarding to teach alongside film music, and a sophisticated exploration of the worth of emotions (and their transnational circulation) is offered in Guy Maddin's *The Saddest Music in the World* (2003).

As the field of film music matures, earlier histories and concepts have been subject to revision. Wagner's influence on film music has been the subject of an early-twenty-first-century anthology (Joe and Gilman). Michel Chion introduced the categories of empathetic and anempathetic film sound and music to describe sound-image relations, suggesting a range of relations rather than those of fixed structural superiority or inferiority often implied by the rubric of parallelism and counterpoint (8–9).

Because of a rising social awareness—a witnessing, if not always a literacy—of the many intersections between music and moving images in everyday media, teaching film music no longer has to rely on exposing "unheard melodies." Still, teaching critical listening and reflection on film music's cultural, emotional, and ideological operations requires more work than many students expect. A practical challenge that continues to face instructors of music and film is the same that film music scholars face: whether students have sufficient formal, historical, and theoretical training in both cinema and music. While some maintain that only those with advanced expertise in both have the proper authority to discuss it, for most of us, film music is too rich, too fundamental to media literacy to leave off-limits. Indeed, the study of film music as a form of aesthetic, industrial, cultural, and ideological expression is a terrific way to foster understandings of both film and music.

Note

This essay does not include studies of film music not available in English.

Works Cited

Alexander Nevsky. Dir. Sergei Eisenstein. Mosfilm, 1938. Film.
Apocalypse Now. Dir. Francis Ford Coppola. Zoetrope, 1979. Film.
Attali, Jacques. *Noise: The Political Economy of Music*. Trans. Brian Massumi. Minneapolis: U of Minnesota P, 1985. Print.
Breathless. Dir. Jean-Luc Godard. CNC, 1959. Film.
Brown, Royal S. *Overtones and Undertones*. Berkeley: U of California P, 1994. Print.
Burt, Peter. *The Music of Toru Takemitsu*. New York: Cambridge UP, 2001. Print.
Chion, Michel. *Audio-Vision: Sound on Screen*. Trans. Claudia Gorbman. New York: Columbia UP, 1994. Print.
Citizen Kane. Dir. Orson Welles. RKO, 1941. Film.
Clockwork Orange. Dir. Stanley Kubrick. Warner Bros., 1971. Film.
The Cobweb. Dir. Vincente Minnelli. MGM, 1955. Film.
Cook, Nicholas. *Analysing Musical Multimedia*. Oxford: Clarendon, 1998. Print.
Coyle, Rebecca, ed. *Screen Scores: Studies in Contemporary Australian Film Music*. Sydney: Australian Film Television and Radio School, 1998. Print.
Creekmur, Corey K. "Popular Hindi Cinema and the Film Song." *Traditions in World Cinema*. Ed. Linda Badley, R. Barton Palmer, and Steven Jay Schneider. Edinburgh: Edinburgh UP, 2006. 193–202. Print.
Dyer, Richard. "Entertainment and Utopia." *Genre: The Musical*. Ed. Rick Altman. New York: Routledge, 1977. 175–89. Print.
Eisler, Hanns, and Theodor Adorno. *Composing for the Films*. New York: Oxford UP, 1947. Print.
Fantasia. Dir. James Algar and Samuel Armstrong. Disney, 1940. Film.
Flinn, Caryl. *New German Cinema: Music, Style, and the Matter of History*. Berkeley: U of California P, 2007. Print.
———. *Strains of Utopia: Gender, Nostalgia, and Hollywood Film Music*. Princeton: Princeton UP, 1982. Print.
Gabbard, Krin. *Jammin' at the Margins: Jazz and the American Cinema*. Chicago: U of Chicago P, 1996. Print.
Gold Diggers of 1933. Dir. Mervyn LeRoy. Warner Bros., 1933. Film.
Gone with the Wind. Dir. Victor Fleming. MGM, 1939. Film.
Gorbman, Claudia. *Unheard Melodies: Narrative Film Music*. Bloomington: Indiana UP, 1987. Print.
Hangmen Also Die. Dir. Fritz Lang. United Artists, 1943. Film.
High Fidelity. Dir. Stephen Frears. Touchstone–Working Pictures, 2000. Film.
Hillman, Roger. *Unsettled Scores: German Film, Music, and Ideology*. Bloomington: Indiana UP, 2005. Print.

Humoresque. Dir. Jean Negulesco. Warner Bros., 1946. Film.
Joe, Jeongwon, and Sander L. Gilman, eds. *Wagner and Cinema*. Bloomington: Indiana UP, 2010. Print.
Kalinak, Kathryn. *How the West Was Sung: Music in the Westerns of John Ford*. Berkeley: U of California P, 2007. Print.
———. *Settling the Score: Music and the Classical Hollywood Film*. Madison: U of Wisconsin P, 1992. Print.
Kassabian, Anahid. *Hearing Film Music: Tracking Identifications in Contemporary Hollywood Film Music*. New York: Routledge, 2001. Print.
Lack, Russell. *Twenty Four Frames Under: A Buried History of Film Music*. London: Quartet, 1997. Print.
Like a Virgin. Dir. Hae-jun Lee and Hae-yeong Lee. CJ Entertainment, 2006. Film.
London, Kurt. *Film Music*. Trans. Eric S. Bensinger. London: Faber, 1936. Print.
Lumby, Catharine. "Music and Camp: Popular Music Performance in *Priscilla* and *Muriel's Wedding*." Coyle 78–88.
Maimets-Volt, Kaire. *Mediating the "Idea of One": Arvo Part's Pre-existing Music in Film*. Talinn: Eesti Muusika, 2009. Print. Estonian Acad. of Music and Theatre Dissertations 4.
Marks, Martin. *Music and the Silent Film: Contexts and Case Studies, 1895–1924*. New York: Oxford UP, 1997. Print.
The Marriage of Maria Braun. Dir. Rainer Werner Fassbinder. United Artists, 1979. Film.
Mars Attacks! Dir. Tim Burton. Warner Bros., 1996. Film.
Monsieur Hulot's Holiday. Dir. Jacques Tati. GBD Intl. 1953. Film.
Nick and Norah's Infinite Playlist. Dir. Peter Sollett. Sony, 2008. Film.
Pennies from Heaven. Dir. Herbert Ross. MGM, 1981. Film.
Pulp Fiction. Dir. Quentin Tarantino. Miramax, 1994. Film.
Richardson, John. *An Eye for Music: Popular Music and the Audiovisual Surreal*. Oxford: Oxford UP, 2011. Print.
Rock Around the Clock. Dir. Fred F. Sears. Columbia, 1956. Film.
Run Lola Run. Dir. Tom Tykwer. Bavaria Film, 1998. Film.
The Saddest Music in the World. Dir. Guy Maddin. IFC, 2003. Film.
Slobin, Mark, ed. *Global Soundtracks: Worlds of Film Music*. Middletown: Wesleyan UP, 2008. Print.
Smith, Jeff. *The Sounds of Commerce: Marketing Popular Film Music*. New York: Columbia UP, 1998. Print.
The Sweet Smell of Success. Dir. Alexander Mackendrick. United Artists, 1957. Film.
Walk on the Wild Side. Dir. Edward Dmytryk. Columbia, 1962. Film.

James F. Lastra

Teaching Film Sound

When it is thought about at all, film sound is usually considered partially, inconsistently, or unsystematically. Unlike the analysis of the image, the study of sound is routinely restricted to an analysis of how a given formal element (dialogue, effects, music) is placed within the film and how it is combined with other sounds or the image. Studies rarely give any consideration to how the sound elements are constructed so that the sort of distinction commonly made between Louis Feuillade's deep frame and Sergei Eisenstein's shallow frame does not exist for sound, and its constructedness is taken as a given. David Bordwell and Kristin Thompson's otherwise enviably systematic *Film Art: An Introduction* provides three exhaustive chapters on the shot (covering mise-en-scène, cinematography, and editing). However, it also offers one of the most thoughtful introductions to film sound, conveying a very useful sense of the primary functions of sound in film despite the baldly inadequate terminology it provides for describing the dimensions of sound, and points to a symptomatic reluctance to take sound seriously as a medium. Therefore I focus here on the materiality and uniqueness of recorded sound as a form of representation. Still, since the Bordwell and Thompson book is unmatched in formal precision and rigor and because it is the most widely taught introductory text, I tailor my suggestions so that they offer a supplement to *Film Art.*

I would suggest that a useful place to start when teaching sound is to compare sound with image to get beyond the idea that sound has no parallels to mise-en-scène, cinematography, or editing. That is, we should disabuse students of the idea that sounds simply have loudness, pitch, and timbre (as if unmediated by the sound apparatus) and instead understand that filmmakers shape or create the loudness, pitch, and timbre (and the space, rhythm, distance, perspective) of every sound. Using the image as a guide, we try to listen to all the ways in which sounds may be shaped for the purposes of different forms of filmmaking. Thus we ask, How do we create sound continuity? How do we enhance or support narration? How can we create the impression of subjectivity? Why is it important to understand that sound is manipulated if we cannot readily perceive these manipulations? How is film sound related to radio, phonography, and popular music recording? Are there different forms of listening?

Much of the task of teaching sound is to recognize that something has been done to design, stage, or manipulate the sound so that it is recognized as a process of representation. While many sound manipulations such as editing are nearly inaudible (especially when compared with the relative visibility of image editing), and some staging (mise-en-scène) such as performing music in a concert hall is culturally transparent, an awareness of how sounds may be shaped helps students become sensitive to the sound track's construction.

Since the publication of Alan Williams's influential essay "Is Sound Recording like a Language?," studies of film sound have encouraged us to understand every sound as an event with a three-dimensional material existence. As Williams argues, every sound event, like every listening event, is unique, since the "entire volume of air that vibrates" in a space constitutes the sound "itself" (53). Likewise, as we all know from our experiences at concerts, where one listens from materially affects the sound one hears. That the listener's location should be so easily forgotten when approaching the highly constructed form of film sound is surprising. To say that sounds inherently possess a pitch, loudness, and timbre encourages us to assume that sounds exist in a realm untouched by mediation and in a single, portable form—regardless of the actual conditions of presentation, representation, or audition. However, just as images are presented from a particular point of view, with scale (close-up, medium shot, long shot) and angle (bird's-eye, from below), sounds are presented from particular points of audition to similar effect.

Orchestral music is recorded from good seats in a good hall, and so it strives to represent the appropriate or ideal experience of the music. Rock music, on the other hand, approaches recording as simply another step in the process of producing electrified music and may manipulate sound by recording it in what may seem unconventional ways to create (rather than reproduce) a specific sound experience. A drum kit recorded from the distant end of a stone hallway produces a distinctive sound, but not one based on a common mode of listening. Similarly, film sound can efface its status as representation by conforming to conventional expectations (such as listening to a conversation from a close distance), or it may foreground its manipulation for effect (dramatizing the conditions of listening so that, for example, we hear a sound as if underwater). Yet however transparent recording seems, it is still a designed experience, and our access to it is shaped in a particular way to achieve particular ends.

As Rick Altman usefully points out in "The Material Heterogeneity of Recorded Sound," the experience that we usually describe as "listening to a recording of a sound" is more accurately understood as "hearing the replay of the recording of the story of a sound event" (28). By way of this deliberately awkward and determinedly sequential list, he means to draw our attention to both the site-specific and temporal dimensions of all acts of listening and the manner in which technological recording listens to an event for us or before we do. Finally, he reminds us that the mechanical process is doubled by our attention to the recording. The wordiness reminds us of the many mediations to which sounds are subject in even the most straightforward recording. Moreover, the awkwardness of the phrase slows us down and makes us reflect on the nature of sound recording. Given that any stage of the process (from the acoustics of the sound stage to the placement of loudspeakers) can powerfully shape our ultimate experience of a sound event, it is best to be aware of the complexity of the process involved in even the simplest film sound.

Perhaps the best pedagogical device for inculcating a sensitivity to sound is focused description. Having students carefully describe what they hear (or what they hear and see) is far more productive than having them memorize taxonomies of diegetic, paradiegetic, meta-diegetic sound-image relationships or lists of microphone types. I do not mean to discount the usefulness of such distinctions in certain cases, but a pragmatic and textually specific approach tends to focus students immediately on formal specifics and locates their effort where it is more likely to pay off in precise description and analysis of how a sound functions in a particular case. Describing carefully what they hear will habituate students to noticing basic sound design techniques and help overcome sound's apparent acoustic transparency. Certain techniques can be illustrated easily in class, with examples from individual music collections and from available films. Whatever the sound example, the most effective question to ask is, What is it doing?, or, What is achieved in this work by constructing these sounds in this manner? Whether the example is a piece of music or a film might necessitate different conclusions (Is this recording meant to replicate a concert hall? Does this sound change how we understand the synchronized image?), but this variation underscores that sound functions differently in different works.

The most important and most easily understood device for shaping the experience of a recorded sound is miking distance or perspective—the point from which the machine "listens to" the source sound and therefore the position we tend to inhabit as auditors. By placing a microphone very close to the actor, the filmmaker typically ensures that dialogue remains intelligible. Orchestras, by contrast, are miked more distantly so that we hear the acoustics and space of the hall, and quartets so that we hear a more intimate setting. Solo instruments like the guitar are typically miked closely to mimic the chamber setting to which they are suited, although a combination of distances may be mixed to "breathe some air" into a recording. Such techniques can be used in film as well. Fred Astaire and Gene Kelly's untrained voices are recorded very closely as if whispering in our ears, while Al Jolson's far less intimate style and more powerful voice sounds better when recorded from a greater distance, as if addressing a vaudeville audience. In each case, the design of the sound experience is supposed to suit an established form of listening. The annoying nasality of Glenn Anders's George Grisby and the smooth baritone of Orson Welles's Michael O'Hara in *Lady from Shanghai* (1947) demonstrate how delivery and microphone placement (close in the latter case, farther in the former) can affect characterization. We want to know O'Hara but recoil from Grisby.

While it is tempting to understand sound scale as directly analogous to shot scale (and we do often use terms like "close-up sound"), close dialogue miking might just as easily be understood as sonic focus, because the goals are usually clarity and directness. In fact, the loudness of dialogue on the final sound track may have more to do with editing and mixing (creating the layered relationships between audio elements) than with microphone placement. The primary advantage to close (detailed) miking is that it allows for a full range of manipulation at later stages of the process. Close-up sound commonly creates what in "Technology of the Voice" Altman calls "for-me-ness" (3), that is, discursivity or, more broadly, salience. Creating structured relationships between sounds given focus and meaning (some of which can be done with miking) and sounds serving a subsidiary function defines the nature of classical (the period 1927–60) film sound.

To the extent that a sound is recorded with great acoustic detail, it can be used flexibly within a sound track and especially as the dominant element in its complex construction. The film sound track is typically constructed of several layers, the primary one in any scene being that which achieves the function desired by the filmmaker, such as narration. There is usually a strong contrast between an acoustic foreground and a less detailed background. Foreground and background are created both by relative volume and by relative clarity or salience, the foreground being either louder or clearer or both. Shaping sound so that the functionally dominant sound speaks most directly to the audience is a complex but systematic practice. Indeed, creating points of sonic emphasis is the basic technique in narrative sound design and can be achieved in any number of ways. By restricting what we otherwise hear in *Play Time* (1967), Jacques Tati can draw our attention to sounds we typically ignore, such as the compression of a seat cushion. Mainstream narrative films use mixing or silence to ensure we always hear the dialogue we need even during a storm or a battle. The same goes for the crucial sound of a door latch opening, which we unfailingly hear during a lull in the sounds of the room. Bringing these structures to students' attention is crucial.

One practical place to start is with the kinds of film sounds that all students know well—dialogue, sound effects, and music. This triad, taken as a given in film production as well as film analysis, is anything but transparent. Although a functional categorization for most classical films, it masks as much as it reveals about film sound. The trio is generally understood as ordered according to formal importance and frequency of use: dialogue takes primacy, effects support dialogue and music, and music intermittently serves as a tonal or emotional foundation. In conventional narrative film, this hierarchy is determined by the supremacy of narration to the formal, institutional, and economic stability of the commercial film industry.

Of course, dialogue is not always the dominant conduit for narrative information. At many moments in individual films and in many genres (melodrama and the horror film come to mind), effects and music may be as narratively essential as dialogue is elsewhere. As Bordwell, Janet Staiger, and Thompson remind us in *The Classical Hollywood Cinema*, the key concept ordering formal choices is a hierarchically ordered paradigm of substitutability. One may achieve a particular function in a variety of ways, but the classical paradigm orders the probability with which they are likely to be used. Particular genres—action films, slapstick comedy, and horror, for example—place a greater than usual emphasis on sound effects as the primary avenue of sonic narration. Others, such as melodrama and romance, may use music as a way of underscoring, indicating, or prompting emotional response of both character and audiences. Likewise, certain sequences—montages, fight scenes, car chases, musical interludes—can diverge from the tendency of the rest of a film. It is important to get students to analyze sound in the context of the film as a whole as well as the particular sequence so that they can understand what a particular film demands at any point and therefore how sound can contribute to it.

In any scene or indeed any film, the layered foreground/background system helps create continuity in two ways. First, a continuous background creates a spatial consistency by persisting uninterrupted during the more extensively edited dialogue or effects tracks. Second, by being temporally continuous like music, a background reinforces the continuity of duration or action. In both cases, sound works in concert with and is redundant with the image. In the classical cinema, redundancy—where the sound track doubles or underscores the functions of the image—is the rule. There are, however, forms of classical sound that go beyond obvious redundancy or expand it. In the most common case, sound can add to the image by creating or signaling off-screen space. The opening of John Stahl's *Imitation of Life* (1934), for example, uses repeated instances of off-screen sound (the splashes and singing of her daughter bathing, a kettle boiling over, a knock at the door, a ringing telephone, and finally the cry of a child falling in the tub) to establish that Bea Pullman's domestic life is out of control, since Bea can never be where the sound demands that she be. Sound can spatialize an image in other ways as well: by providing reverberation, as in *Citizen Kane*'s Thatcher Archive sequence; by creating an ambience redolent of a particular locale, as the clatter of typewriters characterize the newsroom in *His Girl Friday* (1940); or by indicating unseen peril through off-screen space, as in innumerable slasher films. Similarly, both sound effects and music can create emotional tones for a scene, even in contradiction to the image, offering a kind of sonic commentary, either through the familiar romantic underscoring of love scenes, the ironic juxtaposition of images and narration (as in Lockwood's autobiographical introduction to "The Dueling Cavalier" in *Singin' in the Rain* [1952]), or the use of a dominant theme to predict a scene (as when, in *The Road Warrior* [1981], the theme telegraphs who will win a fight).

Sound can also create forms of subjectivity either through sounds that indicate a specific point of listening (say, from behind a door) or by distortions, music, or effects that indicate the mediation of a character's mind or imagination. A voice-over can comment on the action to indicate subjectivity, but a voice-over may as easily indicate the commentator's complete exteriority to the action, as if in a documentary. Nonnarrative relationships are possible, too, and sound can even dominate the image in many ways. In Soviet "asynchronous" or "contrapuntal" sound, in Peter Kubelka's or Larry Gottheim's complex experimental isomorphisms, in song-centered cartoons, and in song-and-dance numbers in musicals, the sound track can be said to dominate the image structurally, motivating the images so that they accompany it.

Three brief examples can give a sense not only of how these techniques are used but also of how they can be used thematically. In *It Happened One Night* (1934), for instance, sound initially seems to play no particular role—it is simply one functional element among others in the production of a narrative. Dialogue dominates the sound track of nearly every scene, with background effects (a yacht, a bus, a car) providing verisimilitude and a context for the action. However, even such formally unexceptional techniques can serve a sophisticated function. While voices are usually set against background meant to substantiate setting, the film makes vocal performance the key measure of the couple's progress. At the outset, Ellen (Claudette Colbert) argues with her father, having no sympathetic interlocutor. Peter (Clark Gable), by contrast, is a master of words but winds up impressing his mates by "winning" an argument with a disconnected phone. Ellen's decreasing social awkwardness is then tracked by her ability to participate vocally in conversation, community, and finally marriage. When she joins in the singing on the bus, she overcomes one obstacle, but when she joins Peter in the give-and-take necessary to avoid discovery, playing at being married, they have found each other as partners. For all his cynicism, Peter, too, learns to participate in genuine conversation—something we sense he is destined to do when he fends off the grating Shapeley who presses his unwanted attentions on Ellen on the bus.

By contrast, the birds' attack on the schoolchildren in *The Birds* (1963), like many of Alfred Hitchcock's set pieces, offers a useful sample sequence for analysis that is not based on the thematic importance of sound. The sequence's images move methodically leftward from slow, long shots, emphasizing duration, through a tense shot/reverse-shot exchange in the classroom, to Melanie's (Tippi Hedren's) protracted wait, spent smoking on a playground bench. The wait is punctuated by crosscutting between closer and closer shots of Melanie and the increasing flock of birds, which, unbeknownst to Melanie, is gathering on the playground. A moving shot joins the spectator's and Melanie's points of view together and reveals even more birds than we had noticed. The effect is of a bow being drawn back to maximum tension—a tension that will be released when the children and adults run downhill. The camera begins tracking right, following Melanie back to the classroom, and then cutting out into the street, where the group breaks into a frantic run down the hill toward a hotel as the camera's movement right and the cutting both accelerate to the point of chaos. The scene ends in a car with Melanie and a couple of girls trapped inside until the birds inexplicably leave.

Sound works in powerful harmony with the image. The opening is quiet, with the distant putter of Melanie's car accompanying a slow pan left. Her exit of the car and entrance into the school is accompanied by a silence broken only by the repeated chorus of the children's nonsense song "Risselty-Rosselty." The song continues faintly while Melanie waits, simultaneously accentuating the duration of the scene to the breaking point and reminding us of the endangered children off-screen right. The apparently endless song, whose repeated chorus delays their escape, offers a powerfully innocent and oblivious counterpoint to the menace of the crows. As Melanie and the camera move right, silence reigns except for the unison response of the students to the teacher's instructions. When outside, the children's suddenly running feet mix indistinguishably with the birds' wings into a frenzied chaos interrupted only by individual screams matched to specific close-ups, culminating in an image that recalls Sergei Eisenstein's famous Odessa Steps sequence in his 1925 film *Potemkin* with a focus on a girl's glasses. The threat posed by the noise increases until the trio finds refuge in a car but can only impotently honk at the attacking flock. The scene ends with a diminishing flutter of wings.

Some films can open to broader questions such as sound's place within urban modernity. In Fritz Lang's *M* (1931), sound works in concert with the image to establish a palpable sense of a threatening and threatened off-screen space. The film begins with the perpetually ascending harmonic and melodic cycles of "In the Hall of the Mountain King," which repeats with the obsessive return of the killer's desire. A group of children sing a repetitive rhyme about the killer, which draws the attention of one of the mothers, who is pulled outdoors by their song. She returns inside, where a series of off-screen sounds (a knock at the door, the chime of a clock, the sounds of feet on the stairs, the honk of a car horn, a policeman's whistle) hail her and draw her attention to that which is just beyond her perception. The same thing occurs in the street, until an off-screen voice solicits a little girl ("Elsie. Elsie Beckmann.") and lures her away from home and toward her death. Back at home, her mother begins to notice signs of absence, culminating in the never-answered call, "Elsie!" which, accompanied by images of absence (an empty plate, a vacant stairway, an unoccupied attic, and an unattended balloon), convey poor Elsie's fate.

M is particularly sensitive to sound and thematizes it beyond this opening by contrasting the state's obsessively visual search of the city, with the underworld's similar effort at mapping urban space. The underworld succeeds more quickly, discovering the killer by means of a sound. The dialectic between sound and image established by the opening is realized by the parallel epistemologies of the law and the outlaw.

In sum, we need always to understand the sound norms appropriate to the sonic world created by a film. Even apparently descriptive terms such as "silence" are typically defined relationally, and a particular film may set its "silence" in terms appropriate to it. Frequently, filmmakers set a sonic floor based on "room tone," or a relative form of quiet that reflects the represented space. A factory might reverberate and feature a faint hum, a seaside setting might consist of the distant roar of waves but no reverberation, an isolated study might include the close, deadened sound of a carpeted and upholstered space, with, perhaps, the buzz of fluorescent fixtures. David Lynch's films, especially his early ones such as *Eraserhead* (1977), *The Elephant Man* (1980), or *Blue Velvet* (1986), often use a low rumble or unsettling hum to set a mood of barely submerged disquiet. Modern sound tracks are more likely to employ such devices, but classical films (from the later 1930s onward) rarely include moments of true silence. Each scene may involve a different sonic floor or background, but there will usually be one. Like the world created in a popular song, the features of a soundscape may range from the nearly documentary to the wholly imaginary, particularly in the modern sound track, which has learned a great deal from the recorded popular song.

The modern sound track mimics the classical but introduces several important shifts in emphasis. First, multitrack mixing and noise-reduction technologies allow for dramatically expanded dynamic and frequency ranges. Lows are lower, highs higher, louds louder, and silences quieter. Indeed, one of the major tendencies of modern sound design is to provide more of everything. The modern track tends to be denser with sound and busier. More sound events occur, and they cover a greater range and leap between extremes. As with the image, modern sound tracks frequently serve as special effects or as sonic spectacle. Action sequences and musical interludes (imagine the air cavalry attack in *Apocalypse Now* [1979] or the hula hoop montage in *The Hudsucker Proxy* [1994]) often allow for a display of sonic might and technique in excess of purely narrative demands. In some ways these sequences are even structurally driven by the sound track (as are music videos and many older cartoons, like the *Silly Symphonies*).

Still, the functions covered by even the most modern tracks are relatively consistent. One domain that has changed, however, is how space is shaped by sound, both on the sound track and in conjunction with the image track. With precise stereo and surround sound placement possible for both release prints and DVDs, ambience and location have been given more and more emphasis. While often a matter of degree rather than kind, stereo surround technology allows for the creation of sonic "landmarks" that anchor us, if not precisely in space, then in a general milieu. Consequently, editors are more able to cut freely and rapidly around a space, knowing that the sound track will continue to help orient viewers. One trend is to emphasize close-ups to a greater degree than in the classical era, with the belief that sound will convey the contextualizing information provided by the establishing, long, or three-quarters shots. It is now also more common to immerse the spectator in the diegesis, often through an exaggerated form of character subjectivity, one that can, in films like *Apocalypse Now*, emulate the "headphone music" of an earlier, more psychedelic era.

Finally, it is often useful to use students' familiarity with other sound forms to advantage. Since the sound track generally aspires to world making, both radio dramas and popular music recordings offer fertile grounds for analysis. Using a highly worked sonic world—such as a Phil Spector track, something like *Sgt. Pepper's*, or even the 1950s and 1960s opera recordings of John Culshaw—it is easy to get students sensitized to both the possibilities of sound manipulations and the parameters that govern a specific sound environment. The same can be said for sound installations, *musique concrete*, or the increasingly common (although still rare) genre of the headphone sound work. Moving your students away from film and out of the theater conceptually, if not literally, makes it easier to understand other sound issues (such as sound's central role in defining the relationship between public and private space, the role of sound proofing or of architecture in shaping the everyday soundscape, or the use of music for coercive purposes, for example) with greater immediacy.

Works Cited

Altman, Rick. "The Material Heterogeneity of Recorded Sound." Altman, *Sound Theory* 15–31.

———. *Sound Theory / Sound Practice*. New York: Routledge-AFI, 1992. Print.

———. "Technology of the Voice." *Iris* 3.1 (1985): 3–20. Print.

Bordwell, David, and Kristin Thompson. *Film Art: An Introduction*. 8th ed. New York: McGraw, 2008. Print.

Bordwell, David, Janet Staiger, and Kristin Thompson. *The Classical Hollywood Cinema: Film Style and Mode of Production, 1917–1960*. New York: Columbia UP, 1985. Print.

Williams, Alan. "Is Sound Recording like a Language?" *Yale French Studies* 60 (1980): 51–66. Print.

Anne Rutherford

Teaching Film and Mise-en-Scène

What is at stake in the ways we teach the formal concepts of film studies? This question always underpins the way I approach teaching mise-en-scène. Are we trying to inculcate students in a set of analytical grids that constitute the received wisdom of the discipline or to teach concepts more dynamically, to get students to think in more open and generative ways? Underlying these questions is a distinction between teaching structure and process: in teaching mise-en-scène, do we focus on breaking it down into static structures, removed from the ways a film engages the spectator, or do we try to get students to immerse themselves in its dynamic construction and unfolding, to come to grips with the way a film plays out in the experiences of viewers?

Mise-en-scène as a concept ranges in its use from the most mechanistic atomized term to the most productive and expansive one. At its most impoverished, mise-en-scène criticism enumerates the contents of the frame, isolates single elements out of the frame, and produces stolid and noncinematic analyses. At its most enabling, it generates vibrant cinematic analyses and gives students a framework to describe the musicality of a film in its expanded sense: the rhythm; the dynamics of space; and the energy of its orchestration of sound and image as the tools out of which narrative is constructed but also as a dimension of experience that runs parallel, not subservient, to narrative. Our understanding of mise-en-scène is constituted in the definition of the term, and only a definition in process—of the operation of mise-en-scène in situ—can fully address its dynamics.

Mise-en-scène has been described as the "grand undefined term" of film theory (Henderson 315). Initially adapted from the stage, the term was popularized in film by the cinephile critics of the journal *Cahiers du cinéma*, in the 1950s and 1960s (see Hillier), to evoke what Adrian Martin calls "that mobile, modulating, sinuous relationship between the camera, the actor, and the environment," the "magic [that is] one of the primal pleasures of cinema, and a great generator of its sensorial and semantic riches" ("Placing"). The French term means literally "what is put onto the stage" or "into the scene," but the *Cahiers* critics avoided a literal transposition of the concept from stage to screen and translated it into a dynamic cinematic concept, one that recognized the pivotal differences between theater and cinema and was productive and open, albeit ambiguous. For the *Cahiers* critics, this was a synthetic concept, used to evoke the fusion of the material dimensions of a film into the elusive flow of energy that sweeps the spectator along in its wake, immersed in the way the rhythmic pulses of light, the choreography of space and movement, and the modulations of color and texture produce an ensemble much greater than the sum of its parts. Mise-en-scène is formulated as an energetic engagement with the spectator, as process, rather than empirical object or technique. Alexandre Astruc wrote that "mise en scène . . . [is] a certain way of extending states of mind into movements of the body. It is a song, a rhythm, a dance" (267). He also maintained, "What pleases me [in a film] is the mise en scène: to make the spectator feel the moment of disequilibrium where everything suddenly falls apart" (qtd. in Bacher 231).

However, in its recent usage in anglophone film studies, the term has been shackled by its heritage in the stasis of the proscenium arch. English-language texts commonly start from a literal translation of the French and apply this formulation mechanically from stage to screen, listing inventories of the "elements of mise-en-scène"—"costume, décor, lighting, camera movement, setting and the behavior of figures"—divorced from their context in the energetic work of the film and from its reception by an audience (Bordwell and Thompson 119).

The emphasis on this theatrical heritage varies in different introductory texts. The most pervasive text, David Bordwell and Kristin Thompson's *Film*

Art: An Introduction, has the narrowest focus on "those aspects of film that overlap with the theater" (176). Bordwell and Thompson separate mise-en-scène from the cinematographic properties of the shot, defining it as equivalent to the profilmic: "all of the elements placed in front of the camera to be photographed: the settings and props, the lighting, costumes and makeup and figure behavior" (504). Susan Hayward adds "movement within the frame" (231). Jill Nelmes refuses the distinction between the profilmic and the cinematographic; she writes of mise-en-scène as "staging": a combination of "what has been filmed (setting props, costumes, etc.) and *how* it is filmed (cinematographic properties of the shot, such as depth of field, focus, lighting, and camera movement)" (460). Bruce Kawin's succinct definition, encompassing both the techniques of theatrical staging and the specificity of the cinematic shot, clarifies this duality:

> In cinema, mise-en-scène is a function of the relations between the scene as a dramatic unit played out in theatrical space (the set or landscape) and the camera that reshapes that space into a two-dimensional rectangle of light and shadow. The cinematic scene is typically divided into several shots, whereas the theatrical scene is played out in the seamless time and space of the stage. Thus each shot also has a mise-en-scène of its own, created primarily by the way a given fragment of action is composed and framed by the camera, selected out of the prefilmic world and given a particular shape and texture. (98)

Kawin's inclusive and dynamic definition focuses on the relation of actors, setting, and camera and the movements of each, as well as "the choice of film stock . . . aspect ratio . . . framing . . . camera placement and movement [and crucially including] sound environment, [and] *the way all of these elements are 'set in motion'*" (98; emphasis mine).

How can the common theatrical understanding of mise-en-scène make sense in cinema? While objects can be put onto the stage in theater and maintain their integrity as inert objects, no such assumption can be made in cinema. An object does not maintain its status once it is in the frame: color or a set are not merely background but part of the experience of the spectator, constituted through the temporal experience of a shot. As Siegfried Kracauer writes, cinema does not just reproduce the material world, but "brings the whole material world into play" (qtd. in Hansen, "'With Skin'" 457).

Robin Wood writes, "mise-en-scène is not all these things considered as separate and detachable items: it is also what fuses all these into one organic unity, and consequently more, much more, than the sum of its parts" (qtd. in Gibbs 57). As John Gibbs explains, "mise-en-scène is sometimes used as a straightforward descriptive term but it is really a concept" (1). By rewriting the concept as simply a set of discrete components, many introductory texts have ignored key strands of mise-en-scène criticism and lost its generative potential. This concept of mise-en-scène brings together several dimensions in a way that no existing English term does, and key to this concept is the integration of space and time.

Sometimes mise-en-scène is described as the art of space, montage as the art of time; James Monaco states, "mise-en-scène is often regarded as static, montage as dynamic" (179). Jean-Luc Godard challenged this polarity, declaring: "montage is above all an integral part of mise-en-scène. Only at peril can one be separated from the other. One might just as well try to separate the rhythm from a melody" (39).[1] Monaco credits Godard with "creat[ing] a dialectical synthesis of these two theses that had governed film theory for so long. This is one of the most important steps in film theory" (411). This synthesis was fundamental to the development of modern cinema and its transformation of cinematic space and time.[2] While the analysis of still frames provides an understanding of pictorial composition, it cannot account for the spatio-temporal dynamics of a shot, since time is integral to the way mise-en-scène works. The long take has been a privileged site for the analysis of mise-en-scène, particularly with the complex spatial relationships made possible by cinemascope and deep-focus cinematography, but the spatiality of the long take cannot be separated from its work with duration.[3]

Adrian Martin describes the "foundational ambiguity" of mise-en-scène, its oscillation between a term that refers to "a quite specific phase in the filmmaking process—which would be the shooting or 'principal photography' phase, in which scenes are blocked and shot within the décor" and one that focuses on the final film, "a looser term, a metaphor almost, for film 'style' taken more broadly and holistically" ("Placing"). He challenges this use of the term as "the catch-all for every notable aesthetic aspect of cinema." At its broadest, it encompasses "the organization of time and space in its entirety" (Gibbs 57). To me, mise-en-scène is a more concrete, nuanced concept than style, which could be understood as extraneous. It is the setting in motion of the spatiotemporal relationships that are the very stuff of our experience of film (Rutherford).

This distinction has major ramifications for the ways we think about the concept. *Film Art*, for example, breaks down the image into a set of production components described for their technical qualities, such as the contrast, color, source, and composition of light. This conceptualization provides a vocabulary to describe material parameters of the image in detail. In a context in which students have commonly been taught an analytical approach that centers on narrative theme and ideology—in which the materiality of image and sound often disappears—this technical focus deflects attention away from the concentration on plot and character, to look at the material and aesthetic dimensions of a film. It offers the tools for breaking down a scene into a shot list, an invaluable task in honing skills of observation and listening. However, dissecting a scene in this way is only the first step toward understanding how it works. As one of my students stated, it is like attempting to understand the act of a juggler by describing the qualities of the individual balls. The next step must be an attempt to grasp how the energetic flow of a scene is built up through the articulation of these material elements together. Exercises that require students to "write the scene from inside"—to develop an analysis of flow—are pivotal here. This focus appears in much of what Gibbs describes as a history of "superb writing [on mise-en-scène] which is alive and sensitive to the complexities of film style" (57).[4]

So how do we teach mise-en-scène, given the proliferation of definitions and uses of the term? One approach is to teach it historically, to discuss its initial theatrical definition, the way it was used by the critics of the French new wave, its adoption into auteurist criticism, its importance for serious consideration of genre cinema, its deployment in polemical debates against montage, its articulation as a cornerstone of Bazinian theories of realism, and the way it has been taught in anglophone film studies (see Gibbs). This reflexive, genealogical approach can reveal why the term has been used in certain ways, release it from these contexts for productive contemporary uses, and contextualize the strictures of its usage in introductory texts.

I prefer to teach the concept polemically, as a contested term, to interrogate the conflict among its different meanings. If we think about mise-en-scène as a set of inert elements in the frame, what does that teach us about the way film works? If, by contrast, we approach it as a dynamic, energetic process, how does this open up our ways of understanding a film? By problematizing the concept at the root, it comes alive pedagogically. Putting it to work in this way demonstrates to students why they need to look and listen closely and to do the work involved in a shot breakdown. It also shows how this process alone can never explain the cinematic alchemy that transforms these elements under the pressure of time and the camera into something new.

Students may not have the conceptual vocabulary to articulate the richness of experience that mise-en-scène generates, but they can feel it. There are countless examples of films that, interrogated experientially, reveal the organic unity of mise-en-scène. One of my favorites is a scene from Wong Kar-wai's *In the Mood for Love* (2000), in which the camera follows Maggie Cheung walking in slow motion down the stairs, into a restaurant, and back up and then follows Tony Leung through the same motions (ch. 9 on the DVD). We could talk about the muted color palette, the dingy light, the texture of the wall or the composition that divides the frame into moving panels, but the fusion of these elements into a whole demonstrates irrevocably the importance of a synthetic understanding of mise-en-scène. The scene is a mesmerizing rhythmic choreography of the relation of figure movement, camera movement, music, and the plasticity of space. The space is performing here as much as the actors are, and we need a performative, temporal understanding of mise-en-scène to grasp how this works, an understanding that mise-en-scène is process, not structure. The role of kinetic rhythm can be a pivotal focal point to ask these questions about the dynamic ways mise-en-scène works.[5]

Is teaching introductory courses, then, a two-stage process in which we teach easy-to-grasp but unproductive concepts and later attempt to break that mold? Or do we lay the foundation from the beginning for dynamic ways of explaining the complexities of cinematic experience? In response to the multiplicity of meanings given to mise-en-scène, introductory texts delimit its meaning into clear-cut uses. However, the complexities of the concept are key to its richness, and its oversimplification actively stultifies thought. *Film Art*, for example, privileges the term as used by production technicians at the expense of the often more dynamic analytical frameworks developed by critics. This presentation insulates the static conceptual framework from the debates across film studies and isolates it from broader aesthetic discourse. With the widespread use of *Film Art* and a generation of film students trained in this approach, mise-en-scène has degenerated in its common usage into a static empirical term.

The attention to questions of reception in film studies since the early 1980s has major implications for the ways we teach mise-en-scène. Methods of analyzing elements in a text in a closed system do not adequately address the experience of images: a film is not simply a text; it is an event. We cannot teach a dynamic understanding of film as event or process if the core concepts we use are static, noninteractive concepts, and there are concerted moves in film studies away from text-based analysis of film toward performative models (see Curtis 45). If we take these moves seriously, their implications must be applied to all our key concepts.

One strength of the concept of mise-en-scène is its materiality. If we focus on the spectator, we risk the loss of this materiality, potentially short-circuiting any real engagement with the film as film; close textual analysis is essential. If the analysis stays with the film as text, however, marginalizing the activation of its energetic charge for the spectator, the understanding of the dynamics of the film can only ever be partial. This difficulty demands a methodology that can hold, in the one frame, the materiality of the film and the materiality of the viewing experience. Mise-en-scène is a linchpin concept here. The ambiguity of the term in its historical usage, encompassing these two ideas at the same time, provides a tool to address this double-edged materiality—how the elements of the material world, rendered cinematic, are both material and energetic. I explain this idea with a scene from *The Thin Red Line* (1998), in which, while the soldiers are reeling in shock from the sudden slaughter of their comrades, the wind ripples up the grassy hillside in a shot that is, at once, kinetic rhythm, flashing light and texture, and intense anxiety that hits the pit of the stomach of the viewer. Mise-en-scène is the only concept we have that addresses that organic unity, that elusive quality of flow and energy that moves a film and moves us as spectators with it.

How do we understand mise-en-scène? Literally, what is put into the scene, but not just what is put into the frame. It is also what is put into the moment of experience, how the spectator is drawn into the scene. We need, therefore, a performative understanding of mise-en-scène, how it draws the spectator into the scene, materially, experientially, as the scene unfolds in time. This approach brings reception into the foreground and restores an understanding of mise-en-scène as energetic process. If we accept this principle, our teaching of mise-en-scène must address how the orchestration of time and space works to draw us as viewers into an embodied engagement with the film, to explore mise-en-scène as a site of intensity. Richard Barsam's introductory text incorporates reception in a rudimentary way into his definition of mise-en-scène:

> the overall look and feel of a movie—the sum of everything the audience sees, hears and experiences while viewing it. A movie's mise-en-scène subtly influences our mood as we watch, much as the décor, lighting, smells and sounds can influence our emotional response to a real-life place. (92)[6]

In *Kill Bill: Vol. 1* (2003), the fight scene with O-Ren-Ishi in the garden opens itself to a close analysis of color, costume, light and choreography of figures. The scene is played out as a conflict between the hot (red/yellow) end of the color spectrum and the cold (blue/green/white) end, culminating in a cryptic, visually striking spray of red blood across the pristine white snow. Yet any close study of this scene reveals the inseparability of image from sound, the importance not only of the music but also of the water feature to the rhythmic articulation of the choreography, punctuating the space and giving it a pulse. This scene, furthermore, relies for its intensity on the heightened sensitivity to color built up through the accumulation of fluctuations, in the previous scene, from full color to black and white to black silhouette on lurid blue. This progression, awakening the senses to an acute awareness of color, demonstrates that the fight scene cannot be analyzed in isolation from the rest of the film or outside the context of reception. Its impact relies on a cumulative sensory training enacted on the viewer.

This importance granted to experience over signification challenges key precepts of conventional thinking about mise-en-scène. Gibbs asserts the value of mise-en-scène criticism for its attention to visual style, but his conclusion is tied to the limited question of how "style determines meaning" (100). Bordwell and Thompson also privilege meaning, considering mise-en-scène as a set of techniques that function to bolster the narrative.[7] This assumed hierarchy has been systematically challenged. Sergei Eisenstein envisaged a film score like an orchestral score in which all of the "various audio-visual elements have equal rights" (Aumont 185). Miriam Hansen has described "classical narrative cinema" as "a scaffold, matrix, or web that allows for a wide range of aesthetic effects and experiences" ("Mass Production" 339). Thomas Elsaesser has explored the "melos" in melodrama—"spatial and musical categories as opposed to intellectual or literary ones" (173)—as a material, affective counterpoint to the linear meaning-producing structures of language, as both an expressive system for that which cannot be articulated through narrative and a dimension of intensity that exceeds the narrative. Martin considers mise-en-scène as a site of an "almost thermodynamic intensity" in the films of Raúl Ruiz:

> [*M*]*ise en scène* becomes a practice radically different to its time-honored dramaturgical understanding and usage if conceived and executed in terms of condensing and displacing, loading and discharging psychic intensities. . . . [Mise-en-scène criticism] would have to trans-

> form itself utterly in order to cope with what is going on here, picking up the road it rarely took when modernist filmmakers began radically reshaping mise-en-scène criticism in the '60s. ("Displacements" 51)[8]

In *Film Art*, the "elements of mise-en-scène" support the narrative largely through their capacity to direct our eye and attention in the frame (Bordwell and Thompson 207). Contemporary film theory has revised this assumption of a disembodied eye, arguing that we not only look at the space of the shot, we inhabit it. Giuliana Bruno, for example, argues that film involves a tactile, kinaesthetic engagement with the environment. This argument challenges understandings of mise-en-scène as static compositions, props, or objects, demanding that space be understood as animate: space moves, shifts with the camera, is malleable; its textures resonate. In my work, I have explored mise-en-scène as a site that enhances "the 'porous interface' between the spectator and the material world that characterizes mimetic experience" (Rutherford 65). I have argued that the sensory-affective experience of mise-en-scène "is the critical link in the relationship between the material dimensions of cinema and its affect" (67).[9] This integration of spectatorship into the core understanding of mise-en-scène characterizes a revitalized mise-en-scène criticism across several contemporary sites (see Bellour).

Working from the concrete, using writing exercises, gestural performance, graphs, diagrams, and metaphors can validate and activate the knowledge students have of the embodied experience of mise-en-scène. Sometimes the best way to evoke the intense spatiotemporal plasticity of a shot like the ten-minute diagonal tracking shot down the street in *Story of Last Chrysanthemums* (1939) is to perform it gesturally, like the conductor of an orchestra. Eisenstein's model of a film score and Hansen's image of a scaffold or matrix can be used to map out, schematically, how mise-en-scène ebbs and flows in a film. Sometimes an analogy from outside the theoretical literature can invoke a greater clarity. I use the model of a crochet hook to describe how a film reaches out and hooks and rehooks the spectator into the web of the film as it moves along. How does it do this? Kracauer writes that film constantly touches the earth, reaches down into our physiological being and so offers us a great model of how mise-en-scène works with the senses and how narrative moves forward through this constant looping into the spectator (qtd. in Hansen, "'With Skin'" 447). Students understand images like this—they remember them and use them as a template that can become a foundation for more sophisticated conceptual work.

Mise-en-scène is one of the most generative of our foundational cinematic concepts. If we teach the concept in a way that challenges and extends how students think, rather than providing them with a simple grid, we offer them the conceptual building blocks that become tools of creative and productive thinking and lead to dynamic analyses. We must find a way to deal with complexity, and the key is in the questions that we ask.

Notes

1. Gibbs gives a good account of the historical contingencies in the polemical opposition set up between montage and mise-en-scène.

2. We can, of course, analyze editing per se, but not in opposition to mise-en-scène. Martin asserts that we need a dialectical term, a marriage between mise-en-scène and theories of montage or at least decoupage, to address modern cinema ("Placing").

3. See Deleuze, ch. 1. Bacher makes a distinction between long-take theories and mise en scène theories, arguing that the former, which derive largely from Bazin's ideas of ontological realism, focus on the long take as a means to preserve the unity of time and space, whereas the latter emphasize the expressive possibilities of mise-en-scène.

4. Gibbs lists what he sees as the best English-language mise-en-scène criticism in an appendix that is useful but British focused and with limited inclusion of contemporary writing. Martin writes that traces of mise-en-scène criticism survive in a "dispersed," "marginal criticism" ("S.O.S.").

5. See also the long take in the opening scene of Andrei Tarkovsky's *Andrei Rublev* (1966) or the virtuoso choreography of the pool room scene in Brian De Palma's *Carlito's Way* (1993; thanks to Adrian Martin for this example).

6. Barsam includes a useful DVD and checklist for analyzing mise-en-scène (136).

7. I use the aquarium scene from *Lady from Shanghai* (1947) to illustrate a dynamic fluctuation of figure and ground as an energetic pulsation that in part drives the scene.

8. See also Martin, "Beyond the Fragments."

9. I use long takes from *Ulysses' Gaze* (1995) to demonstrate the argument that the way mise-en-scène works is not static, contained within a given shot, but relies on cumulatively drawing in the sensory responses of the spectator.

Works Cited

Astruc, Alexandre. "What Is *Mise en Scène*?" Hillier 266–68. Print.

Aumont, Jacques. *Montage Eisenstein*. Trans. Lee Hildreth, Constance Penley, and Andrew Ross. London: British Film Inst.; Bloomington: Indiana UP, 1987. Print.

Bacher, Lutz. *The Mobile Mise-en-Scène: A Critical Analysis of the Theory and Practice of Long-Take Camera Movement in the Narrative Film*. New York: Arno, 1978. Print.

Balcerzak, Scott, and Jason Sperb, eds. *Cinephilia in the Age of Digital Reproduction*. 2 vols. London: Wallflower, 2009. Print.
Barsam, Richard. *Looking at Movies: An Introduction to Film*. 2nd ed. New York: Norton, 2007. Print.
Bazin, André. "An Aesthetics of Reality: Neorealism." *What Is Cinema?* Trans. and comp. Hugh Gray. Vol. 2. Berkeley: U of California P, 2004. 16–40. Print.
Bellour, Raymond. "Figures aux allures de plans." *La mise en scène*. Ed. Jacques Aumont. Bruxelles: De Boeck U, 2000. 109–26. Print.
Bordwell, David, and Kristin Thompson. *Film Art: An Introduction*. 6th intl. ed. New York: McGraw, 2005. Print.
Bruno, Giuliana. *Atlas of Emotion: Journeys in Art, Architecture, and Film*. New York: Verso, 2002. Print.
Curtis, Robin. *Conscientious Viscerality: The Autobiographical Stance in German Film and Video*. Berlin: Imorde, 2006. Print.
Deleuze, Gilles. *Cinema One: The Movement-Image*. Trans. Hugh Tomlinson and Barbara Habberjam. Minneapolis: U of Minnesota P, 1986. Print.
Eisenstein, Sergei. "The Filmic Fourth Dimension." *Film Form*. Ed. Jay Leyda. New York: Jovanovich, 1949. 64–71. Print.
Elsaesser, Thomas. "Tales of Sound and Fury: Observations on the Family Melodrama." Nichols 2: 165–89.
Gibbs, John. *Mise-en-Scène: Film Style and Interpretation*. London: Wallflower, 2002. Print.
Godard, Jean-Luc. "Montage My Fine Care." *Godard on Godard*. Ed. Tom Milne and John Narboni. New York: Viking, 1972. 39–41. Print.
Hansen, Miriam Bratu. "The Mass Production of the Senses: Classical Cinema as Vernacular Modernism." *Reinventing Film Studies*. Ed. Christine Gledhill and Linda Williams. New York: Arnold, 2000. 332–50. Print.
———. "'With Skin and Hair': Kracauer's Theory of Film, Marseille 1940." *Critical Inquiry* 19 (1993): 437–69. Print.
Hayward, Susan. *Key Concepts in Cinema Studies*. London: Routledge, 2000. Print.
Henderson, Brian. "The Long Take." Nichols 1: 314–24.
Hillier, Jim, ed. Cahiers du cinéma*: The 1950s: Neo-realism, Hollywood, New Wave*. London: Routledge; Cambridge: Harvard UP, 1985. Print.
In the Mood for Love. Dir. Wong Kar-wai. Paradis, 2000. Becker Entertainment, 2001. DVD.
Kawin, Bruce F. *How Movies Work*. Berkeley: U of California P, 1992. Print.
Martin, Adrian. "Beyond the Fragments of Cinephilia: Towards a Synthetic Analysis." Balcerzak and Sperb 2: 30–53.
———. "Displacements." *Raul Ruiz: Images of Passage*. Ed. Helen Bandis, Martin, and Grant McDonald. Rotterdam: Rouge, 2004. 45–53. Print.
———. "Placing Mise en Scène: An Argument with John Gibbs's *Mise-en-Scène*." *Film-Philosophy* 8.20 (2004): n. pag. Web. 9 July 2004.
———. "S.O.S." *Film: Matters of Style*. Ed. Martin. Spec. issue of *Continuum* 5.2 (1990): n. pag. Web. 18 Feb. 2005.
Monaco, James. *How to Read a Film: The World of Movies, Media, Multimedia: Language, History, Theory*. 3rd ed. New York: Oxford UP, 2000. Print.

Nelmes, Jill. *An Introduction to Film Studies.* London: Routledge, 2003. Print.
Nichols, Bill, ed. *Movies and Methods.* 2 vols. Berkeley: U of California P, 1985. Print.
Rutherford, Anne. "Precarious Boundaries: Affect, Mise en Scène and the Senses." *Art and the Performance of Memory: Sounds and Gestures of Recollection.* Ed. Richard Candida Smith. New York: Routledge, 2002. 63–84. Print.
Wood, Robin. "New Criticism." *Definition* 3 (1960): 9–11. Print.

Adam Knee

Teaching Film through Stardom

The extremely productive and continually evolving nature of the study of stars and stardom since the mid-1980s suggests its relevance for inclusion in the film studies curriculum. Further compelling reasons to consider employing issues of stardom in teaching film include the intersection of such issues with a large proportion of subdisciplines within the cinema studies field (including many of those represented in this volume) and stars' role as the key means of differentiating and promoting product in many national and regional film industries (including Hollywood). From a practical perspective, students almost invariably already have a substantial degree of factual knowledge about a range of stars, as well as a fairly well-developed understanding of stardom and the present-day mechanics of star promotion. This subject matter, then, readily engages students and always has a strong degree of currency or "liveness"; star case studies unfold in the real world at the same time we examine others in class. Even if the focus in class is on stardom in a past era, the present tends to hold useful parallels or contrasts that students are happy to take up. The aim of this essay is to suggest some of the ways the subject might be introduced in the classroom by, first, outlining key issues, problems, and methods of study within the subfield, selectively noting key texts in the area and, second, illustrating some of these approaches through a short sample analysis of a film that is exemplary in self-consciously foregrounding many of the concerns of star studies: *Being John Malkovich* (1999).

Introducing Star Studies

The works most scholars would describe as being seminal for this subdiscipline are Richard Dyer's *Stars* and *Heavenly Bodies: Film Stars and Society*. The former volume offers an argument for stars as deeply linked to ideology—that is, expressive in various ways of the tensions that exist within human identity under given social conditions—and provides concrete methods for a semiotic reading of star images for their social and ideological meanings. The latter volume builds on this semiotic/ideological approach in providing three extended illustrative case studies and also develops a new emphasis on the importance of distinctive audiences or subcultures in imparting meanings to stars. Dyer's books have been particularly influential in establishing a disciplinary focus on star images as evoking key tensions and preoccupations within the culture that gives rise to them. This area of study has remained fruitful and flexible, and works that are sometimes not categorized as belonging to star studies per se—for example, 1990s studies of gender and race in film—are closely linked to this approach and can sometimes serve as texts for courses concerned with stardom and star images. One anthology that was significant for helping further signpost the various parameters of work in star studies—and that, like the Dyer books, remains in print and useful in the classroom—is Christine Gledhill's collection *Stardom: Industry of Desire*, which features sections on semiotic approaches to reading "star signs" and reading stars as social phenomena, on industrial dimensions of stardom, and on the psychoanalytic mechanisms of desire and identification that stars engender.[1]

What, then, are the things one does when one is "doing star studies"? What follows here is one possible taxonomy or mapping of the field of stardom, a breakdown of the subdiscipline into a set of key (and sometimes overlapping) discourses or foci—some theoretical, others historical, and still others analytical—in an effort to give a clearer view of the star studies landscape, as well as to concretely indicate the kinds of questions and approaches it encompasses (and to note, in passing, some useful works).

Conceptualizations of star *and* celebrity. This focus includes considerations of how the star is defined—by examining the connections among a given performer, his or her on-screen roles, related promotional materials, and entertainment media reporting in the formation of the star image. One also finds broader analyses of what conditions or qualities yield stardom or celebrity within a given context, of how and why the public values it, and of how it may thrive or dwindle. Several of these works come from adjoining disciplines such as media studies and sociology rather than from film studies. Notable examples include Daniel J. Boorstin's discussion of celebrity in his 1962 book *The Image*, Leo Braudy's formidable historical survey of related concepts in *The Frenzy of Renown*, and more recent works by Christine Geraghty, P. David Marshall (*Celebrity and Power*), and Chris Rojek.[2]

Star image as a textual system. This approach is concerned with reading the concrete formal attributes of the star image in the various texts in which it appears and often comes into play as a kind of preliminary foundation for other approaches on this list. Among the formal elements that might be considered are performance style, body image, costuming choices, and typical narrative deployment (see, e.g., Dyer, *Stars*).[3] Issues of stardom and genre also fall within this rubric: To what extent are certain star images genre conventions? What happens in instances when an iconographic star plays against generic type?

Stardom as a historical phenomenon. This discourse concerns such questions as, How have conceptualizations of stardom and practices related to stardom shifted over time? To what degree are they a function of historical context? Some of the specific issues scholars have approached in relation to these questions are the rise of star discourses in the silent era (including the influence of notions of stardom in contemporary theater), the evolution of the relatively formalized star system of the Hollywood studio mode of production, shifts in the star system as the Paramount decrees (and other forces) brought about a change in Hollywood's business model, and the rise of the highly paid blockbuster-era superstar. Richard deCordova and Janet Staiger ("Seeing Stars") are important sources for understanding shifts within early film stardom; analysis of the evolution of the system during the studio era can be found in Thomas Schatz and Joshua Gamson.

Stardom as an economic phenomenon. Central to this area are the specific business practices that have existed in relation to stardom. How and to what extent have film production companies used stars to differentiate and sell their product? How has the availability of stars influenced studios' production decisions? What kinds of contractual arrangements have existed between stars and production companies—and what kinds of struggles between star labor and studio management have arisen from these arrangements? Another area of focus within this category has been the ways stars have been used to help product tie-ins and promotions. (See, e.g., Clark; Eckert; Klaprat; McLean.)

Star-making, promotional, and management machinery. This area includes studies of how studios created and managed their stars during the classical Hollywood era, as well as examinations of how, in a poststudio era, such functions have devolved more to agents and professional publicists, generally working in cooperation with entertainment media organizations. A particularly invaluable case study is Gamson's *Claims to Fame*, which puts twentieth-century star-promotion practices into historical perspective (see also Turner, Bonner, and Marshall). Also within this category are examinations of what happens when this machinery malfunctions—that is, moments of scandal that can lead to valuable insights about what degree of control can be exerted over star images (see McLean and Cook). In the current context of weekly celebrity run-ins with legal authorities, one particularly effective way of engaging students with these issues is to have them remain on the alert for such "scandalous" moments as they arise over the course of a term and to analyze the fallout from the events and the way the stars and managers attempt to "spin" them, as well as the way they are covered on hard news and entertainment news shows and in celebrity-oriented magazines like *People.*

Stardom as a social phenomenon. This particularly central area of study focuses on what kinds of meanings star images carry for a given society. How do star images relate to a society's notions of identity or its constructions of gender, sexuality, race, and class? And, in relation to this, why do some figures happen to become stars in a given context and moment, and others not to the same extent? Much of the scholarship focusing on individual star careers engages this discourse, although these works also tend to take up the issues of the preceding two categories. As suggested earlier, many studies of race and gender in Hollywood films are linked to this discourse as well.

Star audiences. Work within this area is interested in specific audience experiences of and responses to stars. Some are hypothetical (postulating a form of representative spectator), while others are based on various kinds of field work, using interviews, written surveys, or other available evidence of audience activities. This category includes various studies of the activities of fan subcultures, as well as of how members of socially marginalized groups may appropriate mainstream star images to speak to their personal experiences. Among the most often cited scholarship in this area is that of Jackie Stacey, on female spectatorship, and Henry Jenkins, on fan cultures (see also Dyer's chapter on Judy Garland and gay men in *Heavenly Bodies*; Kuhn; Staiger, *Media Reception Studies*).

Stardom and the apparatus. This discourse is concerned with how technologies mediate our connection to stars, an area that has garnered increasing attention as technologies of representation and transfer have continued their rapid development and dispersal. Relevant issues include the psychoanalysis of the viewing context of star imagery (Mulvey), the ways various "leaky" new media engender at once a loss in performer and producer control over star imagery and a gain in audience control, and the possibilities of various forms of virtual stars and stardom (see, e.g., Marshall, "New Media"; McDonald).

Stardom in global, globalized, transnational, or postnational contexts. This discourse has evolved both as the film studies discipline has become slightly more self-aware of its Hollywood bias and as stardom has taken increasingly transnational forms. Thus we have studies of how the star system works differently in various non-Hollywood industries, how the meanings that attach to a given star may shift as she or he operates in different national or regional contexts, how discourses about national affiliation may become an important part of a given star's image, and how the rise of new kinds of global media and labor flows may change stardom (see, e.g., Ciecko; Landy; Miyao).

The foregoing broad listing should suggest the range of analytical paradigms, and of objects of analysis, that studies of stardom may encompass. Indeed, an added pedagogical benefit of teaching film through questions of stardom is that these issues directly point to the importance of sites of analysis other than the traditional filmic text. In examining a given star image, one can readily guide students toward broadening their notions of a filmic text to apprehend the multiple dimensions of the star intertext—not only the filmed roles that the star has played but also the various kinds of publicity for these films, the assorted reviews and press reports that have alluded to or featured the star, and any interviews the star may have given—many of which are sources that students can track down without undue difficulty. Consideration of these numerous intertexts can also be aligned with an examination of the institutions through which stardom operates; the various promotion and publicity strategies employed by either studio or agent; the interactions among these figures, the actor, and the news outlets that circulate information about him or her; and so on. The audience, too, can be readily introduced as a pertinent site of analysis, since it is in many ways the response of an audience that helps endow an actor with star status. It is, moreover, through an examination of audience response that one can most productively glean some of the important resonances and meanings of a given star image for the culture in which it circulates. While gauging audience response can pose some methodological difficulties, an extremely accessible first step for introducing students to this form of analysis is the examination of the readily available wealth of online forums of various kinds devoted to most major stars.[4]

Case Study: *Being John Malkovich*

Offered here is a sample textual analysis, a reading of the film *Being John Malkovich*, to suggest some concrete ways these issues might be taken up either in a course on stardom or in a particular class meeting (or portion of one) where the subject of star studies is engaged in relation to another film or cultural studies topic. Although the film is being used here functionally, largely as a tool to illustrate some of the kinds of things one does when "doing star studies," *Being John Malkovich* merits examination not only because of the way it reflexively meshes with a range of key issues within star studies but also because it is a work of evident complexity and originality that has continued to attract the attention of film scholars—in particular for the ways it explores personal identity (Barker; Shaw). Questions of identity are consonant with some of the fundamental concerns of star studies—the constitution of the star, the star's relationship to the "actual" (biological or legal) subject, and the audience members' personal investments in the star—and therefore provide a useful entry "portal" (to use a term from the film) for this discussion.

In brief, *Being John Malkovich* concerns a down-on-his-luck puppeteer (Craig, played by John Cusack) who, while laboring in a clerical job he has taken up to help support his wife and him, discovers a passageway behind a file cabinet that offers those who enter it the opportunity to briefly experience what it is like to be in the body of the actor John Malkovich—that is, to share the same perceptions and sensations that Malkovich is having at that moment. Craig, as an artist whose work involves the slippage or transference of emotions from his inner self to an externalized medium (the puppet), is quick to articulate how the phenomenon of Malkovich's "portal" (as he dubs it) challenges notions of human identity as stable and unitary. As Craig explains to fellow office worker Maxine, "It raises all sorts of philosophical-type questions, you know, about the nature of self, about the existence of a soul, you know, am I me? Is Malkovich Malkovich? . . . Do you see what a metaphysical can of worms this portal is?" It is important to note, however, that the person whom this narrative endows with a portal is not an ordinary human being but one with a certain measure of celebrity, a condition that de facto opens his life up to access by the public—and also immediately engenders questions of the authenticity of identity, of the extent to which the witnessed Malkovich star persona matches the person named John Malkovich.

The film foregrounds the question of whether Malkovich is Malkovich in several ways, thus highlighting the disjuncture between perceived star image and individual. There is the conceit of having the actual actor John Malkovich play a title character very much like himself, who shares the same name (save for a fictional middle name) and many of the same biographical details, being a star who (in 1999) is well known enough that many people recognize him but cannot recall his name or what films he has acted in (a joke the film brings up repeatedly). The film even makes use of many photographs and biographical details from the "real" John Malkovich's life to illustrate the diegetic Malkovich's earlier years. This device of having characters who directly mirror the actors (or, perhaps, the perceived public image of the actors) who play them extends to other dramatis personae as well: Charlie Sheen plays the character Malkovich's best friend Charlie Sheen, whose bad-boy behavior directly aligns with the real-world Sheen's reputation, and Sean Penn and Brad Pitt appear in cameos of characters who are much like themselves. Yet the fantastic narrative frame of the film highlights the fact that these are of course not the same as the real-life Malkovich and Sheen and Penn and Pitt, despite the ontological confusions engendered here, and this notion is further underscored in the film's simultaneous casting of another actor entirely in opposition to her star image: Cameron Diaz, known for her glamorous looks, straight blond hair, and happy-go-lucky star persona, here plays Craig's frizzy red-haired, dowdy, neurotic wife Lotte—an image so unlike that of "Cameron Diaz" that many viewers at first do not recognize the actress.[5]

Perhaps the definitive moment for highlighting the fragmented nature of John Malkovich—and by implication of any film star—is the scene in which Malkovich enters his own portal and witnesses a restaurant peopled primarily with Malkoviches. The moment speaks not only to the seemingly compromised and uncertain nature of star identity but also to the endless reproducibility of the star image, the potential loss of the aura of authenticity. Significant in this regard is the fact that Malkovich's portal is being used as part of a mass commercial enterprise, with Craig and Maxine offering entry to the public for a fee, and thus we see that a multitude of people are able to purchase the (simulated?) experience of feeling as the star does. A critique of the economics of stardom is also clearly engaged here, with the actor complaining that the portal is being used without his assent; the ersatz company mounted by the entrepreneurs—J.M. Inc.—even takes on his initials, but he has no say in its dealings. Craig defends his actions, noting that it was he who found the portal (read, discovered the star's profit potential), while Malkovich protests, "It's my head." Eventually, however, Craig manages to employ the resources of the portal as a means of bending John Malkovich's actions to his will, acting in effect as agent or producer cum puppeteer, with the star image revealed to be more a function of corporate decision making rather than any preference of a given actor. And when Craig chooses to make Malkovich over as a puppeteer, to make use of his (Craig's) own talents, the film is able to wittily show the star-construction machinery in action, with a perfectly parodied public television–style special touting the actor's new métier.

Still more to the heart of *Being John Malkovich*'s concerns is various characters' fascination with (the diegetic) John Malkovich—and by allegorical extension the cinematic viewer's attraction to the film star. Indeed, the architecture and functioning of the Malkovich portal recall the cinematographic apparatus in several ways: the patron pays a fee before being given admission to a darkened and dirty space in which the eyes have difficulty adjusting, then moves forward to a source of light that turns out to be an emotionally riveting moving image, one that closely simulates (and thus allows identification with) the sensory experiences of another human being—crucially, one who is a star. Maxine only suggests setting up the portal business after she has asked whether Malkovich (whom she is not familiar with) has any celebrity appeal, and the comments of their first customer immediately before entering the portal appear to confirm that part of the attraction is the opportunity to be someone more exceptional than himself, someone of star-like qualities. As the patron says dejectedly, by way of an explanation for his interest in the service, "I'm a fat man . . . I am sad, and I am a fat man."

The film also makes clear, however, that the particular attractions of John Malkovich (and the uses made of his portal) vary according to the audience, with three audiences in particular highlighted: first, the clients of J.M. Inc., who enjoy simply experiencing the sensation of being a star; second, the elderly members of an exclusive group who, like a fan subculture, collect artifacts related to the star, claim to have insider understanding about him, and eventually intend to use his body as a means to extend their youth; and, third, the management group of Maxine, Craig, and Lotte, all of whom develop their distinctly eroticized preoccupations with the use of the portal, while also engaging in a highly unconventional love quadrangle. Lotte is quick to perceive the erotic (and self-actualizing) dimensions of the kind of intimacy with the star that the portal affords. She comments on the vaginal qualities of the opening and finds exciting the fact that Malkovich in effect has both male and female organs.[6] She also receives profound pleasure and fulfillment from the experience of herself possessing a penis, so much so that she decides she ought to undergo gender reassignment procedures. The erotic frisson evidenced here seems to arise first from the fact that this star-based quasi-cinematographic apparatus provides an experience of fluid identity and polymorphous desire—something that even Maxine, who does not enter the portal herself, appreciates.[7] Maxine pursues a sexual relationship with Malkovich not because of any attraction to the actor but because of the distinctive thrill she gets from knowing that Lotte or Craig is inhabiting Malkovich when they are making love. As she reports to Lotte of one such experience, "When I looked into his eyes last night I could feel you peering out. Behind the stubble and the too prominent brow and the male pattern baldness, I sensed your feminine longing. And it just slew me." And Craig, finally, seeks out the Malkovich portal both because it allows him to experience a (mediated) sexual relationship with the woman he most desires (Maxine) and because, making use of his puppetry skills, he is able to develop the ability to manipulate Malkovich's body, to render it in effect his own, and thereby can use Malkovich's celebrity to launch his own puppetry career—one he could not get off the ground when he was not well known (underscoring the fact that modern celebrity does not bear a proportional relationship to talent, as Boorstin observed in his 1962 book).

One key paradox highlighted in this scenario is that while Craig desires to be John Malkovich, it is so that he can then make Malkovich over as another version of himself, his self-perception as a sensitive, suffering, socially committed puppetry artist. On the one hand this use makes literal the notion that the spectator projects himself or herself onto the image of the star (or, in Lacanian terms, that the star image is perceived as a mirror of the self; see Mulvey). On the other hand, it also makes concrete Dyer's notion of the star as embodying the contradictions of living in a given culture, as being in effect a function of the context that gave rise to it. And in either event, it makes eminently clear the dissociation of the real-life actor and human being from the perceived star, since not only are Malkovich's own volitions disregarded but even his too-mortal mid-forties physical habitus is viewed by those using him with some disappointment for its inability to fully meet their needs (it in effect turns out to be too ordinary, un-star-like). These conditions correspond to new economic, informational, and technological contexts in which screen actors are experiencing a diminished control over the formation and circulation of their images, as well as a disconnect from their own ever more mediated (and thereby often eroticized) bodies; audiences, meanwhile, are finding stars ever more theirs to manipulate.

While the foregoing textual analysis focuses for practical purposes on an exceptional case—a film in effect about stardom—the kinds of discussions it provokes and the issues it raises are applicable to most films. For any given film performer, questions can be raised about why we do or do not identify with or feel attraction to him or her, about the ways in which a role relates to the perceived broader star discourse, and about the ways that discourse has been constructed across various intertexts. Moreover, the film text does not have to be the central focus of this kind of inquiry. Star studies, as noted, provides many avenues for moving beyond textual paradigms, for guiding students to explore the assorted media, institutions, audiences, and individuals by way of which historically and culturally inflected star discourses are formed and propagated.

Notes

1. Other, more recent, anthologies that are also useful for teaching and encompass later developments in the subfield include Austin and Barker, as well as Marshall (*Celebrity Culture Reader*) and Redmond and Holmes, both of which extend to nonfilm celebrity.

2. A highly readable synthesis of some of these conceptualizations of celebrity can be found in Turner, well suited for use as an undergraduate text.

3. Issues of film and performance can also constitute a distinctive focus within film studies.

4. See, for example, the forums on Angelina Jolie (e.g., *Angelina: Wuthering Jolie*) or Harrison Ford (e.g., *Harrison Ford Forum*).

5. While Diaz had only been appearing in films for five years at the time of *Being John Malkovich*'s release, her star image had already achieved a wide currency with the success of *My Best Friend's Wedding* (1997) and *There's Something about Mary* (1998).

6. In point of fact, the portal and connected passageway are figured in terms at least as much rectal as vaginal, and the intercourse through it presented as a violation rather than consensual: the dirty, dark passageway leads the spectator up to the point of view of the actor from behind, and the spectator is then somehow excreted out (spent, bedraggled, and slimy) once the allotted time is up. Thus while the interaction is figured as one of erotically charged excitement for the spectator, it is simultaneously one of intimate exploitation for the star.

7. Indeed, at one point the film humorously underscores the potential for the cinematic apparatus to effect a fluidity in subjectivity in allowing us to experience a pet chimpanzee's point-of-view flashback that even features subtitled translations of the animal's parents' vocalizations.

Works Cited

Austin, Thomas, and Martin Barker, eds. *Contemporary Hollywood Stardom*. London: Arnold, 2003. Print.

Barker, Martin. "The Pleasures of Watching an 'Off-Beat' Film: The Case of *Being John Malkovich*." *Scope* 11 (2008): n. pag. Web. 14 Aug. 2008.

Boorstin, Daniel J. *The Image; or, What Happened to the American Dream?* New York: Atheneum, 1962. Print.

Braudy, Leo. *The Frenzy of Renown: Fame and Its History*. New York: Oxford UP, 1986. Print.

Ciecko, Anne. "Muscle, Market Value, Telegenesis, Cyberpresence: The New Asian Movie Star in the Global Economy of Masculine Images." *Global Currents: Media and Technology Now*. Ed. Tasha G. Oren and Patrice Petro. New Brunswick: Rutgers UP, 2004. 186–99. Print.

Clark, Danae. *Negotiating Hollywood: The Cultural Politics of Actors' Labor*. Minneapolis: U of Minnesota P, 1995. Print.

deCordova, Richard. *Picture Personalities: The Emergence of the Star System in America*. Urbana: U of Illinois P, 1990. Print.

Dyer, Richard. *Heavenly Bodies: Film Stars and Society*. New York: St. Martin's, 1986. Print.

———. *Stars*. London: British Film Inst., 1979. Print.

Eckert, Charles. "The Carole Lombard in Macy's Window." *Quarterly Review of Film Studies* 3.1 (1978): 1–21. Rpt. in Gledhill 30–39.

Gamson, Joshua. *Claims to Fame: Celebrity in Contemporary America*. Berkeley: U of California P, 1994. Print.

Geraghty, Christine. "Re-examining Stardom: Questions of Texts, Bodies and Performance." *Re-inventing Film Studies*. Ed. Christine Gledhill and Linda Williams. London: Arnold, 2000. 183–201. Print.

Gledhill, Christine, ed. *Stardom: Industry of Desire.* London: Routledge, 1991. Print.

Jenkins, Henry. *Textual Poachers: Television Fans and Participatory Culture.* New York: Routledge, 1992. Print.

Klaprat, Cathy. "The Star as Market Strategy: Bette Davis in Another Light." *The American Film Industry.* Ed. Tino Balio. Rev. ed. Madison: U of Wisconsin P, 1985. 351–76. Print.

Kuhn, Annette. *Dreaming of Fred and Ginger: Cinema and Cultural Memory.* New York: New York UP, 2002. Print.

Landy, Marcia. *Stardom Italian Style: Screen Performance and Personality in Italian Cinema.* Bloomington: Indiana UP, 2008. Print.

Marshall, P. David. *Celebrity and Power: Fame in Contemporary Culture.* Minneapolis: U of Minnesota P, 1997. Print.

———, ed. *The Celebrity Culture Reader.* New York: Routledge, 2006. Print.

———. "New Media—New Self: The Changing Power of Celebrity." Marshall, *Celebrity Culture Reader* 634–44.

McDonald, Paul. "Stars in the Online Universe: Promotion, Nudity, Reverence." Austin and Barker 29–44.

McLean, Adrienne L. *Being Rita Hayworth: Labor, Identity, and Hollywood Stardom.* New Brunswick: Rutgers UP, 2004. Print.

McLean, Adrienne L., and David A. Cook, eds. *Headline Hollywood: A Century of Film Scandal.* New Brunswick: Rutgers UP, 2001. Print.

Miyao, Daisuke. *Sessue Hayakawa: Silent Cinema and Transnational Stardom.* Durham: Duke UP, 2007. Print.

Mulvey, Laura. "Visual Pleasure and Narrative Cinema." *Screen* 16.3 (1975): 6–18. Print.

Redmond, Sean, and Su Holmes, eds. *Stardom and Celebrity: A Reader.* Los Angeles: Sage, 2007. Print.

Rojek, Chris. *Celebrity.* London: Reaktion, 2001. Print.

Schatz, Thomas. *Boom and Bust: American Cinema in the 1940s.* New York: Scribner's, 1997. Print.

Shaw, Daniel. "On Being Philosophical and *Being John Malkovich.*" *Journal of Aesthetics and Art Criticism* 64.1 (2006): 111–18. Print.

Stacey, Jackie. *Star Gazing: Hollywood Cinema and Female Spectatorship.* London: Routledge, 1994. Print.

Staiger, Janet. *Media Reception Studies.* New York: New York UP, 2005. Print.

———. "Seeing Stars." *Velvet Light Trap* 20 (1983): 10–14. Rpt. in Gledhill 1–16.

Turner, Graeme. *Understanding Celebrity.* Thousand Oaks: Sage, 2004. Print.

Turner, Graeme, Frances Bonner, and P. David Marshall, eds. *Fame Games: The Production of Celebrity in Australia.* Cambridge: Cambridge UP, 2000. Print.

Frank P. Tomasulo

Teaching Film Studies in a Production Context

After a guest lecture at New York University's Graduate Film School, the movie director Susan Seidelman was asked what advice she would give students in the production program. Seidelman replied, "Don't take any film theory classes." Seidelman's comment reflects the attitude of many industry professionals, students, and even some film production professors, but Lev Kuleshov's dictum still holds true today: "Teaching filmmaking without being cognizant of fundamental cinematic theories demeans film craft to the level of an amateur workshop" (qtd. in Petric 2).

Cinema Studies versus Filmmaking?

Despite Kuleshov's sage comment, Dana Polan has observed that the relation between "the critical study of film . . . and practical instruction in filmmaking" has been a source of contestation since the beginning of serious cinema study in the United States (6). In fact, the earliest film production students at the University of Southern California "felt that the emphasis placed on film's cultural and social meanings just was not practical enough" (10). Polan adds that "to a large degree such questions still drive the field" (6).

Indeed they do. Although recent research demonstrates that most major US film schools mandate that film history, theory, and criticism represent ten to twenty percent of the course work toward a BFA or MFA (Tomasulo, "Curricular Survey") and the University Film and Video Association recommends a minimum of "15–20 percent of total required courses" for an MFA (Bukalski et al. 38), several film schools fall far short of this mark—and some have no history and theory requirements. This neglect flies in the face of an Association of American Colleges and Universities report that warns:

> Students in professional fields . . . must learn critical analysis and the capacity to make decisions in uncertain settings. Their future practice must be informed by constant awareness of . . . the aesthetic enhancement or debasement of the work to which they are committing their lives. (2)

One complication that fuels this rift between cinema scholars and film practitioners is that even a curriculum that emphasizes both critical media studies and filmmaking is never "teacher proof." A "studies" instructor who merely screens films and engages in fannish discussion afterward demeans the role of history or theory for production students. Similarly, a cinema professor who uses abstruse vocabulary while spouting incomprehensible theories and who makes no effort to select learning modules that would benefit production students deserves the opprobrium of the filmmaking faculty.

The reverse is also true: a cinematography instructor who fails to explain the aesthetic language of the camera and the historical development of lenses, lighting equipment, film stocks, aspect ratios, and other technical or artistic modes turns his or her classroom into a trade school, not a conservatory. An editing professor who merely teaches nonlinear editing technology without exploring the effect on meaning of every cut ignores the artistic, expressive, and thematic aspects of the cinema to the detriment of a student's creative growth. Ideally, students should internalize aesthetic lessons, so that they become second nature. As the film editor Russell W. Harnden wrote, "The theory and practice ingrained in my mind [in film school] now work on a completely instinctual and subconscious level."

As part of their commitment to support a major in film, universities have a responsibility to make cinema studies education applicable to students who are primarily interested in media production and screenwriting as careers. Crucial to devising a cinema studies course or curriculum that is appropriate for these students is getting them to recognize that a knowledge of cinema history, theory, and aesthetics can help them make better movies, as would an expansive liberal arts education that includes literature, psychology, history, art, music, and languages. As Martin Scorsese has said, "This is what I tell young filmmakers and film students: Do what painters do. Study the old masters. Enrich your palette. Expand the canvas. There's always much more to learn" (Scorsese and Wilson 28).

What Should Be Taught?

D. W. Griffith's oft-quoted credo—"My task is above all to make you see"—can be employed to advantage by film instructors as well as filmmakers. An undergraduate introduction to cinema course may be a first encounter with the notion that films can make us see in new ways rather than according to preconceived or determined patterns. For many, learning to decipher the thematic, formal, and ideological elements in a film is a novel experience, almost a paradigm shift.

Among the challenges for professors of such introductory courses is that most college students, especially those who want to pursue careers in the motion picture or television industry, lost their cinematic virginity long before enrolling in the class. How, then, should the professor "butt in" (Smith 127–28)? What theoretical and practical models of cinematic pedagogy best achieve one's goals? And what are those goals?

Jerome Bruner once theorized, "Any subject can be taught effectively in some intellectually honest form to any [one] at any stage of development" (33). Bruner was concerned with teaching the structure and basic ideas of a discipline, rather than any specific facts or skills. He was interested in transmitting general understanding and training such faculties as analysis, judgment, and memory. Grasping the structure of a subject—understanding it so that other applications can be related to it meaningfully—allows for a continual deepening of one's understanding in a specific class and over a lifetime.

In an effort to make cinema studies courses relevant to film production students, I propose an applied history-theory curriculum. Several books (or sections of books) make excellent required reading in such a program. One is Karel Reisz and Gavin Millar's *The Technique of Film Editing*. This volume traces the history and theory of editing from the beginning of cinema (Lumière, Méliès, Porter, Griffith) to more contemporary times (Antonioni, Godard, Resnais, Truffaut). The book contains brief passages on the practice of film editing and illustrations of the 180-degree rule, but the main focus is on the history and aesthetics of assembling shots to tell a story. Dozens of scenes are presented in full *découpage*, including Lincoln's assassination in *The Birth of a Nation* (1915), the opening of *Great Expectations* (1948), and the jump cuts in *Breathless* (1960).

Of special value to screenwriting students is Lajos Egri's *The Art of Dramatic Writing*, particularly the chapters on premise (1–31), covering themes of tragic and comedic plays, and on character (32–42), in which Egri lists human traits found in the great personages of stage history. These two chapters should be required reading in all screenwriting and introductory cinema studies courses, since they have applicability for both would-be writers and directors and budding cinema historians, critics, and theoreticians.[1]

How Should Cinema Studies Be Taught?

George Bernard Shaw once opined that "fine art is the only teacher except torture" (96). Since Plato's *The Republic*, the notion that art should be the basis of all education has not had many defenders among educational theorists. But John Dewey, Erich Fromm, Herbert Read, Ernst Cassirer, and others who have devoted thought to aesthetic education have increasingly favored using the development of eidetic imagery (that is, visual memory) as a basis for all learning.

But art can do more that merely acculturate students to the status quo. If art is indeed an educator, it can change one's perception, apperception, and conception of the world. In learning how to systematically dissect a film text, students can acquire a means by which to analyze other phenomena, including culture as a whole. Thus a cinema studies course could seek to transform students through learning about learning instead of simply stuffing students full of information (although important facts should be available from textbooks, other readings, and lectures). This process of "critical pedagogy" should not be divorced from sociopolitical and economic issues (Freire 17). Neither should it occur in an aesthetic lacuna that emphasizes only visual literacy and perceptual acumen. Once we pull a film apart, we must be able to put it back together: deconstruction followed by reconstruction.

Providing students with methodologies (structuralism, authorship, formal criticism, ideology, genre, and other paradigms) allows for systematic analysis and eventual synthesis. Films lending themselves to multiple modes of analysis are ideal for this approach. *Johnny Guitar* (1954), for example, can be readily deconstructed from semiotic, historical, genre, gender, ideological, psychoanalytic, and auteurist perspectives.

Essential to addressing the needs of beginning film students is assessing what they know when they enter our classrooms. Previous experience with film and television strengthens students' personal category systems. Thus media educators need to "make strange" some of these preconceptions. A major presumption of beginning film students is that the movies are strictly an entertainment medium. Despite some optimists who insist that students "bring to film a strong visual orientation and at least a rudimentary visual literacy" (Boyum and Pradl 52), the quotidian reality of student papers in an introductory course is enough to call this hopefulness into question. One in-class strategy that I use (usually on the first day) is to hold aloft a replica statue of the Maltese Falcon; I then ask the students to identify this object. Most shout out, "the Maltese Falcon!" In an attempt at humor, I then say that they are all in the wrong class, because they have already been introduced to film. Although this hokey device does not always produce gales of laughter, it does make the point that students do not enter introductory film courses free of preconceptions.

I generally use the classics (an admittedly equivocal term) to break down such preconceptions. Teaching the classics is not part of a knowledge-for-knowledge's-sake philosophy or an attempt to make the student a better person, teacher, or filmmaker. I suggest including canonical movies because they are the best exemplars to reveal structure, style, and theme.[2] It should be of no concern that many of these films are in black and white or foreign languages; it is their structures that make them classics. As Herbert Read said, it is "not the professor, but the artist who is the true schoolmaster" (285).

Teaching students to think cinematically involves giving them practice in using basic concepts and schemes for viewing the film artists they study. In addition, the course outline should allow for a cumulative effect, a buildup of knowledge, with reinforcement and enrichment of many rubrics. After introducing the role and importance of recurring motifs as structuring devices at the beginning of the course (e.g., restaurants, songs, cars, split screens, literary allusions, words, and even lobsters in Woody Allen's *Annie Hall* [1977]), I point out such motifs in other films throughout the semester (e.g., expectorating in James Cameron's *Titanic* [1997], wigs in Norman Jewison's . . . *And Justice for All* [1979]).

Of course, one cannot reach all students in the same manner. Indeed, Diane Carson has demonstrated how the Myer-Briggs inventory (a psychometric questionnaire that measures psychological preferences in how people perceive the world and make decisions) can be used to design assignments, syllabi, and lectures to motivate and enhance each student's learning style (Carson). Although Bruner stated that any subject can be taught, he did not say that every subject can be learned.

Practical Pedagogy

It is one thing to have an explicit or implicit pedagogical philosophy and quite another to accomplish its goals. A few practical ideas might be noted.

First, the instructor can set up each film screening, introducing background information and other topics not covered in the readings, as well as anticipating and alluding to key scenes. This foundation gives the viewing a purposefulness that increases students' awareness and understanding of the film as a constructed entity. Keying students to techniques to watch for also enables them to concentrate on the formal interplay, rather than only the story, characters, and dialogue. Frame enlargements, clips, screenplay excerpts, and other such devices can aid in this preparation enormously. I often screen the credit sequence from . . . *And Justice for All* before showing the entire movie. I then freeze-frame every image in that scene to point out the shift from highly symmetrical compositions to loosely framed, almost sloppy, camera angles. Most students can notice this transition when it is slowed down and discussed in class; they further realize that the change in mise-en-scène is a visual metaphor for the film's major theme: the difference between the balanced ideals of the law and its inexact application in the American judicial system. Eventually, though, as a conscious stratagem, the instructor might gradually wean the students off the pedagogical teat.

Second, a library of slides or frame-grabs from classic films can serve as an important pedagogical resource. Frame-grabs enable students to study the "individual frame life of an image," as Stan Brakhage put it (qtd. in Michelson 37), and write detailed essays. Frame enlargements highlight compositional devices and how meaning is created through lighting, angle, character proxemics, and other techniques. One specific case in point of such a dense image comes from Sam Mendes's Oscar-winning *American Beauty* (1999) (fig. 1).[3]

Third, art works, movie posters, recordings of sound tracks, clips, and other media displays are often useful as preparation for a viewing, especially when they are contextual (Tomasulo, "Teaching"). Each film I screen is

Figure 1. A still from *American Beauty*

Figure 2. *Night,* by Max Beckmann, a contemporary of the German expressionist director Robert Wiene

analyzed not only in terms of its formal and thematic components but also within the larger discourse of its historical, cultural, and ideological framework. I show German expressionist films such as Robert Wiene's *The Cabinet of Dr. Caligari* (1920) with slides of paintings from that period (fig. 2) and discuss the history of the Weimar Republic; conjoin surrealist films with Salvador Dalí paintings; precede Soviet films by Shostakovich symphonies, movie posters, and discussions of dialectical materialism; and give African, Asian, and Cuban films historical and cultural background.

Specifically, playing the musical score from *A Clockwork Orange* (1971) gives the class a greater sense of the psychological and physiological effects of film music, as might data from A. Capurso's study, which quantifies listeners' emotional reactions to various classical and popular melodies. The goal is to help students situate the film in a broader historical and artistic context.

Fourth, cinema professors can show multiple examples of the codes of mainstream filmmaking, the exceptions to the rules, and even the unsuccessful bending of those tenets. One such bad example is *Lady in the Lake* (1947), which uses a subjective camera for its entire running time. Production students who fall in love with the point-of-view shot sometimes overuse it. But twenty wearisome minutes of *Lady in the Lake* will expose the drawbacks of that technique. In the same way, Alfred Hitchcock's experiment with the long take in *Rope* (1948) may suggest the excesses of that style, especially when screened with the unbearable fifteen-minute long take in Brian De Palma's *Snake Eyes* (1998).

Fifth, deadline pressures mean that student filmmakers often resort to imitation and replication of prevailing norms and cinematic clichés. Unfortunately, however, they look rarely to the avant-garde for inspiration and more often to commercial role models. And "shaky-cam" techniques seem to be hot. It is easy, for example, to justify television's *NYPD Blue*'s handheld cinematography on the basis of its New York setting. After all, subways always rumble through Manhattan, shaking the buildings slightly. Similarly, the handheld camerawork in *The Battle of Algiers* (1966) approximates the newsreel footage of its era in an effort to convey verisimilitude. Students might read the Dogme 95 Manifesto and view *Festen* (*The Celebration*; 1998) to see the shaky-cam aesthetic at its finest. But the misuse of that technique should also be explored (e.g., *Rachel Getting Married* [2008]).

Student filmmakers, however, do not always think through the aesthetic implications of their choices. One student, for example, used a handheld camera to shoot a bird resting on a log at the shore of a bucolic lake. The intent was to create a serene mood and show off the beauty of untrammeled nature. My first reaction, though, was "Why is this bird so nervous?" Here the student was using the language of cinema to create a mood of unease, just the opposite of what was intended. Targeted screenings and critiques of films that use good and bad examples of the Steadicam and of shaky-cam effects should provide filmmaking students with a guide on which to base their own stylistic decisions.

Editing is another arena in which clip selection can have an impact on student filmmakers. Although today's Hollywood seems to eschew the 180-degree rule of seamless continuity, when students "cross the line" it is often perceived as a rookie error, not a conscious artistic choice. In fact, when "caught" violating this practice, students often use the excuse that they are just emulating *Stagecoach* (1939) or *Romeo + Juliet* (2002).

Finally, production students are in a vulnerable position with respect to *la règle du jeu* of the industry. If they break or bend certain film conventions, the results are often seen as novice mistakes, yet when Godard used jump cuts in *Breathless* or Gordon Willis did not fully light the backgrounds in *The Godfather* (1972), the effect was hailed as groundbreaking. In *The Godfather*, the darkness that envelops the mafiosi may symbolize the evil that is always part of their lives; noticed in a student production, however, an underlit backdrop reads as careless, unprofessional lighting.

Assignments

I believe that professors should demand grammatically correct, analytical writing in all their courses. With that in mind, I assign three to five major papers in my film studies classes and diligently correct all spelling and grammatical errors. I also work closely with the institution's writing program, referring a certain percentage of students for evaluations of their basic skills. Furthermore, I supply students with a handout—"Guidelines for Writing Papers"—that clearly outlines the dos and don'ts of writing about cinema. This guide serves to discourage imprecise critiques and Roger Ebert–style movie reviews ("Two thumbs up!") and to make up for the inadequate preparation usually provided in high school writing assignments.

I also spend class time explaining how to structure a report—designing a thesis statement, proffering filmic evidence, including appropriate citations, formulating a conclusion, and so on. I place A papers (given students' approval) on reserve (or on *Blackboard*, the online course instrument) so that students who are intimidated by academic writing can study clear, insightful student writing. Sample papers can be obtained from former students, in the chapter "Writing College Papers about Film" in Vivian Sobchack and Thomas Sobchack's *An Introduction to Film*, Timothy Corrigan's *A Short Guide to Writing about Film*, and John Moscowitz's *Critical Approaches to Writing about Film*.

One extremely valuable writing assignment for cinema studies and production students alike is a mise-en-scène exercise that derives from

Louis Giannetti's introductory textbook *Understanding Movies* (96–101). These pages break down mise-en-scène systematically into its fifteen constituent parts (including the dominant, lighting key, camera proxemics, angle, color, framing, depth, character placement) and provide examples of how each element is used in a single frame from *M* (1930). Students are then asked to select a frame of their own choosing, to describe and analyze the fifteen aspects of mise-en-scène in that image, and to submit a two-to-three-page report on the subject, along with a copy of the chosen image (Welsch 103–06). One variation on this project, to make it more worthwhile for production majors, is to have students create their own still images to analyze.

But film students need to read more than just images; they need to embrace ideas, by reading books, articles, scripts, stories, and analytical reports. Even Steven Spielberg recommended reading when he accepted the Irving G. Thalberg Memorial Award in 1986: "I'm as culpable as anyone in exalting the image at the expense of the word. . . . Only a generation of readers will spawn a generation of writers." Therefore, I also require significant reading from textbooks, articles, and handouts. Students are regularly tested on these selections to ensure their rigorous devotion to the course but also to ascertain how well they have mastered the course content week by week. To supplement the assigned reading, I often require students to conduct outside research on nonfilm subjects (e.g., psychology, ideology, history, art, music, politics, gender, and race).

The Role of Television Studies

Today more than ever, faculty members must realize that film and televisual images are converging rapidly. From a pedagogical perspective, a film or media aesthetics course might well use scenes, images, and even entire episodes of television or cable shows to illustrate important foundational aspects of film style and content. (The use of television as a teaching tool is facilitated by the easy availability of entire seasons of a given program on DVD.) Just as important as the theoretical reasons for using television shows in the classroom, there is the practical justification that many film school graduates will be getting their first jobs in television, not in the motion picture industry.

West Wing (1999–2006) can provide numerous examples of widescreen composition and complex mise-en-scène articulations, including the moving camera. The show frequently uses relay-race camerawork, in which two conversing characters are followed through the labyrinthine "corridors of power" in the White House until they come upon two other presidential aides and the camera then follows the new duo, who discuss an entirely separate national issue. These spectacular Steadicam maneuvers are not used merely to show off the cinematographer's expertise. Thematically, these audacious walk-and-talk tracking shots suggest that the West Wing is a carefully reticulated beehive, with everyone working for the common good. The moving camera also conveys the high-stakes pressure and instantaneous decision making that take place.

Law and Order (1990–2010) episodes could exemplify narrative structure, especially since the commercial breaks usually come at major plot points. The story line of *Law and Order* always entails establishing the crime—usually a homicide—before the credit sequence. Then the investigation begins, often by accusing or arresting the wrong suspect by the first commercial break. After that, additional forensic, lineup, or autopsy evidence comes in, leading to the arrest of a more likely culprit. Fade to the second commercial. When we return, the arraignment takes place, usually with a caustic but witty judge on the bench. This scene is followed by the plea bargaining, in which there can be some variations. Inevitably, someone is put on trial, and that court case occupies the final fifteen minutes of the show and customarily ends in a jury verdict. In the final minute, the DA is apprised of the resolution and makes a profound, witty, or cynical point about the legal system. This basic story prototype is almost as immutable as the conventions of Kabuki theater.

One could use almost any episode of *I Love Lucy* (1951–57) to exemplify the trajectory of comedy. I have a schema that I teach—the four Ds of comedy: desire, deception, discovery, and destiny—and Lucy follows that paradigm to the letter. Initially, Lucy almost always has a desire (to break into show business, to get out of the house, etc.), but she cannot attain her goal unless she deceives someone (usually Ricky, but sometimes Fred or Ethel Mertz). In the end, her ruse is discovered, which leads to her destiny, for Ricky to forgive and love her anyway.

Television shows are often even better to use than movie clips for demonstrating editing techniques, especially classical cutting. I have yet to find a totally by-the-book sequence in a major motion picture that perfectly fits the classical regime: eye-line matches, 180-degree rule, continuity cutting, and so on. Yet *The Sopranos* (1999–2007) almost always uses "invisible" editing, with an establishing shot that eventually leads to a *champs-contrechamps* routine and a reestablishing shot at the end.

Conclusion

Certainly, the technical nuts-and-bolts aspects of film production represent important skills to be mastered, but it is just as valuable for production students to realize that the cinema conveys information, ideas, and values. Hence, learning the principles of theme, dramatic structure, visual composition, and editing rhythms is as valuable for production students as being able to write a cute line of dialogue, shoot an in-focus image, or make a nonlinear splice. If the cinema is analogous to a language (as Christian Metz has implied), it has a grammar, vocabulary, and syntax that can be taught and learned. Production and screenwriting students in cinema studies courses thus have a wonderful opportunity to learn about how to translate their ideas into the evolving language of film.

Curricular revision and regular faculty meetings can stimulate the cross-fertilization of ideas between cinema studies programs and production or screenwriting departments. Ideally, all faculty members will be prepared to hold up high standards of scholarly rigor, technical competence, and artistic originality. The integration of theory, history, and aesthetics with production is valuable for its academic sake as well as for enhancing students' professional potential for growth—because only those creative few who can innovate beyond current codes and formulas will ultimately enhance the medium (and their careers). In short, we must prepare students not just for access but also for success in their professional careers or graduate study, not merely for entry-level jobs but also for advancement and growth into leadership positions within the field.

I fervently believe in the need to integrate three models: cinema as an academic, professional, and creative discipline. In today's global film and media climate, with its multitude of trendy critical methodologies, new technologies, and stylistic revolutions, being less than comprehensive would be a disservice to our students, our cinema culture, and ourselves.

Notes

1. In addition, Egri's work has been endorsed by successful writers from Broadway's Moss Hart to Hollywood's Robert Zemeckis.

2. Among the classic films I recommend are *A Trip to the Moon* (1902), *The Birth of a Nation* (1915), *Battleship Potemkin* (1925), *Un chien andalou* (1929), *Triumph of the Will* (1935), *Citizen Kane* (1941), *Bicycle Thieves* (1948), *Tokyo Story* (1953), *Wild Strawberries* (1957), *Blow-Up* (1967), *Ali: Fear Eats the Soul* (1974), *Xala* (1975), *Roger and Me* (1989), *Raise the Red Lantern* (1991), and *In the Mood for Love* (2000).

3. In this example, the dominant focus is the daughter, Jane (Thora Birch) who is centrally positioned behind the brightly lit vase of (American Beauty) roses. Her face is bathed in a warm light while her father's and mother's visages are shadowed and cold. Thus our eyes are directly drawn to Jane, while we perceive the parents, Lester (Kevin Spacey) and Carolyn (Annette Bening), as antagonists. The light behind the mother signifies her dominance within the family unit, while the eye-level camera angle makes it easier to recognize the false, forced intimacy of the scene. The shadows over the lower half of Lester's body subtly suggest that Lester is only half a man in the Burnham household.

In terms of color, the shot is primarily composed of neutral tones except for the most crucial object in the scene (and film): the roses. Their bright redness, affiliated with Jane's inner beauty, is the only contrasting color in the shot, changing the floral symbolism in this scene from the association of roses with female sexuality in other sequences—in particular, those that feature Jane's classmate Angela (Mena Suvari), the object of Lester's fantasies. In a sense, the visual density of this dinner scene conveys the entire narrative situation, including Jane's struggle for compassion and recognition from her physically and emotionally alienated parents, whose contradictions are hidden by the ostensible stability and symmetry of the composition (and Carolyn's rigid insistence on a sit-down dinner). Those antinomies are illuminated by the three separate zones of the dysfunctional triptych, with each character stuck in his or her place, separated from one another by distance, table clutter, and obvious dramatic tension. The lack of background depth suggests the entrapment of the family members, particularly Jane, who is trapped between her parents and the décor of their suburban house. In terms of character placement, Jane faces the viewer directly, allowing for better identification with her. Conversely, Carolyn and Lester are seen in profile, giving the viewer a sense of distance from both adult figures.

Finally, the proxemics of the characters reveals that both parents are equally to blame for Jane's unhappiness. Jane is placed midway between Carolyn and Lester, while they both sit at extreme opposite ends of the table (and the frame), thereby conveying their polar differences and sexual distance. A subtle acting detail is that Jane, although shot leaning away from her mother, also puts up her arm to block any interaction with her father.

Works Cited

Association of American Colleges and Universities. "Statement on Liberal Learning." Washington: Assn. of Amer. Colls. and Univs., 1998. Print.

Boyum, Joy Gould, and Gordon Pradl. "The Necessary Balance in Teaching Film." *English Journal* 63 (1974): 52–57. Print.

Bruner, Jerome S. *The Process of Education*. New York: Vintage, 1960. Print.

Bukalski, Peter J., et al. "University of Film and Video Association Guidelines for MFA Programs." *Journal of Film and Video* 52.1 (2000): 33–47. Print.

Capurso, A. "The Capurso Study." *Music and Your Emotions*. Ed. Emil A. Gutheil. New York: Liveright, 1952. 120–27. Print.

Carson, Diane. "Teaching for Learning: Do They Learn What You Teach?" *Cinema Journal* 36.2 (1997): 109–14. Print.

Corrigan, Timothy. *A Short Guide to Writing about Film.* 6th ed. New York: Longman, 2007. Print.
Egri, Lajos. *The Art of Dramatic Writing: Its Basis in the Creative Interpretation of Human Motives.* New York: Touchstone, 1960. Print.
Freire, Paolo. *Pedagogy of the Oppressed.* Trans. M. B. Ramos. New York: Continuum, 2008. Print.
Giannetti, Louis. *Understanding Movies.* 11th ed. Upper Saddle River: Pearson, 2008. Print.
Harnden, Russell W. Letter to the author. 20 Aug. 2008.
Metz, Christian. *Film Language: A Semiotics of the Cinema.* Trans. Michael Taylor. Chicago: U of Chicago P, 1991. Print.
Michelson, Annette. "Camera Lucida / Camera Obscura." *Art Forum* 11 (1973): 30–37. Print.
Moscowitz, John E. *Critical Approaches to Writing about Film.* Upper Saddle River: Prentice, 2000. Print.
Petric, Vlada. "Relating Courses in Filmmaking and Film Studies." *University Film Study Center Newsletter* 4.5 (1974): 1–3. Print.
Polan, Dana. *Scenes of Instruction: The Beginnings of the US Study of Film.* Berkeley: U of California P, 2007. Print.
Read, Herbert. *Education through Art.* New York: Pantheon, 1958. Print.
Reisz, Karel, and Gavin Millar. *The Technique of Film Editing.* 2nd ed. Woburn: Focal, 2002. Print.
Scorsese, Martin, and Michael Henry Wilson. *A Personal Journey through American Movies.* London: Faber, 1997. Print.
Shaw, George Bernard. "Art Teaching." *Misalliance: A Debate in One Sitting.* By Shaw. New York: French, 1957. 96–103. Print.
Smith, Greg M. "'It's Just a Movie': A Teaching Essay for Introductory Media Classes." *Cinema Journal* 41.1 (2001): 127–34. Print.
Sobchack, Vivian, and Thomas Sobchack. *An Introduction to Film.* 2nd ed. Upper Saddle River: Pearson, 1987. Print.
Tomasulo, Frank P. "Curricular Survey of Top US Film Schools." "Film History and Theory." College of Motion Picture Arts, Florida State U, 2005. 2–6. TS.
———. "Teaching the Introductory Cinema Studies Course: Some Strategies and Resources." *Cinema Journal* 34.4 (1995): 72–78. Print.
Welsch, Tricia. "Teaching Mise-en-Scène Analysis as a Critical Tool." *Cinema Journal* 36.2 (1997): 101–06. Print.
Zemeckis, Robert. Interview by Gil Bettman. University Film and Video Association conference, Chapman U. 4 Aug. 1996.

Tasha Oren

Teaching Screenwriting as Criticism

There are the terminal self-loathers, like Dixon Steele (*In a Lonely Place* [1950]) and Joe Gillis (*Sunset Boulevard* [1950]), or hapless Barton Fink and ill-fated David Kahane (*The Player* [1992]); others suffer from damp desperation, like Charlie Kaufman (*Adaptation* [2002]), or slow-simmering misery, like Christine (*Friends with Money* [2006]). The screenwriter as character is a singularly wretched creature when self-rendered on the screen. Yet the current cultural cachet of the profession is nothing short of remarkable.

In recent years, screenwriting has been riding a crest of hipness as the way in to the film industry. This rise in status is in part due to some high-profile practitioners and the widespread romantic perception that, unlike the collaborative and costly enterprise of making movies, the work of the screenwriter is solitary and requires little experience and even less initial capital. Writing teachers grumble that screenplays all but preoccupy some young would-be writers, who, instead of working on the Great American Novel, now hunch over shooting formats, belabor dialogue beats, and cite Paul Thomas Anderson, Quentin Tarantino, or Alexander Payne as their favorite writers.

While the cultural turn has been to the screenplay as a literary form, the study of screenwriting, as a discipline and a craft, is relatively new to the undergraduate curriculum and is particularly rare in writing programs. With few exceptions, only elite industry-feeder schools offer screenwriting as a professional concentration. In most other institutions, screenwriting—if offered at all—is usually relegated to an elective within creative writing or film production programs.

Despite screenwriting's increasing popularity among students, it holds an uneasy position in the curriculum. Because of the set of tools, objectives, and background the subject requires, production and writing programs are rarely positioned to take on screenwriting as a unique craft. As universities address new demands for film and media writing—and screenwriting slowly moves from its shadowy ad hoc realm to a curricular staple—we will surely see its disciplinary affinities take root. In this essay, I propose teaching screenwriting specifically for film studies students and programs grounded in critical, textual, and theoretical cinema and media studies.

I use the following approach in the hybrid course Introduction to Screenwriting: The Story Structure, which I teach in a humanities-based cinema and media studies program.[1] As a writing workshop, the course instills the fundamentals of writing for the screen and prepares students for the work of crafting a screenplay. The class requires students to develop their own story; turn it into an evolving script in progress; repeatedly read, critique, and help rewrite their classmates' work; pitch story ideas to the class; and craft short treatments with each revision. Below I focus not on the course's utility for budding screenwriters but on how (and why) such fundamentals can (and should) be part of a general film studies curriculum.

Much of our work in undergraduate film courses involves teaching appropriate and holistic perspectives on film and media criticism. Our approaches often combine the various textual, industrial, technical, and historically specific elements that make cinema a significant cultural product, with theoretical lenses and particular strategies for meaning making. As those of us who teach undergraduate classes know, the subtleties of multilayered analysis are particularly challenging to impart; beginning students are often enthralled by heavy-handed symbolism or a blunt approximation of representation study and tend to seize on individual moments (or objects) on the screen for snapshot analysis. Students often struggle to develop a more sustained critical engagement. It may be easier to discuss how camera angles or particular framing convey specific meaning, power relations, or emotional weight in a shot or a scene than to examine how a thematic idea in the film works to make meaning. More taxing still is an investigation of what that meaning is and why it is effective and relevant.

Students' expressive skills can flag when discussing emotional impact; their attentions can sputter midway through a contextual consideration of a character's implicit goals or lose the threads of a theme in the midst of high spectacle. The challenge here is a balancing act: how can teachers highlight a film's position within a network of conditions and dependencies (those of historical and political context; generic and aesthetic form; industrial and technological conventions) while maintaining focus on its interior trajectories (plot structure, character motivation, thematic development)? Further, once we delve into issues of character desire and choice, the escalation of conflict, or the relationship between protagonist and antagonist, how do we keep our students attuned to the narrative's cinematic particularity?

Stepping beyond a how-to practicum, teachers of film studies can embrace an expanded notion of screenwriting as textual study to shed new light on effective story design and the structure of narrative. Unlike traditional screenwriting workshops, screenwriting for film studies aims not to generate a producible, original screenplay but to use this creative process as a framework for the study of film structure and the foundations of filmic storytelling. Through this perspective, students can explore plot and subplots, cinematic principles of character development, the act structure and its internal narrative markers, various approaches and traditions of filmic storytelling and narrative unities, and the particular challenge of telling a story and making meaning cinematically. In short, this approach helps students grasp these fundamentals through a partial inversion of vantage point—from interpretation to construction.

The concept for such a hybrid course is simple: students work on their story ideas—here, story puzzles to be evaluated, tweaked, and resolved collectively—and then apply analytic principles to published screenplays and to films they watch in screenings. The goal of the course is not an oscillating point of view that bobs from creation to criticism but a coalescing new perspective on film scholarship. The hybrid approach focuses not only on the how-to of screenwriting but also asks what a screenplay is, emphasizing its role as a cinematic element rather than as a text in and of itself. In this way, screenwriting is also an excellent primer for follow-up courses in literary adaptation, since it effectively illustrates the fundamental difference (as well as necessary similarities) between writing directly to a readership and writing for cinematic realization.

It should, of course, come as no surprise that the same principles govern the foundation of screenwriting and of story analysis. Yet given the acutely commercial tone and slant of most screenwriting discourse, it seems a stretch to align the craft with film theory. Even among screenwriting approaches that delve beyond step-by-step manuals and the ubiquitous variations on "Secrets to Screenplays That Sell!" the field's notorious stress on formula, conventions, blueprints, and rules tests one's willingness to ascribe resemblance between it and film criticism. A course on screenwriting, however, offers concrete ways to enhance a film studies curriculum. Such a course focuses on the process of textual production (both in terms of original ideas generated and developed by the students and analysis of existing scripts) and the role of the screenplay as a raw map for the creation of a film. Reading a treatment helps students envision how cinematic codes, techniques, and formal elements might be brought to bear on the story, and nothing facilitates discussion of performance, editing, cinematography, or directing more than reading a script—aloud if possible—before seeing the film. When students create a story, they see the process at work and grasp how cinematic codes and the medium's specific characteristics both enable and restrict the kinds of narratives that "work" as films.

The combination of elementary story fabrication with analysis of screenplays and films allows students to reverse engineer a filmic narrative, reducing it to its building blocks and interior dynamics. Beginning with the skeleton of the narrative—characters, conflict, events, and time—students move on to flesh out these basics by exploring setting and genre, themes, resolution or closure, subplot mechanism, parallelism, narration, and audience direction or expectation. Thus the course stages film as a complex, multileveled construction whose quality depends, in large part, on attendance to its formal, narrative structure.

In isolation, such an approach may strike some readers as mechanical, near-sighted, and rigid (indeed, precisely the kind of critique often directed at screenwriting manuals). Yet, in the context of the film studies curriculum, this method moves screenwriting away from formal dogma and toward its utility as one tool in a well-furnished analysis kit. What's more, an instructor can easily stress that classical narrative formulation is only one of several options by adding a few screenings that strain or depart from such a classic model, keeping students from falling into the comfort of prescription, as well as helping them understand how specific alternatives from classic narratives can function as critique.[2]

An education in practical narrative design helps students see a film as a meaningful and decipherable textual construct. Such a tool, in turn, is useful as they develop other critical skills: identifying the protagonist apart from a main character, approaching temporal puzzles or multiprotagonist narratives, or connecting theme to cultural and historical context. For many students, a demystification of story dynamics is accompanied by gaining a new comfort level with theoretical concepts such as Christian Metz's "narrative machine" and apparatus theory, feminist narrative critique, new formalism, and current debates in digital media theory over notions of postnarrative.[3]

The readings for the course include numerous screenplays (both published versions and early drafts), as well as a screenwriting book. I favor *Story*, by Robert McKee, because portions of the book function perfectly as a primer for story analysis and what we call in class "interior" or "forensic" film criticism: a criticism that begins with an evaluation of the narrative structure and the shape of plot and character arcs and moves to the experience of the viewing audience and the kinds of pleasure the texts offer. Along with Syd Field, William Goldman, and Linda Seger, McKee is widely acknowledged as the premier screenwriting coach and instructor. While I find McKee's book works best because of its dramaturgic (as opposed to utilitarian) perspective on screenplay design, teaching McKee to film studies students presents its own pleasures. Notorious after Brian Cox portrayed him as the gruff and impatient screenwriting guru in the most famous contemporary film about screenwriting, Charlie Kaufman's *Adaptation*, McKee is familiar territory to nonwriting film buffs too. That McKee exists beyond the script is often a surprise to my students; that his insistence on form, structure, and emotional truth can lend itself to the kind of Hollywood formula Kaufman spoofs provides an added layer of critical awareness to their reading and discussion.

The course fundamentals are Aristotelian structure, arc-based story design, cause-and-effect chain, protagonist choice as action events, and the notion of conflict as the engine of story. McKee's method also offers students useful terms with which to consider story progression: the inciting incident (the first conflict that sets the protagonist on the story path), characterization versus character, conflict as an "opening gap" between expectation and reality, subtext, choice as value, action as change, and the controlling idea (or theme) that animates the film through dimension and resonance. Once students account for narrative structure as a cinematic element, they can easily think through, say, the protagonist's objective, the setting, or narrative genre conventions as possible paths into critical engagement with film texts. A recent class entered an impromptu discussion about the roles of city space, time, and "quest" arcs, bringing together such far-flung examples as *The Bicycle Thief* (1948), *Run Lola Run* (1998), and *Speed* (1994). Another session featured a lively debate about the convention of the contemporary romantic subplot, incorporating examples from class screenings of *Tootsie* (1982), *Collateral* (2004), *Garden State* (2004), and *The Departed* (2006). Students who would normally shrink from employing a feminist critical perspective by route of ideology and representation were thoroughly engaged with a critical evaluation of the class twist on the "damsel in distress" plot of *Collateral* and the "shared lover" trope in *The Departed*, when these were framed in the instrumental terms of story-structure mechanics.

As in the dictum most often attributed to Alfred Hitchcock, the course subscribes to the approach that a screenplay must be completely written and finished before the dialogue is added. This method is useful for students who have never written a screenplay (and may not ever want to attempt one beyond the scope of the class) and is an all-purpose antidote to a host of pitfalls and writing clichés. Most important, the method emphasizes sustained story, overall plot structure, and cinematic narrative design.

Although significant course time is dedicated to applying critical tools to screenplays and films, students also have the opportunity to work creatively on their own projects. Beginning with a workshop where they work in teams to generate (and then pitch) quick narratives and moving on to a series of exercises exploring setting, character, situations, inciting incident, premise, conflict, and theme, students—even those who have never tackled creative work before—discover the pleasures of discerning the anatomy of storytelling. One particularly effective exercise is my version of Michael Rabiger's improvisational CLOSAT cards.[4] The exercise calls for every student to generate four to eight index cards, each containing a one-sentence character sketch, object, or location. Teams then randomly choose two character cards, one location card, and one object card and have thirty minutes to develop and then pitch their story to the class. Through these individual and collective exercises, students learn the necessary elements of both constructing and telling a story, such as what types of stories generate interest and why, how genre conventions become implicit in story types, and what kind of critical framework applies to evaluating effective stories. What is most valuable, however, is the workshop process itself.

Many film and media students do not have opportunities to work collaboratively or experience their work in a workshop setting and are only exposed to solitary critical writing or research-oriented scholarship. The screenwriting workshop allows students to apply the same critical skills in the live, interactive setting and witness how their ideas and critiques can have immediate and deep impact on an evolving would-be cinematic text. Through such a process, they are often able to engage with the same issues they encounter in other classes from a different vantage point. Representational questions, for example, often prove especially potent. Since texts in progress are, by definition, pliable, representation and its implications (for the story, theme, and audience readings) gain new urgency as students push one another to move a character away from stereotype, rework a "girlfriend" role to emphasize female agency, question a character's matter-of-fact politics, examine the implication of international settings, or point out casual homophobia. There is, of course, nothing new or novel about film studies students' attention to the cultural work of images and portrayals. But the workshop reveals how often particular representational choices—even of minor characters—are fastened to the source mechanics of the story. Repeatedly, students discover how tweaking one character opens a series of domino-like gaps in their narrative, often requiring radical reenvisioning of their original story.

Similarly, students find new understanding of genre not only as a set of conventions and audience expectations but also as a frame of reference for narrative possibility. In story workshop, students challenge one another's pitches by asking about the author's generic intent; in revision, they witness how turning an action this way or that could change the narrative's generic permutation.

Aside from the obvious benefits of creative activity and imaginative story crafting, screenwriting exercises (like writing a scene in the setting where it takes place; writing the same conflict thrice, each time with a different pair of characters; or constructing the same event chain in three different genre styles) allow students to ponder and understand more thoroughly how various material and textual conditions (technology, location, audience expectation, character coherence, story unity) shape every cinematic text. This internal, "inhabited" knowledge they come away with, in turn, affords them a broader perspective and a new comfort with film in their writing, research, and analysis. If nothing else, a course in screenwriting expands our students' expressive and analytical range. Stressing the interrelation of narrative and other filmic elements, such a course cultivates deeper understanding of how cinema tells stories and makes meaning.

Notes

1. The class was developed with the help of Daniel Marcus, who generously shared his class materials, exercises, and readings with me. This note carries my thanks and appreciation.

2. *Junebug* (2005), *Me and You and Everyone We Know* (2005), *Happiness* (1998), or *Lost Highway* (2007) are effective examples, since they are accessible, US-made commercial narratives that stretch the classic structure of a protagonist-driven narrative unity.

3. Among the key texts here are Metz; de Lauretis; Bordwell; and Ryan.

4. In Rabiger's original exercise, *CLOSAT* stands for character, location, object, situation, act, and theme. Players create an "instant story" by picking random cards from each category and weaving them into a coherent narrative.

Works Cited

Bordwell, David. *The Way Hollywood Tells It: Story and Style in Modern Movies.* Berkeley: U of California P, 2006. Print.

de Lauretis, Teresa. *Alice Doesn't: Feminism, Semiotics, Cinema.* London: Macmillan, 1984. Print.

Field, Syd. *Screenplay: The Foundations of Screenwriting.* New York: Delta, 2005. Print.

Goldman, William. *Adventures in the Screen Trade: A Personal View of Hollywood and Screenwriting.* New York: Warner, 1983. Print.

McKee, Robert. *Story: Substance, Structure, Style, and the Principles of Screenwriting.* New York: Harper, 1997. Print.

Metz, Christian. *Film Language: A Semiotics of Cinema.* Trans. Michael Taylor. New York: Oxford UP, 1974. Print.

Rabiger, Michael. *Developing Story Ideas.* 2nd ed. Burlington: Focal, 2006. Print.

Ryan, Marie-Laure, ed. *Narrative across Media: The Languages of Storytelling.* Lincoln: U of Nebraska P, 2004. Print.

Seger, Linda. *Making a Good Script Great.* New York: Dodd, 1987. Print.

Part VI

Film and Media in the Digital Age

Introduction to Part 6

If film has been historically defined as a physical, processed medium, what does it mean, as one author in this section puts it, to "teach an object that no longer has a chemical base, is commonly edited on video, is enhanced with computer graphics or computer-generated animation, and is seen on light-emanating screens of all sizes in all locations?"

No longer confined to the movie theater or to the home living room, film and television are now watched on screens of all sizes, in various settings. They are made, edited, distributed, and marketed in new ways and on a variety of platforms, ranging from broadcast, cable, and satellite television to videotape and DVD. No longer a buzzword, *media convergence* now describes the interrelation of film, telephone, radio, television, and the Internet. Teachers and students today confront the study of the moving image with tools and technologies that provide new resources for teaching as well as new challenges, both practical and conceptual.

Indeed, movies and television shows are more accessible than ever, coming to us on cable television, by mail through services such as Netflix, or online through *YouTube*. Media platforms, such as DVDs, offer students and teachers alike the chance to view a film or television show repeatedly; they can examine shots and sequences in slow motion or freeze-frame and thus perform the kind of close reading nearly impossible before. DVDs also provide other resources for teaching through add-ons or bonus features, as well as through supplementary materials such as directors' and actors' commentaries or scholarly analyses.

And yet for all the pedagogical advantages of DVDs and increased access to films, many of the most influential films in cinema history are not available on DVD or on other media platforms. This is true of many silent films (which no longer exist in any format, even 35mm) as well as international and experimental films, especially those from the 1960s, when the 16mm format flourished throughout the world, offering an inexpensive format for emerging artists and marginalized cultures. DVDs also tend to degrade after about fifteen years. Hollywood feature films, even those "born digital," are currently stored on conventional 35mm film masters as the most effective way to stabilize the digital image. New digital technologies are thus fleeting and ephemeral. We may be using DVDs for teaching film and media now, but only until some new media platform comes along.

The essays here suggest that we adapt to new ways of teaching film and television in a digital age by recognizing film and television as historically specific media forms now contained within newer media that rely on the networks of telephony and the Internet. They provide a variety of ways to help us understand the history of media convergence by situating film and television alongside the emergence and disappearance of new and older technologies (and, in some cases, the theories that explained them). These essays underscore that teaching moving image media requires what it always has; namely, a willingness to adapt to new technologies while exploring the complex status of the moving image as at once an aesthetic, industrial, cultural, and technological form, intimately connected to questions of political economies, media ownership, remix cultures, and notions of taste and aesthetics.

Anne Friedberg

Teaching Media Specificity in an Age of Convergence

As the twentieth century raced toward its end, changes in moving image media occurred at the speed of fast-forward. As we enter this next century, film as a medium and the cinema as a cultural assemblage have lost much of their specificity as they have become embedded—or lost—in new technologies of production, delivery, and display.

Today our students have grown up watching films on broadcast, cable, and satellite TV, on videotape, laser disc, and DVD. They watch them at the movie theater but also on a desktop, laptop, iPod, and gaming console, on their phones, in automobiles and airplanes, on billboards, and at the bank. If film as a medium was historically defined as a strip of photosensitive celluloid run through a camera for exposure, chemically developed, edited, and reassembled to be threaded through a projector and cast on a screen, then what does it mean to study or teach an object that no longer has a chemical base, is commonly edited on video, is enhanced with computer graphics or computer-generated animation, and is seen on light-emanating screens of all sizes in all locations; in other words, that no longer has a film-specific mode of production, delivery, and display (see Friedberg, "End," "Interfacing," *Virtual Window*)?

This essay interrogates the nature of a medium, the historical specificities of old media, and the challenges produced by the new media and then situates the specificities of film and film studies in what some critics have called a "postmedium" age. *Convergence*, once merely a discursive buzzword, has become a literal description of the codependency of the media of telephone, radio, television, and the Internet. In this new media environment, the medium of film exists in a cross-purposed interaction with other media and poses new questions about its technological specificity. How, then, do we teach *film*?

What Is a Medium? Media Specificity and Intermediality

Film was once a medium unto its own. Early theorists of the new medium, from Hugo Münsterberg and Vachel Lindsay to Jean Epstein and Germaine Dulac to Béla Balázs and Rudolf Arnheim, attempted to isolate its essential capacities—its specificity—to campaign for its legitimacy as a new art form different from the established arts (see Lindsay). For Münsterberg, it was film's capacity to objectify the processes of the human mind; for the French theorist-filmmakers Epstein and Dulac, it was the unique rhythmic and visual principles of film, its *photogénie/cinégraphie*; for Balázs, it was the microphysiognomy made possible by the close-up (see esp. 314–15, 315–21); for Arnheim, it was film's peculiar divergence from reality—its lack of sound, its images in black and white, its two-dimensionality. As the technically specific medium of film developed alongside the expanding cultural institution of the cinema, theorists and historians continued to draw from its unique qualities (see Carroll; Marvin). Even the apparatus theories of the 1970s asserted a specificity to the cinematic *appareil*, its ideological effects produced by a combination of the medium-specific configuration of film, projector, screen, and spectator alongside the historically specific conventions of editing, camerawork, and spectator position designed to conceal filmmaking's technical base (see Baudry, "Apparatus" and "Ideological Effects").

But in our current media environment, film is no longer an independent medium. Today films (regardless of what is now referred to as the "capture medium") are almost without exception transferred to video and postproduced electronically; they are delivered on DVDs, through satellite or cable, downloaded or streamed online; they are seen in theaters and on televisions, computers, and an array of portable devices for moving image narratives. Production techniques, display technologies, and delivery platforms have jumbled the predigital/digital divide into uncertain convergences on a rapidly shifting technological terrain. To accurately historicize, theorize, and teach film in the twenty-first century, we need to situate its technical and formal specificities in relation to a range of other media—television and computer-based media but also photography, radio, recorded music, telephony—to assess their shifting intermedial dependencies on one another.

Marshall McLuhan has never been a patron saint of film study; his canonical texts often include writers whose focus is the specificity of filmic media and the cinema as film's historically specific cultural assemblage. Nevertheless, his work on media now provides an important retrospective lens as we address how once historically distinct media have begun to slip into one another. McLuhan's 1964 book, *Understanding Media*, drew attention not only to the mediation that each medium implied but also to the specificity of a long list of separate media—telegraph, photograph, phonograph, typewriter, radio, television, and "the movies." McLuhan analyzed the interrelatedness of these media in an evolutionary scheme, insisting that each new medium would "institute new ratios, not only among our private senses, but among themselves, when they interact among themselves" (53). He believed that the content of each new medium was an old medium: "The 'content' of any medium is always another medium. The content of writing is speech; just as the written word is the content of print, and print is the content of the telegraph" (8). Whether his account of the evolving genealogies of media—in a kind of Chinese box–*matryoshka* doll incorporation—accurately explains the enfolding of one media form into the content of another, McLuhan was keen to establish the historical relations among and between each media form.

McLuhan's prophetic, aphoristic formulations about the manner in which "media" change us—"the medium is the message" and "the global village"—have become a culturally ingrained part of our vernacular. While many of his pop-infused assertions veered to hyperbole or superficiality (the oppositions of hot and cold media never made sense),[1] McLuhan became a necessary predecessor to many recent media theorists, from Friedrich Kittler, Jean Baudrillard, and Paul Virilio to *Wired* magazine. As the term "new media" entered the discursive field, McLuhan's work became an originary site for rethinking the "new ratios" and interactions of previously separate media forms. In their book *Remediation: Understanding New Media*, Jay Bolter and Richard Grusin adopt and adjust McLuhan's model of incorporative and sequential media relations by defining a "medium" as "that which remediates"; that is, each media form is a redo of another and is always a hybrid. Yet as Siegfried Zielinski asserts in his polemic for forging a new historiography of media relations, *Deep Time of the Media*, "we will need a different perspective from that which is only to seek the old in the new" (3). And as "new media studies" answers its need to specify the relation of old to new, a sequential model of media development may overlook the manner in which separate and specific media develop in coconstitutive relations to one another (see Gaudreault and Marion).

Convergence: Toward an Intermedial Methodology

It now appears that the separate historical genealogies of television, film, and computing technologies disregard the intermedial complexity of technological development (see Chun and Keenan; Elsaesser). Instead of conceptualizing each new medium as if it evolved in a series of supercessions in a serial chain, an intermedial historiography situates separate media as coextensive, their histories dovetailing in a complex promiscuity (see Gitelman; Gitelman and Pingree). Friedrich Kittler, in *Gramophone, Film, Typewriter*, argues that the historical synchronicity of inventions in phonography, cinema, and typewriting led not to their interaction but rather to the initial historical separation, or technical autonomy, of acoustic, optical, and written "data flows." In this regard, the disciplinary separation of film, television, and Internet studies may have also functioned to enforce a sense of their media-specific technical autonomy. Kittler argues forcefully that "electric," "electronic," and "digital" technologies ended this separation. "Something is coming to an end," he wrote in his introduction; "the general digitalization of information and channels erases the difference between individual media" ("Gramophone" 102). In the 1990s, as Kittler and others began to assert the "mediumlessness" of digital technology, the digital emerged as a technological determinant that irrevocably changed the interrelations between specific and separate media. Another McLuhan-styled media prognosticator, Nicholas Negroponte, suggested a counter-polemical aphorism, turning McLuhan's "the medium is the message" on its head. "The medium is not the message in the digital world," declared Negroponte. "It is an embodiment of it. A message might have several embodiments automatically derivable from the same data" (71). "Film" as a media-specific term is more and more confined to refer to a delimited technical and historical configuration in the "cinematic century" that has now passed.

Film and the "Postmedium Condition"

Writing about the Belgian artist Marcel Broodthaers in 1999, the art critic and theorist Rosalind Krauss declared that art was afflicted with a "post-medium condition." Krauss detailed how the tenets of high modernism (articulated by Clement Greenberg's 1940 "Towards a Newer Laocoön," which asserted the dependence on the specificities of the materials of each art form) had been forcefully undermined by the art world's embrace of photography and multimedia installation (see Lessing). Contemporary painting, sculpture, and drawing, Krauss argued, were situated in a pluralistic environment where past specificities were muddled into the multimedium. In art criticism, the medium had reached a new state, beyond specificity; it was now a postmedium. Equally, *film* has entered into a slippery semantic freefall as it has lost its singular mode of production, delivery, and display.

To retool our teaching of film—to address its shifting specificities and convergences—the following must be taken into account: the specificity of film or cinema as a medium; the historical relations between film and other media, situating their specificities alongside the emergence and disappearance of other technologies; the role played by digital technology as it has chipped away at the analog base of image production, delivery, and display; and theories of the network that address the emerging rhetoric of interactivity (the do-it-yourself infusion of fan-based culture) that remind us of the mitigation of this development by protocols, codes, and network gates (see Wardrip-Fruin and Montfort).

Teaching Film with Instructional Media Technology

The classroom formats and instructional technologies for the teaching of film have changed dramatically. In many universities, as Dixon and Foster suggest in their contribution to this volume, the video projection of DVDs has replaced 16mm projection. Screen-based pedagogical software (e.g., *PowerPoint*, *Keynote*) allows the instructor to embed moving-image excerpts into computer-driven presentations, while video projection of online sources allows the instructor to project Web pages and to access Web-based archival image streams in the classroom. It would be intellectually dishonest to ignore the specificities of the media that we experience in the classroom—video projection, DVDs, computer-driven visuals and sounds. In the twenty-first century, the teacher needs to situate film among other televisual, computer-based, telephonic, and handheld media to adeptly understand its histories—and its future reach. Of course, there is a certain irony to the set of suggestions I have just made. It has been a decades-long struggle to bring film into the academy as a legitimate object of study (see Polan; Wasson and Grieveson). And, as degree-granting film programs and film departments have become a prominent part of US academia, the National Research Council (NRC) still deems film as an "emerging discipline"—as if the emergence of its study will only occur after its dissolution as a media-specific form. But even as the NRC has not yet sanctioned film studies as an established discipline, the professional organization of film and media scholars, the Society for Cinema and Media Studies (SCMS), celebrated its fiftieth anniversary in 2009–10. In fact, SCMS's recent history marks the historical shifts in our object(s) of study and the method(s) that we have used to approach them. Formed in 1959 as the Society for Cinematologists, the society changed its name to the Society for Cinema Studies in 1969 and for much of its half-century held to that name. In 2002, the society changed its name again, to the Society for Cinema and Media Studies, in a move to annex the media seemingly not included under the rubric "cinema" but that had become key objects of study (i.e., television, video, and other newer forms of moving image media, like the Web, mobile devices, the videogame). With the addition of "media" to the society's name, some felt that the change signaled a disenfranchisement of the society's history and a shift away from the roots and the media specificities of what we study. As someone who strongly advocated that change, I hope that we come to see it as a broadening rather than narrowing of our understanding of the "cinema." In our current context, I would argue that we might redeploy the term "cinematic," a term that includes all moving image media and is not medium based—that is, not photographic film or video or digital technologies. "Cinematic" is an adjective, not a noun; it does not refer to an apparatus, a technology, or a specific medium. "Cinematic" is, instead, a descriptor of the overlapping qualities of many separate media that record and represent movement—with color, sound, three dimensions, and immersive technologies, shown on screens of all sizes and scales and multiples. Film is now best seen as a historically specific media form, contained within newer media incorporations that rely on the networks of telephony or the Internet. In the twenty-first century, the teacher of film needs to parse the specificities and convergences of film, television, and Web-based media.

Note

1. McLuhan's temperature-based differentials were counterintuitive. McLuhan asserted that television was a "cool" medium, while "the movies" were a "hot" medium. A cool medium (like the telephone and television) was one that demanded participation; a hot medium (like radio and the movies) had less intensity of involvement. Perhaps the 1960s context determined his assignation of "cool" to television—and although the telephone's dialogic qualities clearly differentiate it from radio's monologic and less participatory structure, the manner in which television demands participation was explained by McLuhan as deriving from the viewer's perception of the scanning lines. McLuhan was a prophet of the cultural dislocations that occur in the switch from linear, local, and print-based media to nonlinear, global, and electronic media, but his perspective was formed from television, not from other media formations. Reading him now, it is clear that McLuhan had no inkling of the oncoming impact of digital technology.

Works Cited

Abel, Richard, ed. *French Film Theory and Criticism, 1907–1939.* Princeton: Princeton UP, 1988. Print.

Arnheim, Rudolf. *Film as Art / Film Als Kunst.* 1933. Berkeley: U of California P, 1957. Print.

Balázs, Béla. *Theory of Film: Character and Growth of a New Art.* Trans. Edith Bone. New York: Dover, 1953. Print.

Baudry, Jean-Louis. "The Apparatus: Metaphysical Approaches to the Impression of Reality in Cinema." 1975. Braudy and Cohen 760–78.

———. "Ideological Effects of the Basic Cinematic Apparatus." 1970. Braudy and Cohen 345–55.

Bolter, Jay, and Richard Grusin. *Remediation: Understanding New Media.* Cambridge: MIT P, 2000. Print.

Braudy, Leo, and Marshall Cohen, eds. *Film Theory and Criticism: Introductory Readings.* 5th ed. New York: Oxford UP, 1999. Print.

Carroll, Noël. "The Specificity Thesis." *Philosophical Problems of Classical Film Theory.* Princeton: Princeton UP, 1988. Print.

Chun, Wendy Hui Kyong, and Thomas Keenan, eds. *New Media, Old Media: A History and Theory Reader.* New York: Routledge, 2005. Print.

Dulac, Germaine. "The Essence of the Cinema: The Visual Idea." Trans. Robert Lamberton. *The Avant-Garde Film: A Reader of Theory and Criticism.* Ed. P. Adams Sitney. New York: New York UP, 1978. Print.

Elsaesser, Thomas. "Cinema Futures: Convergence, Divergence, Difference." 1998. *Cinema Futures: Cain, Abel or Cable? The Screen Arts in the Digital Age.* Ed. Elsaesser and Kay Hoffmann. Amsterdam: Amsterdam UP, 1998. 9–26. Print.

Epstein, Jean. "Magnification." 1921. Abel 235–40.

———. "On Certain Characteristics of *Photogénie.*" 1924. Abel 314–18.

Friedberg, Anne. "The End of Cinema: Multi-media and Technological Change." *Reinventing Film Studies.* Ed. Linda Williams and Christine Gledhill. London: Arnold, 1999. 438–52. Print.

———. "Interfacing the Screen: CDs, CD-Roms, DVDs." *The New Media Book.* Ed. Dan Harries. London: British Film Inst., 2002. 30–39. Print.

———. *The Virtual Window: From Alberti to Microsoft.* Cambridge: MIT P, 2006. Print.

Gaudreault, Andre, and Philippe Marion. "The Cinema as a Model for the Genealogy of Media." *Convergence* 8 (2002): 12–18. Print.

Gitelman, Lisa. *Always Already New: Media, History, and the Data of Culture.* Cambridge: MIT P, 2006. Print.

Gitelman, Lisa, and Geoffrey Pingree, eds. *New Media, 1740–1915.* Cambridge: MIT P, 2003. Print.

Greenberg, Clement. "Towards a Newer Laocoön." 1940. *Perceptions and Judgments, 1939–1944.* Ed. John O'Brian. Chicago: U of Chicago P, 1986. 23–38. Print. Vol. 1 of *Clement Greenberg: The Collected Essays and Criticism.*

Kittler, Friedrich A. *Gramophone, Film, Typewriter.* 1986. Trans. Geoffrey Winthrop-Young and Michael Wutz. Palo Alto: Stanford UP, 1999. Print.

———. "Gramophone, Film, Typewriter." *October* 41 (1987): 101–18. Print.

Krauss, Rosalind. *A Voyage on the North Sea: Art in the Age of the Postmedium Condition.* London: Thames, 2000. Print.

Lessing, Gotthold Ephraim. *Laocoön: An Essay on the Limits of Painting and Poetry.* 1766. Trans. Edward Allen McCormick. Baltimore: Johns Hopkins UP, 1984. Print.

Lindsay, Vachel. *The Art of the Moving Picture.* 1915. New York: Macmillan, 1915. Print.

Marvin, Carolyn. *When Old Technologies Were New: Thinking about Electric Communication in the Late Nineteenth Century.* New York: Oxford UP, 1988. Print.

McLuhan, Marshall. *Understanding Media: The Extensions of Man.* Cambridge: MIT P, 1964. Print.

Münsterberg, Hugo. *Hugo Münsterberg on Film:* The Photoplay: A Psychological Study *and Other Writings.* Ed. Allan Langdale. New York: Routledge, 2002. Print.

Negroponte, Nicholas. *Being Digital.* New York: Knopf, 1995. Print.

Polan, Dana. *Scenes of Instruction: The Beginnings of the US Study of Film.* Berkeley: U of California P, 2007. Print.

Wardrip-Fruin, Noah, and Nick Montfort, eds. *The New Media Reader.* Cambridge: MIT P, 2003. Print.

Wasson, Haidee, and Lee Grieveson, eds. *Inventing Film Studies.* Durham: Duke UP, 2008. Print.

Zielinski, Siegfried. *Deep Time of the Media: Toward an Archaeology of Hearing and Seeing by Technical Means.* Trans. Gloria Custance. Cambridge: MIT P, 2006. Print.

Wheeler Winston Dixon and
Gwendolyn Audrey Foster

Teaching Film in the Age of Digital Transformation

While we are now firmly anchored in the twenty-first century, the great bulk of films considered in film studies courses were created in the twentieth century. The digitization of the cinematic apparatus has marked the beginning of profound changes in the ways movies are made, edited, distributed, and marketed. What once was considered an experience akin to "truth twenty-four times per second" (in Jean-Luc Godard's famous phrase) has now become a hyperedited construct, replete with computer-generated-imagery effects, MTV-styled cutting, and promotional campaigns that open a film everywhere at once, rather than a traditional theatrical roll out.

Indeed, some distributors are now embracing a model in which a film will open simultaneously in theaters, on the Web, on DVD, and on cable television, such as IFC On Demand. Theatrical motion pictures are even now being streamed directly into theaters by satellite, as a digital signal to be projected directly on the screen, with no film or digital media involved. What we think of as a film has become radically transformed by the culture and language of videogames and interactive Web sites, and now film itself is poised to disappear, an obsolete format in an all-digital world. Viral videos on *YouTube* now spread around the world in a matter of hours, gathering millions of viewers, transforming existing distribution models as well as viewer expectations.

How has our students' visual consciousness been shaped by the tidal wave of imagery from competing sources that sweeps over them, often two and three layers deep? How can we contemplate the delicacy of a shot in a film by Yasujirô Ozu or Vincente Minnelli, for example, with its gravity, depth, and duration, in a culture that values fragments of images over a concrete whole? If one runs an entire motion picture on DVD format without chapter stops, the experience is roughly equivalent to conventional film projection; fragmented, it becomes a different experience altogether. Where we seem only to have time for clips from longer works, we as teachers should argue for the primacy of the complete work as the only true exemplar of the director's vision. We are undergoing a fundamental shift in cinematic reception that distances nineteenth- and twentieth-century cinema from twenty-first-century postdigital cinema. How can we make the works of the past resonant in an atmosphere of constant mutability?

When cinema was first codified as a subject for students at the university level in the mid-1960s, there was usually only one choice when it came to projection formats: 16mm film. Videotape was in its infancy, and except for professional 2" applications used in network television, the quality of its image was poor. First invented in 1923, 16mm was a durable gauge that was reliably used in World War II and in grade school classrooms during the 1950s as the medium of choice for nontheatrical projection. Rental costs were reasonable, and the medium was easy to work with, given a certain level of care and expertise.

Fast-forward forty years, and 16mm is an archival format, used only in classrooms and museums. The photographic images burned on 16mm film have been replaced with digitized ones that form a simulacrum of the original filmic experience; scratches, grain, and other intrinsic filmic characteristics vanish in a new world of pristine digital perfection. As new formats appear in the coming years, all films will be routinely projected with digital equipment, marking a decisive break from the analog past of the cinema.

Once ubiquitous and reasonably priced, 16mm film projection equipment has all but vanished. Indeed, there is currently not one manufacturer left who produces a 16mm projector for classroom use. The format is behind us. While theoreticians and scholars debate the differences between the film and video image, most students and administrators have embraced DVDs as the new standard of our shared visual culture, at least for the moment.

As a platform for the study of the moving image, DVDs offer several immediate advantages. The digital image is sharper, clearer, scratch free, and usually comes with Dolby stereo sound, as opposed to the monaural optical sound track on conventional 16mm film. DVDs are light, convenient to store, and easy to use; they also offer considerable flexibility in the use of subtitles, languages, and screen formats. Projecting 16mm film is a much more exacting task, and the film reels are much bulkier.

Using a large-screen wall-mounted plasma television, such as a 52" or 42" model, a classroom of thirty students can see a film without any projection apparatus. Students also have greater access to the films of the past, as well as to foreign films and experimental films, than at any other time. No longer do they have to travel to archives to see the classics and more marginal films; the films come to them through the mail or over the Web. Using services such as Netflix, students can easily and cheaply rent films online to supplement regular course offerings and pursue independent studies at their convenience. The limited selection previously offered by 16mm rental libraries is no longer an obstacle to the study of film.

Today's improved availability encourages a variety of new approaches to the teaching of film, not the least of which is the inclusion of an increasing number of films by women and minorities, which were formerly excluded from the conventional film canon. Figures such as the pioneering feminist directors Alice Guy Blaché and Lois Weber, along with African American auteurs Oscar Micheaux and Charles Burnett, are now acknowledged as part of film history through the availability of their work. Groundbreaking gay and lesbian films are also available through distributors such as Women Make Movies. In the digital world, all these works are much more accessible. Multiculturalism in film studies is thus encouraged; no longer confined to the storage facilities of film archives, these films and others like them are now free to enlighten and challenge the public.

DVDs are often created from the original 35mm negatives of such films, with digitally remastered sound tracks as well as numerous extras, such as director commentaries or critical appreciations by some of the top historians and theoreticians in the field. The recent reconstructions of classic films for DVD release, such as Fritz Lang's *Metropolis* (1927) and Sergei Eisenstein's *Battleship Potemkin* (1926), include numerous scenes that have previously been considered lost or damaged and give a much more accurate vision of the original film than a battered 16mm print created decades ago. DVDs also offer students the chance to view a film repeatedly, in slow motion, with freeze frames and even blowups, so that they can examine the images in the film in extreme detail.

These capabilities can produce some surprising discoveries. For years, it was held by nearly all film critics that the knife wielded by the character Norman Bates in Alfred Hitchcock's *Psycho* (1960) never actually penetrated the body of Marion Crane (Janet Leigh) during the famous shower murder sequence; the entire scene was discussed as an illusion accomplished by montage and strategic camera placement. Now, it can easily be seen that while most of the sequence is suggested by the violence of Hitchcock's cutting, there is, in fact, one shot in the center of the sequence in which the knife plunges directly into Marion's stomach. This matter may be small, but it is more readily observable when one has the ability to manipulate the image with such freedom.

Students can watch "The Odessa Steps" sequence from *Battleship Potemkin* in slow motion with the same careful attention and more fully appreciate Eisenstein's brilliant cutting; in the past, only an analytic 16mm projector could accomplish the same feat. The same can be said for the signature use of slow motion and reverse motion in Leni Riefenstahl's *Olympia* (1938), particularly the landmark diving sequence, or the intricate cross-cutting in D. W. Griffith's *The Lonedale Operator* (1911) or Jean-Luc Godard's revolutionary jump cuts in *Breathless* (1960). Seen in restored digital prints as part of an analytic screening, these films afford the student a vision of film as a construct, something that is composed of shots, editing points, and a series of conscious decisions—something that is often lost on a viewer who is caught up in a real-time narrative.

Many teachers now routinely require students to subscribe to Netflix, so that they have ready access to the films discussed in class; this process returns the films to the status of being the real texts under consideration. We can thus meet with students during office hours and discuss various films and directors that they may be interested in, so that we can assign a paper on a particular director and then work with them to select a representative group of titles. Students rent the films, screen them, and then we meet again to discuss their impressions, working toward the creation of a final research paper. The opportunity for independent research is thus considerably expanded, since students now have access to nearly the entire history of cinema.

This process teaches students, among other things, about the precedence of the classics; when a student comes to one of us to discuss a remake of a classic film, we direct them to the original and require them to view it, so we can discuss the differences between the two versions. Often students discover that they prefer the original version to the remake. Exploring the history of cinema on their own, while still being directed in their studies, students can enjoy a more egalitarian experience; instead of relying on secondhand accounts of films in books, students can go directly to the source texts, the films in question, and make their own evaluations.

Instructors, in addition to using DVDs both within and without the classroom, can also turn to the Web, which offers a plethora of useful tutorial tools, although they must be used with care and discretion. The Web is still very much in its infancy, but such resources as the *Internet Archive*'s "Moving Images" section offers free, legal downloads of public domain films, from George Romero's *Night of the Living Dead* (1968) to Salvador Dalí and Luis Buñuel's *Un chien andalou* (1929); as of 17 August 2011, the site had some 3,048 full-length titles available. Rick Prelinger, a collector of educational and industrial films that have fallen into the public domain, also offers a collection of short films for free download at the *Internet Archive*; with some 2,141 films available, Prelinger's collection offers an invaluable view into our shared imagist past.

Added to this, one must also consider the large number of films screened on cable television, especially on Turner Classic Movies (TCM), Sundance, and the Fox Movie Channel. Each of these channels is a twenty-four-hour, commercial-free film festival, in which the films are screened in their original aspect ratios, without any cuts or censorship, providing students with a wide variety of films to view. While most of these films are products of Hollywood, TCM does offer some foreign films, as well as special screenings of silent films. The beginning film student could do much worse than watching TCM for a few months to get some idea of the incredible richness of cinema. In fact, we often assign screenings on TCM to our students and find that they enjoy being able to watch these classic films in the privacy of their own homes, with their friends, to study them together as a group.

In addition, diverse film study materials are available on the Web. Journals such as *Senses of Cinema* and *Cinema Scope* provide authoritative essays by top-notch scholars in the field of film studies. *The Internet Movie Database* (*IMDb*) remains problematic, both because of the excessive number of advertisements and commercial tie-ins that the site displays and because it is not edited; anyone can log in with an opinion, no matter how uninformed, and post a review. Nevertheless, in the matter of film credits and running times, *IMDb* is almost unimpeachable, and it has indeed become the standard database for film statistics.

The other factor to consider is that today's students will inevitably go online first for their information and only use printed texts as a last resort. *Wikipedia* is often the first stop for students in search of information on almost any topic. Since *Wikipedia* is also not rigorously reviewed, the entries have to be read with more than a grain of salt. Some essays are detailed and match anything one could find in a conventional encyclopedia; others are, as *Wikipedia* admits, "stubs," constituted mostly of opinions with little factual material. For this reason, we routinely assign at least two or three research papers a semester that require students to use only print sources found in the library, since they are usually more accurate than online materials and are often the only reliable source of detailed critical materials on older films.

At the same time, it must be acknowledged that any responsible film studies program cannot depend solely on DVDs and should also have high-quality 16mm and 35mm projection facilities available for use. Many administrators refuse to acknowledge this need, much to the detriment of the serious study of film. Many of the most influential films in cinema history are simply not available in DVD, nor are they likely to be in the near future. TCM, in particular, often runs films that are unavailable in DVD or 16mm and is thus an extremely useful resource for both teachers and students.

Experimental films tend to be in 16mm, especially those from the great period in the 1960s, when the format flourished throughout the world, offering an inexpensive option for emerging artists and members of marginalized cultures. Canyon Cinema and the Film-Makers' Cooperative are the two key distributors of personal or experimental cinema in the United States. Nearly all their listings are available only in 16mm, although the work of key experimental auteurs, such as Stan Brakhage and Kenneth Anger, is now being released in DVD. To omit these films from any balanced curriculum of film studies would be a serious oversight.

To this discussion, one must add a few words of warning. DVDs are certainly not the end of the line for film studies. BluRay, the new high-definition DVD format, is gaining rapid acceptance as a mass-market medium. In addition, as the media critic Michael Cieply noted, DVDs are not as stable a medium as many would like to believe. In November 2007, the

Academy of Motion Picture Arts and Sciences published a research study entitled "The Digital Dilemma." As Cieply writes, the study notes that "DVDs tend to degrade: according to the report, only half of a collection of disks can be expected to last for 15 years," eventually becoming entirely unreadable, while conventional safety film can last, under optimal storage conditions, for roughly one hundred years without serious damage.

Indeed, for the moment, Hollywood is storing all its feature films—even those "born digital" or shot entirely on high-definition hard-drive video cameras—on conventional 35mm film masters until they can find a more effective way to stabilize the digital image. Thus even as we use the new digital technology in the classroom, we should be aware of its ephemerality. This technology is just what we are using for the moment; some new moving image platform will certainly come along.

Teaching film in the digital age requires what it always has: a willingness to adapt to new technologies, an understanding of how students perceive contemporary film, a desire to share with students the classic films that make up the history of the cinema, and an understanding that just as the platform for the moving image has changed in the twenty-first century, so the overall study of the cinema has been transformed by the digital revolution. Feature films used to be discrete entities, projected first in theaters and later on television. Now, with a host of competing image sources (cell phones, cable, streaming video), the rules of the game have changed. The moving image is everywhere. There are still auteurs making new films, and there will certainly be new theoretical approaches to address as the medium evolves. The only real danger is when one gets stuck in the past and becomes afraid to move ahead with changing technological developments. The digital world is now an accomplished fact, affecting all we see. No doubt the moving image will continue to evolve throughout our lifetime and beyond, offering new challenges and opportunities to those of us in the classroom.

Work Cited

Cieply, Michael. "The Afterlife Is Expensive for Digital Movies." *New York Times.* New York Times, 23 Dec. 2007. Web. 26 Dec. 2007.

Pat Brereton

Teaching with DVD Add-Ons

DVDs have become important for teaching film. In a recent pilot research project, focus groups drawn from university students emphasized the importance of the directors' commentaries contained in DVD add-ons as a significant feature of their favorite DVDs (Kerr, Kücklich, and Brereton). The growing number and range of add-ons certainly appear to strengthen the appeal of the DVD as a teaching tool. Some writers, including Robert Brookey and Robert Westerfelhaus in their 2002 study of *Fight Club* (1999), have suggested that extra features on DVDs can close down meaning, encouraging the viewer to adapt to a predetermined reading. By contrast, I would argue for the overall usefulness and teaching benefits of DVD add-ons. These can be listed under the following broad headings: adaptation and the study of comparative grammars, film style and a reinvigorated auteur theory, political economy and production history, audience reception, and film criticism and theory (see Brereton, *Consumption*).

The so-called smart cinema, which helps categorize the films discussed here, can be defined very loosely as including all new films that are both commercial and independent and feature ostensibly intelligent subject matter that is primarily aimed at a Generation X audience. DVD add-ons have become an important feature of such films. Furthermore, add-ons to even the most mainstream science fiction films can help audiences engage with developments in new technologies, such as special effects. The directors' commentaries in particular can help promote an understanding and an appreciation of the aesthetic mind-set of a new generation of auteurs. This essay explores the benefits of using add-ons, or bonus features, for teaching film, paying special attention to how directors' commentaries can help students situate and interpret film. I use two case studies—*Donnie Darko* (2002) and *Run Lola Run* (1998)—to illustrate how audio commentaries are useful teaching tools.

Adaptation

From the earliest days of cinema to the present, many narrative films have been based on prior literary properties. With so much add-on material from original sources now becoming available on DVD (including excerpts from the original novel alongside the duplication of storyboards), students are in a good position to compare original sources with the final film version in a much fuller way than ever before. Recent science fiction films on DVD, such as *Star Trek: First Contact* (1996), *Artificial Intelligence: AI* (2001), *Minority Report* (2002), and *The Lord of the Rings* trilogy (2001–03), all include extensive and useful analyses of the process of adaptation from original story and storyboard through to the final film version. Film form draws from other media, especially literature, and students can learn a great deal from their interaction. Appropriate add-ons can also help students in film production learn the skills of narrative construction, visual imaging, and script-writing.

Style

The study of film direction and auteur theory, as well as theories of cinematography, music, performance, and stardom, is facilitated by hearing creative personnel discuss their role in the making of a film. These interventions (either as voice-over commentary synchronized to the film or as behind-the-scenes documentaries) often provide useful material to encourage students to learn more about their chosen medium.[1] The auteur theory continues to be a focus for film studies, and directors' commentaries help promote if not validate its importance. In my experience, students frequently identify the audio commentary track as the most useful DVD extra, including the director's and senior crew members' talking the viewer through the movie experience as the film is playing in the background. Such tracks clearly explain the effects created and directors' overall intent, while also revealing various tricks in the filmmaking trade.

Political Economy and Production History

DVD add-ons can also explain the production background that led to the making of a particular film and investigate the economic barometers of success. Again, especially with high-concept, special-effects-driven films, there is often extensive and detailed production history provided in the add-ons. These typically trace major difficulties in bringing the final concept to screen while outlining the considerable use of creative labor involved in the process. An early example is Steven Spielberg's DVD box set of *Jaws* (1975), which includes ample documentary evidence of the trial-and-error process in making the original blockbuster. In the double-disk version of the same director's *Minority Report* (2002), one add-on feature outlines his desire to construct a "believable" future world. We are consequently informed about how Spielberg brought the "best minds" together for a "technological think tank" with the aim of predicting what would be in vogue over fifty years from now. Alongside detailing endless trial-and-error mock-ups of how to visualize this future world, members of the large film production team are shown experimenting on various technical and new aesthetic strategies designed to help underpin Spielberg's and Stanley Kubrick's often contrasting visions of the original short story by Philip K. Dick. Such add-on material helps tease out the process around the conception and execution of new special effects.[2]

Peter Jackson stands out among contemporary directors for his extensive use of add-ons in his films, including supplemental material on the *Lord of the Rings* trilogy and his 2005 *King Kong* remake.[3] Like Spielberg, Jackson celebrates the process of production and adaptation by meticulously documenting every storyboard and every creative decision. Jackson even suggests in his commentary that the format affords him more creative space to showcase his extensive production process; he believes that audience expectations are different for such material. Fans of his films can "wade" through the recorded process of filmmaking and even engage step-by-step with the creative decisions necessary to transform such a mega business project into the final edited version.[4]

At a more macro level, critics have also noted how some DVDs of historical classics have add-ons that provide evidence of the longitudinal placement of the film within the movie company's stable of productions. This information can initiate a useful business case study, as well as expose whether the text fits into predetermined genres.[5]

Film Studies Debates and Audience Reception

Teaching film studies inevitably involves an exploration of debates about how class, race, and gender are represented on film. DVD add-ons can promote group discussion of these issues. Film debates about race have been greatly augmented by excellent historical documentaries, which have accompanied the DVD release of classics like *Birth of a Nation* (1915). Similarly, add-ons can provide useful "raw material" that aid the study of other core debates across a growing catalog of DVDs on the market. Old promotional trailers, when included in class, can enable students to explore the contextual relation of the film and its historical antecedents and to unpack the film's contemporary relevance for audiences. The double-disk release of Alfred Hitchcock's *Strangers on a Train* (1951) or the DVD box set of his films including both *Rear Window* (1954) and *Vertigo* (1958) offer a compilation of trailers.

DVD Add-Ons and *Smart Cinema*

Smart cinema has become a popular term of reference for a broad strand of recent cinema. In addition to viewing add-ons from DVDs, a new generation of students appears to have acquired an aesthetic taste and fascination for consuming such films.[6] Jeffrey Sconce maintains that an ironic stance is a key aspect of this mode of filmmaking. He lists five elements that many of these new films share: a cultivation of "blank" style and incongruous narration, a fascination with "synchronicity" as a principle of narrative organization, a related thematic interest in random fate, a focus on the white middle-class family as a crucible of miscommunication and emotional dysfunctionality, and a recurring interest in the politics of taste, consumerism, and identity ("Irony" 368).

Donnie Darko

While I cannot tease out the full implications of smart cinema here, I can say that it appears to inform a wide range of recent films and, from my teaching experience, seems to speak to a new generational pleasure.

Donnie Darko certainly embodies this trajectory as it plays out its examination of a dysfunctional middle-class high school student, whose pose is simultaneously likable and sardonic and who occasionally forgets his medication. As a consequence, he experiences nocturnal visitations from a "rabbit-wizard" who informs him that the end of the world is near. Sconce suggests that random fate and apparent narrative synchronicity or coincidence are characteristic of smart film as a type; these factors are also critical in driving *Donnie Darko*'s strange fable, as both Donnie and the audience try to make sense of an increasingly enigmatic story line.

Barbara Klinger's research on the consumption habits of students and their repeat home screenings of DVDs suggests that rewatching is becoming more common among new generations of cineastes.[7] Certainly, the complexity of the narrative of a film such as *Donnie Darko* demands multiple viewings to clear up any difficulties the viewer might have in decoding the confusing story line. Repeated viewing is also driven by the audience's desire to use DVD add-on material to maximize their viewing pleasure.

But, first, a few more words on the film itself. The use of irony, as Sconce suggests, is often associated in smart cinema with everything subversive, hateful, and evil linked to the conservative right, exemplified in *Donnie Darko* by the old-fashioned, traditional teacher who is juxtaposed with the more appealing, decadent, secular, young humanist teacher (played by Drew Barrymore). Sconce concludes that for leftist viewers, smart cinema like *Donnie Darko*—particularly in its contrasting representations of teaching—advocates an irresponsible "resignation to the horrors of life under advanced capitalism and an attendant disregard for the traditional villains of racism, sexism and class division" (368). By contrast, for those coming from a more conservative perspective, such films "seem to advance an irresponsible worldview where truth and morality are no longer of concern" (Sconce, "Smart Cinema" 437). Both interventions and contrasting readings help frame a range of new debates around audience consumption and textual analysis across the old/new media divide.

Donnie Darko remains one of the most explicitly intertextual evocations of the new aesthetic as defined by Sconce.[8] The film's DVD add-ons can serve as a useful element for teaching and articulating this apparently new aesthetic and even protocol for engaging with film. I focus here on the opening of the film and Richard Kelly's voice-over. As we learn from his commentary, Kelly was apparently worried he would get into some trouble with the style of the opening credits and its "Arabic" typeface, since the film was released so soon after the 2001 terrorist attacks.[9] The events of 9/11 appear to have affected the fate of the film on several levels, as the scholar Geoff King has made clear (not on the DVD), citing the allegorical significance of a plane engine crashing into Donnie's house.

In the opening scene, in which Donnie wakes up in the middle of a road in the hills overlooking his hometown, the director speaks of the influence of Montgomery Clift in *A Place in the Sun* (1951) and his desire for a stunning opening exposition. The sequence also insinuates a comic book tableau: the main character is summoned up to the mountain (like other mythic comic characters) for reasons he does not understand. Then, after seeing Donnie cycle back down into his hometown (reminiscent of a Spielberg mise-en-scène), we notice his mother reading Stephen King's *It*. This novel, we are informed on the voice-over, is the director's favorite, yet it has nothing to do with the mother's motivation in the scene.[10]

Later, after a family squabble at dinner, we witness Donnie taking his medicine and are informed by Kelly of the difficulty of visually getting the bathroom mirror cabinet framed correctly to reflect Donnie's face, serving to foreground a useful problem-solving cinematographic exercise. The director asserts that the medicine used by Donnie was supposed to be understood by the viewer as a placebo, encouraging the spectator to question Donnie's psychological makeup. This reading, of which there is little evidence on-screen, also raises the question of whether Kelly is foreclosing audience interpretation of the scene. It is now difficult to read the placebo-effect incident without considering whether it was seen pre- or postcommentary. In any case, the expressionist camera setup of the mirror scene insinuates that something is wrong in the protagonist's universe and that he is mentally unstable, while also inferring Donnie has somehow been chosen to do something out of the ordinary.

Later, we are introduced to a slow-motion sequence of a high school locker space that, as several critics have claimed, is deemed to be brilliantly evocative and resonant of so many other filmic interpretations of teen culture. As King describes the scene:

> [I]t begins very distinctively, with the camera positioned on its side as Donnie disembarks from the school bus, before righting itself and moving laterally away to the opening piano notes of "Head over Heels" by Tears for Fears. A new shot picks up Donnie and two friends inside the door, following them and introducing several other characters in an elaborate unbroken series of steadicam maneuvers that includes two near 180-degree rapid pans and sped-up sequences involving the movements of Kitty Farmer and Principle Cole. (82)

King provides this very close reading of the scene in Donnie Darko *(Cultographies)*, a helpful benchmark for film students in developing their writing skills; his work represents the kind of analysis rarely available in DVD add-on material. In most instances, the best critical analysis is still found outside the purview of DVD add-ons. Exceptions include the repackaging of classic box sets, like Hitchcock's, or the repurposing of art house classics from Criterion's back catalog, where film academics have taken charge of writing and framing the add-ons, including the director's commentary and other forms of interpretative analysis, all of which are directly applicable for pedagogic purposes.[11]

Frequently, the director's commentary serves to undercut the multiple meanings of a scene, which paradoxically feed into a film's cult status for audiences. In this process, the voice-over often strives to add apparently irrelevant contextual allusions, which might even serve to make the scene enigmatic and confusing, especially for audiences attempting to reread the film. Yet this somewhat elusive strategy can also be considered part of the new discursive contract with audiences, while consciously affirming the cerebral game of decoding the text. The add-on voice-over provides an insider's point of view of the screen worldview, and, while sometimes sending up authorial seriousness, it also calls to mind various pitfalls in the development of film studies as a discipline, particularly around the primacy of the text versus the "intentionalist fallacy." Kelly's off-the-cuff directorial voice-over recounts numerous naive observations that are avoided in more established critical expositions.

Run Lola Run

While *Donnie Darko* "uses a time-loop strategy to ponder the synchronicity of the universe," *Run Lola Run* "uses a tripartite structure to foreground the fates of synchronicity as a formal and thematic strategy" (Sconce, "Irony" 363). *Run Lola Run* draws on the attributes of smart aesthetics while also foregrounding the structure of game play. It tells the story of a young German woman, Lola, who has twenty minutes to replace one hundred thousand marks that her boyfriend, Manni, lost. She must do so, moreover, before the gangsters (to whom he owes the money) exact the ultimate retribution. Her quest is replayed through the repetition of three slightly different versions of the story as she attempts to get the money from her father. The first ends in the police's capture of her and Manni and in the accidental shooting of Lola. The second ends with the accidental death of Manni after Lola has successfully managed to obtain the money by robbing the Deutsche Transfer Bank where her father works. The third ends with Manni recovering the money and Lola winning the same amount at roulette; both characters are alive in the end.

Run Lola Run is regarded by some as an important crossover narrative between film and video game logic that foregrounds synchronicity in its narrative structure. It has become a core text in much new media research. According to Claudia Mesch, the film depicts its setting as a

> cyberspace obstacle course or environment usually associated with interactive video and computer games. The eerie emptiness of the Berlin of *Run Lola Run*, a fantasy projected onto a city which has been called the single biggest construction site in Europe, is necessary to keep the protagonist Lola moving at high speed from the West to the East part of town and back again—another fantasy which is only possible when the city is recast as a virtual environment. (par. 1)[12]

In the director's commentary on *Run Lola Run*, Tom Tykwer debunks the idea that the film is heavily influenced by game structures or that it is conceived as a critique of more established realist conventions in film. Tykwer's commentary is certainly informative, with lots of interesting elements often missing from the *Donnie Darko* commentary; it also augments the enjoyment of the film. We are informed, for example, that the shooting ratio was around 20 to 1, which is high by any standard and affirms the film's formal experimental strategies and art house credentials. The basic idea for the film came from an image of a girl running. Tykwer states that this iconic image is the "essence of cinema," dramatizing movement and suspense. Many of the background characters are delineated using a very quick "flash-forward" of still images and are designed to illustrate the future for such characters. They are only seen in the background and as backstories, yet they are all well-known German actors who one would expect to be lead performers in any other film. This conceit apparently worked well as an in-house joke for German audiences.

Telling the story three times is also rationalized in various ways. The director says that he was naturally very worried that audiences would become bored, echoing the risk displayed in more established Hollywood-driven films, such as *Groundhog Day* (1993). Hence, it was imperative to have variations in the replay. This strategy corresponds with research carried out on video games, which concludes that each experience of playing a game is different despite the similarity of the broad narrative structure. In turn, this discourse echoes earlier media debates concerning the generic pleasure of repetition and formulaic expression of codes and conventions.[13]

The two examples explored here emphasize the pedagogic usefulness of DVD add-ons, especially the directors' commentaries. Academic film criticism ought to engage with such add-on material in the process of examining the film text and acknowledge its usefulness as part of the process of textual engagement, rather than simply dismiss it as marketing "shovel ware," to use an e-journalism term. Here I have outlined only some of the interconnections between new media pleasures and pedagogy offered by DVD add-ons. I have listed some of the main teaching benefits for harnessing such pleasures for educational objectives while remaining strongly committed to the view that effective media literacy strategies must, where possible, be based on an understanding and legitimation of students' use patterns and preferences. While most of the best critical analysis of film remains outside the DVD package, I would nonetheless suggest that such freely available add-ons help frame how new audiences engage with movies. Even if some add-ons remain self-serving advertisements, many others can affirm the cerebral game of decoding film, which in turn encourages students to test their pleasures while trying to understand the text. Add-ons often strengthen the overall appeal of this consumer-driven medium for audiences and can also have significant educational applications. With a growing interest in convergence within new media research,[14] DVD add-ons provide a bridge to conventional film study and assist in exploring how new generational cineastes connect with the medium.

Notes

My forthcoming book, *Smart Cinema: DVD Add-Ons and New Audience Pleasures*, extends the analysis presented here and examines *Donnie Darko* and *Run Lola Run* across two different chapters.

1. For examples of the quirky subversion of the "serious" exposition around the making of feature films, see *Sideways* (2004), where we witness the crew getting more and more drunk and shooting very little footage, as well as the more conventional if nonetheless offbeat affirmation of the creative process in Michel Gondry's *The Science of Sleep* (2006).

2. For example, the chief designer Alex McDowell is shown explaining the development of the graphic work needed to create the three-legged spider, using graphic animation techniques that interest students of filmmaking. Particularly impressive is the automatic program, which helped build the set in 3-D and can tell the camera how to shoot the shot without making "mistakes."

3. Alternatively, however, note Fox's release of the *Alien* series in 2003, including a nine-disk set containing over fifty-eight hours of *Alien* footage and add-ons. Unlike Jackson's oeuvre, this franchise does not necessarily cohere within authorial terms, since different directors stamped their unique style on the four films in the series.

4. As Pavel Skopal notes, "New Line Entertainment sold over 20 million copies of *The Fellowship of the Rings* (2001) in four versions (on the North American market)" and "Amazon.com offers 16 different DVD products from the franchise, which is extraordinary by any measure of marketing success" (qtd. in Brereton, "Consumption" 117).

5. Paul Grainge traces how the DVD release of *North by Northwest* (1959) was packaged in 2001 with the contemporary logo of Warner Bros. (the MGM back catalog was owned by Turner Entertainment, a subsidiary of Time Warner). By replacing and refreshing old studio signatures, media corporations have been able to claim proprietary rights over Hollywood's past, a form of brand annexation tied to the appropriation and circulation of competing logos (352).

6. For instance, many recent American films call into question the boundaries between perception, memory, and reality, which were previously the preserve of the European art cinema from the 1960s and 1970s. Films such as David Cronenberg's *eXistenZ* (1999), Spike Jonze's *Being John Malkovich* (1999), David Lynch's *Mulholland Drive* (2001), Christopher Nolan's *Memento* (2000), Jonze's *Adaptation* (2002), and Michel Gondry's *Eternal Sunshine of the Spotless Mind* (2004) address similar debates and issues while connecting with a new generation of cineastes and using a range of innovative smart new media techniques. See Allen 139–67 for a broad survey of smart film and its antecedents.

7. Klinger explains how laser disks, which preceded DVDs, offered the contemporary "cinephile" the opportunity to become steeped in a "plethora of seemingly exclusive behind-the-scenes facts" (55). Unfortunately there is little explicit audience study around the use of DVD add-ons, but she speaks convincingly of the enticements to consume film at home, which increased enormously with DVDs. DVD add-ons have become popular with new generations of viewers, much in line with what Klinger equates with interactive or "karaoke" forms of consumption.

8. Incidentally, like many cult classics, it bombed on initial release, and the director Richard Kelly blamed its poor performance on the distribution strategy, arguing that the film was opened too widely (King 19). The film made only $515,545 at the domestic box office but has made more than $10 million in DVD sales stemming from the film's cult following (Beck 57–58).

9. As Sconce suggests, "by the time hijacked planes destroyed the World Trade Centre on September 11, 2001, it was clear that 'irony' had become an extremely charged code word masking a number of larger social, cultural, and aesthetic divisions" ("Smart Cinema" 437). For this reason it is suggested that any reference to planes falling from the sky as in *Donnie Darko* could no longer be regarded as somehow "ironic" and hence audiences did not appreciate the story line and the film failed at the box office.

10. An overt reference is made to Graham Greene's short story "The Destructors." The director tells us in voice-over how it was the best short story he

ever read and serves as a metastory for Donnie to express himself and his postmodern schizophrenic self.

11. Film scholars such as Laura Mulvey, David Bordwell, and others have been engaged by Criterion to edit the add-on material for collectors' box sets of classic films. Richard Dyer's study of David Fincher's *Se7en* (1999) for the British Film Institute and his extensive analysis on the two-disk DVD version of the film are very useful. This linkage between academics and the film industry is pushed one step further in the DVD special edition of *Easy Rider* (1969), which also includes the British Film Institutes's classic monograph on the film by Lee Hill (originally published in 1996). Such innovative cross-fertilizing between the industry and the academy will certainly assist in developing the study of cinema.

12. Meanwhile, David Martin-Jones, in a provocative reading, also suggests that the film focuses "exclusively on the present moment, and does so to offer three possible futures for recently reunified Germany" (100–01).

13. Incidentally, according to Tykwer and his leading actress, Franka Potente, whose commentary is also heard on the add-on, the key sequences for both actor and director were the quiet bed scenes that were shot with a simple red light and counterpointed with the more frequent, high-energy action scenes. Meanwhile, Potente keeps reflecting on the boredom of the filmmaking process, which seems a long way from the ironic playfulness of so-called smart cinema. Yet, instead of demystifying the creative process, such observations serve to stress the effort and care needed to create the final result.

14. See, for instance, Jenkins and Deuze, who suggest that there can and should be a "rapprochement between industry studies and audience research" (5) and that the current global digital culture should be understood as what Lev Manovich "calls a culture of remix and remixibility" (qtd. in Jenkens and Deuze 7). They conclude by asserting that "we need to rethink the categories and perspectives through which we have traditionally framed media phenomena to respond to a profound and prolonged period of media in transition, but we need to do more than that and think more deeply about our roles as academics and our shifting relationships with both media industries and audiences" (11). Understanding the place of DVD add-ons as part of a complex intertexual relation of industry, text, and audiences is part of this new media process and in line with what Jenkins and Deuze suggest.

Works Cited

Allen, Michael. *Contemporary US Cinema*. London: Longman, 2003. Print.

Beck, James C. "The Concept of Narration: An Analysis of *Requiem for a Dream* (.com) and *Donnie Darko*(.com)." *Convergence: The International Journal of Research into New Media Technologies* 10 (2004): 55–82. Print.

Brereton, Pat, ed. *Consumption and Use of DVD Add-Ons*. Spec. issue of *Convergence: The International Journal of Research into New Media Technologies* 13.2 (2007): 115–206. Print.

———. "The Consumption and Use of DVDs and Their Add-Ons." Brereton, *Consumption* 115–17.

Brookey, Robert A., and Robert Westerfelhaus. "Hiding Homoeroticism in Plain View: The *Fight Club* DVD as Digital Closet." *Critical Studies in Media Communication* 19.1 (2002): 21–43. Print.

Grainge, Paul. "Branding Hollywood: Studio Logos and the Aesthetics of Memory and Hype." *Screen* 45 (2004): 344–62. Print.

Jenkins, Henry, and Mark Deuze. "Convergence Culture." *Convergence: The International Journal of Research into New Media Technologies* 14.1 (2008): 5–12. Print.

Kerr, Aphra, Julian Kücklich, and Pat Brereton. "New Media—New Pleasures?" *International Journal of Cultural Studies* 9.1 (2006): 63–82. Print.

King, Geoff. Donnie Darko *(Cultographies)*. London: Wallflower, 2007. Print.

Klinger, Barbara. *Beyond the Multiplex: Cinema, New Technologies, and the Home.* Berkeley: U of California P, 2006. Print.

Martin-Jones, David. *Deleuze, Cinema and Identity: Narrative Time in National Contexts.* Edinburgh: Edinburgh UP, 2006. Print.

Mesch, Claudia. "Racing Berlin: The Games of *Run Lola Run*." *M/C Journal: A Journal of Media and Culture* 3.3 (2000): n. pag. Web. June 2005.

Sconce, Jeffrey. "Irony, Nihilism and the New American 'Smart' Film." *Screen* 43.4 (2002): 349–69. Print.

———. "Smart Cinema." *Contemporary American Cinema.* Ed. Linda Ruth Williams and Michael Hammond. Buckingham: Open UP, 2006. 429–39. Print.

Tara McPherson

Teaching US Television in an Era of Convergence

I have taught Introduction to US Television many times during the past fifteen years. Whether at interdisciplinary academic conferences or at dinner parties (even in Hollywood), the revelation that I teach such a course is often met with a series of bemused questions, including "Do you teach them to use a remote?" and "Do they really get credit for that?" Many humanities departments in US universities have seamlessly integrated the study of film into their curricula, but television has been less successfully or extensively sutured into many of these same departments. This difference derives in part from ongoing and elitist dismissals of television as a low cultural object, as a feminized and thus debased medium (see Petro), a position reflected in those dinner party questions I often hear. In addition, television also poses a difficult problem for the more text-based practices and methodologies dominant in many English or literature departments.

While students might successfully engage a single film in a manner akin to (if still different from) the analysis of a novel, the object of television studies is often called into question. Stephen Heath has observed that television is "a somewhat difficult object, unstable, all over the place" (267). To paraphrase Raymond Williams, is it a technology or a cultural form? His answer is that it is both and more, but this multiple status, coupled with anxieties about television's banality, knocks roughly against many of the methodologies of the humanities. We might understand and interpret a single television series or episode through its formal structures, authorial signature, or aesthetic principles, but television also calls for a more systematic examination that exceeds the contours of any single series, shifting the critical eye toward networks of distribution and enmeshed media practices. Film must also be studied as at once an aesthetic and an industrial form, pushing beyond the singular text toward a variety of systemic analyses.

Indeed, one might argue that the structures of today's globalized media economies reveal the lie behind any curricular fantasy that film and television are discreet or singular systems that might be taught separately. The various audiovisual streams of film, television, popular music, and print publishing exist in tight feedback loops in our contemporary era of media convergence. As a media stream that offers up both discrete texts (including television series that aspire to "art house" status, repackaged in DVD collectors' box sets) and remediated content (revealing complex transmedia flows), the study of television affords students the chance to engage with questions of political economies, media ownership, remix cultures, and taste and aesthetics. In short, television needs to be studied both in its specificity and in its overlaps with other forms of media to engage students in the critical literacies necessary for informed citizenship in the twenty-first century. Perhaps because of television's instability as well as its seemingly endless ability to remediate its predecessors and successors, its study provides students with a robust opportunity for understanding not only television's forms and cultural refractions but also the rapidly shifting media ecologies of the digital era.

This essay addresses the difficulties and advantages of teaching television in a moment of medial remediation by examining a layered approach to the medium that might be adapted in a survey course on American television or in various thematic courses that can bring different media into productive dialogue.

Designing a Survey Course in Television

The last twenty years has seen an explosive growth not only in television, as we have moved to a postnetwork era of literally hundreds of competing channels, but also in television studies. Academic presses now publish several book series focused on television, the Society for Cinema Studies has morphed into the Society for Cinema and Media Studies (SCMS) and has a "scholarly interest group" centered on television, and several ongoing conferences take television as their main focus. *Cinema Journal*, the official SCMS publication, was edited by Heather Hendershot, a television scholar, and has featured special "In Focus" sections on television studies in 2005 and 2008 (see, e.g., Brunsdon). Television studies today has expanded far beyond its earlier social science and mass communication roots, often drawing from contemporary developments in critical theory, film theory, cultural studies, and theories of gender, sexuality, race, and globalization.

In designing a large survey course in US television, I have found it useful to frame the study of television in a layered approach that considers the medium in relation to texts, contexts, and what I would call pretexts, while also drawing out explicit comparisons to film and other media. Across such a syllabus, students are able to come to an understanding of television's complex status as at once an aesthetic, industrial, cultural, and technological form, situating it in relation to other vectors of both old and new media.

Television as Text

Even in the University of Southern California's School of Cinematic Arts (formerly known as the School of Cinema and Television), with a longstanding curriculum in both film and television, students often arrive on campus with a marked preference for the study of film. In such a setting, it is helpful to approach the television text in a comparative mode, drawing out similarities and differences between film and television, particularly in terms of formal analyses, aesthetics, and questions of authorship. A textbook like Jeremy Butler's *Television: Critical Methods and Applications* parallels the analysis of film offered by the now canonical film studies text *Film Art: An Introduction* (Bordwell and Thompson). Working with such a text, an instructor is able to foreground formal, stylistic, and aesthetic analyses of television, engaging such issues as narrative structure, editing, cinematography, mise-en-scène, and performance. Opening a survey class in this manner affords a certain destabilization of the television text, pushing students toward an engagement with television as a formal system of meaning with particular narrative and aesthetic conventions. (This destabilization is particularly important given the widespread tendency among students to see television as ubiquitous beyond analysis, echoing Heath's observations about the difficulty of representing television.) Connecting these conventions to those used by cinema in a comparative mode further allows students to begin to track a history of the construction of the moving image across the twentieth century.

Students are often surprised to see the stability of certain editing, narrative, and stylistic conventions across media forms and historical periods and to realize that such conventions also shape the nonfiction forms of television news and commercials. Once comfortable with such comparative analysis, students also begin to see the blur between media, noting the mutual influence film and television exert on each other, as well as points of important distinction, such as television's segmented narrative or use of different camera setups.

These investigations of the formal structures of the televisual text open a series of related considerations. Students quickly come to realize the importance of the serial form to television, and the examination of the serial points toward nuanced understandings of the relation of narrative structure to constructions of gender. In scholarship ranging from the early work of Tania Modleski on soap operas to later work on the widespread serialization of many television formats (see Joyrich; McPherson), the serial narratives of television bear a privileged relation to how we come to understand femininity, masculinity, and sexuality. In a similar manner, questions of genre are usefully taken up within a discussion of the television text. While some genres may be productively considered alongside those prevalent in film (e.g., comedy, animation, the western) other television genres such as the music video or reality TV offer the opportunity to examine how television functions generatively, particularly in the creation of markets. Finally, analyses of the television text unfold easily into examinations of how television texts relate to one another, setting the stage to talk about the strategies by which television manages time while also staging a specific relation to the now and the live (see R. Williams; Feuer).

Television as Context

This comparative model works equally well when considering television's contexts. Primed to think about differences and continuities between television and film at the level of form, students quickly come to articulate various ways in which we engage each medium. If television's narratives and flow manage and indeed produce time in particular ways, television also bears an interesting relation to constructions of space. Students can come to a rich understanding of television's form when they begin to consider its viewing contexts. Television exists in myriad contexts outside the darkened space of the theater and so does not organize the viewer's engagement in the same way film does, even while both media use overlapping formal techniques. Many scholars have commented on the ways in which television privileges the glance rather than the sustained gaze courted by cinema, partially because of the busy and distracting setting in which television viewing often takes place. Lynn Spigel has analyzed television's place within the home, underscoring the medium's role in consolidating a particular vision of both American domesticity and suburbia. Anna McCarthy, Victoria Johnson, and Mark Williams push these spatial analyses toward the public realm, helping students understand the ways in which television mediates our sense of the local, the regional, and the national. Film scholarship also highlights the role that film plays in constructing a spatial imaginary, but television studies often takes up the interrelation of text and context differently.

If the spatial contexts of television provide productive grounds for engaging students, the commercial context of television also offers a useful springboard for discussion. While film and television are both commercial media, television wears its relation to the commodity in much more obvious ways. The intrusion of the advertisement into the flow of narrative in "typical" broadcast television makes apparent television's dual status as narrative and commodity form and heightens the interplay of text and context. Students are often eager to discuss the tension between television's commercial role and its potential to open up a type of public forum (see Newcomb and Hirsch). Such a focus on context points toward considerations of the many functions television plays not only as a generator of fictional formats but also as a purveyor of news, weather, sports, and "lifestyle" programming, among other types. Considerations of television's commodity status also point to investigations of the television audience and to questions of identity, taste, quality, and fandom. And while the survey course outlined here focuses on US television in a domestic context, American television travels around the globe, and various diasporic televisions are popular in the United States, suggesting strategies for addressing the global flow of media (see Parks and Kumar; Naficy).

While film courses often push beyond textual analyses to consider various cultural contexts of consumption and production, television affords the possibility to address these questions through a variety of lenses. Many contextual approaches meld the methodologies of the interpretative humanities (including analyses of narrative, aesthetics, and textual form) with those more typical of the social sciences. Film and television studies have mined these dual traditions, but television studies owes a greater debt to the social sciences, particularly in ethnographic accounts of the audience (see, e.g., Ang; Seiter) or in works tracking industrial and political economies (see Boddy; Caldwell; Lotz).

Television as Pretext

If considerations of the television text can lead to fruitful engagements with the contexts of television, it is also helpful to think about the ways in which teaching television can serve as a pretext for taking up other pressing questions. Because television is expansive (continually producing new styles and forms) and voracious (repackaging film and other media with some ease), studying television sets the stage for studying shifting media ecologies. Television offers a compelling platform for engaging notions of intermediality; such questions play out as different television series, channels, and formats remediate other media. Television is usefully considered side by side with film, but television is also an electronic medium, as closely tied to radio and to the computer as to cinema. It thus bears a special relation to networked flows of information and to our increasingly digital media environments. As Henry Jenkins, Anne Friedberg, and others have argued, interesting patterns of convergence surface in television. They open up the space to push our students toward important engagements with media and historical specificity and feed back into discussions of text and context, as our students increasingly watch television on a variety of screens and devices.

These patterns of convergence also track to the consolidation of media industries and to the public's right to access information. Because television began as a broadcast medium closely tied to a conception of the airwaves as a public good, the study of television offers a compelling prehistory to contemporary debates of Web neutrality, open access, privacy, and digital transparency. Students may not be easily engaged by what they see as "old media" histories, but they tend to take notice when these histories are tied to current discussions of digital culture, remix, and the future of the Internet.

Using platforms like *YouTube* in class helps drive these points home and opens up conversations about the flow of images across media spaces. As recently as 2000, it was quite challenging to procure materials for television classes. A relatively narrow range of series was available on video or DVD, and the postcable expansion of television had not yet multiplied into a plethora of syndication-driven channels. A small community of television scholars tended to circulate worn copies of a few historical shows and to teach many contemporary texts. The ability to teach television's relation to crisis, to the live, or to politics was often dependent on being by your VCR at just the right time. *YouTube* and similar sites now provide a veritable treasure trove of clips for a television course, and using them in the classroom affords another opportunity to discuss patterns of media ownership, fandom, and convergence culture. In addition, emerging platforms like the Critical Commons project, led by Steve Anderson, provide media scholars the opportunity to archive and share clips used in teaching and research and to engage students in the process. Questions of copyright and fair use lace neatly back into questions of television's texts and contexts.

Beyond the Survey

As the sole essay on television in a volume on teaching film, this essay remains necessarily broad. I have chosen to focus on the survey class to map a general set of conceptual frameworks within which one might teach television within a humanities department and in relation to film and other media. Nonetheless, one might imagine many of these topics addressed within upper-division courses, including courses like Convergence Media; Television and the Commodity Form; Space, Time, and Television; or Television and Media Ecologies. In addition, many of the approaches explored in relation to film in this volume—ranging from explorations of national cinemas to generic conventions to historical analyses to questions of gender, sexuality, or race—might profitably be extended to television courses, or, alternatively, television might be considered within those film courses, introducing an element of intermediality and a comparative framework. A rich body of research on various national television industries and on the global flow of television across borders is now available. Such materials open up new parameters for the study of television's texts, contexts, and pretexts.

Works Cited

Ang, Ien. *Living Room Wars: Rethinking Media Audiences for a Postmodern World.* London: Routledge, 1996. Print.

Boddy, William. *Fifties Television: The Industry and Its Critics.* Urbana: U of Illinois P, 1993. Print.

Bordwell, David, and Kristin Thompson. *Film Art: An Introduction.* 9th ed. New York: McGraw, 2009. Print.

Brunsdon, Charlotte. "Introduction." *Cinema Journal* 47.3 (2008): 122–27. Print.

Butler, Jeremy. *Television: Critical Methods and Applications.* 3rd ed. Mahwah: Erlbaum, 2002. Print.

Caldwell, John. *Production Culture: Industrial Reflexivity and Critical Practice in Film and Television.* Durham: Duke UP, 2008. Print. Console-ing Passions.

Feuer, Jane. "Melodrama, Serial Form, and Television Today." *Screen* 25.1 (1984): 4–16. Print.

Friedberg, Anne. *The Virtual Window: From Alberti to Microsoft.* Cambridge: MIT P, 2006. Print.

Heath, Stephen. "Representing Television." *Logics of Television: Essays in Cultural Criticism.* Ed. Patricia Mellencamp. Bloomington: Indiana UP, 1990. 267–300. Print.

Jenkins, Henry. *Convergence Culture: Where Old and New Media Collide.* New York: New York UP, 2006. Print.

Johnson, Victoria. *Heartland TV: Prime Time Television and the Struggle for US Identity.* New York: New York UP, 2008. Print.

Joyrich, Lynne. *Re-viewing Reception: Television, Gender, and Postmodern Culture.* Bloomington: Indiana UP, 1996. Print. Theories of Contemporary Culture.

Lotz, Amanda. *The Television Will Be Revolutionized.* New York: New York UP, 2007. Print.

McCarthy, Anna. *Ambient Television: Visual Culture and Public Space.* Durham: Duke UP, 2001. Print. Console-ing Passions.

McPherson, Tara. "'The End of TV As We Know It': Convergence Anxiety, Generic Innovation, and the Case of *24*." *Oxford Handbook of Film and Media Studies.* Ed. Robert Kolker. London: Oxford UP, 2008. 306–26. Print.

Modleski, Tania. *Loving with a Vengeance: Mass Produced Fantasies for Women.* Hamden: Archon, 1982. Print.

Naficy, Hamid. *The Making of Exile Cultures: Iranian Television in Los Angeles.* Minneapolis: U of Minnesota P, 1993. Print.

Newcomb, Horace, and Paul Hirsch. "Television as a Cultural Forum." *Quarterly Review of Film Studies* 8 (1983): 45–55. Print.

Parks, Lisa, and Shanti Kumar, eds. *Planet TV: A Global Television Reader.* New York: New York UP, 2003. Print.

Petro, Patrice. "Mass Culture and the Feminine: The 'Place' of Television in Film Studies." *Cinema Journal* 25.3 (1986): 5–21. Print.

Seiter, Ellen. *Television and New Media Audiences.* London: Oxford UP, 1999. Print.

Spigel, Lynn. *Make Room for Television: Television and the Family Ideal in Postwar America.* Chicago: U of Chicago P, 1992. Print.

Williams, Mark. "Entertaining 'Difference': Strains of Orientalism in Early Los Angeles Television." *Living Color: Race and Television in the United States.* Ed. Sasha Torres. Durham: Duke UP, 1998. 12–34. Print.

Williams, Raymond. *Television: Technology and Cultural Form.* London: Fontana, 1974. Print.

Michael Aronson

Teaching Film and the Internet

My students call it "going down the rabbit hole." It began as an exercise that I created for an advanced undergraduate course on film historiography, but it is now something that I have almost all my students do, from graduates in seminars to freshmen in my 250-student "history of film" lecture. The assignment starts with the title of an individual film and the film's associated entry on *Wikipedia*. In a course on Warner Bros. and the history of the studio system, the film selected was *The Jazz Singer* (1927). Each student is required to choose three pieces of information about the film found on the *Wikipedia* page; past examples include a name associated with the production of the film, a statement about the film's initial reception, or even an image of a poster, a ubiquitous element for film entries on *Wikipedia*. The assignment is then to attempt to trace this fact or object back to an original source, a primary document. Students may, if possible, accomplish this task entirely online or, if truly desperate, walk across campus and physically enter the university's library. Finally, they post the results of their labor on the course's internal wiki page about the film. They are expected to include a reflective narrative tracing out their research process, and its results, including all relevant citations, as well as, if they are successful, a PDF attachment or embedded video providing visual evidence of the primary sources they located. Questions they must ask and answer of their sources include the following: Who wrote or made this? Who is the intended audience for it? What did its maker want? What rhetorical strategies are embedded in this object? The collective result of the students' individual efforts ends up being a kind of historiographic mirror held up to the original *Wikipedia* entry, although the image it reveals almost always ends up much messier and less cohesive, revealing gaps, fissures, and many a frustrating dead end. This complex outcome, I teach them, is a good thing.[1]

Today, most teachers have developed an opinion about the place of *Wikipedia* in the research process, particularly when it comes to the work of their students. Some instructors may be of the belief that it represents the intellectual downfall of humankind (or at least the undergraduate percentage of it) and may even attempt to ban its use by students doing research-based assignments for their courses (which likely results only in students not citing their use of it; see Cohen). Others have clicked through to an entry from a *Google* search enough times in both our academic and everyday lives to come to the conclusion that *Wikipedia* as a resource is uneven, productive and surprisingly enlightening in places, banal or plain wrong in others. Many of us explain to our students the problematic of non-peer-reviewed, crowd-sourced material and urge them to at least look to the bottom of the page for citational evidence that demonstrates that the entry is derived from reliable sources, those that can be trusted to provide accurate information.

This is what I used to do. But as I came to realize over the last few years, mostly while in the process of engaging in my own research, the definition of terms like "reliable sources" and "accurate information" (even if you are not a poststructuralist) are particularly slippery when digging into the rapidly expanding, ever changing digital landscape of online material related to the study of film. How can we teach students to judge for themselves which citation at the bottom of the *Wikipedia* page is reliable? When looking at the copy of a poster on the screen, or, more likely, the copy of a copy of a copy, how exactly does one determine provenance—what exactly counts as a primary or reliable source these days? How can we teach our students not just to retrieve information but also to evaluate both its provenance and value? In an era in which students can access content almost as fast (or faster) than we can teach it, how can we use online resources to close the gap between the habits of mind we wish to impart and the activities students perform? It was with these questions in mind that

I created the "rabbit hole" exercise, not simply to highlight for students the specific strengths and weaknesses of *Wikipedia*, but rather to begin teaching them how to effectively tackle the problems, possibilities, and pleasures of all forms of online film research.

This exercise, it should be said, takes time, time that could be used for other things, including teaching content. Even in my large historical film survey course, my lectures now include fewer dates, fewer names, and even fewer clips. Instead, my teaching in the classroom is designed to model the historical-critical thinking I want students to bring to their work, the mastery of a process rather than a particular body of information. The time I save lecturing content I now most often use in a series of how-to sessions that range from the pragmatic instruction in particular databases or digital tools to inspirational-oriented lectures on how to think about the past and become a film historian. It should be said that my decision to shift away from content in the classroom was not made lightly and certainly not without a considerable amount of internal anguish, particularly when it came to the showing of films or clips of films. But this change resulted in part from the recognition that changes in technological infrastructure—such as the pervasiveness of campus wifi and most students' regular access to high-speed Internet—meant that my students could and would watch many more films than in the past without my having to press "play" for them.

The emergence of vast digital repositories have immeasurably enriched film studies, and students today can access critical primary texts, images, and films while sitting on the couch at home, on the bus to work, or even in your classroom while you are lecturing on the subject. What once required weeks, if not months, of carefully worded correspondence and the expense, time, and energy of travel to far-flung institutions by scholars who have invested years in a project is now sometimes available to freshmen taking their very first film class, often at the click of a mouse. There are a seemingly never-ending variety of good, bad, and problematic sources and tools online for the study of film, and in the remainder of this essay I share several of those that my students and I have found most productive. Some of these resources are very established (at least two years old) and likely will survive long enough for this essay to be published; others are potentially more transient, but exciting or useful enough to recommend and risk highlighting the increasingly anachronistic folly of writing about online research in a to-be-printed-with-ink, sit-on-a-shelf-made-of-wood book. Yet there are more serious issues to overcome than just mentioning a dead link or two. For teacher and student alike the potential wealth of online sources and tools is tempered by the challenges of a digital environment that presents a bewildering set of new genres of objects and archives of ambiguous origin accessed through a diverse range of often nonintuitive interfaces. It is into this digital environment of enormous complexity that we turn students loose, expecting them to know what to do.

Whether you are reasonably comfortable in this environment or apprehensive about entering it, most of us assume that our students have strong technical skills and are comfortable enough with computers to readily adapt to anything we might do technologically in the classroom or ask them to do outside class. This assumption is incorrect. What my experience has taught me is that, while students have had significant exposure to computers (and to other digital tools such as smart phones), their range of technology use is fairly narrow even just online. Students are generally quite good at word processing, using e-mail (less and less), texting (more and more), and making use of social network platforms such as *Facebook*. Beyond that, however, their skills are limited. Working with wikis and blogs is something new to many (though their familiarity with word processing helps them quickly adapt), and citation software like *Zotero* or *EndNote* is beyond anything most of them have encountered before (though most of them are quite taken with its ability to create bibliographies).

So, my pedagogy has gone from just telling students about good tools and pointing them to appropriate databases to teaching the use of these resources and even getting students set up with their own accounts. For the tools that I expect my students to access repeatedly, I now create online tutorials using a program like *ScreenSteps. ScreenSteps* allows you to capture part (or all) of your computer screen, annotate what you capture, generate the HTML for your step-by-step instructions, and then upload them as a Web page.

A helpful librarian introduced me to the possibility of creating this kind of tutorial, and it is important to recognize that university librarians are often key players in navigating and helping you teach your students to navigate the technological changes occurring on campus and online. Because of this, I design my courses so that students spend a considerable amount of time interacting with librarians; it is a librarian that familiarizes my students with the three different databases that I want them to regularly engage and master: *ProQuest*, *FIAF*, and the *AFI Catalog*.

ProQuest is actually a search platform for an aggregate of hundreds of databases with literally billions of records used by scholars in almost every discipline, but its interface is not necessarily intuitive and its size can be overwhelming to many students (and even their instructors). My particular goals are to use digital sources to expose students to the complexity of the past and to teach them how to formulate strategies to interpret primary sources in an attempt to gain a social, economic, or political perspective on the culture and history of film. For these purposes, the *ProQuest* search platform can be engaged within its more manageable historical newspaper database; it currently encompasses thirty-six American titles, including its "Black Newspaper Collection," which provides page-to-page coverage of, among others, the *Chicago Defender* (1910–75). Newspapers have always offered film scholars a potential ocean of information, but a lack of a comprehensive index for many papers made this form of primary research a lengthy hit-or-miss process for most scholars. *ProQuest* and other newspaper databases, however, offer almost instantaneous keyword- and subject-searchable access to articles, editorials, ads, reviews, and even photographs, providing instructors and their students with a rapid and productive entry into the use of primary documents and their power to reveal information and ideas about a particular moment in time. In *The Jazz Singer* assignment, for instance, my students were able to easily compare and discuss initial reviews of the film in the *New York Times* in relation to later reactions from black critics writing for both Baltimore's *Afro-American* (1893–1998) and Pittsburgh's *Courier* (1911–2002).

While *ProQuest* provides swift entry into the past, the strength of the *FIAF* database lies in its purposefully narrow attention to secondary sources of film and television scholarship written after 1971. Produced by the International Federation of Film Archives, the database includes indexing to over three hundred international periodicals on film and television, popular and academic, as well as selected bibliographies and a directory of archives and research centers. This database is a critically valuable resource for teaching film studies, since it indexes important resources not indexed in more generalist aggregate databases that are often used by the humanities and social sciences, such as the *MLA International Bibliography* or *Academic Search Premier*. It is here that I most often locate peer-reviewed articles to use while teaching, and it is here that I send students to find out what has already been written about a particular topic or film when they begin to research a new project.

If their project is about a specific American film produced before 1971, my students have learned that their best first stop is often the *AFI Catalog*, compiled by the American Film Institute. The online catalog is a filmographic database that includes extensive entries on over 32,000 American feature-length and 17,000 short films produced from 1893 to 1970. Unlike the *Internet Movie Database* (*IMDb*), a free (and often useful) database that is largely the result of crowd sourcing, the *AFI Catalog* is professionally researched and provides extensive citations of the primary sources that have been used to gather information on cast, crew, plot summaries, subjects, genres, and historical notes about each film entry. For *The Jazz Singer*, it was here that my students first came into contact with reference to trade papers other than the ubiquitous *Variety*, including journals like the *Hollywood Reporter* and *Moving Picture World*. A number of students, in attempting to follow the rabbit down the hole, sought out copies of these journals, only to find that they are currently available only on microfilm. This limitation led to their using a microfiche machine for the first time, as well as prompting a productive class discussion of how uneven and incomplete the digital archive remains and the results this might have on the histories we write.

My students have come to realize that this unevenness also applies to the available online archive of moving images. Because of issues of ownership and technological hurdles, the availability of online moving images remains relatively limited, even with thirty-five hours of video being uploaded on *YouTube* every minute ("Great Scott!"). Started in 2005, *YouTube* qualifies as an established online archive, and its uses and problems as a resource for the study of film could productively fill a book. One of the most consistent but solvable complaints I hear from other instructors is about the transience of this archive. Clips posted by a particular user may be there one day and gone the next, either removed by the user or pulled down by *YouTube* for a potential copyright violation. *YouTube* videos, and most of the other streaming images found online, are presented in the flash video (FLV) format and cannot be downloaded with a simple right-click. However, saving copies of online video for use in teaching can be accomplished in two other ways, either with screen or audio capture software such as *SnapZ Pro* (Mac) or *Camtasia* (Windows) or, even easier, with a browser-based helper site such as *YouTube Downloader*, which inputs the URL associated with the video and allows users to download its file to their computers for personal archiving and repeated use for teaching. Most educational institutions, many instructors, and even a few students are concerned enough about the complex tangle of copyright law, academic exemption rights, and fair-use rules to be uncomfortable with personally downloading videos from *YouTube*. While, in almost every case, making and using copies of clips or films for the limited use of teaching falls safely within the boundaries of existing academic exemption rules, there are other rich online archives that only provide access to media that is within the public domain or that has been licensed under an agreement that allows for redistribution, such as Creative Commons.

The largest of these types of online depositories is the *Internet Archive*, a not-for-profit digital library of everything from copies of traditionally printed books to vintage video games with the umbrella mission of "universal access to all knowledge." Its moving image media collection allows for the easy (and legal) download of copies of newsreels, classic cartoons, pro- and antiwar propaganda, and some two thousand "ephemeral" films from the *Prelinger Archives*, such as advertising, educational, and industrial films and amateur and home movie collections. The *Prelinger Archives*, a subcollection available through the *Internet Archive*, is a suggestive case in point regarding the limited but rich possibilities that currently exist as online teaching resources for the study of film. Beginning in 1983, Rick Prelinger saved, collected, and preserved some sixty thousand "ephemeral" films, works typically produced to fulfill specific purposes at specific times, many of which exist today only by chance or accident. The Library of Congress, recognizing the importance of these objects to the history of film as well as the wider history of American culture, acquired the collection in 2002. The vast bulk of the collection, however, with the exception of those two thousand films available in digital form, have yet to be processed and so are still unavailable even for onsite research by academic scholars. The result is that only one in approximately thirty films in the Prelinger collection can be seen today, and the only way to see them is in digital form as found online.

The reverse is more typical of the contents of traditional media archives, and until recently most archives did not provide much if any of their moving image collections online. For instance, the George Eastman House has an important archive of over twenty-eight thousand titles, particularly rich in content from the history of silent era, but it offers almost no online access to any of their films. Many archives, however, are beginning to make material available online; *Europa Film Treasures*, for example, offers an exciting glimpse into what could be the digital future for film scholarship. Presented by a consortium of approximately thirty European film archives, public and private, the cooperative site offers about one hundred fifty of the collections' films ranging in production date from 1895 to 1970. All films have been restored, many of the silent films have had new music scored and recorded for them, and each includes production details and a history of the film designed to situate the film in both its sociological and technological context. The videos are designed as stream-only but are of high enough quality to present full-screen in a typical classroom situation.

Of course, one advantage of digital resources and tools is that they allow us to easily move our pedagogy, and our students' engagement with it, beyond the classroom. As I mentioned earlier, I show fewer clips in the classroom than when I first began teaching film studies courses and increasingly offer students the option of watching clips online. But how and where does this viewing occur? In my large undergraduate course on world film history, the somewhat unfortunate answer is within the omnipresent *Blackboard* site associated with the class. Among *Blackboard*'s media-related features are the ability to post media files, to create links to movies streaming online but outside the *Blackboard* system, or even to embed windows and create direct access to videos on *YouTube* and other sites. These capabilities are all possible and relatively easy for an instructor to accomplish. Yet while this sharing of media content is theoretically also available to students in collaborative areas of the course site (e.g., within a wiki module), in practice the interface makes such sharing difficult for all but the most tech savvy to accomplish. Students in my large lecture no longer post videos with their wiki work, after having learned the videos cause the site to crash. Programs and platforms change often, and we can hope that in the future *Blackboard* may offer a more useful and simpler interface for students to share moving images within its system. For now, however, in all but the largest lecture courses, I have moved my online component of coursework to commercial (largely no- or low-cost) platforms that provide intuitive interfaces for students to engage in collaborative work, including the sharing of moving images, resources, and ideas. With the dramatic rise in popularity of social networks, these types of Web-based programs are rapidly developing and evolving. The platform that I currently use, *Ning*, has proven itself to be both stable and intuitive for creating film-related content by my students and me. The *Ning* site created for each class enables students to post and annotate images, moving and still, write individual blog posts about their research, and participate in discussion forums about multiple topics related to the course. Easy content creation, the ability to share materials online, and a collaborative workspace for developing ideas about a particular film or concept do not, of course, necessarily make for better students or even better teachers. But increasingly I find that using these types of digital tools and resources in the study of film have allowed me to teach my students to engage more effectively in the process of working analytically, of reading and interpreting primary documents and moving images, and to write as a process of learning and disciplinary thinking.

Note

1. It is worth noting that the current *Wikipedia* page for *The Jazz Singer* (1927) is, if not comprehensive, a substantial entry that includes fifty citations of almost two-dozen sources, among them reviews contemporary to the film's initial release, scholarly works on the history of sound technology, and critical analysis of blackface performance and genre development of the Hollywood musical.

Works Cited

Cohen, Noam. "A History Department Bans Citing Wikipedia as a Research Source." *New York Times*. New York Times, 21 Feb. 2007. Web. 12 Jan. 2010.
"Great Scott! Over Thirty-Five Hours of Video Uploaded Every Minute to YouTube." *YouTube Blog*. YouTube, 10 Nov. 2010. Web. 1 Sept. 2011.
"*The Jazz Singer* (1927 film)." *Wikipedia*. Wikimedia, 28 Dec. 2010. Web. 3 Jan. 2009.

Appendix 1: Going Down the Rabbit Hole

The following is an actual example of a student's participation in the "rabbit hole" exercise for the film *The Jazz Singer*. This particular student opted to trace out the sources for a single sentence in the section of the *Wikipedia* entry devoted to the film's initial exhibition and reception.

> I decided to choose: "After the show, the audience turned into a 'milling, battling, mob', in one journalist's description, chanting 'Jolson, Jolson, Jolson!' " I thought I could try to track down the original newspaper reporter this might have come from and maybe even find the actual article. For this sentence, the Wiki author cites "page 140" of the following book:
>
> Eyman, Scott. *The Speed of Sound: Hollywood and the Talkie Revolution,* 1926–1930. New York: Simon and Schuster, 1997. Print.
>
> Using the online catalog I found the book in our library. The book is a historical narrative of film during the transition from silent to "talkies." The book is divided into chapters based on years and there is a chapter for 1926–1930. It seems to me to be a pretty concise historical overview and the language in it doesn't seem to be overly academic, it seems to be a popular text on film of the period. One difficulty in this text is the author's lack of citations. He doesn't footnote any of the quotations that he uses and only mentions a quotation's author within the text.

In the actual book I located the paragraph that the wiki cites: "By the film's end, the . . . audience, transformed into what one critic called 'a milling, battling mob,' stood, stamped, and cheered 'Jolson, Jolson, Jolson!'" (139–40)

Eyman, the author, doesn't mention where this quote is from or whom it came from. From the book's bibliography my best guess at where this quotation would come from is the following:

Goldman, Herbert G. *Jolson: The Legend Comes to Life*. New York: Oxford University Press, 1988. Print.

This book was also in our library. *The Legend Comes to Life* is a comprehensive biography of Al Jolson. It seems like a pretty reliable biographical source. The language is a bit dense and there's a lot of information in it, encompassing all of Jolson's life. Part of the quotation in *Wikipedia* does, in fact, appear in this text, as follows: "A mob—'one of those milling, battling mobs that used to blockade cinema premieres to watch the stars pass by in the days before they moved all the studios to Hollywood' was the way that Richard Watts, Jr., described it in the New York *Herald Tribune*—flooded the sidewalk and street in front of the Warner Theatre that night" (152).

From here I decided to look up the original article from the *Tribune*, which we have on microfilm in the library. I assumed that the review would've appeared the day after the premier so I went to the October 7, 1927 issue of the newspaper and found the original article. Here is the citation:

Watts, Richard, Jr. "'The Jazz Singer' with Al Jolson Opens at Warner." *New York Herald Tribune* 7 October 1927: 18. Print.

The original quote from this, the primary source, is at the beginning of the article: "One of those milling, battling mobs that used to blockade cinema premieres to watch the stars pass by in the days before they moved all the studios to Hollywood grouped itself menacingly in front of the Warner Theatre last night, grimly determined to prevent the entrance into the house of those who proudly possessed tickets to the opening of the Vitaphoned Mr. Al Jolson in a screen version of 'The Jazz Singer.' Yet it is to be expected that few of the surviving blockade runners who finally managed to fight their way into the theater felt that their battle was in vain" (paragraph 1). Interestingly, this article does not contain the "Jolson, Jolson, Jolson!" part of the quote that is part of the *Wikipedia* entry though, so that must've come from a different source.

So while the Wiki uses this example from the original premier to illustrate crowd hysteria after the movie, the activity actually took place before the movie started. A small shift, but one that changes history, at least a little bit.

Appendix 2:
Resources and Tools

Databases

Institutional subscriptions to the databases discussed in this article may vary considerably, and specific license cost is dependent on several factors. If, however, your institution does not currently subscribe to a particular database, all the ones mentioned here are available for free trials by your library and, in my experience, librarians are always eager to try out new resources.

ProQuest Historical Newspapers
Searchable database, full text or image, of thirty-six American newspapers, ranging in publication from 1764 to 2008.
FIAF International Index to Film Periodicals
Includes more than three hundred popular and academic journals on film and television.
AFI Catalog
Contains comprehensive production information for 48,300 films from the period 1893 to 1973. Institutional subscriptions to the database are currently managed by ProQuest.

Tools

ScreenSteps Desktop
Software for creating tutorials (Mac or Windows, academic license).
Camtasia
Screen or audio capture software for creating personal archives of online videos (Windows, academic license).
SnapZ Pro
Screen or audio capture software for creating personal archives of online videos (Mac).
YouTube Downloader
Web-based service for creating downloadable video files from *YouTube.*
Ning
Online platform for the creation of specific and limited social networks. See http://education.ning.com/ for an example focused on using the platform in educational environments. Ad-supported networks are provided at no cost to users.

Online Archives (Besides *YouTube*)

Internet Archive
http://www.archive.org
Prelinger Archive
http://www.archive.org/details/prelinger

Europa Film Treasures
http://www.europafilmtreasures.eu/

Online Resources regarding Copyright and Fair Use

Creative Commons
http://creativecommons.org/
Electronic Frontier Foundation
http://www.eff.org/work
Critical Commons (from the Society of Cinema and Media Studies)
http://criticalcommons.org/blog/content/fair-use-guidelines-from-scms-1

Notes on Contributors

Mark Lynn Anderson is associate professor of film studies in the Department of English at the University of Pittsburgh. He has published articles and chapters on the early Hollywood star system, motion-picture censorship, celebrity scandals, and early film education. He is the author of *Twilight of the Idols: Hollywood and the Human Sciences in 1920s America*.

Dudley Andrew is the R. Selden Rose Professor of Film and Comparative Literature and chair of the Comparative Literature Department at Yale University. He began his career with three books that commented on film theory and included a biography of André Bazin. He is the author of *What Cinema Is!*; the editor of *Opening Bazin: Postwar Film Theory and Its Afterlife*; and the author of *Mists of Regret: Culture and Sensibility in Classic French Film* and *Popular Front Paris and the Poetics of Culture*. He is completing a book, "Encountering World Cinema."

Michael Aronson is associate professor of English and cinema studies at the University of Oregon. He is the author of *Nickelodeon City, Pittsburgh at the Movies, 1905–1929*. His "Silent Cine Tip o da Day," a daily *Twitter* feed about online early film resources, can be followed @MichaelAronson.

Edward Branigan is professor in the Department of Film and Media Studies at the University of California, Santa Barbara. He is the author of *Projecting a Camera: Language-Games in Film Theory*; *Narrative Comprehension and Film*; and *Point of View in the Cinema: A Theory of Narration and Subjectivity in Classical Film*. With Charles Wolfe, he is the general editor of the American Film Institute Film Readers series.

Pat Brereton is senior lecturer in communications and film and associate dean of research for the faculty of Humanities and Social Sciences at Dublin City University. His books include *Hollywood Utopia: Ecology in Contemporary American Cinema*, *Continuum Guide to Media Education*, and, with Roddy Flynn, *Historical Dictionary of Irish Cinema*. He is working on a study of "smart cinema." He has edited a special issue of *Convergence: The Journal of New Media* on DVDs and smart cinema.

Steven Cohan is professor of English at Syracuse University. His books include *Screening the Male*; *The Road Movie Book*; *Masked Men: Masculinity and the Movies in the Fifties*; *Hollywood Musicals: The Film Reader*; *Incongruous Entertainment: Camp, Cultural Value, and the MGM Musical*; *CSI: Crime Scene Investigation*; and *The Sound of Musicals*.

Timothy Corrigan is professor of English, cinema studies, and history of art at the University of Pennsylvania. His books include *New German Film: The*

Displaced Image; *The Films of Werner Herzog: Between Mirage and History*; *Writing about Film*; *A Cinema without Walls*; *Film and Literature*; *The Film Experience* (with Patricia White); *Critical Visions in Film Theory: Classic and Contemporary Readings* (edited with White); and *The Essay Film: From Montaigne, after Marker.* He is an editor of the journal *Adaptation* and an editorial board member of *Cinema Journal.*

Peter Decherney is associate professor of cinema studies and English at the University of Pennsylvania. He is the author of *Hollywood's Copyright Wars: From Edison to the Internet* and *Hollywood and the Culture Elite: How the Movies Became American*. He has been an Academy of Motion Picture Arts and Sciences Film Scholar and an American Council of Learned Societies Fellow.

David Desser is emeritus professor of cinema studies, University of Illinois. He has written and edited nine books, including *The Samurai Films of Akira Kurosawa*; *Eros Plus Massacre: An Introduction to the Japanese New Wave*; *Reframing Japanese Cinema: Authorship, Genre, History*; *Cinematic Landscapes: Observations on the Cinema of China and Japan*; and *The Cinema of Hong Kong: History, Arts, Identity.*

Wheeler Winston Dixon is the James Ryan Endowed Professor of Film Studies, professor of English, and coordinator of the Film Studies Program at the University of Nebraska, Lincoln. He and Gwendolyn Audrey Foster are editors in chief of the *Quarterly Review of Film and Video.* His books include *A History of Horror*; *Film Noir and the Cinema of Paranoia*; and *A Short History of Film*, written with Foster. His films are in the permanent collection of The Museum of Modern Art, following a career retrospective at the museum in 2003.

Nataša Ďurovičová is the editor of *91st Meridian*, the online journal of the International Writing Program at the University of Iowa and associate faculty in the Department of Cinema and Comparative Literature there. With Kathleen Newman she is the editor of *World Cinemas, Transnational Perspectives.*

Lucy Fischer is Distinguished Professor of English and Film Studies at the University of Pittsburgh. She is the author of *Jacques Tati*; *Shot/Countershot: Film Tradition and Women's Cinema*; *Imitation of Life*; *Cinematernity: Film, Motherhood, Genre*; *Sunrise: A Song of Two Humans*; *Designing Women: Art Deco, Cinema, and the Female Form*; and *American Cinema of the 1920s: Themes and Variations.* With Marcia Landy, she is the editor of *Stars: The Film Reader.*

Caryl Flinn is professor in the Department of Screen Arts and Cultures at the University of Michigan, Ann Arbor. She is the author of *Strains of Utopia: Gender, Nostalgia, and Hollywood Film Music*; *Brass Diva: The Life and*

Legends of Ethel Merman; and *New German Cinema: Music, History, and the Matter of Style* and the coeditor of *Music and Cinema*.

Gwendolyn Audrey Foster is professor in the Department of English at the University of Nebraska, Lincoln. Her books include *A Short History of Film*, with Wheeler Winston Dixon; *Class-Passing: Social Mobility in Film and Popular Culture*; *Identity and Memory: The Films of Chantal Akerman*; *Women Filmmakers of the African and Asian Diaspora: Decolonizing the Gaze, Locating Subjectivity*; and *Women Film Directors: An International Bio-critical Dictionary*. She is coeditor in chief of the *Quarterly Review of Film and Video*.

Anne Friedberg was professor and chair of critical studies in the School of Cinema-Television at the University of Southern California. She is the author of *Window Shopping: Cinema and the Postmodern* and the editor, with Laura Marcus and James Donald, of *Close Up, 1927–1933: Cinema and Modernism*. Her most recent book is *The Virtual Window: From Alberti to Microsoft*.

E. Ann Kaplan is Distinguished Professor of English and Comparative Literary and Cultural Studies and director of the Humanities Institute at Stony Brook University. She is the author of *Trauma Culture: The Politics of Terror and Loss in Media and Literature*; *Looking For the Other: Feminism, Film and the Imperial Gaze*; *Playing Dolly: Technocultural Formations, Fantasies and Fictions of Assisted Reproduction*, edited with Susan Squier; *Feminism and Film*; and *Trauma and Cinema: Cross-Cultural Explorations*, edited with Ban Wang.

Adam Knee is associate professor in the Division of Broadcast and Cinema Studies in the Wee Kim Wee School of Communication and Information at Nanyang Technological University, Singapore. His writings have appeared in the anthologies *Framing Celebrity*, *Acting for America: Movie Stars of the 1980s*, and *Glamour in a Golden Age: Movie Stars of the 1930s*. He serves on the editorial board of the journal *Celebrity Studies*.

Mark Langer teaches film studies at the School for Studies in Art and Culture at Carleton University. His articles have appeared in anthologies and in *Cinema Journal*, *Animation Journal*, and *Screen*. He has curated animation retrospectives for museums and festivals, including the Museum of Modern Art and the Cinémathèque Française. He is president of the Ontario Confederation of University Faculty Associations.

James F. Lastra is associate professor in the Departments of Cinema and Media Studies and English at the University of Chicago. He is the author of *Sound Technology and the American Cinema: Perception, Representation, Modernity*. He is completing a book entitled "Why Is This Absurd Picture Here? Buñuel, Cinema, and the Persistence of Surrealism."

Adam Lowenstein is associate professor of English and film studies at the University of Pittsburgh. He is the author of *Shocking Representation: Historical Trauma, National Cinema, and the Modern Horror Film*, as well as essays that have appeared in *Cinema Journal*, *Representations*, *Critical Quarterly*, *Boundary 2*, *Post Script*, and numerous anthologies. He is an interviewed scholar in the documentary *The American Nightmare* and in articles for the *New York Times* and the *Village Voice.*

Neepa Majumdar is associate professor of film studies in the English Department at the University of Pittsburgh. Her research interests include star studies, film sound, South Asian early cinema, and documentary film. She is the author of *Wanted Cultured Ladies Only! Female Stardom and Cinema in India, 1930s to 1950s.*

Paula J. Massood is professor in the Department of Film at Brooklyn College, City University of New York, and professor of film studies in the doctoral program in theater at the Graduate Center. She is the author of *Black City Cinema: African American Urban Experiences in Film* and the editor of *The Spike Lee Reader.* She served as the film and theater subject editor for the African American National Biography project.

Tara McPherson is associate professor in the School of Cinematic Arts at the University of Southern California. She is author of *Reconstructing Dixie: Race, Gender, and Nostalgia in the Imagined South*; coeditor of *Hop on Pop: The Politics and Pleasures of Popular Culture*; editor of *Digital Youth, Innovation, and the Unexpected*; and coeditor of the forthcoming *Interactive Frictions.* She is the founding editor of the multimedia journal *Vectors* and a founding coeditor of the *International Journal of Learning + Media.*

Hamid Naficy is professor of radio, television, and film and the Sheikh Hamad bin Khalifa Al Thani Professor of Communication at Northwestern University. His English language books include *An Accented Cinema: Exilic and Diasporic Filmmaking*; *Home, Exile, Homeland: Film, Media, and the Politics of Place*; *The Making of Exile Cultures: Iranian Television in Los Angeles*; and the four-volume *A Social History of Iranian Cinema.*

Scott Nygren is professor of film and media studies in the Department of English at the University of Florida. He has been involved in developing international programs at the university's Paris Research Center in France. He is the author of *Time Frames: Japanese Cinema and the Unfolding of History* and has published essays in a number of books and journals.

Tasha Oren is associate professor of film and media studies and director of the graduate studies program in the Department of English at the University of Wisconsin, Milwaukee. She is the author of *Demon in the Box: Jews, Arabs, Politics and Culture* and coeditor of *East Main Street: Asian American*

Popular Culture; *Global Currents: Media and Technology Now*; and *Global Television Formats.*

Patrice Petro is professor of English and film studies at the University of Wisconsin, Milwaukee, where she is also vice provost for International Education. She is the author of *Aftershocks of the New: Feminism and Film History* and *Joyless Streets: Women and Melodramatic Representation in Weimar Germany* and the editor of several books, including *Idols of Modernity: Movie Stars of the 1920s*; *Rethinking Global Security: Media, Popular Culture, and the War on Terror*; and *Global Currents: Media and Technology Now.* She is past president of the Society for Cinema and Media Studies.

Raphael Raphael is lecturer in film and media studies at the Center on Disability Studies at the University of Hawaiʻi at Mānoa. He is working on a book about the cultural work of the American freakshow and is coediting three forthcoming books on issues in transnational genre and culture and representations of disability. He serves as media specialist in Eurasia for the not-for-profit corporation International School Services. His tweets on film and media may be located @raphaelspeak.

Michael Renov is professor of critical studies and associate dean of the School of Cinematic Arts at the University of Southern California. He is the author or editor of seven books, including *Hollywood's Wartime Woman: Representation and Ideology*, *Theorizing Documentary*, *Resolutions: Contemporary Video Practices*, and *The Subject of Documentary.* He cofounded Visible Evidence, an international documentary studies conference, and is an editor of the Visible Evidence book series.

Eric Rentschler is Arthur Kingsley Porter Professor of Germanic Languages and Literatures at Harvard University. His books include *West German Film in the Course of Time* and *The Ministry of Illusion.* He is the editor of *German Film and Literature*; *West German Filmmakers on Film*; *Augenzeugen* (2nd ed., with Hans Helmut Prinzler); and *The Films of G. W. Pabst.* His book projects are "Haunted by Hitler: The Return of the Nazi Undead" and "Courses in Time: Film in the Federal Republic of Germany, 1962–1989."

Anne Rutherford is senior lecturer in cinema studies at the University of Western Sydney. She is the author of *"What Makes a Film Tick?": Cinematic Affect, Materiality and Mimetic Innervation* and has published numerous essays and interviews on cinematic affect and embodiment, cinematic materiality, aesthetics, mise-en-scène, film sound, and documentary. She has also made several short films.

Zoran Samardzija is assistant professor of film and video at Columbia College Chicago. He has published articles on the films of Andrei Tarkovksy, the use of historical and national myths in the films of Theo Angelopoulos, representations of exile and migration in Balkan cinemas, and David Lynch's embrace of the Internet and commercial grade video.

Garrett Stewart is James O. Freedman Professor of Letters at the University of Iowa. He is the author of *Between Film and Screen: Modernism's Photosynthesis* and *Framed Time: Toward a Postfilmic Cinema*, as well as several books on fiction and literary theory, most recently *Novel Violence: A Narratography of Victorian Fiction*. He was elected to the American Academy of Arts and Sciences in 2010.

Frank P. Tomasulo teaches film courses at City College of New York and graduate seminars for National University. He is the author of 70 articles and 160 academic papers. He served as editor of *Journal of Film and Video* and *Cinema Journal* and coedited *More Than a Method: Trends and Traditions in Contemporary Film Performance*. He received the University Film and Video Association's Teaching Award and the Georgia State University Outstanding Teacher Award.

Maureen Turim is professor of English and film and media studies at the University of Florida. She is the author of *Abstraction in Avant-Garde Films*; *Flashbacks in Film: Memory and History*; and *The Films of Oshima: Images of a Japanese Iconoclast*. She has published over eighty essays in anthologies and journals on a wide range of theoretical, historical, and aesthetic issues in cinema and video, art, cultural studies, feminist and psychoanalytic theory, and comparative literature.

Cristina Venegas is associate professor in film and media studies at the University of California, Santa Barbara. She teaches Latin American film and media, Spanish-language media in the United States, digital media, international cinema, and cultural studies. She is the author of *Digital Dilemmas: The State, the Individual, and Digital Media in Cuba*.

Patricia White is professor of film and media studies at Swarthmore College. She is the author of *Uninvited: Classical Hollywood Cinema and Lesbian Representability* and is completing a book on global women's filmmaking in the twenty-first century. With Timothy Corrigan, she is author of *The Film Experience* and editor of *Critical Visions in Film Theory: Classic and Contemporary Readings*. She is a member of the editorial collective *Camera Obscura* and serves on the board of Women Make Movies.

Index

Modern Language Association of America
Options for Teaching

Teaching Film. Ed. Lucy Fischer and Patrice Petro. 2012.

Teaching Seventeenth- and Eighteenth-Century French Women Writers. Ed. Faith E. Beasley. 2011.

Teaching French Women Writers of the Renaissance and Reformation. Ed. Colette H. Winn. 2011.

Teaching Law and Literature. Ed. Austin Sarat, Cathrine O. Frank, and Matthew Anderson. 2011.

Teaching British Women Playwrights of the Restoration and Eighteenth Century. Ed. Bonnie Nelson and Catherine Burroughs. 2010.

Teaching Narrative Theory. Ed. David Herman, Brian McHale, and James Phelan. 2010.

Teaching Early Modern English Prose. Ed. Susannah Brietz Monta and Margaret W. Ferguson. 2010.

Teaching Italian American Literature, Film, and Popular Culture. Ed. Edvige Giunta and Kathleen Zamboni McCormick. 2010.

Teaching the Graphic Novel. Ed. Stephen E. Tabachnick. 2009.

Teaching Literature and Language Online. Ed. Ian Lancashire. 2009.

Teaching the African Novel. Ed. Gaurav Desai. 2009.

Teaching World Literature. Ed. David Damrosch. 2009.

Teaching North American Environmental Literature. Ed. Laird Christensen, Mark C. Long, and Fred Waage. 2008.

Teaching Life Writing Texts. Ed. Miriam Fuchs and Craig Howes. 2007.

Teaching Nineteenth-Century American Poetry. Ed. Paula Bernat Bennett, Karen L. Kilcup, and Philipp Schweighauser. 2007.

Teaching Representations of the Spanish Civil War. Ed. Noël Valis. 2006.

Teaching the Representation of the Holocaust. Ed. Marianne Hirsch and Irene Kacandes. 2004.

Teaching Tudor and Stuart Women Writers. Ed. Susanne Woods and Margaret P. Hannay. 2000.

Teaching Literature and Medicine. Ed. Anne Hunsaker Hawkins and Marilyn Chandler McEntyre. 1999.

Teaching the Literatures of Early America. Ed. Carla Mulford. 1999.

Teaching Shakespeare through Performance. Ed. Milla C. Riggio. 1999.

Teaching Oral Traditions. Ed. John Miles Foley. 1998.

Teaching Contemporary Theory to Undergraduates. Ed. Dianne F. Sadoff and William E. Cain. 1994.

Teaching Children's Literature: Issues, Pedagogy, Resources. Ed. Glenn Edward Sadler. 1992.

Teaching Literature and Other Arts. Ed. Jean-Pierre Barricelli, Joseph Gibaldi, and Estella Lauter. 1990.

New Methods in College Writing Programs: Theories in Practice. Ed. Paul Connolly and Teresa Vilardi. 1986.

School-College Collaborative Programs in English. Ed. Ron Fortune. 1986.

Teaching Environmental Literature: Materials, Methods, Resources. Ed. Frederick O. Waage. 1985.

Part-Time Academic Employment in the Humanities: A Sourcebook for Just Policy. Ed. Elizabeth M. Wallace. 1984.

Film Study in the Undergraduate Curriculum. Ed. Barry K. Grant. 1983.

The Teaching Apprentice Program in Language and Literature. Ed. Joseph Gibaldi and James V. Mirollo. 1981.

Options for Undergraduate Foreign Language Programs: Four-Year and Two-Year Colleges. Ed. Renate A. Schulz. 1979.

Options for the Teaching of English: Freshman Composition. Ed. Jasper P. Neel. 1978.

Options for the Teaching of English: The Undergraduate Curriculum. Ed. Elizabeth Wooten Cowan. 1975.